Behavioral Self-Management

Strategies, Techniques and Outcomes

Edited by

RICHARD B. STUART, D.S.W.

University of Utah and
Weight Watchers International, Inc.

BRUNNER/MAZEL, *Publishers* • New York

SECOND PRINTING

Library of Congress Cataloging in Publication Data

Main entry under title:
Behavioral self-management.

    Includes bibliographies and index.
    1. Behavior modification.   I. Stuart, Richard B.
BF637.B4B453   158   77-23501
ISBN 0-87630-148-0

Copyright © 1977 by BRUNNER/MAZEL, INC.
Published by
BRUNNER/MAZEL, INC.
19 Union Square W., New York, N. Y. 10003

Distributed in Canada by BOOK CENTER
1140 Beaulac St., Montreal, Quebec H4R-1R8

MANUFACTURED IN THE UNITED STATES OF AMERICA

Preface

This is one in a continuing series of publications sponsored by the Banff International Conferences on Behavior Modification. The conferences are held each spring in Banff, Alberta, Canada, and serve the purpose of bringing together outstanding behavioral scientists to discuss the present data related to emergent issues and topics in the field of behavior modification. Thus, the International Conferences, as a continuing event, have served as an expressive "early indicator" of the developing nature and composition of behavioristic science and scientific application.

Distance, schedules, and restricted audiences preclude wide attendance at the conferences. Consequently the publications have equal status with the conferences proper. They are not, however, simply publications of the papers presented at the conference. Major presenters at the Banff Conferences are required to specifically write a chapter for the forthcoming book, separate from their informal presentation and discussion of the topic at the conference itself.

Past conference topics and faculty were:

1969: I. IDEAL MENTAL HEALTH SERVICES

Nathan Azrin   Todd Risley
Ogden Lindsley   Richard B. Stuart
Gerald Patterson

1970: II. SERVICES AND PROGRAMS FOR EXCEPTIONAL CHILDREN AND YOUTH

Loren and Margaret Acker   Ogden Lindsley
Wesley C. Becker   Patrick McGinley
Nancy Buckley   Nancy J. Reynolds
Donald Cameron   James A. Sherman
L. Richard Crozier   Richard B. Stuart
David R. Evans   Walter W. Zwirner
Leo A. Hamerlynck

1971: III. IMPLEMENTING BEHAVIORAL PROGRAMS
FOR SCHOOLS AND CLINICS

Joe A. Cobb
Rodney Copeland
R. Vance Hall
Ogden Lindsley
Hugh McKenzie
Garry L. Martin

Jack L. Michael
Gerald R. Patterson
Ernest G. Poser
Roberta S. Ray
Richard B. Stuart
Carl E. Thoresen

1972: IV. BEHAVIOR CHANGE: METHODOLOGY, CONCEPTS,
AND PRACTICE

Eric J. Mash
S. M. Johnson and
O. D. Bolstad
K. D. O'Leary and
R. Kent
K. Skindrud
R. Jones
L. A. Hamerlynck
G. C. Davison
G. R. Patterson
H. Hops and J. A. Cobb

J. B. Reid and
A. F. C. J. Hendriks
R. B. Stuart
Lee C. Handy
H. M. Walker and H. Hops
J. LoPiccolo and W. C. Lobitz
D. L. Fixsen, M. M. Wolfe and
E. L. Phillips
L. L. Weiss, H. Hops and
G. R. Patterson

1973: V. EVALUATION OF BEHAVIORAL PROGRAMS IN COMMUNITY,
RESIDENTIAL AND SCHOOL SETTINGS

Richard R. Jones
Siegfried Hiebert
Bryan C. Smith
Aldred H. Neufeldt
Peter D. McLean
Robert Paul Liberman,
William J. DeRisi,
Larry W. King,
Thad A. Eckman and
David Wood
Srinika Jayaratne,
Richard B. Stuart and
Tony Tripodi
William B. Neenan

Michael F. Cataldo and
Todd R. Risley
Robert L. Kahn and
Steven H. Zarit
Rosemary C. Sarri and
Elaine Selo
H. S. Pennypacker, Carl H. Koenig and
W. H. Seaver
William W. Cooley and
Gaea Leinhardt
James R. Barclay
Charles Windle and
Peter Bates

1974: VI. BEHAVIORAL MODIFICATION AND FAMILIES

Frances Degen Horowitz
Todd R. Risley,
Hewitt B. Clark and
Michael F. Cataldo
Elaine A. Blechman and
Martha Manning
L. Keith Miller,
Alice Lies,
Dan L. Pettersen and
Richard Feallock
John B. Conway and

Bradley D. Bucher
Stephen M. Johnson,
Orin D. Bolstad and
Gretchen K. Lobitz
Sander Martin,
Stephen Johnson,
Sandra Johansson and
Gail Wahl
Martha E. Bernal,
Leo F. Delfini,
Juell Ann North and

Susan L. Kreutzer	Gerald R. Patterson
Paul M. Rosen	John A. Corson
Lief Terdal,	Victor A. Benassi and
Russell H. Jackson and	Kathryn M. Larson
Ann M. Garner	Robert F. Peterson

and

BEHAVIOR MODIFICATION APPROACHES TO PARENTING

Donald R. Green,	Virginia Tams and
Karen Budd,	Sheila Eyberg
Moses Johnson,	Karen E. Kovitz
Sarah Lang,	Barclay Martin and
Elsie Pinkston and	Craig Twentyman
Sara Rudd	Wallace L. Mealiea, Jr.
Barbara Stephens Brockway and	Martin E. Shoemaker and
W. Weston Williams	Terry L. Paulson
Edward R. Christophersen,	Joe H. Brown
James D. Barnard,	A. M. Gamboa, Jr.,
Dennis Ford and	John Birkimer and
Montrose M. Wolf	Robert Brown
Buell E. Goocher and	Margaret Steward and
David N. Grove	David Steward
Merihelen Blackmore,	Peter D. McLean
Nancy Rich,	W. Doyle Gentry
Zetta Means and	Allison Rossett and
Mike Nally	Todd Eachus

1975: THE BEHAVIORAL MANAGEMENT OF ANXIETY, DEPRESSION AND PAIN

Donald Meichenbaum and	Peter Lewinsohn,
Dennis Turk	Anthony Biglan and
Ernest G. Poser	Antonette M. Zeiss
Peter McLean	Wilbert E. Fordyce

Many people have donated their energies and talents to the continued success of the Banff Conferences on Behavior Modification. Primarily, of course, we must acknowledge the guest faculty who develop, present, and discuss topics found in this volume.

The Banff Conferences have been more than places at which theories and research data are presented and discussed. The Conferences have stimulated planning and research in selected areas and have helped to bring together policy makers, program administrators, researchers and clinicians in an effort to stimulate adoption in practice settings of many of the programs that have been discussed during its proceedings. The success of this effort has been aided in great measure by the material support and the technical guidance of the University of Calgary's Division of Continuing Education and by the staff and resources of the Banff School of Fine Arts which has been the site of the Conferences since their inception.

Other members of the Conference Committee deserve to be singled out for their substantial help and guidance. They are Drs. Gus Hamer-lynck and Park O. Davidson and Ms. Donna Fraser, who both helps in the planning and also oversees every aspect of the administration of the Conference.

R.B.S.

Contents

Introduction

Some psychologists are concerned with explaining but not with influencing human behavior. Applied psychologists, however, are committed to the pursuit of practical understanding or the explanation of behavior leading to its control. From its beginnings in a few scattered clinics and laboratories about 20 years ago, behavior modification has risen to become one of the major forces in this applied attempt to influence human behavior in personally and socially productive ways.

Since its start, behavior modification has been concerned with 1) attempts to change specific behaviors, 2) through use of definable technologies, 3) leading to desirable outcomes. Operational definition and measurement have been two of the benchmarks of the development of behavior modification. Another abiding concern of behavior modifiers has been their attempt to offer services to their clients in such a manner as to fully respect their clients' rights to share to the extent of their abilities in all decisions regarding treatment planning (Davison & Stuart, 1975).

Within behavior modification, two rather different traditions have flourished. One, generally termed "behavior therapy," draws upon classical conditioning procedures. It sought to disinhibit some responses by desensitizing the emotional responses that prevent their occurrence and to inhibit others by associating them with aversive events. Later, behavior therapists also stressed efforts to change thoughts about action alternatives as another technique of behavior change. "Applied behavior analysis" is the other tradition. It draws upon operant conditioning procedures in its effort to strengthen some responses and weaken others through the rearrangement of the environmental contingencies that control their occurrence.

These two traditions lived in relative harmony during the early days when behavior modification struggled to differentiate itself from the non-empirically based approaches to human services. Soon after they had established their separate identity, however, the two traditions turned their energies toward differentiating themselves from one another with ever increasing vigor. Extreme positions developed on both sides. Many behavior therapists claimed to change people, not places, and played down the role of environments in human action. On the other side, behavior analysts sometimes disregarded the role of thought and feeling in determining human behavior.

Fortunately, the basic respect for data shared by both groups has helped to reunite the behavior modification movement. This volume is but one expression of that reunion. All of the papers presented here accept the phenomenology of thoughts and feelings as they prompt and reinforce action and they accept the role of the natural environment in blocking, promoting and/or maintaining behavior change.

The *behaviors* with which papers in this volume are concerned range from consumatory responses like smoking, drinking alcohol, and eating to health, mental health and community oriented responses. All are overt and measurable. All are changes selected by the clients themselves.

All of the papers in this volume are addressed to producing either self-initiated or self-maintained changes in these behaviors. The word *"self"* has as yet no precise meaning either within or beyond behavior modification. Behavior modifiers generally agree with Skinner's (1953) position that we are what we do. Analogous to the "state" theories of personality, many define self as consistent patterns of action, recognizing that these can change dramatically from time to time. Self can also be considered to be analogous to the "trait" theories of personality by those who regard self as the potential for action, implying some large measure of cross-situational consistency. We do tend to behave with some consistency, a fact that is not readily explained by the state approach, but we are also subject to dramatic behavior change, a fact that does not set well with the trait approach.

Beyond the definitional problem there is also some difficulty in understanding the interface between self and environment. We would all like to think of ourselves as the masters of our own fate. But it has been shown that not only our actions fall under the control of our environment (Stuart, 1972a; Jones, Nelson & Kazdin, 1977) but even our decisions about how to act are environmentally influenced if not determined (Bandura & Perloff, 1967). Therefore, the extent to which behavior is ever "self"-controlled is still unknown. Nevertheless, by including self-management in our theories of intervention, we can at least preserve a definitional place for the individual in the process of behavior change and we can strive to heighten, to the greatest extent possible, the role of individuals as arbiters of their therapeutic experiences.

Finally, the *management* of behavior is an important common theme in the following papers. Behavior modification involves three clusters of techniques aimed at promoting behavior management: 1) Some techniques create a readiness to accept influence; 2) other techniques are the core of the behavior change effort; and 3) still other techniques are oriented to maintaining behavior change (Stuart, 1972b). Some of the papers explore means through which clients' readiness to accept change can be enhanced. These techniques may be concerned with the creation of an environment in which instigations for new behaviors can be presented in the most relevant and least threatening way. Other techniques are concerned with efforts to improve the precision of the instigations given and to reduce the "noise" that might interfere with their being correctly understood. For some the treatment session becomes the ultimate environment for change while other papers display ways through which the synthetic quality of the intervention environment can be muffled so that the transfer of responses to the natural environment can readily occur.

The change technologies presented in this volume represent all four of the behavior control options: 1) Some of the chapters offer techniques through which clients are helped to relabel their experience—these are the deconditioning techniques; 2) some of the chapters offer techniques through which clients can change their expectations about the outcome of possible actions—these are the cognitive control techniques; 3) some of the chapters train clients to change their behaviors so that they can modify their natural behavioral environments—these techniques involve well-known instigation procedures; and 4) some of the techniques change environments directly either by transforming the treatment environment into the natural environment for the client or by putting therapists in control of aspects of the situations in which clients' lives are naturally lived.

Finally, several of the chapters in this volume are concerned with the question of measurement and maintenance of post-therapeutic behavior change. One can imagine a series of models of maintenance services. The most ideal model would feature a treatment produced effect that would be sustained through years without further intervention. While clearly the standard against which all treatments are measured, this standard may be naive insofar as it fails to account for the power of environments to thwart the best of behavioral change intentions. The other models would therefore feature a series of different patterns of follow-up services which are planned adjuncts to the original behavior change effort. Indeed, based upon the follow-up data that have been collected for many different intervention methods, both part of and beyond behavior modification, it would seem that this continued contact model is certainly the most reasonable alternative. While this is not stressed as strongly as would be desired, many of the authors of the papers presented herein are attentive to the question of maintenance effects and technology and some may point the way toward advances in this important area.

In the first chapter, Kanfer characterizes the efforts of an individual to change his or her behavior as requiring a two-stage model: The first stage involves choice of one from a set of several behavioral objectives; the second stage involves a protracted effort to persevere along the direction that has been chosen. Kanfer clearly shows the role of ideas and values in guiding the initial choices and the role of self and environmentally produced consequences in sustaining these choices. For Kanfer, all behavior change efforts can be located at some point on a continuum in which the variance for a decision at any point is determined by a greater or lesser amount of self (internal) versus other (environmental) stimulation.

In the second chapter, Schwartz focuses upon the psychobiology of behavior. He illustrates the way in which response patterns can go astray when the proprioceptive feedback which guides them is inadequate due to insufficiency or inaccuracy. He then illustrates the way in which biofeedback training serves as a prosthesis that elicits and properly directs the behavior control center's error in reducing feedback about the direction of that behavior.

In the third chapter, Risley demonstrates some empirical constraints upon the "self" as a control center. His data show that, while individuals may appear to control their own behavior, the goals that they select, the methods that they use, and their willingness to continue acting in the same way are all very much under the influence of external events. These data revive but, of course, do not resolve the classic free will-determinism debate insofar as they show that choice is never free because it is always influenced by environmental influences; however it is never fully determined—one is always free to thwart the flow of environmental pressures and to give up proffered pleasures or to accept predictable pain as a consequence of nonconforming action.

The next series of papers illustrates data-based attempts to enable individuals to gain lasting control over their own behaviors. The papers by Goldfried, Marlatt and Marques, and Miller all illustrate different methods of attempting to enable clients to control emotions that interfere with productive behavior. Goldfried refines the technique of helping individuals to dissociate crippling emotional reactions to challenging events by systematically desensitizing these events—a kind of emotional sanitizing with very precise referents. Marlatt and Marques show how generalized emotional control can be taught as one means of neutralizing potentially troublesome emotional action triggers. The method that they evaluate is meditation which has a broad-spectrum mood-controlling effect. While Goldfried attempts to neutralize emotions, and Marlatt and Marques attempt to make emotions positive, Miller's paper illustrates an attempt to create a negative reaction to a previously positive event in order to redirect behavior.

Five of the papers in this volume illustrate different approaches of efforts to change thought patterns as a means of promoting behavior change. McFall illustrates the role of self-produced behavioral feedback as data that cue and reinforce behavior change. Goldfried demonstrates a system for redirecting counterproductive thought patterns based upon the observations some years ago by Kelly (1955) that our behavior is channeled by our preception of alternatives for action. Goldfried recognizes that if we erroneously clog one of the channels of action by a faulty belief, action in that direction can be impossible with sometimes unfortunate effects. The papers by Bootzin, Miller, and Heckerman and Prochaska all take a proactive approach to the role of cognition in behavior control: Each of them illustrates a different way in which individuals can be helped to analyze their own interaction with the events that influence their behavior, and then to use this information to reprogram environmental events so that desired behaviors are more likely to occur.

All of the foregoing papers, except Risley's, utilize the traditional therapist-client interaction. Clients present themselves to therapists for rational discussion of change alternatives; they receive instigations that suggest innovative behaviors in their natural environments, often with some practice in these behaviors during the treatment session itself; and then they are encouraged to put the therapeutic recommendations into practice. In the next chapter, Suedfeld recognizes that this may not be the most efficient technique for instigating change. Drawing upon research from a number of settings, he reasons that the therapist could do things to the process of instigation that would increase the likelihood that the client will follow through. He presents data to show that by creating a climate of sensory deprivation in which distractions are at a minimum, and by offering an intensive exposure to instigative messages over time, the probability of client behavior change can be increased. Research such as that by Suedfeld can go far toward encouraging behavior modifiers to think of creative ways to increase client compliance with their instigations through improved service delivery techniques.

The next three chapters are also concerned with the settings in which service is delivered. The papers by Buhler and McKay and Stuart illustrate conventional self-help efforts to promote behavior change where professional services have been found lacking. The self-help model employed features professional-conceived services that are delivered by lay people. Self-help services of this sort are likely to be highly relevant to the efficient needs of their recipients; they are cost efficient and are accepted with less resistance than many professional services which often better serve institutional than client needs, are expensive and build the barriers that stimulate self-help groups to action.

The Vancouver Health Collective described by Buhler and McKay and Weight Watchers programs described by Stuart are organizations in which present or former clients offer service to others. Then the Vancouver Mental Patients Association describes its ultimate step toward self-help. In the VMPA model, the servers are the served: The group both offers and receives treatment. The gap between treatment conception and client need can therefore never be smaller than it is in this approach, and the model is one that merits very careful examination and considerable experimentation.

Finally, Stunkard addresses one of the most neglected issues in the behavior modification literature: the problem of maintaining change. He offers a comprehensive model of the etiology and control of obesity and then presents his format for comparing the effects of various treatment approaches. While recognizing the complexity of maintenance evaluation which must take into account client differences, treatment factors, treatment duration and factors in the treatment such as therapist characteristics, method and duration of contact, Stunkard offers a rather simple model that contrasts pounds lost at the end of treatment with the follow-up results, ignoring intervention differences. While not a final answer, Stunkard moves further toward offering a framework of comparing long-term treatment outcomes than has been offered before. His paper should stimulate considerable thought in the years ahead.

In general, behavior modifiers are faced with the task of choosing the least intrusive treatment method having the longest lasting effect. Like the task of selecting the deepest lake at the highest altitude, the task is never satisfactorily done because every choice is arbitrary. In this technique-focused volume, suggestions are made for procedures that cover a broad spectrum with regard to the intensity with which they are offered. Some of the least intrusive techniques may not have the staying power offered by other procedures that are more pervasive. On the other hand, high intrusiveness in intervention may lead to overdependency and lessened maintainability over the long haul. We still do not have studies involving multi-method comparisons with clients of known characteristics as sources of data for choosing intervention methods. The cost of this research and the kaleidoscopic changes that take place in the developing theory and practice of behavior modification may prevent a data base from ever being available. Nevertheless, it is hoped that researchers, theorists and clinicians alike will turn to volumes such as this as a catalog of the possible in their efforts to choose the best.

REFERENCES

BANDURA, A. and PERLOFF, B.: Relative efficacy of self-monitored and externally imposed reinforcement systems. *Journal of Personality and Social Psychology*, 1967, 7, 111-116.

DAVISON, G. C., and STUART, R. B.: Behavior therapy and civil liberties. *American Psychologist*, 1975, 30, 755-763.

JONES, R. T., NELSON, R. E., and KAZDIN, A. E.: The role of external variables in self-reinforcement: A review. *Behavior Modification*, 1977, 1, 147-178.

KELLY, G. A.: *The Psychology of Personal Constructs*. New York: W. W. Norton, 1955.

SKINNER, B. F.: *Science and Human Behavior*. New York: Macmillan, 1953.

STUART, R. B.: Situational versus self control. In: R. D. Rubin, H. Fensterheim, J. D. Henderson, & L. P. Ullmann (Eds.), *Advances in Behavior Therapy*. New York: Academic Press, 1972a.

STUART, R. B.: The role of social work education in innovative human services. In: F. W. Clark, D. R. Evans, & L. A. Hamerlynck (Eds.), *Implementing Behavioral Programs for Schools and Clinics*. Champaign, Illinois: Research Press, 1972b.

Contributors

CATHY BATTEN
*The Vancouver Mental Patients'
Association*

DAVE BEAMISH
*The Vancouver Mental Patients'
Association*

RICHARD R. BOOTZIN
Northwestern University, Evanston

LYNN BUHLER
*Vancouver Women's Health
Collective*

MOLLY DEXALL
*The Vancouver Mental Patients'
Association*

MARVIN R. GOLDFRIED
*State University of New York
at Stony Brook*

CAROL LANDAU HECKERMAN
Butler Hospital, Providence

JACKIE HOOPER
*The Vancouver Mental Patients'
Association*

FREDERICK H. KANFER
*University of Illinois at
Urbana-Champaign*

G. ALAN MARLATT
University of Washington, Seattle

JANICE K. MARQUES
University of Washington, Seattle

GORDON MCCANN
*The Vancouver Mental Patients'
Association*

RICHARD M. MCFALL
University of Wisconsin, Madison

RETA MCKAY
*Vancouver Women's Health
Collective*

WILLIAM R. MILLER
The University of New Mexico

FRANCES PHILLIPS
*The Vancouver Mental Patients'
Association*

TOM POLLOK
*The Vancouver Mental Patients'
Association*

JAMES O. PROCHASKA
University of Rhode Island

TODD R. RISLEY
University of Kansas

xvii

GARY E. SCHWARTZ
Yale University

RICHARD B. STUART
University of Utah

ALBERT J. STUNKARD
University of Pennsylvania

PETER SUEDFELD
The University of British Columbia

1

The Many Faces of Self-Control, or Behavior Modification Changes Its Focus

FREDERICK H. KANFER

INTRODUCTION

If a practitioner of behavior therapy had decided to take a long leave of absence in 1965 and returned today, he would be astonished and confused. The multitude of books and articles on behavior modification contains contradictions and complexities that represent many of the positions which the systematic approach of the conditioning therapies had attempted to avoid. For example, use of self-reports for assessment and treatment, methods designed to alter thinking and imagery, concern with the client's attitudes toward himself and motivation to change, and stress on the patient's self-management of the treatment program are new ingredients of behavior therapy. These techniques seem to be flourishing and gaining wide acceptance by clinicians of all orientations. While the precariously thin theoretical and research base has made many psychologists uneasy, many contemporary behavior therapists seem all too eager to absorb, compromise, integrate or incorporate all the concepts and methods of traditional systems, which focused on the "processes-in-the-head" (and perhaps in the heart and hormones) as the primary determinants of action.

This interest in covert processes may reflect a growing maturity and

1

sophistication of a neo-behavioral approach, if it leads to an expansion of the basic learning model, which includes modifying variables, associated with cognitive activities, as they are needed to improve prediction of human behavior. But the understanding of covert processes has been the unresolved core problem of psychology for centuries. So far, no satisfactory methodological or substantive models have been developed that can objectively assess private events or even answer simple questions about the nature of memory, the genesis and use of language, or the processing and categorizing of perceptual information. The advances of the last few decades may have prepared us to recognize the complex interactional nature of behavior-in-environment, as well as the inadequacy of previous models of processes-in-the-head. But acquiring knowledge for the engineering of practical behavior change programs must be distinguished from having knowledge about fundamental psychological processes on which the techniques are based. Treatment by behavior therapy has expanded in scope to cover the full range of problems encountered in clinical, counseling and consultative practices. But it is important that principles from the learning laboratory be integrated with research findings from all other areas of psychology to yield a conceptual model, not only of the learning changes in the patient, but also of the total context of the intervention process. It is essential that the broadening framework and its complex procedures, however effective, be as carefully tested, in all aspects, as was the simple conditioning paradigm.

Despite the rapprochement with the domain, contents, and methods of other therapies, the behavioral approach has maintained most of its characteristic features. In treatment, the focus on behavior, the pretreatment commitment to methods, objectives and treatment rationales, and the continuing assessment of change remain at the heart of the approach. But at times, the attempt to expand behavior therapy into new areas has led to problems that have often been bypassed rather than resolved.

In essence, self-management therapy represents a new stage in behavior therapy. It emphasizes an active rather than a passive model of man and leans heavily on an interactional view of personality. In addition, it includes target behaviors which are not directly observable, but can only be inferred from subsequent actions or, in some cases, from self-reports. Self-management therapy also involves the use of the same person as subject and therapist in the execution of the treatment program.

The success of self-management techniques has encouraged clinicians and investigators to expand rapidly, resulting in a widening gap between clinical methods and a supporting theoretical framework securely anchored in research. Cognitive techniques and attention to a person's self-generated behavior introduce a critical departure from earlier efforts to derive methods and explanations solely from a conditioning model. Use of these techniques requires a shift toward research on those psychological processes on which the new treatments are based. While learning theory, research on anxiety and some areas of social psychology were adequate for environmentally-induced behavior change methods, self-management therapy, reattribution therapy, use of coping strategies, or covert conditioning require recourse to research on the specific processes by which individuals modify simple input-output relationships and organize individual repertoires—a domain that has generally been covered in the study of personality. And, if it is necessary to understand the organization of a person's behavior repertoire in all its complexity, then the prevailing research makes a mediational or a cognitive behavior model more attractive than a simple S-R model.

The complex methodological problems in this area lend themselves to an easy temptation to foresake observation or low-level inference for constructs and analogues with a long history and wide popular appeal. Thus, it becomes especially important to describe fully the processes about which we speak, and not to accept their existence mainly by postulation or on the grounds of common experience. It is, in fact, this insistence on empirical verification that is a *sine qua non,* the pillar of a behavioral approach. To talk about thinking, belief-systems, self-control or attribution, we must therefore gain knowledge about the characteristics of the behavioral processes to which these terms refer—and the variables which affect them. Clearly, there is much to be done before this can be accomplished.

In simplest terms, the field of behavior modification has moved away from a relatively restricted conditioning model, be it respondent or operant, toward engineering a) the patient's contribution to his own treatment, and b) the effects of the social and therapeutic context on various sections of the treatment process. Behavior modification has now placed itself in the same arena with competing and encompassing systems which have taken a stand on critical issues related to a model of Man (for example, the origin and function of behavior variations, the optimal goals of life, etc.). While this development robs the approach of some of its simplicity, it also permits behavior modifiers to expand their research and to develop new techniques and procedures. It promises to bring the entire clinical enterprise into one theoretical framework and thus guide research toward new areas. This trend should end a period in which behavioral clinicians were forced to rely on clinical folklore or on traditional personality theories for guidance in structuring intervention programs or selecting critical behavioral contents for evaluation. But it also demands a new data base for the expansion.

From a different point of view, the new developments move behavior modification closer to the type of field model that has been anticipated by such field theorists as Kantor (1924) and others. The early conditioning model, not very different from the analytic paradigm which it attempted to replace, put its explanatory mechanisms into a linear personality model. Input variables were related to the organism's output without much consideration of the constant dynamic interplay among variables both in the environment and in the individual. Current research in personality makes it clear that the environment-organism interplay requires careful examination of the interactional setting factors of behavior (Bowers, 1973; Cronbach, 1975; Ekehammar, 1974; Mischel, 1973). The complexity of behavior and its susceptibility to continuing change in the social environment may well preclude the construction of any broad and lasting generalizations. For the practical setting, the most precise guide we may ever hope to establish is a set of working hypotheses which require affirmation anew as the client and the context change (Cronbach, 1975).

The emphasis on the reciprocal interaction between a person and his environment implies the need for a thorough investigation of the "pull value" of a client's behavior on his social environment and a careful assessment of the attitudes and actions which the client elicits from the people with whom he interacts. While both protagonists and critics of the behavioral model have stressed the organism's dependence on the environment, behaviorists like Skinner have also called attention to the reciprocal relationship. A person is the product of his environment. His behavior, in turn, shapes the environment and, thus, the individual is able to modify the conditions under which he lives. It is this second direction of behavioral effects on which the methods of self-management therapy concentrate.

A philosophy that credits a person with potential for active alteration of his environment and his own behavior is the very antithesis of a mechanistic, passive, environmentally determined picture of Man—a concept of man-as-machine which has its modern roots in Watsonian classical behaviorism. The goal of self-control methods is to train individuals to become better problem-solvers and behavior analysts. These methods are designed to help them become more independent of the immediate environment (Goldiamond, 1965). It is too easy, however, to conceptualize the treatment process in terms of a single curative feature. Skill training in problem-solving or covert sensitization surely can be critical elements in treatment, but no method is so powerful that it can be applied universally, without regard to its context. We consider the client's motivation to change a prerequisite for effective self-management therapy. Consequently, with many clients any behaviors or conditions which enhance or oppose change become the primary targets before the problem behavior *per se* is attacked. In this connection, other factors must be considered: the ratio of payoffs for present behavior in relation to the anticipated payoffs for change; the client's reason for coming to therapy; his available behavioral skills for self-change; the availability of motivational resources for acquiring and maintaining a change; acquaintance with persons knowledgeable about therapy; and the probable support of the changed behavior by the social environment. These are just a few of the factors which can affect the results of the selected treatment methods.

In the following section, the central theme is the theoretical and empirical base of self-regulation processes. Then, the concept of self-control is re-analyzed and the role of contracts in self-regulation is considered. Finally, some clinical issues in self-management therapy and the implications of our analysis are discussed.

SELF-REGULATION

For purposes of organization, it is helpful to conceptualize differences among the multiple influences on behavior in terms of their current origin. We have suggested that situational (alpha), self-generated (beta) and biological (gamma) variables are in constant flux with regard to their joint impact on behavior at a specified time (Kanfer & Karoly, 1972). Rather than postulating a dichotomous division between external and self-generated factors, a dynamic model that assumes a changing range from a minimal to a maximal contribution of each set of independent variables seems to fit the empirical facts. It also is probabilistic rather than definitive with regard to behavior predictions. While the gamma variables can never go to a zero value, their contribution may momentarily be fixed across many situations and for a wide range of phenomena.

Thus, they may be of little interest to the observer. Similarly, alpha and beta variables may assume major or minor importance in affecting a given behavior in a given situation.

This view tends to distinguish between different emphases of clinical approaches. Broadly, environmentally anchored change programs (commonly represented by operant control) illustrate the focus on alpha variables. Self-management methods exemplify the use of beta factors and some techniques for anxiety reduction or change of emotional arousal illustrate the emphasis on gamma variables. But it is essential to note that a) no event is likely to be under total control of only one set of variables, and b) these influences constantly interact and moderate the final effect. The observations of counter-control in token economies and the effects of self-generated verbal instructions on arousal level are selected instances which illustrate both the multiply determined and complex nature of the phenomena.

The degree of influence changes across time and events. Consequently, we cannot expect to predict more than probable effects of any of the three sets of controlling variables. Neither external nor self nor physiological control can ever be wired permanently into the organism or the situation! From this viewpoint many questions about self vs. external control are as empty as those posed earlier in the nature-nurture controversy. For clinical purposes the effects of proper combinations of the three sets of determinants need to be evaluated for their utility in achieving a desired effect. Clearly, if the influences of these sets of variables are in opposition, as they frequently are in human problems, then any shift in the magnitude of one determinant could alter the behavior. Self-regulation methods in socialization, as in therapy, are often aimed at reducing the effects of temporary fluctuations in alpha and gamma variables on a person's behavior, thereby increasing individual continuity and consistency.

Among the natural sciences psychology has been especially burdened by its historical link with philosophy, theology and common sense. As a result, the domain of psychology, as well as its methodology and its terminology, has been continually influenced by the social and cultural matrix in which investigations take place. Not only the professional but also the scientist have yielded to social and philosophical pressures in the organization of the domain and in the selection of the phenomena which they investigate. The attempt to analyze events in the area of self-regulation has been affected by these pressures. As a result, currently used constructs and conceptualizations have been heavily contaminated by the investigator's biases, derived from membership in a society which has very definitive notions about this domain and its relevance to human behavior and to social organization. Despite the efforts to provide some empirical data on which an analysis of self-regulation phenomena could be based, questions repeatedly are raised that are irrelevant to a scientific analysis. These questions reflect our extra-scientific concerns and deserve to be answered, but perhaps not until they have been rephrased in a manner that makes them amenable to empirical investigation. It therefore is necessary to redefine the domain and to use such terms as self-direction and self-control only to designate an area of interest rather than as constructs, mechanisms or psychological forces.

A general three-stage model of self-regulation has previously been described (Kanfer 1970, 1971, 1975; Kanfer & Karoly, 1972) as a heuristic framework for organizing research. The domain of self-control has been differentiated as a special case of self-regulation, to which the model can be adapted. The domain covers self-directed behavior sequences in which a person is exposed to conflict and to the requirement for taking actions which initially alter the likelihood of executing a previously highly probable response. Thus, in self-control the criterion for performance represents the attainment of some complex goal that is contrary to previous or concurrent behavioral standards and may have conflicting consequences. Examples of such situations are the reduction of food intake, the tolerance of the pains of a medical procedure, the failure to approach an attractive sexual object or the inhibition of a physical attack. The self-regulation model, however, also includes situations such as new learning, complex problem-solving in which the criterion-attainment is generally either neutral or favorable.

There are at least three reasons why self-control is a domain of special interest to psychologists as well as to students of social organizations. *First,* traditional views stress the importance of the individual's capacity to regulate his own behavior, particularly to control his inclination to gain immediate personal benefits. Such capacity is critical for group survival, since the interests of an individual often conflict with the interests of his social group. From Freud's early emphasis on the struggle between id impulses and ego demands to current research on the socialization of the young child, personality theorists have been aware of the importance of the balance between the achievement of immediate individual satisfactions and the impact of such gains on the social structure and the welfare of others. The human condition also includes numerous situations in

which immediate satisfactions are achieved at the cost of long range aversive consequences, not only to society but also to the individual himself.
In societies in which individuals are encouraged to plan ahead to maximize overall benefits, an understanding of psychological and social processes that facilitate such behaviors as delay of gratification, resistance to
temptation, tolerance of aversive situations and similar such conditions is
essential.

The development of self-regulation also becomes essential in complex
societies in which external control is neither desirable nor feasible. In fact,
it might be posited that as social surveillance increases there is a decreased
need for self-regulatory behaviors.

A *second* reason for concern about self-control stems from its association with the concepts of responsibility and morality. Sacrifice, delay of
gratification, restraint and moderation in the enjoyment of worldly goods
have been the guiding principles of theologians and moral philosophers
of many different persuasions. The current value system in the United
States in the 1970s, despite recent attacks and rapid shifts, still accepts
restraint, moderation, resistance to temptation and sacrifice as inherently
good and desirable. As Skinner has indicated in *Beyond Freedom and
Dignity* (1971), considerable credit is given for behavior that appears to
be relatively independent of environmental controlling contingencies.
Admiration goes to persons who sacrifice immediate reinforcers or tolerate aversive consequences for the sake of some greater, nobler social good.
As Mischel and Mischel have recently pointed out (1976), self-regulatory
behaviors are also required to achieve the moral ideals that are prescribed
by our culture.

A *third* reason for the interest in the area of self-control relates directly
to psychological theory. At the turn of the century, psychodynamic theory
suggested essentially an interaction between two major personality systems; the self-system, an intrapersonal system that represents the core of
personality, and a more superficial system that deals with the social and
physical environment. Theorists differ with regard to the degree to which
they see the self-system resulting from the environment's shaping of the
individual's potential. Most personality theorists clearly give priority to
psychological phenomena (including cognitive structures, constellations
of motivational forces, or other processes) that are attributed to intrapersonal development, be it genetic, biological or socially assisted. Secondary
emphasis is given to the habit pattern which the individual learns, in conformity with his social environment, to express or moderate these intra-

personal factors. Behavioristic approaches characteristically differ in that they clearly give priority to the role of the environment in shaping the broad and unchanneled potentials of the individual. In behavioristic theory the development of individual learning patterns, the acquisition of skills in dealing with others, and even the development of cognitive behaviors, fantasies, dreams and emotional reactions have been attributed heavily to learning experiences. It is clear therefore that the area of self-regulation and self-control represents a field of contest for opposing points of view and is critical not only for our understanding of specific behaviors in limited situations but also for our conceptualization of personality.

In the following sections I will review some recent studies evaluating the relationship among the components of the self-regulation model. The subsequent brief discussion of research and issues in self-monitoring and self-reinforcement is directed mainly toward the potential clinical application of these procedures.

RELATIONSHIPS AMONG THE SELF-REGULATION MODEL COMPONENTS

Behavior modification techniques were originally derived from conditioning models and clinicians limited themselves to a research base that supported the particular learning techniques used in a treatment. Because of our awareness that all components of the total clinical enterprise may be important in influencing treatment progress, the research and theoretical base for self-management therapy has been broadened now to include almost the entire field of human psychology. For example, the client's expectation of therapy, his relationship to the therapist and the social context are considered critical features that may determine treatment success (Kanfer & Phillips, 1970; Gottman & Leiblum, 1974). However, the most closely related areas of interest are those that examine the processes by which a person modulates or counteracts the influence of environmental inputs, or integrates them with prior experiences to form an important set of determinants of his behavior.

Attempts to explain the processes describing the organization and use of environmental inputs have created the widest conceptual disagreements among students of human behavior. These questions about the essential nature of man may seem philosophic, but they have a direct bearing on the clinician's conceptualization of his clients, on the development of techniques of behavior change, and on the justification for the use of various treatment methods.

Setting aside the monumental task of explaining these processes, we will limit our discussion to a model which we have used to study self-regulation processes. This model assumes the utility (though by no means the veracity) of a behavioral analogue for covert processes. It assumes that, until we have evidence to the contrary, cognitive activities can be treated as behavior, even though specific parameter and process conditions might be unique to this class of events (see Mahoney, 1974 for a summary of some supporting evidence). It aims solely at constructing a framework for integrating observations and directing research. This model, which has been described in detail elsewhere (Kanfer, 1971, 1975; Kanfer & Karoly, 1972), proposes three related stages in self-regulation, self-monitoring, self-evaluation, and self-reinforcement. It is based on earlier research of the component processes. Since its first presentation, a number of variables have suggested themselves for inclusion in the model.

The original presentation of the self-regulation model did not consider attribution. As Bandura (1971) has suggested, the administration of self-reinforcement may depend not only on achieving a standard set by oneself but also on the importance of that achievement to the person. Specifically, attribution of a monitored performance to a person's own skills or effort, to some change factor, or to the task difficulty might alter the occurrence or the magnitude of a self-reward. Some support for this relationship between success attribution and self-reinforcement has been reported by Weiner, Heckhausen, Meyer, and Cook (1972, Exper. I). In a recent paper, Rehm (1975) has further suggested that the self-evaluation stage in the model be reconceptualized to apply only when the performance is internally attributed. This redefinition invokes consideration of another source of possible problems in self-regulation of clients, namely that faulty attributions might affect self evaluation and influence a self-control program. To date it is not clear at which stage of the model the attribution is more important. The above hypothesis suggests that only self-attributed performance is related to self-set standards (and monitoring of externally attributed behaviors would not contribute to self-evaluation). A second possibility is that attribution affects only the subsequent self-reinforcement stage. Thus self-reward or self-criticism *following* self-evaluation would depend on the attribution. The former view implies that self-monitoring has differential, selective effects on self-evaluation as a function of attribution; the latter view predicts differences only at the point of dispensation of self-reinforcement. Of course, it is possible that the attribution influence is of importance at both stages.

In our laboratories, two attempts were made to examine the effects of attribution on self-reinforcement. In an unpublished experiment subjects were given a complex Braille-like task, and told that their scores depended on ability, effort or luck. After training with true feedback they were asked to self-evaluate and self-reward. Although group differences in the expected direction were found on early trials, these effects quickly dissipated. From post-experimental questionnaire data we concluded that the subjects did not adopt our causal ascriptions because of the lack of stable feedback consistent with the attributions made on the basis of our instructions.

In a later study (Newman & Kanfer, 1976), variable feedback and stable feedback were introduced as experimental conditions. In a pseudo-perceptual task, the scores were also said to be the subject's or those of another subject and external reward in training was correlated or uncorrelated with feedback. It was found that subjects did not make differential attribution in the different conditions, nor were there significant main effects of attribution on self-evaluation or self-reward. These attempts have led us to be cautious about assuming the ease with which subjects accept attributions. But they have not furthered our knowledge about the role of attribution in self-regulation. Several recent studies have contributed toward further clarification of the relationships between the component processes of the model. One important question concerns the contributions of the separate components to the effectiveness of the total process. Others deal with the clinical utility of a program designed on the basis of the variables specified in the model.

Spates and Kanfer (1977) tested the relative contributions of the self-monitoring, criterion setting, self-evaluation and self-reinforcement components in the learning of a simple arithmetic task in first-graders. Five- to six-year-old children were selected for the study, after they failed a criterion-task of addition. A *control* group observed the experimenter carry out 12 addition problems while verbalizing only the numbers which he added. For a *self-monitoring* group the experimenter verbalized the operations which he carried out. In a *criterion setting* group the experimenter modeled the criteria for proper addition. In a *self-monitoring* plus *criterion setting* group the experimenter self-monitored his actions and verbalized the proper criteria. Finally, the *self-evaluation plus self-reinforcement* group observed the experimenter carry out self-monitoring, criterion setting and saying "I am right" or "I am wrong" subsequent to each component operation. All groups practiced the proper procedure until they could perform it correctly. Thus, training consisted of teaching the child to generate different self-instructions while doing the task. No feedback on arithmetic accuracy was given. The children were not required to verbalize aloud the previously trained self-instructions.

The results indicated significant differential improvement among the groups. The control and self-monitoring groups differed only marginally in improvement (p <.08). Both the control and the self-monitoring groups differed significantly from all other experimental groups in the amount of improvement on the post-test. The inclusion of criterion-setting in training was the most significant feature. Training in additional components, i.e., self-reinforcement and self-monitoring plus criterion-setting, yielded no further significant reduction in errors. While the pretest scores for all children ranged from 8 to 12 errors on 12 trials, on the post-test the groups which had been trained either in criterion setting or in self-evaluation made between 0 and 3 errors. In contrast, the control group and the self-monitoring-only group averaged 6 to 8 errors, respectively, on the 12 post-test trials. Omega Squares were computed for the within group changes and indicated that training in additional components of the model increased the percentages of variance accounted for. The control procedure accounted for 0.7% of the variance; training and self-monitoring accounted for 20.9%; training in criterion-setting accounted for 89.3%; training in self-monitoring plus criterion-setting accounted for 90.3%; and training in self-evaluation plus self-reinforcement accounted for 99.3% of the variance. These results suggest that the establishment of a criterion against which a person can test his current performance is a critical element in the effectiveness of self-regulation for improved performance.

In a doctoral dissertation, Greiner (1974) addressed a similar question in a clinical analogue. He examined the relative effectiveness of the basic components of the model in a study skills program. In addition, he compared the effectiveness of a program designed on the basis of the model with the standard SQ3R program. The subjects were undergraduates who had poor study habits and low grade point averages (GPA). They were asked to report their GPA and their performance on their first quiz in Introductory Psychology. They also took a questionnaire assessing motivation to change study habits and the Brown and Holtzman Survey of Study Habits and Attitudes (SSHA). Each subject's scores on these variables were weighted and summed to yield a weighted score. On the basis of these scores, subjects were randomly assigned to one of six groups. In the first part of training all students were given a lecture on how to use Robinson's SQ3R method, and asked to keep outlines on chapters in the Introductory Psychology text and use the text workbook. They were then divided into the following groups: Group I was given further tips on how to take examinations but no training in self-control techniques. Group II was given the same training but also a strong expectancy that the program would result in better grades and study habits. In Group III, subjects were given the same training but they were also taught to self-monitor and record their study activities. In Group IV, training in self-reward strategies was added to the training of the preceding groups. In Group V, subjects were given the same training as Group IV and were also trained how to plan strategies, that is to set criteria for scheduling their work and attaching contingencies for successfully completed tasks. Group VI was a control group which received no further training.

At the end of the training session, all subjects were given contracts which specified what was expected of them during the academic quarter. They were also promised research credit. They returned after two weeks to review the major points of the SQ3R method and the particular self-control techniques in which they had been instructed. At that time they took a brief quiz on the SQ3R method. During the last week of the academic quarter all subjects took the SSHA again and another version of the study questionnaire. In addition, workbooks, outlines, and other products of their study activity were collected. The data analysis was carried out separately for process and outcome measures. With regard to process, it was found that the group which was given the basic techniques and also instructed to set standards by planning their work and rewarding themselves for reaching their criteria performed significantly better on all of the measures than did the groups that had been taught to self-monitor only, or to self-monitor and self-reward. The latter two groups did not differ significantly from each other, and the self-monitor only group did not differ from the groups that had only gotten information, or information plus an expectation for improvement. These results are quite consistent with the data obtained in the Spates and Kanfer (1977) study. They suggest that the establishment of criteria for performance represents a critical feature when the self-regulation model is applied in a behavior change program.

The analysis of outcome measures was quite similar. The group that had been helped to plan criteria setting for their studying showed the highest increase in all outcome measures, performing significantly better than all other groups. Consistent with the findings of some other clinical studies and the data reported above in the Spates and Kanfer study, self-monitoring alone had little effect on study activity or outcome. The addition of self-reward showed superiority over the self-monitoring and information group only on a few process measures but not on outcome measures. Essentially, the subjects who used self-reward seemed to improve their study habits but this did not assist them in studying effectively.

Effectiveness of the procedure for the planning group cannot be attributed to the criterion setting alone, however, since the design combined added components in succeeding groups. Thus, the addition of a strategy for planning might potentiate the effects of self-monitoring and self-reward. Alternately, training in planning strategies alone may represent a sufficient factor. These two hypotheses could not be differentiated on the basis of Greiner's design. Taken together, however, the results of the two studies strongly suggest that the self-evaluative component plays a critical role in the application of self-directing procedures. In fact, it is reasonable to speculate that the divergent results of reported studies on self-monitoring and self-reward might well be due to the role of self-evaluation. When a procedure for self-monitoring and for self-reward aids subjects to generate their own criteria, greater effectiveness would be expected than in a procedure in which no criteria are specified or none can be generated by subjects. The discussion of inconsistent outcome data in the self-monitoring literature (e.g., Nelson, 1975; Kazdin, 1974; Kanfer, 1970; Lipinski & Black, 1975) suggests that in some cases the context of self-monitoring may be sufficient to provide subtle criteria for the subject, even though they are not regarded as part of the experimental variable.

SELF-MONITORING

In the clinical area, the parameters of self-monitoring have recently undergone extensive study, since this technique is critical as a means of collecting information from a client in self-management therapy. Reviews by Kazdin (1974) and Nelson (1975) have begun to clarify the conditions which enhance the therapeutic effects of self-monitoring. For clinical purposes, it is well to remember that self-monitoring probably always implies some goal. Therefore, it is difficult to isolate this activity from some self-evaluative reaction to the products of self-monitoring. For these reasons it is not surprising that the motivation of the person to alter the monitored behavior, the selection of a positively or negatively valued behavior for monitoring, the availability of particular goals for change of the monitored behavior and the potential function of the observing response as a reinforcer are among the variables affecting the role of self-monitoring in behavior change. In addition, individuals differ in rates of self-monitoring (Snyder, 1974).

Various studies tend to agree that in clinical programs self-monitoring is most effective in the early stages but does not maintain a behavior change very long (Kazdin, 1974). Several important questions remain to be resolved for effective clinical application. How does the arousal level associated with the monitored behavior affect the faithfulness and reactivity of self-monitoring? For instance, are these effects different for monitoring study habits than for anxiety-related behaviors? Other critical questions deal with the role of self-monitoring as a means of establishing a client's active role in a treatment process, initiating other beneficial processes such as the self-attribution of any generated change, or increasing awareness of the antecedents of target behaviors. Finally, the requirement to attend to target behaviors which result in strong aversive consequences may result in learned avoidance of the monitoring activity, as suggested by the studies on selective attention to the self (Mischel & Ebbesen, 1970; Byrne, 1964).

Horan and his coworkers have addressed this problem experimentally (Horan, 1974; Horan & Johnson, 1971; Horan, Baker, Hoffman, & Shute, 1975; Horan, Smyers, Dorfman, & Jenkins, 1975). They found that obese persons are less willing to tolerate observation of their image than average weight persons. Subjects also tend to resist or quit programs that require focusing on aversive aspects of their person or behavior. Just as other component activities in self-management therapy may require the use of new skills, renewed motivation, or environmental support to overcome the initial resistance to behavior change, the monitoring task, *per se,* may have to be treated as a problem in self-control. Specifically, in some cases the requirement that a client self-monitor, or carry out an assigned task, or change a contingency for rewarding a spouse, can be defined as a problem in self-control if 1) the client is in conflict because a change may bring both positive and negative consequences; 2) the client is asked to initiate a new behavior on his own; and 3) a well over-learned chain of behaviors must be interrupted to carry out the new task. The techniques for assuming self-control must then be introduced in connection with the therapy assignment.

A recent dissertation by Kirschenbaum (1975) contributes further to analysis of the connection between self-monitoring and the other stages of the self-regulation model. The model suggests that self-monitoring is an essential feature in the total process. Consequently, Kirschenbaum argued that the value of the monitored behavior might be an important factor since self-monitoring of aversive events, compared to self-monitoring of positively valued behavior, should result in an unfavorable self-evaluation. As a result, positive self-reinforcement should be reduced and negative affect increased. Execution of such behavior should be aversive and should eventually be stopped. Kirschenbaum hypothesized further that the difficulty of the task would interact with self-monitoring. Negative self-monitoring on a difficult task might be detrimental to performance and tend to reduce self-monitoring because of the subjects' perception of the hopelessness of their efforts. However, on an easy task negative self-monitoring should increase self-monitoring and facilitate performance.

The subjects in Kirschenbaum's study were student volunteers who planned to take admission tests to graduate programs and who were promised some opportunity to practice problems in the mathematical area. All subjects were pretested in small groups on math problems of medium difficulty. In subsequent individual sessions, subjects were divided into three groups according to their math ability. A second between-groups factor was the task difficulty (easy or difficult). Finally, there were four different self-monitoring conditions. In a *positive self-monitoring* group, the subjects could monitor only correct responses, in the *negative self-monitoring* group only incorrect responses. A *performance feedback control* group was given feedback about their overall performance and their individual responses but did not self-monitor. *Control* subjects obtained overall performance feedback (as all other groups), but received neither feedback on individual responses nor self-monitoring opportunities. There were three problem-solving sessions, each followed by a period for answering questions and a free time period. Self-monitoring consisted of self-initiated replay of a videotape of the prior performance on either correctly or incorrectly solved problems. Subjects were also invited to make notes on the videotape replay. Performance measures, self-evaluation measures, measures of assigned self-reward or self-penalty and anxiety checklists represented the additional dependent variables.

The results indicated that subjects who monitored only incorrect performance evaluated themselves less favorably than subjects in all other groups. In addition, subjects who monitored incorrect responses also tended to decrease their reported self-reward level over blocks of trials in comparison to an increase in self-reward by subjects who self-monitored correct responses. Further, all subjects who worked on difficult tasks reported higher anxiety levels than those who worked on the easy tasks. There was a trend in the association of greater self-reported anxiety for subjects who monitored incorrect responses than those who observed their correct responses.

On the difficult task, positive self-monitoring resulted in increased accuracy of performance as compared to negative self-monitoring. Finally, on the easy task, negative self-monitoring led to more self-monitoring on later trial blocks than positive self-monitoring. However, negative self-monitoring was also associated with poorer performance. These findings clearly show that the various components of the self-regulation model affect each other; further, the relationship is modified by such variables as task difficulty and, perhaps, by the anxiety arousal level induced by the difficulty of the problem. For clinical applications, the study suggests that care must be taken in selecting target behaviors for self-monitoring because of the probable effects on subsequent self-evaluation and self-reinforcement by the subject. As we have indicated earlier, Horan's findings (Horan, Smyers, Dorfman, & Jenkins, 1975) of treatment avoidance after use of negative coverants support this suggestion.

SELF-REINFORCEMENT

Most self-management programs utilize self-reinforcement as a means of motivating and maintaining behavior change. Although there is a large literature on the determinants of self-reinforcement, on its effect on behavior and its role in clinical and personality processes (Bandura, 1971; Kanfer, 1970, 1975; Masters & Mokros, 1974; Mahoney & Thoresen, 1974), several problems arise in the clinic which require clarification. As a technique, self-reinforcement operations can be used for the initiation of a new behavior or long-term maintenance of a response. Apart from the need for distinguishing between various classes of objects and events which can be used as reinforcers (cf. Kanfer, 1975), there is also a difference in two types of cases. If used to acquire a new (and initially low probable) response, the procedure often involves the establishment of criteria for the contingency and the prior deprivation of the event until the contingency is met. For example, rewarding oneself with dinner only after completing the task of answering several letters requires delay of food when hungry and evaluation of the achievement of the criterion. Thus, the procedure meets the conditions which define a self-control problem in that a current noxious state is tolerated for a later positive outcome. Two studies in which self-reward was contingent on an external criterion are discussed in a later section on resistance to temptation.

In contrast to the problem of delay in contingent self-reward, following a habitual task—such as a daily routine of hygiene—with a self-reward which is not related to a deprivation, or giving noncontingent self-rewards at predetermined intervals simply requires that the client remember to take the reward. In both cases the reward may have informational or motivational properties, or both. The degree to which the therapist's help will be needed to establish the procedure will differ in the two cases. There are currently no data that compare the effectiveness of these different procedures on the target behavior, or indicate which of the many possible combinations of procedures and types of self-reward is most effective in long-term programs. Similarly, although clinical lore suggests a gradual shift from material to symbolic self-rewards and from a dense to a lean schedule as most desirable, empirical support for these choices is weak.

SELF-CONTROL

Despite the wide interest in self-control, a conceptual analysis of the underlying psychological processes is still lacking. A rough boundary of the area is given by a widely accepted definition of the domain of self-control as covering psychological processes that involve behavioral shifts in which external influences (alpha variables) are supplemented by self-generated cues and reinforcers (beta variables) in cases where conflict between possible behavioral choices exists. The outcome of these processes can be described in two ways: 1) the probability of a response with initial high likelihood of occurrence is decreased, or 2) the probability of a response with initially low likelihood is increased, by the execution of self-generated behaviors. Most commonly, the initial behaviors are well established by prior learning, have been supported for a long time by immediate reinforcement, or have been maintained by socially or physiologically determined contingencies.

The common element in all situations in this domain involves a *change* of what was initially either a very stable or a very gratifying state of affairs. We have taken the view that this type of situation requires analysis, as any other behavioral episode, in terms of the variables affecting a person's initiation and maintenance of new behaviors. Therefore we talk about behavioral changes that can be brought about by a combination of external (alpha), self-generated (beta), and organismic (gamma) variables. The model requires inclusion of beta processes which may have been learned in previous social interactions but which are now functioning as independent variables, in the absence of momentary environmental influences.

Several research paradigms have developed in this area and generalizations have been made to the entire domain from the results of different studies. However, an analysis of the experimental paradigms reveals that they include different critical variables. It is not clear whether the variables found to be effective in one set of experiments have the same effect under different conditions, or whether the same psychological processes are operating in all the diverse situations. We suspect that interactional effects between the experimental conditions and the independent variables occur and often modify the outcomes. Further, current research efforts have not yet provided sufficient evidence to determine whether consistent person variables may indeed contribute significant variance across situations, or whether individual behavior is highly specific to the various situations which have been used as experimental tests of "self-control."

In any case, a decision needs to be made as to which types of situations are to be included in the domain of self-control, since all the reported experiments, case studies and anecdotes concerning self-control include some degrees of alpha control. For example, in human and animal studies, as well as clinical cases, external control is generally necessary to motivate a subject to initiate a behavioral change and to provide support for the new behaviors.

Our conceptualization also suggests that the effectiveness of beta variables will be limited by the degree to which the influence of alpha and gamma variables are introduced in any future situations. For instance, self-generated control over a social behavior such as stealing may be ineffective when physiological variables, such as hunger, or alpha variables, such as peer approval, are strongly increased. Although it has been suggested that individuals may differ in their sensitivity to alpha and gamma control (e.g., external-internal control, susceptibility to somatic stress, etc.), there is no good indication of the particular behavioral dimensions on which such individual differences occur.

Two Stages in Self-Control

A pragmatic organization of self-control processes results from an analysis of the total sequence within a two-stage model (Kanfer & Karoly, 1972; Mischel, 1974; Premack & Anglin, 1973; Marston & Feldman, 1972). Although many life situations involve both stages, research efforts have focused on them separately. Further, the possibility that each stage may be influenced by different determinants (some due to the inherent difference in the two situations) requires separate treatment. The first stage is characterized by the requirement for a clear and momentary decision to choose among alternatives. In the experimental paradigm of *decisional self-control* (e.g., Mischel, 1966; Grusec, 1968; Rachlin, 1974; Tarpy & Sawabini, 1974; Renner, 1967; Maltzman & Wolff, 1970), a subject is usually presented with two choices. He can obtain immediate reinforcement (either positive or aversive) or delayed delivery of a reinforcer which is usually quantitatively larger. The critical feature of the situation is that only a single response needs to be made. Once a decision has been made, the consequences to the individual are no longer under his control. In other words, the conflict occurs at the choice point. The subject's later fate, such as obtaining a reward or a shock, is under alpha control.

However, in an important variation of decisional self-control the choice of the subject consists of a commitment or contract for his future performance. The variables affecting the act of commitment are of interest in their own right, although they may be different from those which affect the person's later behavior in carrying out the contracted behavior (Kanfer & Karoly, 1972). If the contract involves conflictful behavior and its execution is not fully dependent on environment cues and monitors, the person may then find himself in the second stage, *protracted self-control*. Until the contract requirements are reached, invocation of various self-generated techniques for maintaining the new behavior (competing with strongly established alternatives) may be required. There are several clinical examples of this type of situation. For instance, contracts with others and oneself, the establishment of contingent self-reward (in which the reward is freely available but not taken until the criterion is reached), instances of self-monitoring in which the immediate effects are aversive, or carrying out therapist-suggested, self-initiated novel behaviors—all may involve self-control. In these situations, the commitment (itself a self-control problem) sets the stage for the execution of a protracted series of new behaviors of varying aversiveness, primarily under short-term beta control.

Several groups of experiments have focused on the processes and strategies by which a subject prolongs a waiting period for a future reward or delays escape from a noxious stimulation (e.g., Mischel, 1974; Kanfer & Seidner, 1973). Most studies have examined the effects of various variables on the duration of the subject's endurance or the frequency of success in reaching a pre-set criterion. Although there is no direct evidence on the moment-to-moment events during the interval between commitment and fulfillment, observation and self-reports of human subjects, and data from delay of reinforcement studies in animals have suggested shifts in the incentive values of the alternatives over time (Ainslie, 1975). Within our self-regulation model, it is not unreasonable to hypothesize that subjects continually monitor, evaluate, and reinforce their behavior. Further, with the passage of time changes in criteria may also result from self-evaluation. If a subject continually compares his current achievements with the outcome of any future actions, the discrepancy between the criterion and the result of a contemplated or completed action may represent a source of motivation for the individual to maintain a controlling response or to engage in a transgression. Of course, additional variables such as the intensity of concurrent aversive stimulation, temporal factors, and other variables may further affect his behavior with regard to the initiation of various controlling responses or termination of the situation. The presence of competing responses (and their strength in maintaining the "temptation-resisting" behavior) should further affect this self-regulatory process. These speculations clearly suggest the many variables that require examination as critical determinants of processes and outcome in self-control paradigms.

Decisional Self-Control

We have previously suggested (Kanfer, 1970) that self-regulation processes are not acting continuously. They are primarily activated when well trained behaviors are interrupted or impossible. A large research area on self-control has dealt with different paradigms in which the person is required to act in contrast to his usual and most probable behavior. Extensive discussions of definitions of self-control can be found in numerous recent sources (e.g., Kanfer & Phillips, 1970; Thoresen & Mahoney, 1974; Goldfried & Merbaum, 1973). Unfortunately, the research area has grown around paradigms and it is difficult to compare results because of a lack of analysis of the different elements that constitute the various paradigms.

One large research area concerns a paradigm in which an organism is required to make a choice between two possible responses, one of which brings immediate access to a small amount of reward, while the other leads to a larger reward but only after a specified requisite waiting period. The reward magnitudes and delay intervals of the choices are usually communicated to the subject. This paradigm we have called *decisional self-control*. It is applicable when the net outcomes (i.e., combinations of choices and delays) are sufficiently similar to present some conflict to the person.

Numerous studies have been reported (e.g., Rachlin & Green, 1972; Ainslie, 1974; Mischel & Staub, 1965; Mischel & Gilligan, 1964; Mischel & Grusec, 1967; Seeman & Schwarz, 1974; Grusec, 1968), which have investigated various determinants of the choice behavior. The results of most of these studies have been reviewed by Mischel (1966, 1974) and will not be repeated here. We are concerned primarily with the fact that all of these experiments represent a paradigm that involves a popular concept of self-control because the organism, animal or human, foregoes immediate satisfaction for the sake of a larger reward at a later time. Such "impulse control" has also been scrutinized because of the hope that commitment to wait for a delayed reward may relate to personality variables, to prior experiences with delays, to the organism's behavioral repertoire in reducing the aversiveness of the delay period, and the particular temporal parameters associated with delay of reinforcement. If the choice cannot be reversed, the domain of self-control and its associated processes and variables would seem to have no bearing on what happens thereafter. That is, once a person chooses a delayed reward and cannot change this decision, the conflict element, which, by definition is a component of the self-control situation, is removed as a determinant of further action. Postdecisional theories, such as dissonance, deal with this area of behavior.

In contrast, resistance to temptation or tolerance of pain over a prolonged interval, during which the conflicting response tendencies are continuously acting, requires *persistent* use of controlling responses. The separation of decisional and protracted self-control suggests itself since different variables may be relevant for each paradigm. Furthermore, persons may differ in their performance within each experimental paradigm as a result of their prior history or laboratory training. For example, different variables (and programs) may be used to induce a person to make a commitment not to drink and turn down invitations to go to a tavern, as opposed to asking him to join his companions at a tavern all evening and not drink alcoholic beverages. It is this difference in paradigms that contrasts the approaches to self-control provided by, for example, Rachlin (1974) and Ainslie (1975), and the work on delay of gratification by Mischel (1974), Hartig and Kanfer (1973) and others. In the former paradigm the research task is to explain what variables are most potent in affecting a desired choice, while in the latter paradigm the task is to determine what variables affect the moment-to-moment decisions to wait for some expected terminal reinforcer.

Protracted Self-Control

Resistance to Temptation. Our earliest work on resistance to temptation resulted from our experiments on self-reinforcement. When a subject can administer a reward to himself but does it only on reaching some self-selected or externally imposed criterion, he can be said to be exercising self-control, since the situation involves a choice between various outcomes that contain positive, aversive and sometimes punishing elements. Taking an immediately available reward represents a highly attractive response alternative, in conflict with the delay of self-reward. One would expect that the attractiveness of the reward, the difficulty of the task, the duration of the delay, past experience of the subject with postponing rewards, and fear of punishment for the transgression would affect the probability that a subject will adhere to executing the contingency prior to administering self-reward. Two studies (Kanfer, 1966; Kanfer & Duerfeldt, 1968) illustrate the effects of situational and person variables on this behavior.

Children in classes were asked to reward themselves in a guessing game in which the probability of correct guesses was near zero. The children were certain that the experimenter could not monitor their adherence to the prescribed standard for self-reward. This was accomplished by asking children to guess quietly, in advance, the number from zero to one hundred which the experimenter would draw on each trial from a lottery box. If the child had guessed accurately, he could credit himself with a point score. Due to inherent probabilities, a correct guess by the child was extremely unlikely. It was found that the frequency of undeserved self-reward for the "cheating" score varied as a function of age. Second graders cheated on over half of the trials, fourth graders cheated on approximately 20% of the responses, while older children cheated only 10% of the time. Further, brief observation of an adult model who administered self-rewards quite liberally resulted in increased cheating in all children. The magnitude of the reward (candy versus points) affected children only at the lower grades. Finally, it was found that children who had been characterized by their teachers as performing in the upper half of their class transgressed significantly less frequently than children who were judged to be in the lower half of their class. In a separate experiment the same children were given an individual learning task in which undeserved self-rewards could be taken. Low ranking children performed as well as high ranking children, but took more undeserved self rewards. The frequency of taking undeserved self-rewards correlated 0.45 in children across the two experiments.

In a second study (Kanfer & Duerfeldt, 1968), the aversiveness of the transgression was emphasized by labeling it clearly as cheating. Further, the children were asked to write down the guessed number prior to the experimenter's announcement. This procedure aimed to enhance the child's commitment to his guess by adding visual cues on which to base his judgment of a match with a criterion for a deserved self-reward. However, it was also clear that the experimenter could not monitor the child's actual score. Frequency of undeserved self-rewards was again found to be a function of age. The prior written commitment to a score, forcing a clear self-evaluation by comparing the written records and the experimenter's announcements, significantly reduced the children's tendency to cheat. The child's standing in his class, as rated by his teachers, was also significantly related to his cheating behavior. Low achievers consistently had higher cheating scores in all grades. Finally, when one group of children was given their backup candy rewards after the first half of the trial, cheating increased in all children subsequent to the redemption of the recorded score for candy. The actual size of this increase, however, was relatively small.

These results suggested that resistance to temptation in children is the result of the joint interaction of situational variables, age and other person variables. These findings are consistent with the results reported by Mischel and Gilligan (1964). The authors found that classification of scores in a game of skill for which criteria had been set was related to the children's tendency to prefer immediate over delayed rewards in a prior choice situation and to the child's score on a need achievement measure. Our primary concern, however, had been the exploration of situational variables as determinants of children's resistance to temptation, since previous research had focused heavily on personality variables and such historical variables as parental training.

These studies suggested the appropriateness of a self-control model in a situation involving contingently administered self-reinforcement when there was little risk in being caught in failing to fulfill the contingency. This area is of critical interest to clinicians, since current self-management programs widely use procedures in which a person is given the task to establish self-reinforcement contingencies for executing low probability new behaviors. Our earlier studies, and those of other investigators, have examined variables affecting immediate self-reinforcement under conditions in which the criterion for such self-reward was intentionally ambiguous in order to examine the effects of these variables on the rate of self-reinforcement. Later studies added a conflict elment to the situation, by introducing a temptation to engage in a pleasant activity, contrary to established rules (e.g., studies on the "Forbidden Toy Paradigm;" Ebbesen, Bowers, Phillips & Snyder, 1975; Hartig & Kanfer, 1973).

If the temptation situation involves a prolonged exposure to the conflict arousing stimuli, an interesting question arises about the nature of the processes and behaviors that modulate the person's tolerance of the waiting interval. Most studies have focused on the variables which reduce the probability that the person will transgress or give up the expected larger reward for an immediately available smaller one. There are numerous studies which have shown that self-instructions, distractions and other cognitive behaviors can serve as controlling responses. In addition to the contents of the self-instructions, the type of activity in* which the child could engage in during waiting, and the role of the adult during the *practice* of controlling responses appear critical. Kanfer and Zich (1974) found that first graders who were trained to use verbal controlling responses in order to avoid turning around to look at a toy display resisted temptation longer when training was carried out in the absence of an experimenter than when the adult was present in the back of the room. Current work in this area (e.g., Mischel & Baker, 1975) has begun to focus on a fine-grain analysis of the various dimensions affecting the utility of the controlling responses in resisting temptation.

Tolerance of Noxious Stimulation. This situation usually occurs on a choice between several aversive stimuli including some positive elements. It is desirable to know what training procedures are most effective for altering the undesirable escape behavior. Within the protracted self-control paradigm two different experimental procedures have been developed, requiring a) delay of a positive reinforcer; b) tolerance of an aversive situation. Both procedures introduce an ongoing aversive situation. In resistance to temptation a person is encouraged to inhibit transgressing (leaving the situation or choosing a less desirable reward) and to look forward to the future outcome. In variations of this laboratory procedure, failure to tolerate the delay can be followed by immediately available smaller **rewards**, or by explicit or implicit punishment for transgression. The relationship between endurance and the consequence of yielding to temptation has not been examined systematically.

Resistance to temptation presents an interesting paradox. A person begins a waiting interval for a large reward and, after having spent some time in waiting and getting closer to the reward, he gives up the reward and takes a smaller reward or risks punishment by transgression. In laboratory studies, the delay interval prior to achieving the anticipated reward is usually not known to the subject. Consequently his momentary decision to wait or take a smaller reward, or—in some cases—risk being caught in yielding to the temptation cannot be influenced by less proximity to the desired larger reward. We know of no human study which systematically investigated the relationship between magnitude and length of delay interval for choice A or choice B in order to predict duration of delay tolerance. When a paradigm involves a prior choice of A but an abandonment of that choice during a delay interval, the interesting problem concerns the variables leading to this change. It is possible that a) the distant goal becomes less attractive than an alternative as time progresses; b) the immediately available option gains in incentive value; c) the hoped-for event increases in value but gradually frustration increases beyond the person's limit of tolerance, or d) the aversiveness of waiting (frustration) for the larger reward builds until it is sufficiently great to occasion an escape response. These alternative explanations require thorough study for theoretical as well as practical reasons.

In addition to earlier explanations in terms of Pavlovian theory (Luria, 1961, 1969), the most common explanation of a person's behavior in this situation has been given by Mischel. It suggests that with increasing delay, frustration is also increased. While this explanation appears reasonable, it has not been directly tested. Another possibility is that the incentive value of the delayed reinforcer changes relative to the immediately available outcome as time elapses (Ainslie, 1975). Neither theoretical explanation has been sufficiently supported by empirical work to warrant immediate acceptance. From a pragmatic point of view one can question the need for a theoretical explanation, as long as techniques are proposed which offer means for enhancing the subject's ability to tolerate delay. Actually, however, the two divergent theoretical positions would lead to different clinical procedures. For example, a frustration hypothesis might suggest that reduction of frustration may be more reliable and effective than self-instructed interpolated activity. If the temporal hypothesis is correct, however, introduction of cognitive activity that further alters the relative incentive values would be advisable.

There is another group of complex choice situations in which tolerance of a noxious event is required for the sake of an ultimate favorable outcome. Endurance of physical stress in sports and exposure to dental work are examples of these situations. In our studies we have chosen the cold-pressor task as a laboratory vehicle to represent this paradigm because of its ethical acceptability to subjects and its convenience and suitability for introducing different variables and measuring their effects on tolerance. If we accept the frustration hypothesis for resistance to temptation, then the two situations become less sharply differentiated. However, the similarity is limited. For example, in tolerating a pain stimulus, subjects tend to concentrate on the current event, while the anticipation of a delayed positive reinforcer invites attention to the future event. In the cold-pressor paradigm, termination of the waiting interval brings relief from the pain stimuli, but no other positive reinforcer. Perhaps additional positive future outcomes are provided by the subject. For instance, self-generated standards for pain tolerance are very common in adult subjects. The situation is viewed as a challenge and long tolerance is self-rewarded. Thus, avoidance of self-criticism as well as criticism by others might enhance pain tolerance, while resistance to temptation may not be affected by this variable to the same degree. Clues about the relative effectiveness of self-generated standards as challenges in the two different situations come from the finding that children use self-evaluative statements as controlling responses to resist temptation (Hartig & Kanfer, 1973). No significant differences in tolerance duration were found between groups in which self-evaluative statements emphasized either the positive feature "I will be a good boy (girl)," or the negative aspect, "I will be a bad boy (girl) if I look at the toys." Further, children who were trained to stress personal competence tolerated a totally dark room significantly longer than children who were trained to emphasize the benevolent aspects of the dark (Kanfer, Karoly, & Newman, 1975). These data suggest that self-generated challenges may be more effective in the tolerance of noxious stimulation than in the tolerance of a delay interval for positive outcome.

Our earliest study with the cold-pressor test indicated that distracting slides which competed with the subject's attention to the painful stimulation were most effective in enhancing tolerance. In contrast, attending to the pain stimulation by describing momentary sensations reduced duration below the level of a control group (Kanfer & Goldfoot, 1966). We noted in all studies that subjects bring with them a variety of controlling responses which they used in addition to the experimental treatment. Essentially, those responses consisted of a variety of competing cognitive and motor behaviors. Thus, as in clinical practice, the results always represent the net effect of the systematic introduction of a treatment variable in addition to, or in place of the subject's own self-controlling mechanisms.

In subsequent work (Kanfer & Seidner, 1973), it was found that the effectiveness of the controlling response was increased when the person perceived himself to be in control of the presentation schedule for the stimuli which set the occasion for the controlling response. Further, even the presence of very simple controlling response—a number naming task —significantly increased duration of pain tolerance. Further, when a light was previously conditioned positively or negatively, its later contingent administration for a controlling response affected pain tolerance. The positive conditioned reinforcer resulted in longest tolerance, the negative reinforcer in shortest tolerance. Comparison with the various control groups also indicated that the conditioned reinforcer did not affect tolerance of the ice water directly, but was effective by increasing the strength of the number naming as a controlling response. These findings support the theoretical suggestion that the effectiveness of a competing controlling response may depend on its inherent attractiveness or value as a reinforcing event.

Both the resistance to temptation and the tolerance of noxious stimulation procedures involve a delay interval. Recent research has progressively sharpened the differences between cognitive and behavioral explanations for the hypothesized processes *during* that interval. For example, Mischel (Mischel & Baker, 1975) has chosen to describe these processes in terms of cognitive structures and activities, emphasizing the quality of the subject's ideation during the interval. As a result, the recent experiments from this group attempted to specify the characteristics of the subject's cognitive activities in terms of strategies, such as cognitive transformations. A behavioral analysis, as derived from Skinner's conceptualization (1953) and refined in later work by others (Kanfer & Goldfoot, 1966; Mahoney & Thoresen, 1974), selects the relationship between the controlling response and the response to be controlled as the focus of study. For example, in our laboratory we have attempted to detail the specific characteristics of the controlling response, in terms of its inherent power to compete with the undesirable response. From this standpoint, the reinforcing properties of a controlling response (Kanfer & Seidner, 1973), its availability to the subject (Berger & Kanfer, 1975), and its ease of execution are of special interest for study. But, this focus does not deny the importance of other relevant variables, such as the demand characteristics of the situation, the prior experience with the experimenter and other factors.

A recent study by Grimm and Kanfer (1977) illustrates this approach. The experiment attempted to differentiate between the distracting quality of a controlling response and its inherent positive (reinforcing) value in increasing pain tolerance in the cold-pressor task. College students were first given a base trial. They were then divided into five groups. The *positive content* group was trained to think of a pleasant activity during the later test trial. The *neutral content* group was trained to rehearse a counting and alphabet reciting task. An *expectancy* group was told to expect decreases in discomfort due to physical adaptation. In addition, it was of interest to note whether subjects who were asked to view the task as a *challenge* would be able to provide their own effective controlling responses for enhancing tolerance. Finally, a group was added to examine whether external pressure (by the experimenter) would be more effective than self-control procedures in enhancing tolerance. This *instructional control* group was urged to keep their hand in the water as long as they possibly could. The results indicated that the controlling response with positive content was significantly superior in comparison to the neutral content. It also increased tolerance in contrast to the expectancy group. However, while positive content enhanced tolerance over the challenge group, the differential increment on the second trial was not statistically significant. Further, the neutral content and expectancy groups did not differ from each other, but both showed significantly lower tolerance than the challenge group. As expected, the instructional control group also displayed significantly greater tolerance than the neutral content and the expectancy groups but their performance was considerably, though not significantly, lower than for subjects in the positive content and challenge groups.

An interesting suggestion about the critical dimension in training comes from replies on a post-experimental questionnaire. The distractive quality of the controlling response was rated very high in the positive and challenge groups, but considerably lower in the remaining groups. In addition, the enjoyment rating of the controlling response was highest for the positive content group. The results suggest the critical importance of the content of the controlling response in enhancing pain tolerance. Thus, it is not simply the amount of cognitive activity in which the subject engages during the waiting interval that is important, but also the quality of the controlling response. A follow-up study is currently in progress in which attempts are made to differentiate further between the distractive and rewarding qualities of the controlling response, as determinants of the duration of tolerance. Along similar lines, a recent study by Horan and Dellinger (1974) also reported greater effectiveness of *in vivo* emotive imagery over a distraction group. Thus, the relative rewarding value of the controlling response may be a critical property defining its effectiveness.

Training for Delay Tolerance. In addition to providing the subject with controlling responses, or cognitive activities, or coping behaviors that compete with a high tendency to respond in an undesirable manner, several attempts have been made to heighten resistance to temptation by prior training with various reinforcement schedules. There are many reports of animal studies on the effectiveness of training procedures in overcoming the aversiveness of delayed reinforcement. Renner has suggested that the result of such training is to help the animal "to place a particular value on a given outcome in a consistent way, and to combine those outcomes into an overall net value . . . (the rat) also carries with it an integrated set of experiences which form a value system and which give long-term coherence and self-direction to its behavior" (Renner, 1971, p. 1). Bandura and Mahoney (1974) trained pigeons and a dog to observe contingency relationships for self-discrimination of freely available food rewards by use of initial punishment for undeserved self-reward. In a later study (Bandura, Mahoney & Dirks, 1975), pigeons learned to adhere to self-reward contingencies with the aid of contextual cues and periodic negative consequences for transgression. However, withdrawing contextual cues or response consequences eventually tended to dissipate self-control. Punishment for transgression on a partial schedule was most effective in maintaining contingent self-rewarding.

In a study with first grade children, Newman and Kanfer (1976) pretrained different groups on a simple discrimination task, with various fixed delays, progressively decreasing delays, or progressively increasing delays of reinforcement for correct choices. The delay intervals ranged from 0 to 60 seconds. Following training, all children were exposed to a resistance to temptation test in which the child could obtain one candy immediately or delay his request and receive increasingly more candy. A second test replicated the same procedures with toys as rewards. The duration of fixed delay in training did not significantly affect resistance to temptation, nor were fixed delay groups significantly different from the decreasing delay groups. However, the group which had been trained with increasing delays demonstrated significantly superior resistance to temptation on both self-control tests. The data nicely support the self-control program outlined by Skinner (1948) in *Walden Two,* for increasing tolerance for annoying experiences by gradually increasing the delay interval between the discriminative stimulus and the reward. Before proposing a possible clinical application of training by such increases in delayed reinforcement, however, we must remember that the few available animal and human studies in this area have focused on acquisition of such a response pattern. Before attempting to utilize a progressively increasing delay of reinforcement program in the clinic, research evidence of the longevity of the effects would be desirable. Of course, the evidence for maintenance of self-control is not much clearer for the effects produced by training of other self-controlling responses except by inference from clinical reports. On follow-ups clinical studies of overeating and smoking have repeatedly shown decline of the initial gains.

CONTRACTS AND SELF-REGULATION

A contract serves two functions in self-regulation. The process of negotiating a contract in a therapy program permits the clarification of the possible outcomes, their associated requirements and expected consequences dependent on the person's choice of one of several alternatives. It can serve to motivate a person toward a commitment to change, to establish the supporting contributions he can expect from others, and to make concrete a previously vague intention or decision to alter one's behavior. This function relates the contract to decisional self-control in that the acceptance of a set of conditions represent choices to the person which usually involve a momentary commitment and specify some later consequences which are no longer under the person's complete control.

A second function of the contract lies in the provision of a clear statement of the specific objectives of a change program and the means by which it is achieved. This feature relates to our self-regulation model in that it provides the performance criterion for self-evaluation, defines the target behaviors to be monitored and provides the basis for self-reinforcement contingencies.

A contract is relevant to self-control only if it specifies actions which require a reversal of the relative order of pre-existing response probabilities. Other contracts or commitments may serve to organize or direct behavior or to establish reciprocal reinforcement contingencies between two parties without introducing conflict or self-generated controlling responses. The study of such "social contracts" can assist in formulation of hypotheses about procedures or variables relevant to contracts in clinical cases.

Further, the contract conceptualization can be extended to provide a framework for dealing with situations in which a person establishes his own standards for behavior, albeit nonverbally and often not very concisely. Such self-made contracts may have functions similar to public contracts but involve other considerations. Clinically, their effectiveness may be enhanced by training. However, their inaccessibility has created many problems; for instance, in private intra-person contracts the established performance level can be continually modified without much consequence. A smoker may promise himself in the morning that he will smoke no more than three cigarettes that day. Given the effects of numerous alpha and beta variables, reinstatement of cues associated with smoking, or physiological conditions that had earlier been related to smoking, the smoker may alter his contract as the day progresses, raising his smoking quota "as an exception." Once a person engages in this behavior pattern, as Ainslie (1975) has suggested, the program is jeopardized. Various ways in which a person can bargain with himself and still permit loopholes without excessive jeopardy to the total program are described by Ainslie. While private redefinition may also occur with public contracts, the following studies give good evidence of the overall effects of public contracts on the occurrence of self-control behaviors.

It should be noted that the establishment of a contract is itself an interactional process which is subject to numerous variables. Acceptance of a contract by a client can be influenced by various manipulations, but such a commitment does not necessarily guarantee that the contracted behavior will be executed. In a laboratory study using the cold-pressor test as the experimental vehicle (Kanfer, Cox, Greiner, & Karoly, 1974), it was found that tolerance of ice water was significantly longer when an explicit written contract was signed by the subjects than when the same information was communicated by oral instructions. When a person believes that he has failed to meet the contract requirements, his subsequent behavior is affected by the source to which he attributes the failure. Subjects who believed that their failure to meet the contract criterion was due to their own action, tolerated ice water exposure on a second trial longer than subjects who believed that it was the experimenter's fault. The role of timing receipt of anticipated reinforcement also appears to be of critical importance. When subjects anticipated reinforcement after fulfilling their stated contract, they tolerated the cold-pressor test longer than subjects who were not reinforced, or received reinforcement immediately after stating their intention to tolerate the cold-pressor test.

In a clinical situation different desirable outcomes can be selected for inclusion in the contract. While it seems most plausible to contract for change in the target behavior that represents the client's problem behavior, the activities which constitute participation in the therapy program can themselves be the subject of contracts. If a client is not highly motivated, then the requirement to execute certain self-managed techniques will probably not be achieved. Some evidence on the relative effectiveness of contracting for the client's achievement of a therapeutic goal or for his participation in required therapeutic activities has been presented in a dissertation by Seidner (1973). The study investigated the role of two components of the therapeutic contract: 1) the degree of therapy structure communicated to the client; and 2) the requirement to work toward long-term therapeutic goals or to carry out the specific activities during the beginning phase of the program.

Two studies were carried out, both with college students who volun·teered for a program in improving their study habits. In the first study, women students were selected on the basis of low scores (below the 50th percentile) on the Brown and Holtzman Survey of Study Habits and Attitudes. They were seen for two sessions, one week apart. All subjects were shown a videotaped interview in which the experimenter described the program to a model (student). In Groups 1 and 2, minimum information was given about the program. In Groups 3, 4, and 5 maximal information was given. Subsequently, Groups 2 and 4 were asked to write a contract that stated the goal for the program, and specified the daily time of effective studying they hoped to accomplish by the end of the program. Group 5 signed a parallel contract that specified intended study time *during* the program period. Groups 1 and 3 had no contract. All subjects were given taped instructions for completing a daily inventory about their study behaviors. A pamphlet about study habit improvements was casually offered. On their return a week later, each subject turned in her self-monitoring sheets, was given a brief quiz on the pamphlet and repeated the SSHA under two instructional sets: one describing her current study habits and the other her expected study habits at the end of the program. Subjects were also asked to mail a prepaid postcard to the experimenter at the end of the academic quarter indicating their latest grade point average. Two optional sessions were held in the following weeks. In Study 2, the procedure was quite similar, except that two levels of 1) information about program strategies, and 2) specification of the changes to be expected as a result of the program were combined in a factorial design. A fifth group was not exposed to the videotape that contained information about the program structure and anticipated behavior changes. Data were collected on 22 measures about client effort, interview involvement, and perceived improvement of study habits. These data were grouped into eight clusters of independent factors by a principal component factor analysis.

The results of Study 1 indicated that subjects who received maximum information about the program obtained significantly higher scores than those who received minimum information. Various indices of the amount of work spent on a self-monitoring task were affected both by the information and contract variables. Introduction of a goal-oriented contract under maximal information tended to lower self-monitoring, whereas the contract to carry out program activities enhanced this behavior. Structure also affected interview involvement and attitudes. The task-oriented contract groups showed greater involvement with the program as judged by an interview. The results clearly supported the hypothesis that increased structure resulted in beneficial results in seven of the eight clusters of variables. Signing of a contract also reduced within group variance and resulted in performance which more closely approximated the program standards. Interestingly, subjects who signed a contract to work toward the goal of effective study hours self-monitored significantly less carefully than subjects who did not sign a contract. In Study 2, information about therapy strategies had significantly greater influence on the measures than information about what to expect of the program. The group which obtained maximum information, both about therapy strategies and expectations, had the highest scores of all groups.

In general, these findings suggest that a contract focusing on participation in various treatment activities was more effective in promoting efforts in therapy than a contract that specified long-term goals. Further, providing a client with a high degree of information about treatment strategies and expected goals enhanced client efforts. This study is limited to an examination of an initial stage in therapy. However, it clearly indicates the role of contracts as specific standards that the client can set for himself. The contents of the contract also differentially affected client participation in the program. What remains to be studied are the effects of various types of contracts on long-term changes, and on the range of behavior that is affected by different contracts. It seems that clinicians must decide carefully whether they wish to enhance treatment participation at first, or contract immediately for changes in symptomatic behavior. The Seidner study makes it clear that contracting for vague long-term change is not a very effective procedure.

The use of contracts in treatment may be limited by the client's previous experience with contracts and the degree to which he trusts his therapist. It is conceivable that clients who have had repeated experiences in their social history in which mutual agreements were consistently broken by others may not respond favorably to the use of contracts. Both Patterson and Stuart, who have used contracts with families and with delinquents, have emphasized the critical importance of contract fulfillment by *all* contracting parties.

In two laboratory analogs with children, an attempt was made to ascertain the effect of the adult's prior fulfillment of his side of the contract on later task requirements. Karoly and Kanfer (1974) asked girls between eight and twelve to play a "scarecrow game" in which they were required to extend their arms horizontally, "perfectly straight for as long as possible." After a base line trial the children were divided into four groups. On a monotonous letter crossing task the children were promised candy on each of six trials. In the kept-contract group the promise was fulfilled. In the broken-contract-negative group the children were given less candy than promised; in the broken-contract-positive group they were given more candy than promised; and in the double message group they were given the promised candy but also a mild verbal criticism for their performance. Subsequently, the scarecrow game was played again. The results indicated that the broken-contract-positive group increased their tolerance of the progressively aversive scarecrow game, while the other contract groups maintained approximately the same level.

In an attempt to clarify these findings, Beiersdorf (1975) repeated essentially the same procedure but introduced several additional variables. First and fourth graders were used; contract fulfillment was under or over paid by large amounts. In addition, the child's level of aspiration and judgment of his class performance by teachers were introduced as personality variables. The findings were consistent with the earlier results in some respects. Underpayment of the contract resulted in significantly lower performance on the scarecrow game than either overpaid or accurately paid performance. These findings were obtained both for the younger and older children. Further, the older children who were in the lower half of their class and whose contracts were overpaid maintained their arms in a horizontal position longer than the older children with the same contract experience who had been judged to be in the upper half of their class. The older children with higher aspiration levels also tolerated the scarecrow game longer on the second trial than children of the same age with average aspiration levels.

The results of these studies suggest that the previous contract experience may affect the degree to which a person carries out a task that involves tolerance of painful stimulation. Further, they indicate that children react positively (by greater compliance to the request for prolonged tolerance) to an adult's excessive payment of a contract but do not react negatively when the adult fails to fulfill his promise. Perhaps this relates to the likelihood that most children experience broken promises more frequently than excessive rewards. Finally, the interactions with the personality variables suggest the interactive effects of particular contract experiences on a child's later willingness to carry out a required unpleasant task.

These studies illustrate research in which we have attempted to specify an increasingly larger number of variables that need to be taken into consideration when we ask about the probable effect of contracts. As stated above, contracts can aid in the setting of specific standards and goals for later performance. In this sense, they can become components of the self-regulation process. However, both the overall self-regulation model and each of its components are further affected by a host of variables, many of which still require exploration. The model seems to be accomplishing its heuristic purpose of providing a loose framework for the detailed analysis of the complex processes that are involved in self-regulatory behavior. Perhaps it is disappointing that the conceptualization does not permit simple and sweeping generalizations. For the clinician it can serve as a guide in examining the various component processes and the possible deficits in any or all of them. It can also help in the development of clinical techniques for remedying such deficiencies. However, it is clear that the model represents only an incomplete summary of the complex variables that originate in the immediate situation, in the subject's personal history, and in the interaction between them. Nevertheless, evaluation of research in this area certainly suggests that contracts represent a pivotal element in self-regulation.

SOME CURRENT CLINICAL ISSUES

We have previously pointed out the importance of integrating clinical treatment methods with the characteristics of their user (the clinician), and their beneficiary (the client) and of fitting the interactions among the three within the same comprehensive system (Kanfer & Phillips, 1966). The preceding review has indicated a direction in gradual development of a base for behavior therapy which transcends the earlier conditioning models. However, even without consideration of the role of the clinician (and the wider influence of the mental health professions and their presumed mission), just the closer analysis of the client as an active participant in treatment has presented numerous problems and stimulated new research directions. Only a few which are particularly relevant for self-management methods will be discussed in this section.

The increasing use of self-management techniques has highlighted the need for detailed consideration of several problems in the integration of treatment methods with other features of the total intervention process. Among these issues is the development of a theory of behavioral assessment which would indicate what behavioral dimensions should be evaluated in order to predict treatment success with various self-directed procedures. Since several recent papers deal with this issue (Bellack & Schwartz, 1976; Meichenbaum 1976), I will not discuss it further.

Another important issue concerns the choice of treatment objectives. In the basic conditioning model the choice is clear. The patient's symptom becomes the target behavior. A behavioral analysis, however, often leaves the clinician with several choices. He can attack a specific problem behavior, or he can attempt to alter a wide range of inefficient behaviors of which the problem constitutes a product. For example, aggressive behavior toward a spouse can be directly attacked by reinforcing incompatible responses, by attaching aversive consequences to such behaviors, or by other direct techniques. A choice at another level might be to modify critical interactional behaviors between husband and wife that represent the antecedent of the aggressive behaviors.

In self-management therapy an even higher level in the hierarchy of the behavioral repertoire may be chosen as a target. For example, situationally determined aggressive behavior might be altered by training the client to observe and correct his inefficient cognitive and interactional behaviors, and by using problem-solving or previously rehearsed behaviors when the problematic situation is identified. Perhaps the recent success of the numerous treatment programs, books, and workshops to increase assertiveness suggests the popularity of the widely applicable "packaged" approach. A standardized program can be offered with the hope that an increased assertive repertoire would resolve many different individual problems. In a culture in which assertiveness is often punished in childhood and praised in adulthood, such an approach is frequently successful.

In anxiety reduction, the specific target approach is well illustrated by the use of systematic desensitization. A broader attack is made by training the client to cope with his anxiety in a wide range of fear-arousing situations (Suinn & Richardson, 1971) or to restructure his thinking about the fear-arousing situation (Goldfried & Goldfried, 1975). In the case where related or antecedent behaviors are modified, rather than the specific problem behavior, the assumption is often made about a causal chain of partly overt and partly covert behavior sequences and about the intraindividual organization of experiences that permits intervention at one point of the chain or in one life segment to affect targeted behaviors that are presumed to be linked to the point of intervention. For example, sexual problems in a married couple (with intact repertoires for lovemaking) may be changed by altering aversive social interactions or training them to resolve conflicts about economic or vocational or familial decisions. Or conversely, other interpersonal problems may be changed by training in satisfactory sexual behaviors. Unfortunately, though such distant interventions often work well, the rules for proper loci of application are not available on the basis of empirical knowledge. Clinical decisions, based on thorough analysis of the connections in individual cases, need to be supplemented by process and outcome research on these problems.

An important issue concerns the choice of problems and client populations for whom self-management methods are most effective. This issue can also be considered from the view of the proper development of assessment methods and criteria which would permit early prediction of the client's response to these techniques (Bellack & Schwartz, 1976).

We have previously suggested that self-regulatory processes are activated only when there is some disruption in the smooth flow of well-learned behaviors (Kanfer & Karoly, 1972). For the clinician it is also important to note the disruptive influences of conditions that may reduce self-regulatory functions, since the dominance of control by alpha or gamma variables in some situations may lead to untoward consequences. Our model suggests that in any situation in which a person is highly motivated by the availability of external reinforcers, the self-regulatory feedback loop may be short-circuited. For example, when a person is highly motivated to obtain praise, monetary rewards or other external reinforcers, behavior may be shown that is exclusively directed toward attainment of these reinforcers and remains primarily under control of situational cues. In clinical situations, this can lead individuals to behave in ways that lead observers to describe the person as "not being himself," that is to behave inconsistently with respect to the standards which the person has set for himself and which have guided his behavior on many previous occasions. Prediction based on knowledge of the moderating effects of the person's past history, therefore, would become less reliable as the current situational cues become determinants of the behavior. Thus, a person who has established high standards of moral behavior for himself may, under the influence of very strong alpha variables, engage in acts which are inconsistent with such standards. The common adage "every person has his price" and the frequent observation of responses that deviate from the person's habitual behavior when unusual external reinforcement contingencies are available illustrate this hypothesis. Similarly, strong gamma variables, such as in acute anxiety or pain, may guide the person's behaviors primarily toward reduction of such aversive inputs, regardless of his long-standing criteria for action in a given situation.

The past success of a client in using controlling responses in different life situations, his attitude toward treatment as guidance toward self-change, his past skills in self-monitoring, evaluating and reinforcing his own behavior and his dependence on his social environment may be fruitful predictors for investigation. While the current mood is toward increasing the client's cooperation, responsibility and control in behavior change programs, there is little research evidence that a) all clients can acquire the necessary skills to do so, and b) that this approach is most effective in facilitating desired changes.

While increasing experimental evidence has shown the role of both alpha and beta variables, very little attention has been paid to the role of gamma variables in clinical treatment. For example, just as the additional support by alpha variables, such as the use of prescribed diets, time-locked cigarette cases or therapist reinforcement for a behavior change can contribute to the acquisition and maintenance of controlling responses, so a change in physiological conditions might serve to facilitate behavior change. However, the role of affective arousal, or fatigue, or tranquilizing or sedative drugs in timing the training of self-control procedures has not yet been studied. Of course, such research would have to distinguish the effects of biological variables on self-control training from their effects on the conflicting consequences in the problem situation. For example, adding quinine to food may alter eating behavior but the self-control feature concerns only the person's act of adding the substance prior to eating. As soon as this is done (as in pouring out the contents of a whiskey bottle) the subsequent behavior is simply controlled by alpha variables.

The role of organismic variables in self-regulation has been studied in a series of experiments which focus on the effect of affect on the dispensation of self-rewards (e.g., Mischel, Coates & Raskoff, 1968; Underwood, Moore & Rosenhan, 1973; Masters & Peskay, 1972; Masters, 1972). These laboratory studies with children suggest that preceding experiences of success or instruction-induced "happy thoughts" tend to increase the child's generosity in administering non-contingent self-rewards. The implications of these findings need to be tested for the clinical situation in which the increase in the rate of self-rewards may be a treatment target. Some steps in this direction have recently been made. Rozensky, Rehm, Pry and Roth (1975) demonstrated differences in self-reinforcement behavior between depressed and non-depressed subjects. Fuchs and Rehm (1975) compared a six-week therapy program that focused on modifying self-monitoring, self-evaluation and self-control skills with a general group therapy program in depressed women. Self-control subjects showed greater improvement in self-reports, behavioral measures and MMPI scores. In a recent paper, Rehm (1975) analyzes depression as a problem in self-regulation and reviews evidence of the differential reactions of depressed and normal persons at various stages of self-regulation.

In a recent laboratory study (Grimm & Kanfer, 1977) we investigated the effects of subject-induced changes in heart-rate on tolerance of pain in the cold-pressor task. Subjects were given brief relaxation training in which they learned to lower their heart rate significantly before a second exposure to the ice water. A group which was trained in the use of verbal controlling responses, between test trials, also reduced their heart rate significantly. Neither a control group nor an expectancy-suggestion control showed such changes. The critical finding of the study was that, despite these similarities in heart rate decreases, the group trained in relaxation did not differ from the control groups in duration of tolerating the painful stimulation on the test trial, while the group trained in using a verbal controlling response significantly increased their tolerance, enduring over twice as long as the other groups.

These laboratory findings suggest that the ability of a person to lower his physiological arousal (as in transcendental mediation, yoga, relaxation and similar methods) may not necessarily have any significant effects on the tolerance of pain per se, although the use of self-generated verbal controlling responses has similar effects on heart rate *and* also increased tolerance. Such findings suggest that the active or necessary component in therapy methods reducing autonomic arousal may be the cognitive concomitant (cf. Goldfried, 1971). While currently available studies in this area permit only limited conclusions, they call attention to the need for further consideration and study of the role of physiological variables in the clinical use of self-control methods, and the interaction between self-generated and biological variables.

In self-management therapy, attribution of change to the client's own actions has been considered an important feature. The motivational effects of self-attribution have been described in many studies. It has been shown that even in such purely chance tasks as selecting a lottery ticket, persons have a higher expectation of success when they had some part in selecting the ticket, giving an illusion of control (Langer, 1975). Tolerance of noxious stimulation (Averill, 1973), effects of self-attributed behavior changes in insomnia (Davison, Tsujimoto, & Galros, 1973), and other behaviors seem to be strongly influenced by the person's belief about the source of control. These data lead to the clinical emphasis on self-attributed success experiences to enhance change. Further, the total structure of self-management therapy stresses the client's active participation in treatment, be it in the choice of goals, in selecting parameters of a contract, or in the choice of the particular contents in a treatment method, or in the evaluation of his progress. Willingness to accept responsibility for treatment procedures and for progress in treatment may affect the effectiveness of the methods. Therefore, this approach requires special attention to the initial motivation of the client and his reasons for seeking assistance, and may require that the increase in such dispositions be the major focus in the initial phase of treatment. However, these strategies are currently based on extrapolations from laboratory data and require further examination in clinical cases.

EPILOGUE

This chapter has attempted to cover some highlights of the complexities of research in self-regulation, their implications for behavior theory in general, and some of the accomplishments that are leading the way toward an eventual understanding of this area. Experimental re-evaluation of several clinical techniques (e.g., Goldfried, DeCenteceo & Weinberg, 1974; Foreyt & Hagen, 1973; Goldfried, 1971) has suggested that various experimental paradigms proposed under the title of self-control might be embedded in more complex procedures. In addition, there are probably other situations to which the term self-control has been applied and which have not yet been brought under experimental scrutiny. For example, I do not know of any experiments that parallel the common problem of stopping an enjoyable activity for the sake of long-term benefits or the avoidance of aversive consequences. Mother's problem in getting her child to stop an exciting game in order to come into the house to wash up, or the gourmand's problem of pushing away a rich dessert illustrate this dilemma. In general, such situations have been handled by looking at an earlier time interval, namely the problem of resisting the temptation to *begin* a pleasurable activity.

Another problem, barely touched in this paper, is the analysis of the social and cultural context that necessitates the use of beta control. Advertising of cigarettes or alcohol, manufacture of sexually attractive clothing and cosmetics, and numerous other features of our social system present the individual with the dilemma of developing a set of controlling variables to counteract the purpose of such social enticements. Moderation represents a challenge to develop behavior patterns that handle conflicting environmental stimulation. The achievement of moderation represents one of the critical tasks of the socialization process.

A practical approach is also needed for handling situations in which aversive or positive consequences of an individual's behavior affect not only him but other members of the society. A beginning has been made by a model suggested by Platt (1973) for the case of self-control for the benefit of the social environment and some recent studies (Dawes, 1973; Kelley & Grzelak, 1972; Meux, 1973) derived from game theory. The bridge between self-control research and the area of altruism and egocentrism remains to be built.

To summarize, I have attempted to show the complexity of the domain of self-control, as the term has been popularly used to encompass a vast range of different situations. Its relationship to self-regulation was briefly described. Further, it was pointed out that a complex set of variables needs to be investigated to ascertain their effects on the various components of the self-regulation process. These factors include variables related to the particular situation, to the context in which the phenomenon is observed, to the prior history of the individual under observation, and to the relationship among various components over a temporal interval, extending in some cases over repeated episodes or long time periods.

For purposes of analysis, research programs were divided by their experimental paradigms. Some emphasize decisional self-control, others deal with protracted self-control. In the latter group, one can further distinguish between situations that call for resistance to temptation and those that involve tolerance of a current noxious stimulation.

Finally, some increment in our knowledge of the determining factors in the many different situations subsumed under the term self-control is regarded as prerequisite for achieving good effectiveness of self-regulation procedures in clinical or other practical settings. In practical application it is also critical to differentiate between situations which may appear similar to an observer. While some problems involve self-generated controlling events, others simply are maintained by operant reinforcement from external agents. Such clinical problems as aggressive behaviors, sexual behaviors, or other interactional behaviors are frequently also under multiple control. Finally, the continuity of research between this area and other fields, such as personality or social psychology, requires a broadening of inquiry of relevant variables and related phenomena.

REFERENCES

AINSLIE, G. W.: Impulse control in pigeons. *Journal of the Experimental Analysis of Behavior,* 1974, 21, 485-489.
AINSLIE, G.: Specious reward: A behavioral theory of impulsiveness and impulse control. *Psychological Bulletin,* 1975, 82, 463-496.
AVERILL, J. R.: Personal control over aversive stimuli and its relationship to stress. *Psychological Bulletin,* 1973, 80, 286-303.
BANDURA, A.: Vicarious and self-reinforcement processes. In: R. Glaser (Ed.), *The Nature of Reinforcement.* New York: Academic Press, 1971.
BANDURA, A., MAHONEY, M. J., and DIRKS, S. J.: Discriminative activation and maintenance of contingent self-reinforcement. *Behavior Research and Therapy,* 1975.
BANDURA, A. and MAHONEY, M. J.: Maintenance and transfer of self-reinforcement functions. *Behaviour Research and Therapy,* 1974, 12, 89-97.
BEIERSDORF, D.: *Die Auswirkungen unterschiedlicher Vertragserfahrungen auf das Selbstkontroll-verhalten.* Unpublished doctoral dissertation, University of Köln, 1975.
BELLACK, A. S., and SCHWARTZ, J. S.: Assessment for self-control programs. In M. Hersen and A. S. Bellack (Eds.), *Behavioral Assessment: A Practical Handbook.* New York: Pergamon Press, 1976, 111-142.
BERGER, S. and KANFER, F. E.: Self-control: Effects of training and presentation delays of competing responses on tolerance of noxious stimulation. *Psychological Reports,* 1975, 37, 1312-1314.
BOWERS, K. I.: Situationism in psychology: An analysis and a critique. *Psychological Review,* 1973, 80, 307-336.
BYRNE, D.: Repression-sensitization as a dimension of personality. In B. A. Maher (Ed.), *Progress in Experimental Personality Research,* Vol. 1. New York: Academic Press, 1964.
CRONBACH, L. J.: Beyond the two disciplines of scientific psychology. *American Psychologist,* 1975, 30, 116-127.
DAVISON, G. C., TSUJIMOTO, R. N., and GALROS, A. G.: Attribution and the maintenance of behavior change in falling asleep. *Journal of Abnormal Psychology,* 1973, 82, 124-133.
DAWES, R. M.: The commons dilemma game: An N-person mixed-motive game with a dominating strategy for defection. *ORI Research Bulletin,* 1973, 13, No. 2.
EBBESEN, E. B., BOWERS, R. J., PHILLIPS, S., and SNYDER, M.: Self-control processes in the forbidden toy paradigm. *Journal of Personality and Social Psychology,* 1975, 31, 442-452.
EKEHAMMAR, B.: Interactionism in personality from a historical perspective. *Psychological Bulletin,* 1974, 81, 1026-1048.
FOREYT, J. P. and HAGEN, R. L.: Covert sensitization: Conditioning or suggestion? *Journal of Abnormal Psychology,* 1973, 82, 17-23.
FUCHS, C. and REHM, L. P.: *The Treatment of Depression Through the Modification of Self-Control Behaviors.* Paper presented at AABT, San Francisco, December 12, 1975.
GOLDFRIED, M. R.: Systematic desensitization as training in self-control. *Journal of Consulting and Clinical Psychology,* 1971, 37, 228-234.
GOLDFRIED, M. R., DECENTECEO, E. T., and WEINBERG, L.: Systematic rational restructuring as a self-control technique. *Behavior Therapy,* 1974, 5, 247-254.
GOLDFRIED, M. R. and GOLDFRIED, A. P.: Cognitive change methods. In F. H. Kanfer and A. P. Goldstein (Eds.), *Helping People Change.* New York: Pergamon Press Inc., 1975.

GOLDFRIED, M. R. and MERBAUM, M.: *Behavior Change through Self-Control.* New York: Holt, Rinehart and Winston, Inc., 1973.

GOLDIAMOND, I.: Self-control procedures in personal behavior problems. *Psychological Reports,* 1965, 17, 851-868.

GOTTMAN, J. M. and LEIBLUM, S. R.: *How to Do Psychotherapy and How to Evaluate It.* New York: Holt, Rinehart and Winston, Inc., 1974.

GREINER, J. M.: *The Effect of Self-Control Training on Study Activity and Academic Performance.* Unpublished doctoral dissertation, University of Cincinnati, 1974.

GRIMM, L. and KANFER, F. H.: Tolerance of aversive stimulation. *Behavior Therapy,* 1977, 593-601.

GRUSEC, J.: Waiting for rewards and punishments: Effects of reinforcement value on choice. *Journal of Personality and Social Psychology,* 1968, 9, 85-89.

HARTIG, F. H. and KANFER, F. H.: The role of verbal self-instructions in children's resistance to temptation. *Journal of Personality and Social Psychology,* 1973, 25, 259-267.

HORAN, J. J.: Negative covariant probability: An analogue study. *Behaviour Research and Therapy,* 1974, 12, 265-266.

HORAN, J. J., BAKER, S., HOFFMAN, A. M., and SHUTE, R. E.: Weight loss through variations in the covariant control paradigm. *Journal of Consulting and Clinical Psychology,* 1975, 43, 68-72.

HORAN, J. J. and DELLINGER, J. K.: "In vivo" emotive imagery: A preliminary test. *Perceptual and Motor Skills,* 1974, 39, 359-362.

HORAN, J. J., and JOHNSON, R. G.: Covariant conditioning through a self-management application of the Premack principle: Its effect on weight reduction. *Journal of Behavior Therapy and Experimental Psychiatry,* 1971, 2, 243-249.

HORAN, J. J., SMYERS, R. D., DORFMAN, D. L., and JENKINS, W. W.: Two analogue attempts to harness the negative covariant effect. *Behaviour Research and Therapy,* 1975.

KANFER, F. H.: Influence of age and incentive conditions on children's self rewards. *Psychological Reports,* 1966, 19, 263-274.

KANFER, F. H.: Self-management methods. In F. H. Kanfer and A. P. Goldstein (Eds.), *Helping People Change.* New York: Pergamon Press, Inc., 1975.

KANFER, F. H.: Self-monitoring: Methodological limitations and clinical applications. *Journal of Consulting and Clinical Psychology,* 1970, 35, 148-152.

KANFER, F. H.: Self-regulation: Research, issues and speculations. In C. Neuringer and J. L. Michael (Eds.), *Behavior Modification in Clinical Psychology.* New York: Appleton-Century-Crofts, 1970, 178-220.

KANFER, F. H.: The maintenance of behavior by self-generated stimuli and reinforcement. In A. Jacobs and L. B. Sachs (Eds.), *The Psychology of Private Events.* New York: Academic Press, 1971, 39-57.

KANFER, F. H., COX, L. E., GREINER, J. M., and KAROLY, P.: Contracts, demand characteristics and self-control. *Journal of Personality and Social Psychology,* 1974, 30, 605-619.

KANFER, F. H. and DUERFELDT, P. H.: Age, class-standing and commitment as determinants of cheating in children. *Child Development,* 1968, 39, 545-557.

KANFER, F. H. and GOLDFOOT, D. A.: Self-control and the tolerance of noxious stimulation. *Psychological Reports,* 1966, 18, 79-85.

KANFER, F. H. and KAROLY, P.: Self-control: A behavioristic excursion into the lion's den. *Behavior Therapy,* 1972, 3, 398-416.

KANFER, F. H., KAROLY, P., and NEWMAN, A.: Reduction of children's fear of the dark by competence-related and situational threat-related verbal cues. *Journal of Consulting and Clinical Psychology,* 1975, 43, 251-258.

KANFER, F. H. and PHILLIPS, J. S.: Behavior therapy: A panacea for all ills or a passing fancy? *Archives of General Psychiatry*, 1966, 15, 114-128.

KANFER, F. H. and PHILLIPS, J. S.: *Learning Foundations of Behavior Therapy*. New York: John Wiley & Sons, Inc., 1970.

KANFER, F. H. and SEIDNER, M. L.: Self-control: Factors enhancing tolerance of noxious stimulation. *Journal of Personality and Social Psychology*, 1973, 25, 381-389.

KANFER, F. H. and ZICH, J.: Self-control training: The effects of external control on children's resistance to temptation. *Developmental Psychology*, 1974, 10, 108-115.

KANTOR, J. R.: *Principles of Psychology*. Bloomington, Ind.: The Principia Press, 1924.

KAROLY, P. and KANFER, F. H.: Effects of prior contractual experience on self-control in children. *Developmental Psychology*, 1974, 10, 459-460.

KAZDIN, A. E.: Self-monitoring and behavior change. In M. J. Mahoney and C. E. Thoresen (Eds.), *Self-control: Power to the Person*. Monterey: Brooks/Cole, 1974.

KELLEY, H. H. and GRZELAK, J.: Conflict between individual and common interest in an N-person relationship. *Journal of Personality and Social Psychology*, 1972, 21, 190-198.

KIRSCHENBAUM, D. S.: *When Self-Regulation Fails: Tests of Some Preliminary Hypotheses*. Unpublished doctoral dissertation, University of Cincinnati, 1975.

LANGER, E. J.: The illusion of control. *Journal of Personality and Social Psychology*, 1975, 32, 311-328.

LIPINSKI, D. P., BLACK, J. L., NELSON, R. O., and CIMINERO, A. R. The influence of motivational variables on the reactivity and reliability of self-recording. *Journal of Consulting and Clinical Psychology*, 1975, 43, 637-646.

LURIA, A. R.: Speech development and the formation of mental processes. In M. Cole and I. Maltzman (Eds.), *A Handbook of Contemporary Soviet Psychology*. New York, 1969.

LURIA, A. R.: *The Role of Speech in the Regulation of Normal and Abnormal Behavior*. New York: Liveright Publishing Corporation, 1961.

MAHONEY, M. J.: *Cognition and Behavior Modification*. Cambridge, Mass.: Ballinger Publishing Company, 1974.

MAHONEY, M. J. and THORESEN, C. E.: *Self-Control: Power to the Person*. Monterey, Calif.: Brooks/Cole Publishing Company, 1974.

MALTZMAN, I. and WOLFF, C.: Preference for immediate versus delayed noxious stimulation and the concomitant GSR. *Journal of Experimental Psychology*, 1970, 83, 76-79.

MARSTON, A. R. and FELDMAN, S. E.: Toward the use of self control in behavior modification. *Journal of Consulting and Clinical Psychology*, 1972, 39, 429-433.

MASTERS, J. C.: Effects of success, failure, and reward outcome upon contingent and noncontingent self-reinforcement. *Developmental Psychology*, 1972, 7, 110-118.

MASTERS, J. C. and MOKROS, J. R.: Self-reinforcement processes in children. In H. Reese (Ed.), *Advances in Child Development and Behavior* (Vol. 9). New York: Academic Press, 1974.

MASTERS, J. C. and PESKAY, J.: Effects of race, socioeconomic status, and success or failure upon contingent and noncontingent self-reinforcement in children. *Developmental Psychology*, 1972, 7, 139-145.

MEICHENBAUM, D.: A cognitive-behavior modification approach to assessment. In M. Hersen and A. S. Bellack (Eds.), *Behavioral Assessment: A Practical Handbook*. New York: Pergamon Press, 1976, 143-171.

MEUX, E. P.: Concern for the common good in an N-person game. *Journal of Personality and Social Psychology*, 1973, 28, 414-418.

MISCHEL, W.: Processes in delay of gratification. In L. Berkowitz (Ed.), *Advances in Experimental Social Psychology* (Vol. 7). New York: Academic Press, 1974.

MISCHEL, W.: Theory and research on the antecedents of self-imposed delay of reward. In B. A. Maher (Ed.), *Progress in Experimental Research* (Vol. 3). New York: Academic Press, 1966, 85-132.

MISCHEL, W.: Toward a cognitive social learning reconceptualization of personality. *Psychological Review*, 1973, 80, 252-283.

MISCHEL, W. and BAKER, N.: Cognitive transformations of reward objects through instructions. *Journal of Personality and Social Psychology*, 1975, 31, 254-261.

MISCHEL, W., COATES, B., and RASKOFF, A.: Effects of success and failure on self-gratification. *Journal of Personality and Social Psychology*, 1968, 10, 381-390.

MISCHEL, W. and EBBESEN, E. B.: Attention in delay of gratification. *Journal of Personality and Social Psychology*, 1970, 16, 329-337.

MISCHEL, W. and GILLIGAN, C.: Delay of gratification, motivation for the prohibited gratification, and responses to temptation. *Journal of Abnormal and Social Psychology*, 1964, 69, 411-417.

MISCHEL, W. and GRUSEC, J.: Waiting for rewards and punishments: Effects of time and probability on choice. *Journal of Personality and Social Psychology*, 1967, 5, 24-31.

MISCHEL, W. and MISCHEL, H. N.: A cognitive social learning approach to morality and self-regulation. In T. Lickona (Ed.), *Morality: A Handbook of Moral Behavior*. New York: Holt, Rinehart & Winston, 1976, 84-107.

MISCHEL, W. and STAUB, E.: Effects of expectancy on working and waiting for larger rewards. *Journal of Personality and Social Psychology*, 1965, 2, 625-633.

NELSON, R. O.: Methodological issues in assessment via self-monitoring. In J. D. Cone and R. P. Hawkins (Eds.), *Behavioral Assessment: New Directions in Clinical Psychology*. New York: Brunner/Mazel, 1977.

NEWMAN, A. and KANFER, F. H.: Self-control in children: The effects of training under fixed, decreasing and increasing delay of reward, *Journal of Experimental Child Psychology*, 1976, 21, 12-24.

PLATT, J.: Social traps. *American Psychologist.* 1973, 28, 641-651.

PREMACK, D. and ANGLIN, B.: On the possibilities of self-control in man and animals. *Journal of Abnormal Psychology*, 1973, 81, 137-151.

RACHLIN, H.: Self-control. *Behaviorism*, 1974, 2, 94-107.

RACHLIN, H. and GREEN, L. Commitment, choice and self-control. *Journal of the Experimental Analysis of Behavior*, 1972, 17, 15-22.

REHM, L. P.: *A Self-Control Model of Depression.* Unpublished manuscript. University of Pittsburgh, 1975.

RENNER, K. E.: *Coherent Self-direction and Values.* Paper presented at New York Academy of Science Conference on "Patterns of Integration from Biochemical to Behavioral Processes," New York, N.Y., May, 1971.

RENNER, K. E.: Temporal integration: An incentive approach to conflict resolution. In B. A. Maher (Ed.), *Process in Experimental Personality Research* (Vol. 4). New York: Academic Press, 1967.

ROZENSKY, R. H., REHM, L. P., PRY, G., and ROTH, D.: *The Assessment of Level of Depression and Self-Reinforcement Behavior in Hospitalized Patients.* Unpublished manuscript, University of Pittsburgh, 1975.

SEEMAN, G. and SCHWARZ, J. C.: Affective state and preference for immediate versus delayed reward. *Journal of Research in Personality*, 1974, 7, 384-394.

SEIDNER, M. L.: *Behavior Change Contract: Prior Information About Study Habits Treatment and Statements of Intention as Related to Initial Effort in Treatment.* Unpublished doctoral dissertation, University of Cincinnati, 1973.

SKINNER, B. F.: *Beyond Freedom and Dignity.* New York: Alfred A. Knopf, 1971.

SKINNER, B. F.: *Science and Human Behavior*. New York: The Macmillan Company, 1953.

SKINNER, B. F.: *Walden Two*. New York: The Macmillan Company, 1948.

SNYDER, M.: Self-monitoring of expressive behavior. *Journal of Personality and Social Psychology*, 1974, 30, 526-537.

SPATES, C. R. and KANFER, F. H.: Self-monitoring, self-evaluation and self-reinforcement in children's learning: A test of a multi-stage self-regulation model. *Behavior Therapy*, 1977, 8, 9-16.

SUINN, R. M. and RICHARDSON, F.: Anxiety management training: A non-specific behavior therapy program for anxiety control. *Behavior Therapy*, 1971, 2, 498-510.

TARPY, R. M. and SAWABINI, F. L.: Reinforcement delay: A selective review of the last decade. *Psychological Bulletin*, 1974, 81, 984-997.

THORESEN, C. E. and MAHONEY, M. J.: *Behavioral Self-control*. New York: Holt, Rinehart & Winston, Inc., 1974.

UNDERWOOD, B., MOORE, B. S., and ROSENHAN, D. L.: Affect and self-gratification. *Developmental Psychology*, 1973, 8, 209-214.

WEINER, B., HECKHAUSEN, H., MEYER, W. R., and COOK, R. E.: Causal ascriptions and achievement behavior: A conceptual analysis of effort and reanalysis of locus of control. *Journal of Personality and Social Psychology*, 1972, 21, 239-248.

2

Biofeedback and the Self-Management of Disregulation Disorders

GARY E. SCHWARTZ

In one way or another, almost everything man does involves corrective information or feedback, both external and internal (Wiener, 1948). The concept of feedback in its simplest form is so obvious that it is often overlooked by health professionals and laymen alike. Everyone knows that it is essential to have external visual feedback and internal kinesthetic and proprioceptive feedback to learn to tie a knot or to serve a tennis ball. Placed in a more neurophysiological perspective, it becomes clear that the brain requires feedback of what it is doing and of its surroundings in order to appropriately regulate itself and its body (Schwartz, 1977).

The recent product of 20th century biomedical technology, biofeedback is a special form of information. With the aid of modern electronics it is now possible to accurately monitor a variety of internal physiological processes and to convert these signals into novel forms of visual or auditory information that can be consciously perceived and processed by the brain, and consequently self-regulated by the brain. From an evolutionary perspective this is a unique event in human history, for man has provided the brain with a dynamic form of bioinformation not part of its original biological structure (Schwartz, 1976).

This capacity for new perception and regulation of the brain and body has stimulated extensive research on the voluntary control of neural, visceral and skeletal responses (Schwartz & Beatty, 1977), and the application of biofeedback to the behavioral treatment of psychophysiological disorders (Birk, 1973). Although I emphasize a neurophysiological interpretation of biofeedback and its application to the treatment of functional (Whatmore & Kohli, 1974) or disregulation (Schwartz, 1977) disorders, this approach is recent in origin and does not reflect the historical development of biofeedback (Kimmel, 1974).

Much of the early research was derived from learning theory, emphasizing the application of instrumental (Miller, 1969) or operant (Shapiro, Crider, & Tursky, 1964) conditioning procedures. As noted by a number of authors (Lang, 1974; Schwartz, 1974; Shapiro & Surwit, 1976), investigators taking a feedback approach emphasize the role of information in self-regulation, whereas researchers taking a learning approach tend to emphasize incentives or motivation in the development and maintenance of self-control. As we will see, information and incentives are *both* important to the clinical application of biofeedback procedures, and their integration is emphasized in current neurophysiological theory.

Yogis and meditators have long claimed unusual powers of voluntary control over physiology and consciousness, but until recently these claims were dismissed by the scientific community. The theories or paradigms of the researchers could not explain such claims, and therefore they were dismissed as being inaccurate or fraudulent (Kuhn, 1967). Not only did paradigms in medicine disallow the voluntary control of visceral and glandular responses, but so did the prevailing conditioning paradigms in psychology. However, with the development of biofeedback, coupled with advances in neurophysiology, new paradigms have evolved which seek to explain and extend these observations. In the process, this information is revising our conceptualization of health and disease, and therefore the means by which we treat disease.

Unfortunately, the fervor for biofeedback is so strong that it has become almost fanatical. The popular press has at times been filled with uncritical enthusiasm for any speculated application of biofeedback techniques. The electronics industry has taken advantage of this interest and has exploited biofeedback in both the medical and lay markets. At one extreme there are those today who argue that biofeedback can enable us to control any aspect of our biology at will; at the other extreme, a growing number dismiss biofeedback as a useless gimmick. It is this writer's opinion that neither of these extremes is appropriate, and that current research on biofeedback from a neurophysiological perspective not only expands our understanding of human self-regulation and its applications to medicine, but helps us recognize its limitations (Schwartz, 1975).

In order to more fully appreciate the potential and limitations of bio-feedback for the treatment of psychosomatic disorders, it is essential to view biofeedback within a broader psychobiological perspective. Towards this end a brief introduction to psychosomatic disorders from the perspective of feedback and disregulation is presented. The relevance of this model to the development of more holistic approaches in medicine becomes clear when we consider how the traditional medical model is inadvertently perpetuating physiological disregulation by ignoring the role of negative feedback in homeostasis (Schwartz, 1977).

DISREGULATION: A NEUROPHYSIOLOGICAL MODEL OF PSYCHOSOMATIC DISORDERS

The concept of feedback is central to our understanding of health and disease. As originally posited by the French physiologist Claude Bernard in the last century, and elaborated by Walter Cannon in his classic volume, *The Wisdom of the Body* (1939), there is a biological necessity to maintain physiological variables within adaptive limits for the purpose of survival. This is accomplished by homeostasis, a process requiring an intact nervous system. Homeostasis, therefore, is an *internal* negative feedback mechanism, devoted to the maintenance of the internal organs. It is negative in the sense that the feedback acts to dampen overresponding in a corrective and stabilizing manner.

However, what happens if the protective negative feedback circuit or loop is altered or made ineffective? It follows logically that normal self-regulation will not occur, and the system will become unstable. I have called this instability "disregulation" (Schwartz, 1977); the concept is similar to Miller and Dworkin's (1977) "anti-homeostasis."

The basic model is as follows: When the environment places demands on a person, the brain performs the necessary regulations to meet the specific demands. Depending upon the nature of these stresses, certain bodily systems will be activated, while others may simultaneously be inhibited. However, if this process is sustained to the point where the organ becomes damaged, the negative feedback loop of the homeostatic mechanism will normally be accentuated, forcing the brain to change its course of action. Often this negative feedback loop results in the experience of pain.

For example, if a person is very active and eating on the run, the stomach may fail to function properly. Consequently, the stomach may

ORGANISM

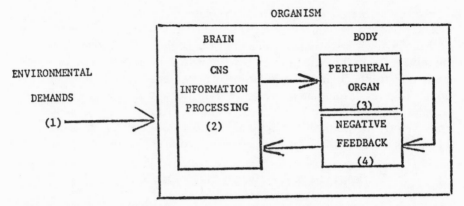

FIGURE 1. Schematic representation of four stages when disregulation can be produced, illustrating environmental demands (external, Stage 1), entering via sensory inputs (not shown), the CNS information processing system (the brain, Stage 2), which regulates a particular organ in the body (only one shown, Stage 3), and is provided with information about the state of the organ via negative feedback (Stage 4).

generate sufficient negative feedback to the brain, which is experienced as a stomachache. This corrective signal should serve the important function of causing the brain to change its regulation in specific ways, such as leading the person to slow down and to allow digestion to occur more normally. The pain serves a second function in that it "teaches" the brain what it can and cannot do if the stomach is to work properly. The adaptive brain is one that can learn through its mistakes, and learn to anticipate the needs of its organs for the sake of their health.

However, the brain may fail to regulate itself effectively to meet the stomach's needs. The reasons for this can be quite varied. There are four major stages where disregulation can occur (Schwartz, 1977).

Stage 1: Environmental Demands. The stimuli from the external environment may be so demanding that the brain (Stage 2) is *forced* to *ignore* the negative feedback (Stage 4) generated by the stomach (Stage 3). This is the classic case of the person placed in unavoidable stress who must continue to act in certain ways despite negative feedback to the contrary. Many previous theories of psychosomatic disorders have emphasized this factor.

Stage 2: CNS Information Processing. The brain may be so programmed, initially through genetics and/or subsequently through learning, to respond inappropriately to the stimuli in the external environment. This is what we typically refer to as personality or life-style. Thus, although feedback from the abused organ may be present, the person's brain may fail to react to it appropriately.

Stage 3: Peripheral Organ. The organ in question may itself be hyper- or hypo-reactive to the neural or hormonal stimulation coming from the brain. This is the literal translation of what has sometimes been called the "weak organ" theory of psychosomatic disorders. It can explain why, in response to the same environmental stress, people differ in the organ that ultimately becomes dysfunctional. From this perspective, it is possible that the brain cannot regulate itself to compensate for the altered feedback it is receiving from the given organ, or in the case of a diseased organ, finds itself no longer capable of modifying the functioning of the organ.

Stage 4: Negative Feedback. Finally, the negative feedback derived from the organ in question may itself be inappropriate. In other words, it is possible for the protective negative feedback system to become less effective and, in extreme cases, be inactivated. An extreme example of this condition can be seen in persons born without the normal pain response system (Melzack, 1973). These individuals are constantly in danger of severely injuring themselves, for they lack the protective mechanism for detecting and coping with injury.

Although the etiology of disregulation can occur at any of these four stages, the general consequence of disregulation is the same in each case. By not responding appropriately to the negative feedback (Stage 4), the brain (Stage 2) fails to maintain stable regulation of the organ in question (Stage 3) and disregulation (with its accompanying instability) occurs.

It is important to recognize that not only can disregulation occur at each of the four stages in the system, but it is also possible for problems to occur simultaneously at multiple stages. In the extreme case, if a person was 1) exposed to demanding stimulation in his environment, requiring continued adaptation (Stage 1), *and* 2) his brain processed the sensory information and reacted inappropriately due to genetic and/or learning factors (Stage 2), *and* 3) the peripheral organ itself reacted inappropriately due to genetic and/or maturational factors (Stage 3), *and* 4) the feedback mechanism derived from this organ was also ineffective (Stage 4), this *pattern* would combine so as to increase the likelihood that the person would develop a specific psychosomatic disorder. Since the brain and body are composed of multiple systems that must be coordinated in an integrated fashion, it becomes necessary to examine *each* of the components and then consider how they *combine* so as to produce the final outcome or disease.

This holistic perspective to psychosomatic disorders illustrates how the functioning of a *system as a whole* requires the adaptive coordination of all of its components in responding to a variety of environmental demands. By emphasizing the concept of feedback, the disregulation model provides a framework for understanding how biofeedback is viewed as the addition of a new corrective feedback loop to augment those inherent in man's natural biological structure (Schwartz, 1977). By taking a neurophysiological, multi-process perspective, the disregulation model also helps to delineate conditions under which biofeedback will be ineffective as a clinical tool. However, before we consider biofeedback's role in the treatment of disregulation, it is instructive to consider how the traditional medical model approaches these disorders.

MEDICINE AND THE PERPETUATION OF DISREGULATION

One novel and somewhat disturbing implication of the disregulation model is that, due to incomplete diagnosis and treatment of functional disorders, the traditional medical model inadvertently leads to the enhancement of disregulation, not only of bodily disease but of human behavior as well (Schwartz, 1977).

As we have seen, disregulation can be initiated and perpetuated at four stages. Often, the disregulation is initiated by stimulus demands from the outside environment (Stage 1), coupled with the brain's reaction to them (Stage 2). If the brain is exposed to (or exposes itself to) environmental conditions which ultimately cause an organ system (Stage 3) to break down and develop a functional disorder, the appropriate internal negative feedback loops are activated (Stage 4). This negative feedback serves a vital function, since it directs the brain (Stage 2) to take corrective action if the organ is to survive. Even if the brain is busy attending to other stimuli in the outside environment, and thus fails to recognize the breakdown of a given organ, at some point the organ (if its negative feedback loop is intact) will generate sufficient negative feedback to redirect the brain's attention. Anyone who has experienced a strong stomachache caused by overeating, eating under the wrong circumstances, or eating the wrong food, knows the power that negative feedback can have in commanding our attention and our subsequent behavior.

What *should* the brain's response be to this internal stimulation? From a neurophysiological perspective, it becomes clear that the brain should either change the external environmental demands (Stage 1) or its behavior (Stage 2) to maintain the health of the organ (Stage 3). Consequently, the intrinsic pain of the disturbed stomach (Stage 4) can help to keep our behavior in check by forcing us to stop eating, or to stop running while we are eating, or to not eat the dangerous food again.

However, for many sociological reasons, man is not content to follow his initial biological heritage. He either feels no longer competent to change his environment or behavior, or simply does not want to. However, due to his highly developed brain and the resulting development of culture, he is no longer constrained to deal with the negative feedback by responding to organ dysfunction in terms of the body's normal structure. Instead, the typical patient would rather change his body structure (Stages 3 or 4) than change his life-style (Stage 2) or his environment (Stage 1), the two factors which together augment or cause the bodily dysfunction in the first place. Simply stated, man may choose instead to modify Stage 3 and/or 4 by *extrinsic biological intervention.* As would be predicted from the disregulation model, by artificially removing the negative feedback mechanisms, the brain is freed to continue behaving in *maladaptive* ways that could ultimately be deleterious to its survival. Lacking the stabilizing impact of the negative feedback regulation, the brain (and therefore its expression as behavior) thus goes more and more out of control (Schwartz, 1977).

Consider again the basic stomachache. At no time in human history has human culture so reinforced the practice of taking drugs to eliminate stomachaches caused by the brain's disregulation. The antacid commercials of the 1970s exemplify this value system. We see an obese man stuffing himself with apple pies or spaghetti. When he gets a functional stomachache, the conclusion is not, "The stomach and the rest of the body were not meant to eat like that—your stomachache represents the necessary biological feedback mechanism that will help keep you from further abusing your body." Instead, what we hear is "Eat, eat—and if you get a stomachache, don't change your external environment or behavior—rather, eliminate the internal discomfort artificially by taking a pill." Or, we see a family shopping at Christmas time, surrounded by crowds, struggling to hold the packages, rushing from counter to counter, continually inhibiting aggression caused by being bumped or offended in other ways. And, in the process, one of the members of the family gets a stomachache. The conclusion to this scenario based on the disregulation model, "The stomach and the rest of the body were not meant to live like that—your stomachache represents the necessary biological feedback mechanism that will help you from further abusing your body," is not the message of the commercial. Rather, what we are told is "Shop, shop—and if you get a stomachache, don't change your external environment or behavior—rather, eliminate the discomfort artificially by taking a pill."

Simple antacids are mild drugs, and do not always work. When this happens, medicine comes to the rescue with stronger medication to quell the pain. Then, when the organ becomes sufficiently abused so that an ulcer develops and internal bleeding occurs, does the person now listen to his stomach and radically change his external environment and behavior? Often not—what he does instead is to go to his surgeon and have the stomach repaired. Medicine, by dint of its continued ingenuity, is developing new and finer means of bypassing the normal adaptive feedback mechanisms. Thus, in extreme cases a patient can have a vagotomy, thereby eliminating the brain's capability to directly regulate the stomach. And if the trend in modern medicine continues, man in the future can look forward to the day when he can simply go to his local surgeon and be fitted with a new, artificial stomach.

Now we have a brain that is no longer constrained by the needs of its natural stomach. Consequently, according to the disregulation model, this brain is free to continue and even expand upon the inappropriate disregulation that was the initial cause of the problem. The stomach is only one organ, however, whereas modern medicine is using the same strategy for many of the systems of the body. Our culture is continually reinforcing the idea that if the brain and its body cannot cope with its external environment, then the body and brain will simply have to be altered medically to adjust to the increasing maladaptive demands of the environment. According to the disregulation model, this prospect carried to its extreme would have serious consequences for the structure and survival of the human species as we now know it.

The reader should not be left with the conclusion that I am against all medical intervention. On the contrary, a disregulation analysis helps delineate under what select conditions it is adaptive, not only in the short run but more importantly in the long run, for pharmacological and surgical intervention to be used. My point is that we should not come to the oversimplistic conclusion that the correction of Stages 3 and 4 of disregulation using external medical intervention should be the *sole* approach to treatment. Rather, it may be necessary for us to accept and respect the wisdom and limitations of the body as it was originally designed (Cannon, 1939) even though this may require more active self-regulation on the part of the brain to keep the health and behavior of the human organism intact. Biofeedback could play a role in helping to reinforce this conclusion.

BIOFEEDBACK AND PHYSIOLOGICAL SELF-REGULATION: BASIC RESEARCH

There are now hundreds of studies demonstrating increased physiological control with feedback and reward. The list of responses brought under self-control includes systolic and diastolic blood pressure, heart rate, blood flow, sweat gland activity, skin temperature, body temperature, respiratory functions, genital responses, stomach motility, fine skeletal muscle control (including single motor units) and various changes in the electrical activity of the brain. Many of these studies are reprinted in a set of *Biofeedback and Self-Control* volumes (Barber et. al., 1971; Kamiya et al., 1971; Stoyva et al., 1972; Shapiro et al., 1973; Miller et al., 1974; DiCara et al., 1975) and are critically evaluated elsewhere (Schwartz & Beatty, 1977).

A useful example of basic biofeedback research concerns blood pressure self-regulation in normotensive subjects. It is now well established that normal subjects can learn to regulate their systolic and diastolic blood pressure depending upon the nature of the feedback and instructions used. If subjects are given simple binary (yes-no) feedback for relative increases or decreases in systolic pressure at each beat of the heart, and are given minimal instructions about what they are to do (they are not told what specific response they are to control, nor are they told in what direction their physiology is to change), subjects learn in 25 one-minute trials to increase or decrease voluntarily their systolic pressure without producing similar changes in heart rate (Shapiro et al., 1969; Shapiro, Tursky & Schwartz, 1970a). Conversely, if the feedback is provided for increases or decreases in heart rate, and minimal instructions are again used, subjects rapidly learn to increase or decrease their heart rate without similarly changing their systolic pressure (Shapiro, Tursky & Schwartz, 1970b). These data illustrate how biofeedback procedures can enable subjects to learn to control *specific* responses associated with the feedback. In more neurophysiological terms, if the brain is required to process the external feedback without any "preconceived notions," it readily learns to regulate those specific neural processes required to activate the periphery and thereby control the feedback.

Subjects can learn to regulate two or more responses simultaneously if feedback and reward are given for the desired *pattern* of responses. For example, if subjects are given feedback only when their systolic blood pressure and heart rate simultaneously increase (BP^{up}HR^{up}) or simultaneously decrease (BP$_{down}$HR$_{down}$) subjects now learn to regulate both responses (Schwartz, 1972). Interestingly, teaching subjects to control patterns of responses uncovers biological linkages and constraints between systems not readily observed when controlling the individual functions alone (Schwartz, 1974, 1975, 1976). For example, when subjects are taught to lower both their systolic pressure and heart rate simultaneously, they tend to show more rapid learning, produce somewhat larger changes, and experience more of the subjective concomitants of relaxation than when they are given feedback for either function alone (Schwartz, 1972). When subjects are given pattern biofeedback for making these responses go in opposite directions (BP^{up}HR$_{down}$ or BP$_{down}$HR^{up}), regulation of the two responses is attenuated. These observations are important because they highlight the concept of physiological *patterning* in both basic research and clinical treatment (Schwartz, 1974, 1975, 1976) and emphasize natural physiological constraints that must limit the degree of neural control possible.

In all of the above mentioned studies, subjects were given minimal instructions about the task. When subjects are specifically instructed to control their heart rate or blood pressure, however, they may demonstrate physiological control even in the absence of any feedback (Bell & Schwartz, 1975). However, it is a mistake to conclude that instructional control is identical to regulation gained through biofeedback. Whereas single system biofeedback leads to learned specificity, instructions often lead to more complex patterns of responses. Hence, the verbal instruction to control blood pressure leads to control of heart rate as well, whereas single system biofeedback for blood pressure with minimal instructions can lead to blood pressure control in the absence of heart rate control. It follows that the precise nature of the biofeedback *and* the specific instructions used *both* contribute to the final *pattern* of responses that the subject will learn to regulate. It should not be surprising for us to recognize that instructions differentially influence physiology, since the average adult brain can draw on a variety of neural strategies in its conscious repertoire to control the feedback, and depending upon the specific nature of the instructions, the strategies will vary.

This issue is of more than academic importance. For example, in certain cases of hypertension the goal may be to lower peripheral resistance in the absence of heart rate changes, whereas for the treatment of angina pectoris the goal may be to lower the pattern of blood pressure and heart rate since the product of these two functions leads to reduced work of the heart and consequently reduced pain (Braunwald et al., 1967). At the present time, however, we can only speculate as to what kinds of biofeedback procedures and instructions are best combined to produce these two different cardiovascular results, for there are as yet no controlled clinical studies on this issue.

CLINICAL APPLICATIONS OF BIOFEEDBACK: A CRITICAL OVERVIEW

At the present time there are over 50 published papers on clinical applications of biofeedback techniques. Most of these papers are based on collections of case studies, and it is difficult to interpret them. Several critical reviews have been written which cover a wide variety of clinical applications (Birk, 1973; Shapiro & Surwit, 1976; Miller & Dworkin, 1977; Shapiro & Schwartz, 1972; Blanchard & Young, 1974), including tension headache, asthma, bruxism, muscular rehabilitation, epilepsy, hypertension, cardiac arrhythmias, Raynaud's disease, migraine, sexual responses, pain and anxiety. Many of these reports represent only pilot studies and, while suggestive, all require carefully controlled clinical trials to evaluate them.

The clearest evidence for the efficacy of biofeedback therapy grows out of research on the regulation of skeletal muscle activity. This should not be surprising, since of all the bodily systems the skeletal muscles are under the most voluntary control, and feedback of their activity (both external and internal) is most extensive and available to the conscious brain. A clinical example is tension headaches, where the major symptom (pain) is often due to excessive and prolonged tension of the muscles in the forehead and neck. Stoyva and Budzynski have demonstrated that biofeedback for changes in frontalis muscle activity can enhance a patient's ability to voluntarily decrease forehead tension, which in turn leads to reduced pain. In one experiment, they found that clinical improvement was significantly greater in the frontalis biofeedback treatment group compared to two control groups, one given false biofeedback, the other given no treatment at all (Budzynski et al., 1973).

There is little question that biofeedback can enhance the self-regulation of muscle activity. In fact, it has been demonstrated that subjects can gain control of individual motor units within a single muscle when provided with the appropriate biofeedback, even though these changes are well below the level of normal awareness (Basmajian, 1972). However, Stoyva and Budzynski are careful to point out that gaining control over frontalis tension with biofeedback in the laboratory is but a prerequisite for clinical improvement. Patients must also practice self-regulation in real life situations outside of the laboratory in order for the biofeedback training to have any long-term clinical value. This observation is understandable within the disregulation model, since there is no reason to expect that enhancing self-regulation via the addition of external feedback will in and of itself compensate for headache disregulation, especially if the etiology and maintenance of the disorder involve excessive environmental stresses (Stage 1) or a maladaptive life-style (Stage 2). Stoyva and Budzynski are careful to tell their patients that they should use the enhanced awareness of muscle tension in their daily life as a signal for them to change their environment and/or their life-style (including coping style) in order to maintain low tension levels. If they do not, disregulation will continue and their headaches will likely return.

There are numerous other applications of muscle tension biofeedback under investigation, including applications to various neuromuscular disorders such as hemiplegia due to stroke; reversible physiological blocks due to edema; and Bell's palsy (see Blanchard & Young, 1974). The extent of muscle retraining depends in large measure on the precise nature of the etiology, including the extent of central (Stage 2) and peripheral (Stages 3 and 4) damage. It is likely that such work will continue to progress, and that feedback techniques may become a standard adjunctive treatment in physical rehabilitation.

There are other more general muscle biofeedback applications of relevance to psychosomatic medicine and psychiatry. Whatmore and Kohli (1974) claim that the training of whole body muscle relaxation can be used as a treatment for such skeletal, autonomic and affective disorders as functional backache and neck pain, hyperventilation syndrome, hypertension, ulcers, anxiety and depression. Like Jacobson (1938) before them, they argue that chronic muscle tension in various parts of the body plays an important role in the development and maintenance of disregulation disorders, and through muscle biofeedback these functional disorders can be eliminated. Their neurophysiological model of "dysponesis," including case studies involving prolonged muscle retraining collected over a 20-year period, is described in *The Physiopathology and Treatment of Functional Disorders* (1974). While their approach is promising, particularly in their consideration of possible neurophysiological mechanisms and their emphasis on multi-process treatment programs, it must be recognized that their conclusions are based entirely on uncontrolled case reports. Carefully designed outcome studies have yet to be carried out demonstrating that the use of biofeedback training in the regulation of muscle tension has a central role in the treatment of these disorders.

A second major area of biofeedback therapy involves feedback for electroencephalographic (EEG) activity of the brain. The best documented studies are those by Sterman and colleagues (1977) in which biofeedback training for EEG activity recorded from the scalp over the sensory/motor cortex is used to reduce specific epileptic seizures. Sterman claims that one particular sensory motor rhythm (SMR) between 12 and 14 hz must be regulated by the patient in order for reduction of seizures to occur. However, this conclusion may be premature, since other rhythms in this same region, such as sensory/motor alpha (8-13hz), may reflect similar brain processes. In any event, Sterman claims that when selected patients learn to inhibit sensory motor processes, reductions in seizures can occur. What is not known is whether training in general muscle relaxation (which by definition involves regulation of the sensory motor cortex) is sufficient for obtaining clinical improvement.

Like biofeedback for peripheral skeletal motor responses, it should not be surprising to learn that biofeedback for various EEG changes results in rapid self-control. This is because surface EEG typically reflects complex neural processes underlying normal voluntary control by the brain of its sensory, attentional, cognitive and skeletal processes (Schwartz, 1977). However, the claim that training for EEG alpha (without regard for cerebral localization) will lead to general relaxation and altered states of consciousness (Kamiya, 1969) is now recognized as being too simplistic (Schwartz, 1975, 1976). Furthermore, altered states of awareness can so readily be achieved through simple cognitive, attentional and somatic exercises already under a person's voluntary control (e.g., Davidson & Schwartz, 1976; Benson, 1975) that biofeedback for EEG may be irrelevant to this goal.

Stoyva and Budzynski (1974) point out, however, that for certain patients (e.g., those with insomnia) a multi-stage training procedure may be needed for inducing low arousal, drowsiness and sleep: 1) training in forearm muscle relaxation (which is quite easy), followed by 2) training in frontalis muscle relaxation (which is more difficult), followed by 3) training in EEG theta (4-7hz) activity (which is quite difficult). What becomes clear is that blanket statements for or against the use of biofeedback techniques are premature and probably incorrect.

The last class of biofeedback applications involves feedback for visceral and glandular responses regulated by the autonomic nervous system. One major area of application under investigation involves the treatment of migraine headache. In an uncontrolled clinical trial Sargent and colleagues (1973) have claimed that training migraine patients to simultaneously increase warmth in the fingers and decrease warmth in their forehead region using pattern temperature biofeedback leads to the reduction of migraine headaches. They combined biofeedback with instructions to imagine that one's hands were heavy and warm, based on a cognitive self-regulation therapy called autogenic training (Schultz & Luthe, 1969). The rationale for using "autogenic-feedback" training was suggested to them by the experience of a research subject who, during the spontaneous recovery from a migraine attack, demonstrated considerable flushing in her hands with an accompanying 10°F rise in two minutes. In subsequent work with 19 patients with migraine headache, Sargent et al. reported improvement in 63%.

Despite these encouraging findings, it is not known whether these same results could have been obtained with autogenic phrases alone, or if comparable results might have been observed through spontaneous remission and/or a "placebo" effect. Again, the issue is not simply whether biofeedback can be used to regulate temperature. As recently reviewed by Taub (1977), highly localized control of skin temperature can be trained with temperature biofeedback. What is not clear is whether temperature biofeedback training is necessary and/or sufficient for the treatment of migraine. Nor is it known whether biofeedback for other parameters such as blood flow in the inflicted area will be more beneficial. In this regard biofeedback for temperature and blood flow are currently considered as a potential adjunctive treatment for Raynaud's disease. Successful cases have been described (Taub, 1976; Surwit, 1973; Schwartz, 1973), but the interpretation of these cases is unclear.

Biofeedback for disorders of cardiac rhythms such as tachycardias and preventricular contractions (PVCs) has been investigated by Engel and

Bleecker (1974). There is little question that certain patients can reduce the frequency of PVCs by regulating heart rate. Interestingly, for some patients this is accomplished by decreasing sympathetic tone; for others it is achieved by decreasing parasympathetic tone. It appears that, depending upon the specific etiology of the arrhythmia, different components of the neural innervation must be self-regulated to achieve clinical improvement.

A major application of autonomic biofeedback involves feedback for blood pressure in the regulation of essential hypertension. Based on our blood pressure findings obtained in normotensive subjects (Shapiro et al., 1969; Shapiro, Tursky, & Schwartz, 1970a, 1970b; Schwartz, 1972), we studied seven patients with essential hypertension (Benson et al., 1971). After between five and 16 control sessions, patients were given daily biofeedback sessions for lowering systolic pressure. Large decreases in pressure were obtained in five of the patients, ranging from 16 to 34mmHg after 12 to 34 training sessions. Using a more sophisticated within-subject design where patients were taught to both decrease and increase pressure with systolic blood pressure biofeedback, Kristt and Engel (1975) have replicated and extended these findings. In their study, daily blood pressure readings were obtained outside of the laboratory with a three-month follow-up. These data suggest that blood pressure biofeedback can be used to help hypertensive patients regulate their pressure. However, it is not known whether blood pressure biofeedback is either necessary or sufficient for achieving clinical improvement. For example, Jacobson (1938) reported that large blood pressure decreases could be obtained through general muscle relaxation, and Whatmore and Kohli (1974) have extended this observation using biofeedback for muscle tension.

The utility of biofeedback in visceral self-regulation appears to be especially well documented in the training of rectosphincteric responses for the treatment of fecal incontinence. Engel and colleagues (1974) used pattern biofeedback for training external sphincter contraction in synchrony with internal-sphincter relaxation in six patients with severe fecal incontinence. During follow-up periods ranging from six months to five years, four of the patients remained completely continent and the other two were definitely improved. The technique was simple to apply and learning occurred within four sessions or less. Engel and colleagues emphasize that not only can sphincter activity be brought under voluntary control (a phenomenon long recognized), but that this control can be reintroduced in patients with chronic fecal incontinence, even when the incontinence is secondary to organic lesions. Clearly, the capacity for neural control must have been present in these patients for the biofeedback to have been effective.

A final example concerns the possible use of intestinal biofeedback in the treatment of functional diarrhea. Furman (1973) reports that subjects can rapidly learn to reduce stomach and colon activity when given auditory biofeedback using a simple, electronic stethoscope. Furman applied this procedure to five patients with functional disorders of the lower gastrointestinal tract who manifested no organic findings. Response to treatment was uniformly positive. Furman claims that even patients who had experienced a lifetime of functional diarrhea and who had been virtually toilet bound are now enjoying normal bowel function. Although controlled studies have yet to be carried out using this technique, Furman's study illustrates how simple modes of feedback may be utilized by the patient and therapist as a team to aid in regaining control over a functional disorder.

THE PLACE OF BIOFEEDBACK IN THE SELF-MANAGEMENT OF DISREGULATION DISORDERS

It is clear that there are many potential applications of biofeedback in the treatment of physiological disorders. It is also clear that the exacting work of conducting controlled clinical studies to determine the validity and limitations of biofeedback for specific disorders with particular patients is just beginning. It will be years before definite conclusions can be drawn. Issues of expectancy, placebo responses, spontaneous remission and others must be considered (Schwartz, 1977; Miller & Dworkin, 1977; Shapiro & Schwartz, 1972), since they apply to any behavioral or biological treatment in psychiatry and medicine.

However, biofeedback research is providing more than just a potential clinical technique. It is providing a new research tool for understanding functional disorders and, as I have illustrated, it is stimulating new neurophysiological analyses of normal and abnormal physiological self-regulation (Schwartz, 1977). These analyses, in turn, serve to illuminate both the potential and the limitations of biofeedback as a self-regulation therapy. They emphasize how biofeedback must be viewed as only one component of multi-process approach to treatment if long-term clinical gains are to be obtained.

For example, one issue of historical relevance to the development of biofeedback therapy concerns the so-called direct versus indirect approach

(Schwartz, 1973; Lazarus, 1975). The simple, direct approach is to provide the patient with feedback for a specific symptom for the purpose of self-regulating the symptom. Once self-regulation is acquired, the hope is that the symptom will remain under control and disappear. The indirect approach is broader in scope; it argues that patients should learn to regulate as many of the underlying components or processes contributing to the disorder as possible, including environmental and behavioral factors.

The indirect approach argues that biofeedback can be used to signal both the therapist and the patient that the patient is currently thinking, feeling or doing specific things that are detrimental to his physical or emotional health. A well-known example of this approach is the use of feedback in the treatment of obesity. In the same way that a scale helps direct the therapist and his obese patient in learning how to reduce food consumption and/or to increase exercise in order to reduce weight (rather than having the patient spending hours on the scale attempting to lower his weight by thought processes alone), biofeedback for physiological disorders can similarly determine the course of treatment. By means of the immediate, augmented feedback (with its associated increased bodily awareness), the patient can learn new ways of coping cognitively and behaviorally with his environment (Stage 2 CNS information processing) and/or he can learn to alter his environment (Stage 1) in such a way as to keep his physiological processes (Stage 3) within safer limits. In this respect biofeedback is similar to current psychotherapies, for they all provide corrective feedback (Schwartz, 1973) in the cybernetic sense (Wiener, 1948).

By recognizing that disregulation disorders can have multiple etiologies requiring a multi-process treatment program, it becomes possible to determine more precisely what combination of factors is contributing to the disorder in the individual patient, and what combination or pattern of treatment approaches should be used in each individual case (Schwartz, 1977). For example, if it were found in a given hypertensive patient that the high pressure tended to occur in anger arousing situations, the therapist could employ a variety of cognitive and behavioral approaches, including, for instance, role playing, as a means of teaching the person better ways of handling his aggression. Or, if the patient had difficulty relaxing in situations of moderate stress, the therapist could employ a variety of cognitive and behavior relaxation procedures, including muscle relaxation and meditation procedures, as a means of teaching the person better ways of reducing excessive tension. As part of the treatment, however, both the therapist and patient would profit from intermittent bio-feedback (augmented Stage 4) of blood pressure to ensure that the treatment regime was effective. This use of feedback is similar to what the physician normally does when he monitors the patient's pressure as a means of titrating drug effects. The difference here, however, is the emphasis on the patient, via the negative feedback (Stage 4), taking a more active role in monitoring his physiological processes (Stage 3) and in self-regulating his behavior (Stage 2) and environment (Stage 1).

There are numerous issues that need to be resolved, not the least of which is economy. Is biofeedback too expensive to be considered on a large-scale basis, especially if nonelectronic relaxations procedures in and of themselves prove sufficient to produce clinically significant long-term changes (Benson, 1975)? It seems probable that certain patients with certain disorders will not require augmented biomedical instrumentation to achieve improvement, but at this point it is premature to conclude that this will be the case for all patients. The disregulation model helps us to appreciate the multiplicity of factors contributing to functional disorders, and helps us place factors such as secondary gain and suggestion (Stage 1) and peripheral organpathology (Stage 3 and/or 4) into a total treatment approach (Schwartz, 1977). To the extent that severe pathology reduces the brain's ability to regulate the diseased organ via normal and humoral factors, the limitations of biofeedback and other behavioral approaches can be estimated. The theme of self-regulation (broadly defined) and bio-feedback (in particular) provides the impetus for developing a field of "behavioral medicine" (Birk, 1973). It places more responsibility for both sickness and health in the hands of the patient, and suggests new directions for preventive medicine by manipulating Stages 1 and 2 before organic pathology in Stages 3 and 4 has a chance to develop.

However, when we view functional disorders in terms of four stages of disregulation, and when we recognize that a *combination* of stages can contribute to the final disorder in the individual patient, it becomes clear why increasing external feedback in and of itself may not be sufficient for long-term clinical gains, even with the use of home trainers and ambulatory feedback devices. As mentioned earlier, the corrective internal negative feedback loop (Stage 4) in normal homeostasis not only provides information, but, with few exceptions, also provides a strong incentive (i.e., pain), for the brain (Stage 2) to regulate itself for the sake of the organ's health (Stage 3) and therefore ultimately its own. For this reason it is necessary for the therapist to consider both the information value and incentive value of biofeedback in the total treatment program. If the latter is lacking, the former will be short lived at best.

In cases of extreme pain or embarrassment (such as in fecal incontinence), this adaptive mechanism provides a strong incentive for the patient to seek treatment and follow the regime. In these instances biofeedback may be particularly effective in aiding the patient to gain self-control. Unfortunately, in other disorders, such as essential hypertension, this adaptive mechanism is minimal or lacking. As a result, not only does the patient lack the feedback that something is wrong, but when he receives this feedback from his physician, he still lacks the built-in internal negative feedback which would motivate him to recover.

A good illustration of this point comes from one of our hypertensive patients who, during the feedback sessions, was successful in lowering his pressure (Schwartz, 1973). Over the five daily sessions of a typical week, he would lower his pressure by 20 mmHg and thus earn a total of over $35.00 for participating in the research. However, we consistently noticed that, after the weekend, he would enter the laboratory on Monday with elevated pressures again. In interviews with the patient, the problem became clear. After earning a sizeable amount of money, the patient would go to the race track on the weekend, gamble, and invariably lose. The likelihood of teaching this patient to "relax" through simple laboratory blood pressure feedback while losing at the race track would seem slim, indicating that there is a need to change other aspects of the patient's total life-style and to develop some enduring incentive system for sustaining his health.

The motivation issue helps clarify the distinction between *learning* a self-regulation skill versus *using* that skill for the continued maintenance of one's health. The long-term effectiveness of biofeedback or, for that matter, any behavioral or biological treatment program involving self-control (e.g., taking drugs) ultimately depends on the patient's motivation and ability to continue using the self-regulation skill. This distinction is an important one, for it helps us recognize the difference between developing behavioral procedures for helping patients to help themselves, as opposed to developing educational and social programs for leading patients to make effective, long-term use of the new behavioral technology. This writer is of the strong opinion that we are closer to solving the former than the latter. The ultimate clinical value of biofeedback and other self-regulation procedures for the treatment of disregulation disorders will hinge on our success in solving both of them.

REFERENCES

BARBER, T. X., DiCARA, L. V., KAMIYA, J., MILLER, N. E., SHAPIRO, D. and STOYVA, J. (Eds.): *Biofeedback and Self Control 1970: An Aldine Annual on the Regulation of Bodily Processes and Consciousness.* Chicago: Aldine-Atherton, 1971.

BASMAJIAN, J. V.: Electromyography comes of age. *Science,* 1972, 176, 603-609.

BELL, I. R. and SCHWARTZ, G. E.: Voluntary control and reactivity of human heart rate. *Psychophysiology,* 1975, 12, 339-348.

BENSON, H.: *The Relaxation Response.* New York: Morrow, 1975.

BENSON, H., SHAPIRO, D., TURSKY, B., and SCHWARTZ, G. E.: Decreased systolic blood pressure through operant conditioning techniques in patients with essential hypertension. *Science,* 1971, 173, 740-742.

BIRK, L. (Ed.): *Biofeedback: Behavioral Medicine.* New York: Grune and Stratton, 1973.

BLANCHARD, E. B., and YOUNG, L. C.: Clinical applications of biofeedback training: A review of evidence. *Archives of General Psychiatry,* 1974, 30, 573-589.

BRAUNWALD, E., EPSTEIN, S. E., GLICK, G., WECHSLER, A. S. and BRAUNWALD, N. S.: Relief of angina pectoris by electrical stimulation of the carotid-sinus nerves. *New England Journal of Medicine,* 1967, 227, 1278-1283.

BUDZYNSKI, T. H., STOYVA, J. M., ADLER, C. S., and MULLANEY, D. J.: EMG biofeedback and tension headache: A controlled outcome study. *Psychosomatic Medicine,* 1973, 35, 484-496.

CANNON, W. B.: *The Wisdom of the Body.* New York: W. W. Norton, 1939.

DAVIDSON, R. J. and SCHWARTZ, G. E.: Psychobiology of relaxation and related states: A multi-process theory. In D. Mostofsky (Ed.), *Behavior Control and Modification of Physiological Processes.* New York: Prentice Hall, 1976.

DiCARA, L. V., BARBER, T. X., KAMIYA, J., MILLER, N. E., SHAPIRO, D. and STOYVA, J. (Eds.): *Biofeedback and Self-Control 1974: An Aldine Annual on the Regulation of Bodily Processes and Consciousness.* Chicago: Aldine, 1975.

ENGEL, B. T. and BLEECKER, E. R.: Application of operant conditioning techniques to the control of the cardiac arrhythmias. In P. A. Obrist, A. H. Black, J. Brener and L. V. DiCara (Eds.), *Cardiovascular Psychophysiology.* Chicago: Aldine, 1974.

ENGEL, B. T., NIKOOMANESH, P. and SCHUSTER, M. M.: Operant conditioning of recto-sphincteric responses in the treatment of fecal incontinence. *New England Journal of Medicine,* 1974, 290, 646-649.

FURMAN, S.: Intestinal biofeedback in functional diarrhea: A preliminary report. *Journal of Behavior Therapy and Experimental Psychiatry.* 1973, 4, 317-321.

JACOBSON, E.: *Progressive Relaxation.* 2nd Ed. Chicago: University of Chicago Press, 1938.

KAMIYA, J.: Operant control of the EEG alpha and some of its reported effects on consciousness. In C. Tart (Ed.), *Altered States of Consciousness.* New York: John Wiley and Sons, 1969.

KAMIYA, J., DiCARA, L. V., BARBER, T. X., MILLER, N. E., SHAPIRO, D., and STOYVA, J. (Eds.): *Biofeedback and Self-Control: An Aldine Reader on the Regulation of Bodily Processes and Consciousness.* Chicago: Aldine-Atherton, 1971.

KIMMEL, H. D.: Instrumental conditioning of automatically mediated responses in human beings. *American Psychologist,* 1974, 29, 325-335.

KRISTT, D. A. and ENGEL, B. T.: Learned control of blood pressure in patients with high blood pressure. *Circulation,* 1975, 51, 370-378.

KUHN, T.: *The Structure of Scientific Revolutions.* Chicago: University of Chicago Press, 1967.

LANG, P. J.: Learned control of human heart rate in a computer directed environment. In P. A. Obrist, A. H. Black, J. Brener and L. V. DiCara (Eds.), *Cardiovascular Psychophysiology*. Chicago: Aldine, 1974.

LAZARUS, R. S.: A cognitively-oriented psychologist looks at biofeedback. *American Psychologist*, 1975, 30, 553-561.

MELZACK, R.: *The Puzzle of Pain*. New York: Basic Books, 1973.

MILLER, N. E.: Learning of visceral and glandular responses. *Science*, 1969, 163, 434-445.

MILLER, N. E., BARBER, T. X., DiCARA, L. V., KAMIYA, J., SHAPIRO, D., and STOYVA, J.: *Biofeedback and Self-Control 1973: An Aldine Annual on the Regulation of Bodily Processes and Consciousness*. Chicago: Aldine, 1974.

MILLER, N. E. and DWORKIN, B. R.: Critical issues in therapeutic applications of biofeedback. In G. E. Schwartz and J. Beatty (Eds.): *Biofeedback: Theory and Research*. New York: Academic Press, 1977.

SARGENT, J. D., GREEN, E. E., and WALTERS, E. D.: Preliminary report on the use of autogenic feedback training in the treatment of migraine and tension headaches. *Psychosomatic Medicine*, 1973, 35, 129-135.

SCHULTZ, J. H. and LUTHE, W.: *Autogenic Theory* (Vol. I). New York: Grune and Stratton, 1969.

SCHWARTZ, G. E.: Voluntary control of human cardiovascular integration and differentiation through feedback and reward. *Science*, 1972, 175, 90-93.

SCHWARTZ, G. E.: Biofeedback as therapy: Some theoretical and practical issues. *American Psychologist*, 1973, 29, 666-673.

SCHWARTZ, G. E.: Toward a theory of voluntary control of response patterns in the cardiovascular system. In P. A. Obrist, A. H. Black, J. Brener and L. V. DiCara (Eds.), *Cardiovascular Psychophysiology*, Chicago: Aldine, 1974.

SCHWARTZ, G. E.: Biofeedback, self-regulation, and the patterning of physiological processes. *American Scientist*, 1975, 63, 314-324.

SCHWARTZ, G. E.: Self-regulation of response patterning: Implications for psychophysiological research and therapy. *Biofeedback and Self-Regulation*, 1976, 1, 7-30.

SCHWARTZ, G. E.: Psychosomatic disorders and biofeedback: A psychobiological model of disregulation. In J. D. Maser and M. E. P. Seligman (Eds.). *Psychopathology: Experimental Models*. San Francisco: W. H. Freeman, 1977.

SCHWARTZ, G. E. and BEATTY, J. (Eds.): *Biofeedback: Theory and Research*. New York: Academic Press, 1977.

SHAPIRO, D., BARBER, T. X., DiCARA, L. V., KAMIYA, J., MILLER, N. E. and STOYVA, J.: *Biofeedback and Self-Control 1972: An Aldine Annual on the Regulation of Bodily Processes and Consciousness*. Chicago: Aldine, 1973.

SHAPIRO, D., CRIDER, A. B., and TURSKY, B.: Differentiation of an autonomic response through operant reinforcement. *Psychonomic Science*, 1964, 1, 147-148.

SHAPIRO, D. and SCHWARTZ, G. E.: Biofeedback and visceral learning: Clinical applications. *Seminars in Psychiatry*, 1972, 4, 171-184.

SHAPIRO, D. and SURWIT, R. S.: Learned control of physiological function and disease. In H. Leitenberg (Ed.), *Handbook of Behavior Modification and Behavior Therapy*. New York: Prentice-Hall, 1976.

SHAPIRO, D., TURSKY, B., GERSHON, E. and STERN, M.: Effects of feedback and reinforcement on the control of human systolic blood pressure. *Science*, 1969, 163, 588-590.

SHAPIRO, D., TURSKY, B., and SCHWARTZ, G. E.: Control of blood pressure in man by operant conditioning. *Circulation Research* (Supplement I). 1970, 26-27, 27-32 (a).

SHAPIRO, D., TURSKY, B., and SCHWARTZ, G. E.: Differentiation of heart rate and systolic blood pressure in man by operant conditioning. *Psychosomatic Medicine,* 1970, 32, 417-423 (b).

STERMAN, M. B.: Clinical Implications of EEG Biofeedback Training: A Critical Appraisal. In G. E. Schwartz and J. Beatty (Eds.) , *Biofeedback: Theory and Research.* New York: Academic Press, 1977.

STOYVA, J. and BUDZYNSKI, T.: Cultivated low arousal—an antistress response? In L. V. DiCara (Ed.), *Limbic and Autonomic Nervous Systems Research.* New York: Plenum, 1974.

STOYVA, J., BARBER, T. X., DiCARA, L. V., KAMIYA, J., MILLER, N. E., and SHAPIRO, D. (Eds.): *Biofeedback and Self-Control, 1971: An Aldine Annual on the Regulation of Bodily Processes and Consciousness.* Chicago: Aldine-Atherton, 1972.

SURWIT, R. S.: Biofeedback: A possible treatment for Raynaud's disease. *Seminars in Psychiatry,* 1973, 5, 483-490.

TAUB, E.: Self-regulation of human tissue temperature. In G. E. Schwartz and J. Beatty (Eds.), *Biofeedback: Theory and Research.* New York: Academic Press, 1977.

WHATMORE, G. E. and KOHLI, D. R.: *The Physiopathology and Treatment of Functional Disorders.* New York: Grune and Stratton, 1974.

WIENER, N.: *Cybernetics or Control and Communication in the Animal and Machine.* Cambridge: M.I.T. University Press, 1948.

3

The Social Context of Self-Control

TODD R. RISLEY

How can you insure that desired behaviors will occur at times and places where you can neither prompt nor reinforce the behaviors? How can you get someone to do something—over there in some other time and place—when you cannot directly intervene over there in that setting?

The straightforward operant approach would rely on generalization— that is, you train and reinforce the behaviors in settings you can control and hope that the behaviors will generalize to new settings. With careful stimulus programming, this paradigm works well when the behavior is actually functional in the generalization setting. In other words, there must be "natural" reinforcers in that other time and place which will maintain the behavior once it occurs. However, if there are no rein- forcers for the behavior in that setting, the operant generalization para- digm is largely ineffective, as discrimination rapidly occurs.

But there are occasions when behavior must occur in settings where there are no functional immediate reinforcers for the behavior. On these occasions society appeals to internal attributes to account for the occur- rence of desired behaviors. When someone is seen working hard and there are no operant prompts or supports for that behavior, or when someone is seen resisting temptation, that is, not complying with imme- diate pressures nor seeking immediately available reinforcers, that person is attributed with willpower, altruism, ethics, or more recently, self- control.

As behaviorists we cannot accept simply labeling a phenomenon, espe-

71

cially with a label that assumes an internal state of the organism. As behavior therapists we must know how to produce the phenomenon which society calls altruism, the protestant ethic, or self-control when needed. As scientists, we must understand this important human phenomenon.

Although the simple operant generalization paradigm appears insufficient to account for this phenomenon, an alternative paradigm, equally familiar to psychology, may give us some leads. This alternative paradigm is the therapy paradigm, where the individual meets regularly with a therapist, is taught to describe desired behaviors and commits himself to perform those behaviors in other settings.

It is frequently assumed that what a person says he has done or will do relates to what he actually has done or will do. Much of psychotherapy—even the new "behavior" therapy—is based on the assumption that reorganizing and restructuring a patient's verbal statements about himself and his world will result in a corresponding reorganization of the patient's behavior with respect to that world. The problem with this paradigm is that there may be no correspondence between the person's verbal commitment in the sessions and his actual behavior in the other settings.

We have found this lack of correspondence to be almost universally true with young children. Although children can learn to describe or report on features of their own behavior, our research has consistently shown that discussions of what a preschool child has done or should do in another setting have little or no effect on what the child actually does there. Similarly, studies by Lovaas (1961, 1964) and Sherman (1964) found that when reinforcement procedures were applied in the modification of verbal behavior alone little increase in related nonverbal behavior of preschool children resulted. Therefore, we set out to determine how the therapeutic paradigm could be made effective for young children and to thereby determine how verbal discussion in one setting could be made to influence behaviors in another setting.

Our initial work on this paradigm began when we were attempting to teach young preschool poverty children to describe events in their life with more detail and elaboration. We were successful in producing extended narrations but noted that the long and specific descriptions they were producing had little relationship to the events that actually occurred in their life (Risley & Hart, 1968). While pursuing this observation we stumbled upon the procedures which would allow us to, in effect, determine what situations they sought out and what behaviors they emitted in their daily activities at the preschool. The report of our first series of studies of this paradigm (Risley & Hart, 1968) contains an examination of virtually every feature we have found to be critical to the paradigm in all of our subsequent analyses. However, our subsequent work has led us to a substantially different interpretation of this phenomenon. Let me therefore skip the several years of intervening research and exemplify this paradigm with two studies which were designed to illustrate our present conceptualization of this phenomenon.

Francisco Montes, who was then the director of the Turner House Preschool, and I noted that the preschool playground was full of trash and litter. Such littered playgrounds are common to most urban areas and the presence of litter on a playground has no apparent effect on the children's use of those playgrounds. The litter did not appear to make play on our playground any less reinforcing and indeed may have represented some actual reinforcers for the children, as they occasionally incorporated bits of litter in their playground activities. Thus, at mid-morning the children played happily for a half-hour period on their littered playground while their teacher stood near the unused garbage can placed in the middle of the playground. Each day about an hour and a half after the playground period, just before the children left the preschool, they assembled in two groups of eight children in two different locations in the day care center for a brief discussion session with two teachers. For 20 days (Figure 1, school days 114-134) we simply counted the number of children who deposited trash in the playground garbage can. None of the children was ever observed to do so.

On the 135th school day we began to direct the conversation in the daily discussion groups toward the desirability of maintaining a clean environment. As can be seen in Figure 1, within a very short period the children in both discussion groups were describing the value of picking up trash. The teacher would call on each child in turn as they raised their hands and ask, "What should we do when we see trash lying around on the ground?" The children would proudly describe in virtuous tones that, whenever we see trash lying around on the ground we should always pick it up and thereby improve the environment and make our neighborhood a pleasant place to live. During this time, on the playground, these same children, in spite of their virtuous discussion at the end of each day, were never observed to once pick up any trash on the playground and put it in the garbage can (Figure 1, school days 135-151

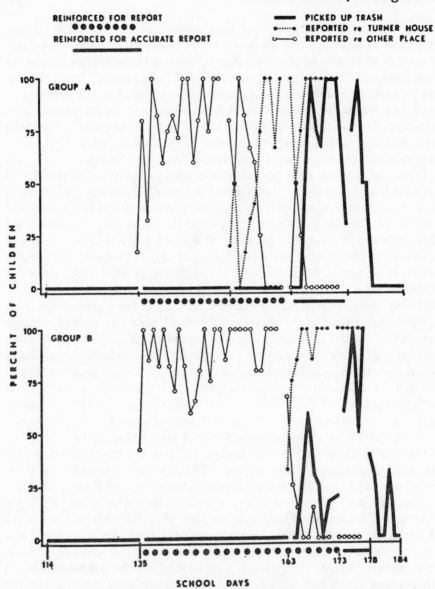

FIGURE 1. Percent of children who stated in group discussion that they should pick up trash anywhere (open circles) or specifically on the playground (closed circles), and percent of children who picked up trash from the playground (solid line). After a baseline period the teachers prompted and socially reinforced the children's verbal statements about trash pick-up during group discussions at the end of the school day ("REINFORCED FOR REPORT"), and then added confirming or disconfirming comments on the correspondence between each verbal statement a child made about trash pick-up and that child's behavior during the morning's outdoor play period ("REINFORCED FOR ACCURATE REPORT").

Group A, school days 135-162 Group B). Even when we guided the discussions to be more specific to the playground at the preschool—such that the children were then describing how whenever they saw trash on their playground at the preschool they should always pick it up so that the playground would look better—no child was observed to pick up the trash and deposit it in the garbage can (Figure 1, Group A, school days 152-162). Indeed our previous work had indicated that the form of the verbal statement alone makes little difference. Whether the statement is an abstract statement of value (as, "Whenever one sees ......, one should always do ...."), or is a presumed report on past activities ("Yesterday, when I saw ......, I did ...."), or a promise of future activities ("Tomorrow when I see ......, I will do ...."), seems to make little difference in producing any effect on the behavior of the children.

However, when the discussion session was also used as an opportunity to give feedback on the correspondence between the verbal commitment and the actual behaviors in the other setting, the behaviors there began to occur. The teacher simply began to comment during the discussion sessions on the correspondence or discrepancy between the child's verbal statement about picking up trash in the playground and his actual behavior on the playground. When a child virtuously stated, "Whenever we see trash on our playground we should always pick it up and put it in the garbage can," the teacher would simply comment, "Yes, but this morning on the playground there was trash around and I didn't notice you picking up any, did I?" The child would usually hang his head slightly and mumble, "No, no, I didn't." In Group A this correspondence feedback was begun on the 163rd day of the preschool year. Several children picked up trash two days later. When they virtuously described what children should do when they see trash on the playground in the end-of-the-day discussion, the teacher was able to comment to these children, "Yes, that's right and I noticed you picking up some trash on the playground this morning." The next day all of the children in Group A picked up trash at least once during the playground period and most continued to do so each day as long as the discussions about trash with correspondence feedback were continued (Figure 1, school days 163-173 Group A). It is interesting to note that in Group B, where during this time, discussions focused simply on what one should do when he sees trash on the playground without receiving any correspondence feedback from their teacher, some children picked up some trash for the first time. This appeared to be a modeling effect: In observing Group A children picking up trash, a few Group B children once in a while would also pick up trash and throw it in the garbage can. But this effect was very weak (Figure 1, school days 163-174 Group B). However, when correspondence feedback was introduced in Group B on the 173rd day of the preschool year, most children began picking up trash each day on the playground. It's important to note that in both groups when the discussion sessions were discontinued the virtuous behavior of picking up trash on the playground also ceased.

This paradigm has been applied across longer periods of time, more difficult behaviors, and more independent settings in many other studies. For example, Patricia Krantz and I selected poor, black children in an inner city public school kindergarten classroom, and sought to influence their school behavior only by things we did with them in an after-school day care center which they also attended. The data were collected throughout the three-hour kindergarten class each day by trained observers who were seen by the children only in that setting. The children were told the observers were "watching in order to learn how to be teachers" (average agreement between the observers exceeded 80% on all measures and conditions during all three experiments). Although the children were randomly assigned to experimental and control groups, the kindergarten teacher was unaware of this assignment, and all children also participated in the same after-school day care program activities together. The only time the experimental and control groups were separated was during the 15- to 20-minute daily group discussion sessions at the day care center. During the session, the control group children listened to and discussed children's stories.

This experiment focused upon the use of polite expressions to the kindergarten teacher. After a baseline period (Figure 2, school days 1-12) children in the experimental group were directly taught to use verbal etiquette to caregivers at every opportunity in the day care center. This training had no effect at all on their politeness in public school (Figure 2, school days 13-62). The experimental group was then prompted and socially reinforced in their daily discussion session for describing how one should try to be polite to their school teacher and for providing examples of verbal etiquette (please, thank you, excuse me, good morning, good-bye, etc.) to use for various occasions in the public school (entering the classroom, receiving materials, interrupting or walking in front of the teachers, etc.).

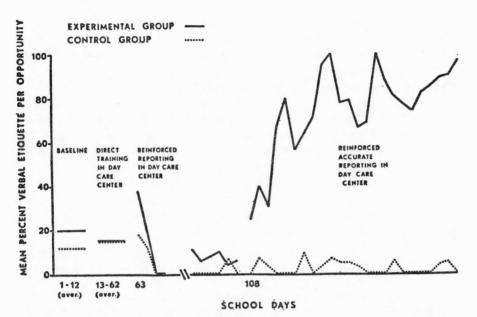

FIGURE 2. Average use of verbal etiquette statements by children to their kindergarten teacher, per opportunity for such statements.

They soon could describe at length that teachers (particularly *their* kindergarten teacher, Ms. Punitive Neurotic) liked it when children were polite to them, and so whenever they left for the day they should say "good-bye" to her, and when they asked her for something they should say "please" and when they belched in her presence they should say "excuse me," etc., etc. Although these discussions on politeness to their kindergarten teacher persisted for 45 days (Figure 2, school days 63-107), their verbal etiquette to the teacher actually declined (as did that of the control group—and no wonder as this kindergarten teacher was the worst teacher we have ever observed).

Finally, of course, the caregiver conducting the discussion sessions began to give correspondence feedback to their statements. She would usually present one or more confirming and one or less disconfirming comments to each child's statements. ("Yes, and this morning you *did* say good morning to Ms. Neurotic. That was very good." "But when she handed you your drawing paper after recess you didn't say thank you, did you?") The experimental group children immediately began saying polite things to their kindergarten teacher. They continued to improve until they were displaying verbal etiquette on over 80% of their opportunities throughout their half-day kindergarten class (Figure 2, school days 108-125). Meanwhile, the control group children continued to use verbal etiquette on only 3% of their opportunities.

Let us examine this now sufficient therapeutic paradigm. A person is brought to publicly describe the problem situation and to describe what he should and should not do in the situation to an audience of one or more persons. The audience comments on the correspondence or discrepancy between the person's verbal statements and specific instances of his actual behavior in other settings. His behavior in other settings then will change to correspond with his verbal behavior.

After having used it many times with many children over many behaviors the following components seem to emerge as critical:

1. The discussion sessions must predictably occur: Therefore they must be reinforcing or occur in a reinforcing context if attendance is voluntary. (Although food reinforcers were contingent upon desired statements in our early studies, they were later found unnecessary—so long as children could be required or enticed to attend the discussion sessions. However, school children would sometimes avoid coming to the day care center for after-school play, snack and discussion session on the day they had done poorly on the school behavior being discussed.)

2. The verbal statements themselves must be guided and reinforced—otherwise the verbal statements will alter to match the target behavior rather than the target behavior altering to match the verbal statements. That is, people will only talk about things they are already likely to do, unless statements of more ambitious goals are encouraged (see Risley & Hart, 1968, Experiment I).

3. The audience in the sessions must be able to have some independent information about the person's performance in the other setting—especially early in the program, but at least occasionally thereafter—to provide accurate comment on the correspondence or discrepancy between verbal statements and performance. Otherwise increasing discrepancy between verbal and nonverbal behavior may develop (see Risley & Hart, 1968, Experiment III).

Using this paradigm, we have been able to produce substantial changes in many behaviors of many disadvantaged children in many remote settings without directly intervening in those settings.

With preschool children we have also used brief discussion sessions to produce use of more varied materials in free play, to promote better hygiene habits in the bathroom, to eliminate disruptive behavior when the teacher was out of the room, to eliminate the theft of preschool materials, and to increase eating of more nutritious food at lunch.

With kindergarten and first grade children we have also increased the amount of time spent attending to their seatwork assignments, and to their teachers' instructions and lectures throughout the public school class periods, reduced dangerous pedestrian behavior when leaving school, and promoted picking up neighborhood litter after school.

Across our investigations of this paradigm a notable developmental phenomenon has emerged: After repeated use, simply getting a child to describe what he should do begins to have an increasingly greater effect on what he actually does—even *before* he is given feedback on the correspondence between those descriptions and actions. With preschool children, simply repeating the basic paradigm—generating discussion and description of desired behavior first, and then providing correspondence feedback on the congruence or discrepancy between their descriptions and their performance of desired behavior—across three or four examples of behavior, will predictably result in discussions of new desired behavior providing an immediate improvement in the performance of that behavior (see Risley & Hart, 1968, Experiment II; and Risley, Hart, & Doke, submitted). Thus, a child's verbal descriptions of desired behavior—*to an audience which has provided correspondence feedback in the past*—will markedly influence his actions.

In other words, when this paradigm is used frequently, a generalized behavior class will begin to form—if such a class is not already formed, as probably it is at some level in most adults. (A generalized behavior class is formed when many individual behavioral units are strengthened which have one or more common characteristics. Other behavioral units with the same characteristics are also thereby strengthened. Once such a generalized behavior class is established, intermittent reinforcement of some occurrences of old or new behaviors in that class will maintain the integrity of that generalized behavioral class and the strength of all individual behaviors contained within it. Baer, Peterson, and Sherman (1967) provide an analogous example of the formation of the generalized behavioral class of imitation.) Such a general class of correspondence between descriptions and actions, once formed, can be maintained by intermittent correspondence feedback from any recurring social audience which maintains discussion about appropriate behavior and values.

Our program of research has shown the power of a "self-control" paradigm in supporting desired behaviors of children across many different types of behaviors and in many different settings. More importantly, our research, I think, has suggested some general conclusions about the basis of self-control.

The primary conclusion is that instances of functional self-control should be considered to be individual examples of a general behavioral class of correspondence between words and deeds. As in all such behavioral classes, the strength of the class, and the variety of behaviors which are contained will differ according to the individual history of each person. However, deliberate programming can both strengthen the class and extend it to include any behavioral target for which self-control is lacking. As in any such behavioral class, the intermittent strengthening of some behaviors in the class will similarly strengthen all other behaviors in the class.

One method of strengthening the behavioral class called self-control requires establishing a predictable social context in which public descriptions of desirable performance are prompted and supported and the person's actual performance is publicly related to his descriptions. When a person exhibits a problem relating to the lack of self-control, this problem can be interpreted as resulting from the absence of predictable informed audiences in his normal life with whom to discuss his affairs and ambitions, and/or to a weak general relationship between his words and his deeds.

People's problems in governing their own behavior in situations where their desired behavior is not supported by immediate consequences may be best handled by providing them with a regular social context in which values and goals are predictably discussed and deliberately related to their performance. Therapy is one such social context for self-control —poorly functioning individuals who seek therapy may be functioning poorly because they have few such social contexts in their normal lives. Therapy should, however, be viewed as the artificial provision of such an audience. For durable therapeutic effects, the therapist should introduce the client into more durable social contexts and audiences which already exist.

REFERENCES

BAER, D. M., PETERSON, R. F., and SHERMAN, J. A.: The development of imitation by reinforcing behavioral similarity to a model. *Journal of the Experimental Analysis of Behavior*, 1967, 10, 405-416.

LOVAAS, O. I.: Interaction between verbal and non-verbal behavior. *Child Development*, 1961, 32, 329-336.

LOVAAS, O. I.: Control of food intake in children by reinforcement of relevant verbal behavior. *Journal of Abnormal and Social Psychology*, 1964, 68, 672-678.

RISLEY, T. R. and HART, B.: Developing correspondence between the non-verbal and verbal behavior of preschool children. *Journal of Applied Behavior Analysis*, 1968, 1, 267-281.

RISLEY, T. R., HART, B. and DOKE, L. A.: The development of "self" control. Submitted.

SHERMAN, J. A.: Modification of non-verbal behavior through reinforcement of related verbal behavior. *Child Development*, 1964, 35, 717-723.

4

The Use of Relaxation and Cognitive Relabeling as Coping Skills

MARVIN R. GOLDFRIED

In the late 1920s, Edmond Jacobson (1929) published *Progressive Relaxation,* in which he described in detail how relaxation training may be used in dealing with a wide variety of psychological problems. The impact that Jacobson's book made on the field was singularly unimpressive. From a practical point of view, Jacobson's suggestion that approximately 50 to 200 training sessions were required to produce beneficial effects no doubt discouraged many therapists from employing this procedure. Perhaps more important, the *Zeitgeist* within professional circles at that time was such that a therapeutic procedure merely entailing relaxation training probably made little sense in light of the influence of the psychoanalytic paradigm for the treatment of neurotic behavior. Consequently, relaxation training was not used professionally to any great extent until some years later, when Wolpe (1958) simplified the procedure and incorporated it into systematic desensitization.

Although it is not clear exactly how relaxation training lowers anxiety (Davison, 1966; Davidson & Schwartz, 1976), there is little doubt that it does. In addition to subjective reports of anxiety-free states from individuals following a relaxation training session, research has shown that

Preparation of the paper was supported in part by Grant MH24327 from the National Institute of Mental Health. The author would like to thank Sharon Foster and Richard Stuart for their helpful comments on an earlier draft of this chapter.

muscular relaxation has definite physiological consequences, including decrease in pulse rate, blood pressure, and electrodermal activity (Jacobson, 1938; Paul, 1969). The initial investigations into the effects of relaxation procedures that extend beyond the immediate training session, however, yielded less impressive results. Reports by several investigators (Davison, 1968; Lang, Lazovik & Reynolds, 1965; Rachman, 1965) consistently pointed to one conclusion: Relaxation training is not very effective in reducing anxiety when used as a therapeutic procedure in and of itself. In some situations, however, relaxation training *was* found to have positive therapeutic effects (Davison, 1965; Gray, England & Mahoney, 1965; Jacobson, 1938; Lazarus, 1958; Snider & Oetting, 1966; Weil & Goldfried, 1973). Additional evidence from post-treatment questionnaires in controlled outcome research revealed that successfully desensitized individuals did report the use of relaxation as a self-control skill for coping with anxiety (Bootzin & Kazdin, 1972; Paul & Shannon, 1966; Sherman, 1972). Therapeutic impact was also found to be enhanced when relaxation skills were presented to subjects within a self-control context (Davison, Tsujimoto & Glaros, 1973).

In applying systematic desensitization clinically, I have noticed an interesting phenomenon regarding the clinical effectiveness of relaxation training. After relaxation training has begun, but prior to desensitization proper, clients frequently report: "The treatment is really working. I find myself becoming less anxious in a number of situations." Upon first hearing some of these comments, I found myself most confused. After all, the desensitization has not yet taken place, and the available texts and research on the procedure seemed to suggest that relaxation alone should be ineffective. These clients had not been reading the behavioral literature! Instead, they apparently had been learning a method that I had not been deliberately teaching—they had begun to use relaxation as a means of actively coping with their problems. In reviewing the hierarchy items immediately prior to desensitization, such clients would frequently indicate that many of the situations that were originally included in the hierarchy no longer posed any problems, in that they had successfully been able to cope with these situations on their own.

Other behavior therapists have also noted that, even when they have presented desensitization as a counter-conditioning procedure for the elimination of specific fears, clients frequently interpret the beneficial effects as being due to having learned a strategy for coping with stress in general (e.g., Bootzin & Kazdin, 1972). For example, in their study on the effect of group desensitization, Paul and Shannon (1966) report:

> . . . subjects in the group seemed to perceive the desensitization method as an active mastery technique which they could acquire and use themselves, more than in the individual application. Client's descriptions of utilizing desensitization training to master anticipated areas of stress themselves suggest the development of a confidence-building "how to cope" orientation (pp. 133-134).

Another illustration of this serendipitous finding appears in a report by Sherman (1972), who found that subjects desensitized to fear of water indicated that their ability to relax helped them in such diverse situations as test-taking, speech-giving, and sleeping at night.

Extrapolating from the findings described above, it appears that relaxation training may have greater clinical utility than was heretofore recognized when it is viewed by clients as a procedure for providing them with a skill for coping with their anxiety.

CLINICAL IMPLEMENTATION OF SELF-CONTROL DESENSITIZATION

In conceptualizing relaxation as a coping skill, I have hypothesized that imaginal desensitization actively teaches clients to relax in response to experienced tension (Goldfried, 1971). That is, desensitization trains clients to become more attuned to their sensations of tension, and to react to these experiential cues with their newly acquired skill of relaxation. Within this context, several modifications in the standard desensitization procedure would seem to enhance the establishment of generalizable relaxation skills (Goldfried, 1971; Goldfried, 1976; Goldfried & Davison, 1976).

1) *Presentation of rationale.* The desensitization procedure is presented to clients with a coping orientation. Specifically, they are told that in order to effectively reduce their anxiety in real-life situations, they will be asked to practice during the consultation sessions. This rehearsal will both prepare them for various specific life events and it will give them practice in coping with anxiety in general. In this regard, relaxation training is structured in such a way that it not only emphasizes training the clients to voluntarily relax, but also helps them become more sensitive to the sensations of tension. These sensations of tension will eventually be experienced as a signal for voluntary relaxation.

2) *Hierarchy construction.* Much of the original desensitization literature emphasized the importance of carefully selected hierarchies, each of which reflected a single theme or dimension. When a client experiences a number of different fears or phobias, it has typically been recommended that several different hierarchies be drawn up, each reflecting a particular phobia. If one assumes that passive deconditioning underlies the efficacy of desensitization, then this procedure makes considerable sense. If, however, one assumes that desensitization provides a training regimen for coping with anxiety in general, there is no reason why different fears or phobias cannot be placed within a single multidimensional hierarchy, particularly if the *perceived sensations of tension* are viewed as the relevant cues for responding with relaxation. Thus, it is the proprioceptive feedback associated with anxiety, and not the external situation that originally created the anxiety, which is the relevant "stimulus." (See Goldfried [1973] for a case illustration of this modification).

3) *Self-control desensitization proper.* According to the procedure outlines by Wolpe, the aversive hierarchy image must immediately be discontinued if the client experiences anxiety during the presentation of the scene. In contrast, the self-control approach to desensitization suggests that it is entirely appropriate to require clients *to stay in the imaginal situation* and to make attempts to cope with it by relaxing away the tension. In essence, this is the type of behavior one wishes clients to use when confronted with an anxiety-producing situation in real life.

In structuring self-control desensitization as a behavior rehearsal for eventual performance in criterion situations, individuals sometimes find it difficult to continue to imagine themselves in the aversive situation while at the same time attempting to relax away their tension. This difficulty can be resolved by instructing clients to imagine themselves in the situation, and if they experience anxiety, to imagine themselves relaxing away the anxiety while still in the situation. Thus, if a businessman reports feeling anxious while imagining sitting at his desk the day before having to give a presentation at a meeting, he is told to continue to imagine himself at the desk, but relaxing away any experienced anxiety. By structuring the image in this manner, clients typically report that the task of maintaining an image and coping at the same time presents fewer problems.

4) *Use of coping relaxation in vivo.* As noted above, relaxation training during consultation sessions enables clients to rehearse the behavior they will ultimately use in their natural environment. Consequently, prompting

clients to apply relaxation skills in real-life anxiety-provoking situations is essential to self-control desensitization. As part of the relaxation training *per se*, clients can be instructed in what Jacobson has called "differential relaxation," which involves relaxing only those muscles not required to carry out the client's ongoing activity. In addition, it is advisable to forestall the discouragement clients sometimes report when initially attempting to relax away anxiety in real-life situations by emphasizing that relaxation is a complicated skill and requires a certain amount of practice before it may be most effectively employed.

Concurrent with desensitization proper, clients are given specific homework assignments. If the hierarchy contains frequently occurring situations, or situations in which clients can readily place themelves (see Goldfried & Davison, 1976), then it is possible to have them confront *in vivo* the events described in completed hierarchy items. The initial portion of each session is set aside for discussing the clients' attempts at applying relaxation *in vivo*, and the clear expectation is established that such between-session activities play an essential role in the treatment.

In this regard, Kanfer and Phillips' (1969) concept of "instigation therapy" captures the essence of this aspect of the treatment package. In this model, the therapist must instigate clients' behavior change attempts between sessions, have clients monitor their performance and reinforce themselves for their achievements, prompt them to become aware of how their performance might be improved in the future, and provide reinforcement for each of these activities. The nature of the therapeutic relationship becomes particularly crucial at this point, when the therapist must rely heavily on his or her persuasive and reinforcing abilities to encourage such between-session behavior.

Empirical Support

Although no one would deny the subjective and physiological impact of any single relaxation session, research evidence concerning the more long-term clinical status of relaxation training has been unclear. Some of these conflicting findings have been described above. The confused status of relaxation as an effective clinical procedure is exemplified by the fact that certain studies have employed relaxation as the primary treatment procedure (e.g., Snider & Oetting, 1966), while others have construed it as an attention-placebo control (e.g., Trexler & Karst, 1972).

A possible reason for the conflicting findings on the effectiveness of relaxation training may be the different sets with which clients approach the learning and utilization of relaxation skills. To investigate this possibility, Goldfried and Trier (1974) investigated the effect that the training procedure had on speech-anxious subjects' eventual use of relaxation as a coping skill. Subjects were assigned to one of two relaxation treatments or to an attention placebo control, each of which was carried out in five group sessions. The first relaxation condition utilized standard relaxation training. Subjects in this group were told that the training procedure would have the effect of automatically lowering their overall tension level, so that it would be easier for them to deal with a wide variety of anxiety-provoking situations, including those involving public speaking. Subjects in the second group, the self-control relaxation condition, were told that the purpose of the training procedure was to provide them with a coping skill, which they could actively employ in relaxing away tension in a variety of anxiety-provoking situations, including those involving public speaking. In both the standard and the self-control relaxation group, relaxation training was carried out during each session, as well as twice a week between sessions with the aid of taped instructions. From the second session on, however, subjects in the self-control group were also encouraged to apply the relaxation skills *in vivo*, whenever they felt themselves becoming tense.

A discussion group condition, modeled after the attention-placebo control, used by Meichenbaum, Gilmore, and Fedoravicious (1971), dealt with relatively impersonal topics (e.g., Should marijuana be legalized?). Subjects in this condition were told that the purpose of the discussions was to allow them to express their opinions in group settings and to help them to improve their communication skills, which should result in their becoming less anxious in public speaking situations.

On most of the dependent measures, the greatest improvement occurred in the self-control relaxation condition. These measures included a Behavior Checklist, the S-R of Anxiousness (Endler, Hunt & Rosenstein, 1962), the Personal Report of Confidence as a Speaker (Paul, 1966), and the Trait Anxiety Inventory (Spielberger, Gorsuch & Lushene, 1970). Furthermore, when subjects were asked during the follow-up to rate how satisfied they were in the amount of change they had seen in themselves at that point in time, responses revealed a striking and highly significant difference in favor of subjects in the self-control relaxation condition. Self-control relaxation has similarly been found more reflective than standard relaxation in the case of test anxiety (Chang-Liang & Denney, 1976). In general, then, it would appear that presenting relaxation as training in an active coping skill can increase its effectiveness above that of relaxation training which is presented in a more traditional manner.

A growing body of corroborative evidence further supports the effectiveness of a self-control variation of desensitization and some of its basic assumptions. For example, Meichenbaum (1972) demonstrated that test-anxious subjects treated by desensitization with a "coping" orientation manifested greater anxiety reduction than individuals treated by standard systematic desensitization. However, Meichenbaum's variation also included both cognitive restructuring and instructions for subjects to focus on the task at hand while continuing to imagine themselves in the test-taking situation. In an outcome study with acrophobics, Jacks (1972) compared traditional and self-control systematic desensitization, where subjects in the self-control condition were asked to maintain the image and "relax away" any experienced anxiety. While subjects in both conditions did not differ in their actual performance on the avoidance posttest, only individuals in the self-control condition reported significant decreases in subjective anxiety while in the criterion situation, a possible indication of the active use of relaxation skills. In addition, follow-up assessment revealed that self-control subjects reported continued anxiety reduction, which was significantly greater than that indicated by subjects having undergone standard desensitization. Denney and Rupert (1976) found self-control desensitization to be superior to standard desensitization in reducing test anxiety, which is consistent with similar trends obtained by Spiegler, Cooley, Marshall, Prince, Puckett and Skenazy (1976) in their work on test anxiety.

While self-control desensitization is based on the premise that individuals are being trained to actively respond to their proprioceptive anxiety cues, standard desensitization assumes a conditioning of the relaxation response to the external situation that elicited tension. As mentioned earlier, this implies that the clear delineation of hierarchies reflecting clinically relevant themes may be relatively unimportant. Raising similar questions about the importance of hierarchy construction, Suinn and Richardson (1971) compared systematic desensitization with an Anxiety Management Training Program in which test-anxious subjects were trained to use relaxation and positive imagery to cope with anxiety-inducing images unrelated to test anxiety. Subjects in both treatment conditions showed significant and comparable reductions in anxiety, although the brief treatment duration (between two and a half and four and a half hours) limits the extent to which these findings can be generalized to lengthier clinical interventions with different populations and presenting problems. Studies by Meichenbaum and his colleagues (Meichenbaum & Turk, 1976), and Tunner, Oelkers, Ferstl, and Birbaumer (1973), further support the contention that a target-relevant hierarchy may not be required when teaching anxiety-reduction skills.

A recent investigation by Zemore (1975) is worth noting in this regard. This study was designed to test the importance of the hierarchy in standard and self-control desensitization, focusing particularly on the extent to which there would be differential generalization to target behaviors that were not the actual focus of treatment. Using subjects who were anxious in both public-speaking and test-taking situations, Zemore used a factorial design to compare the relative effectiveness of the two desensitization procedures that used either target-relevant or target-irrelevant hierarchies. He predicted that greater generalization would occur with the self-control procedure, as it presumably provided subjects with a general anxiety-reducing skill. However, the findings failed to reveal any difference between the two therapeutic procedures, in that comparable reduction in speech anxiety was observed for subjects treated with a test anxiety hierarchy, and similar improvement for the two procedures was noted in test anxiety for subjects exposed to a speech anxiety hierarchy. However, the study does not provide an adequate test of the relative effectiveness of the two approaches to desensitization, as one may always argue that even with a passive deconditioning model, generalization might be expected along a social-evaluative dimension. A further limitation in Zemore's study is the fact that there was no follow-up, particularly since findings by Goldfried and Trier (1974) and Jacks (1972) indicate that subjects going through a self-control program for anxiety reduction continue to improve between posttest and follow-up. With continued practice, subjects receiving self-control training may be expected to become more adept in their coping skills.

Goldfried and Goldfried (1977) recently provided a more stringent test of the importance of hierarchy content in the self-control of anxiety. A comparison was made between two self-control desensitization procedures in the treatment of speech anxiety—one with a hierarchy relevant to speech anxiety, and the second involving a hierarchy of fearful situations totally unrelated to public speaking. A third treatment condition involved presentation of speech-relevant hierarchy items without relaxation, and was included as a control for the prolonged exposure associated with the target-relevant desensitization condition. No waiting list group was used, since past research on speech anxiety has indicated that no change occurs among waiting list subjects (Meichenbaum et al., 1971; Paul, 1966; Trexler & Karst, 1972). Subjects in the study were self-referred men and women from the community. Each treatment was group-administered one hour weekly for seven weeks. Measures included self-report questionnaires and behavioral ratings of a four-minute videotaped speech, and were collected immediately before and after treatment, with a questionnaire follow-up two months after termination.

The findings indicate that a significant reduction in speech anxiety occurred across most measures for all three therapeutic procedures, although fewer within-group changes occurred for the prolonged exposure condition. No differences were found between the two desensitization procedures. Differences between groups emerged only when desensitization and prolonged exposure conditions were compared according to subjects' subjective impression of improvement and willingness to participate in public speaking situations. During the follow-up assessment, subjects in the two desensitization conditions reported that therapy had been significantly more successful in helping them to overcome their anxiety in public speaking situations compared to the reports of subjects in the prolonged exposure group. Similarly, when asked how many times, if any, they had been involved in public speaking situations since posttesting, subjects in both desensitization conditions reported involvement in significantly more speaking situations than subjects in the prolonged exposure condition.

The consistent reduction in speech anxiety within the two desensitization conditions, together with the absence of between-group differences, indicates that the generally accepted procedure of using carefully delineated hierarchies may *not* be an important component of desensitization, at least as presented within a self-control framework. These findings are consistent with Goldfried's (1971) hypothesis that desensitization entails learning to relax when anxious, rather than automatically substituting non-anxiety for anxiety linked to specific stimulus-situations. The absence of an attention placebo condition clearly warrants caution in interpreting what is essentially a confirmation of the null hypothesis. However, past investigations of the treatment of speech anxiety (e.g., Goldfried & Trier, 1974; Meichenbaum et al., 1971) have revealed that subjects in attention placebo conditions fail to improve at follow-up, in contrast to the significant improvement manifested by the treatment groups in this study.

Interestingly, the results of Goldfried and Goldfried (1977) demonstrated that prolonged exposure subjects did, in fact, improve significantly on several measures, although they showed fewer within-group changes than did subjects who used relaxation together with an imaginal exposure to these same hierarchy items. The fact that exposure alone—particularly prolonged exposure—is a potentially effective means of reducing anxiety has been observed by other investigators (Aponte & Aponte, 1971; Barrett, 1969; Calef & MacLean, 1970; D'Zurilla, Wilson & Nelson, 1973; Malleson, 1959; McGlynn, 1973; Mylar & Clement, 1972, Raimy, 1975). In fact, in reviewing animal research that addresses the theoretical assumptions underlying desensitization, Wilson and Davison (1971) concluded that nonreinforced exposure to conditioned aversive stimuli may be the crucial component of the anxiety reduction process. They further hypothesized that relaxation may enable fearful individuals to tolerate an anxiety-producing situation long enough for extinction to take place.

Regardless of the theoretical underpinnings of desensitization, the findings of the present study offer some important pragmatic directions for anxiety reduction. Namely, by employing an approach to desensitization that focuses on the active use of relaxation skills in coping with the sensations of anxiety per se—regardless of the external situation eliciting the anxiety—one has available an effective self-control procedure that can generalize both over situations and time. These findings add to what appears to be an increasing body of evidence supporting the clinical utility of relaxation as a method for the self-management of anxiety.

RATIONAL RESTRUCTURING AS A COPING SKILL

Despite the effectiveness of relaxation in coping with anxiety, instances undoubtedly exist where this clinical procedure may not be the optimal treatment strategy. For example, the use of relaxation could help an individual temporarily cope with anxiety, while not resolving the "basic problem" or "underlying cause" that precipitates the anxiety reaction. Although some behavior therapists are undoubtedly reluctant to conceptualize problems in these terms, it nonetheless is becoming increasingly clear that any sophisticated approach to clinical behavior therapy may at times have to focus not only on target behaviors themselves but on other variables believed to be functionally linked to such targets. This point has been made numerous times before (Bandura, 1969; Goldfried & Davison, 1976; Goldfried & Sprafkin, 1976; Mischel, 1968; Peterson, 1968) by authors who emphasize the importance of using a functional analysis to pinpoint the important variables currently maintaining the presenting problem. Within this context, this section focuses on cognitive variables, their functional influence on anxiety, and their manipulation in therapeutic intervention.

Theoretical and Research Foundations

That an individual's attitude or set can have profound effects on his or her behavior and emotional reactions is hardly new to psychology. Numerous studies have clearly demonstrated that the way an individual perceives a situation, typically manipulated by experimental instructions, can alter that person's subsequent behavior. Extrapolating from these basic research findings, as well as from a related body of literature on attitude formation, it is not unreasonable to assume that early social learning experiences lead individuals to develop generalized cognitive sets regarding various situations or social interactions in their lives, and that these expectancies somehow mediate their emotional and behavioral reactions. Dollard and Miller (1950) speculated on this issue when they considered the potential importance of covert labeling, and Ellis (1962) has more recently described how this orientation may be incorporated into therapeutic intervention.

It is of considerable interest to observe the trends in behavior therapy, especially the increasing receptivity to cognitive conceptualizations that currently characterizes the field. Just as relaxation training did not readily fit into the prevailing therapeutic paradigm of the first half of this century, so behavior therapy initially resisted any allusion to cognitive metaphors. Breger and McGaugh's (1965) arguments against the narrowness of a learning theory orientation to therapy and deviant behavior were severely criticized by behavior therapists a decade ago. Yet, in rereading their critique, many of their suggestions are most compelling, particularly when they observe that a peripheralist approach to learning theory is giving way to a more centralist orientation. No doubt behavior therapists at the time lacked the appropriate "cognitive set" for incorporating such new information.

In describing how a cognitive relabeling procedure may be used clinically, it is only natural to turn to the writings of Albert Ellis (1962), who has long recognized the therapeutic significance of modifying inappropriate expectations and beliefs as a means of anxiety reduction. Illustrative of his basic orientation is the following premise:

If . . . people essentially become emotionally disturbed because they unthinkingly accept certain illogical premises or irrational ideas, then there is a good reason to believe that they can be somehow persuaded or taught to think more logically and rationally and thereby to undermine their own disturbances (Ellis, 1962, p. 191).

There are some interesting observations one may make with regard to this statement. Ellis clearly presented a viewpoint in 1962 that is consistent with a cognitive behavior therapy orientation, and one that has considerable relevance for self-management procedures (Goldfried & Merbaum, 1973). What is particularly interesting, however, is that, until very recently, Ellis' therapeutic approach has not been incorporated into the mainstream of behavior therapy. In fact, Bandura's (1969) classic work, which emphasizes both the importance of cognitive processes and the issue of self-control, has no reference at all to Ellis or rational-emotive therapy. The difficulty in incorporating Ellis' approach into a behavioral orientation has been due, no doubt, to the lack of clear specificity of therapeutic procedures, as well as the absence of any empirical data base for its clinical effectiveness. The situation is clearly changing, and steps are currently being taken to incorporate many of Ellis' concepts and procedures into the field of cognitive behavior therapy (Beck, 1976; Goldfried & Davison, 1976; Goldfried, Decenteceo, & Weinberg, 1974; Meichenbaum, 1972). As Meichenbaum and Turk (1976) noted at the Seventh Banff International Conference on Behavior Modification:

Behavior therapy, as psychology in general, is going cognitive . . . What the client says to himself (i.e., his appraisals, attributions, self-evaluations), or the self-statements and images that he emits prior to, accompanying, and following his overt behavior are becoming an increasingly important area for therapeutic intervention (p. 1).

The basic assumption that the way individuals label or evaluate situations can differentially determine their emotional reactions to those situations underlies any cognitive relabeling procedure used to reduce anxiety. That covert verbalization can elicit emotional reactions has been confirmed in a number of studies. One experimental test of the effect of self-verbalizations on mood states was carried out by Velten (1968). Subjects were asked to read self-referent statements which reflected elation ("This is great—I really do feel good"), depression ("I have too many bad things in my life"), or neutral feelings ("Utah is the beehive state").

Subjects' moods and behavior changed in a positive or negative direction as function of the content of the statements they had read. These changes were measured by the subject's verbal report, as well as by indirect behavioral indicators of mood, such as writing speed, decision time, reaction time on a word association task, and spontaneous verbalizations. In a related study, Schill, Evans, Monroe, and Ramanaiah (1976) similarly found that rational self-statements facilitated performance on a mirror-tracing task, whereas irrational self-statements interfered with task performance. Rimm and Litvak (1969) also investigated the effects of self-verbalizations on emotional arousal, and found that affect-related statements elicited significantly greater emotional reactions (as indicated by breathing rate and depth) than did neutral sentences. May and Johnson (1973) similarly found that affectively-toned self-verbalizations resulted in increased heart rate and respiration. Changes in skin conductance have also been found when subjects are presented with verbal representations of situations previously labeled by them as troublesome, but not when they read statements of neutral, nonemotional content (Russell & Brandsma, 1974). Hence, the basic assumption that self-statements are capable of eliciting emotional responses appears to have empirical support.

Although these studies clearly point out the influence of covert statements on emotional arousal, research is also needed to determine the consequences of individual variations in self-statements as they occur in the natural environment. Ellis (1962) hypothesizes that individuals' maladaptive emotional reactions are mediated by the nature of their beliefs or expectations about emotionally arousing situations. More specifically, Ellis maintains that certain individuals have a tendency to hold certain irrational beliefs. Among the various irrational ideas described by Ellis is the expectation that it is essential to be loved and approved of by others, and that one should achieve competence and perfection in all one's undertakings. According to Ellis, people who maintain these and other irrational beliefs tend to covertly verbalize their irrational ideas in the situations that produce overemotional responses. To the extent that individuals maintain expectancies that are not consistent with the real status of the world around them, they are more likely to experience disappointment and upset.

Goldfried and Sobocinski (1975) studied the relationship between irrational beliefs and emotional arousal in various types of situations. In a correlational study, significant positive relationships were found between the tendency to think irrationally, as measured by a paper-and-pencil test of irrational beliefs (Jones, 1968), and measures of interpersonal anxiety, test anxiety, and speech anxiety. In a second experiment, Goldfried and Sobocinski focused on one specific irrational belief—the overriding importance of social approval—and investigated the likelihood of emotional arousal occurring among individuals who subscribe to this belief.

Two groups of subjects, scoring either high or low on the social approval belief, were asked to imagine themselves in several different situations. The first of these consisted of a neutral scene, in which subjects were asked to visualize themselves in a bookstore, looking at several books on the shelves. Following this baseline scene, subjects were administered the Multiple Affect Adjective Checklist (Zuckerman & Lubin, 1965) to assess the extent to which they felt anxious, depressed, and angry. They were then asked to imagine themselves in five social situations in which they might conceivably perceive social rejection. One of these situations was as follows:

> One of your girlfriends has invited you to come to a party. Think of
> of a girl you know. You get to her house and you walk through the
> door. You're standing there now at the door just inside her house.
> Look around you and you'll see a number of people—people whom
> you have not met before. And now your girlfriend is walking over to
> you. She says "hello" and takes your coat. Try to see her face as
> vividly as you can. She goes to put your coat away. You're standing
> there by yourself, and when she comes back out she walks over to
> some other people and starts talking to them. Try to stay in this
> situation, standing there by yourself, seeing your girlfriend talking
> to these people, and you're there alone looking around. Just notice
> how you feel in that situation (Goldfried & Sobocinski, p. 507).

Other situations included not being complimented on one's physical appearance, being excluded from a conversation, being alone on a Saturday night, and not receiving positive feedback during a job interview. The Adjective Checklist was administered at the completion of all five situations. Subjects were then presented with a therapeutic release situation, where they were asked to imagine themselves lying on the beach in the summertime without having any responsibilities or concerns. As is depicted graphically in Figure 1, subjects who strongly believed in the importance of receiving approval from others reported feeling more anxious than did subjects for whom this belief was less salient. As can be seen in the figure, after imagining themselves in the therapeutic release situation, all subjects returned to their baseline scores. Similar findings were found with subjective reports of hostility.

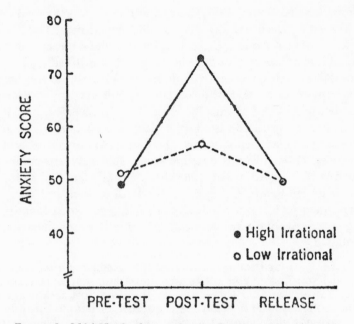

FIGURE 1. MAACL Anxiety rating at baseline, following the imaginal presentation of social rejection situations, and the therapeutic release situation for both high and low irrational conditions (Goldfried & Sobocinski, 1975, p. 508).

Although these findings shed some light on the differential suscepti-bility to emotional arousal as a function of different types of beliefs, the exact nature of any irrational self-statements generated in response to the experimental conditions was not studied directly. Thus, it is impos-sible to determine whether the high irrationality subjects had a *greater tendency to perceive* the situations as entailing social rejection, or whether the upset was primarily a function of the high irrationality subjects' *over-generalization* of what was observed, such as telling themselves that their rejection in this particular situation was proof of their basic inadequacy as a person. The results obtained by Goldfried and Sobocinski should also be interpreted in light of the correlational nature of both studies. Even in the case of the second experiment, it is possible to argue that height-ened emotional arousal in social situations sensitizes an individual to certain irrational beliefs, rather than the reverse being the case. However, findings from other research (May & Johnson, 1973; Rimm & Litvak,

1969; Russell & Brandsma, 1974; Velten, 1968) also support the contention that self-statements do have the potential for eliciting emotional reactions.

Further support—albeit indirect—for the assumption that irrational beliefs precede emotional arousal comes from several clinical outcome studies that have demonstrated that various forms of social-evaluative anxiety may be alleviated by the direct modification of irrational beliefs. Before reviewing some of these studies, however, actual procedures for the clinical implementation of rational restructuring will be outlined.

Clinical Implementation of Rational Restructuring

As noted in the case of self-control desensitization, a given principle may be translated into a therapeutic technique in numerous ways. With rational restructuring this translation raises the issue of the most effective methods of persuading or teaching clients to think more reasonably and rationally. Systematic procedures incorporating the basic tenets of Ellis' therapeutic approach within a more clearly defined social learning framework have been successfully employed both clinically and in outcome research. These have been outlined in greater detail elsewhere (e.g., Goldfried, 1976; Goldfried & Davison, 1976; Goldfried, Decenteceo, & Weinberg, 1974; Goldfried & Goldfried, 1975), and will only be touched upon briefly here.

A typical approach to the implementation of rational-emotive therapy to date has been frequently characterized by heated arguments in which the therapist attempts to convince clients that unreasonable beliefs are responsible for their emotional reactions to problematic situations. Often, the arguments reflect disagreement on several different issues, which might be better dealt with in a more systematic and Socratic fashion. Specifically, the steps that are associated with *systematic rational restructuring* are as follows:

1) *Helping clients to accept the assumption that self-statements mediate emotional arousal.* The initial discussion leading to this acceptance is generally more theoretical than personal. The therapist's goal is to help clients recognize the general assumption that their emotions can be directly influenced by their labels, expectations and beliefs. It should be emphasized that many of such assumptions occur more or less automatically, rather than being carefully thought out. Thus, it is important that clients accept the premise that even though they may not deliberately "tell themselves" certain things prior to or during emotionally upsetting situa-

tions, they nonetheless react disproportionately "as if" they view the situation in a given way. When this basic premise is presented in a simple and objective manner, it is rare to find clients who cannot accept it.

2) *Helping clients to see the irrationality in certain beliefs.* Once the clients have agreed that their emotional reactions can be mediated by thoughts and self-statements, it is important to have them acknowledge the irrational or unrealistic nature of a series of beliefs that individuals frequently hold. The two beliefs that most typically appear in clinical cases are a) the expectation that it is essential to receive approval and love from others in order to have any feelings of self-worth, and b) the notion that perfection is required in all accomplishments in order to see oneself as anything but a failure.

Instead of trying to verbally convince clients that these thoughts are irrational, the social psychological literature suggests that the therapist could more effectively promote attitude change by having the clients *themselves* offer arguments to support the irrationality of these beliefs (Janis & King, 1954; King & Janis, 1956). Thus, the therapist can play devil's advocate, giving clients the task of providing as many reasons as possible to convince the seemingly irrational therapist that his or her views are untenable. The ultimate objective of this step is to prompt clients not only to agree that certain beliefs are irrational, but also to generate specific reasons—which may later be used as coping self-statements—for the unreasonableness of these views.

3) *Helping clients to understand that their own maladaptive emotions are mediated by irrational self-statements.* Following the second step, some clients spontaneously acknowledge that they can see where certain irrational assumptions are particularly relevant to their own emotional reactions. In other cases, it may be necessary to systemtically explore various emotionally arousing situations of the clients' current life, in an attempt to investigate and enhance their awareness of the irrational expectations influencing their anxiety. Typically, after clients are gradually and systematically guided through this third phase, they conclude that they need to learn how to stop thinking irrationally in problematic situations.

4) *Helping clients to modify their irrational self-statements.* Up until this point, much of what has gone on during the clinical interaction has been intellectual and theoretical. In much the same way that relaxation

skills are not particularly effective in reducing anxiety if they are not *used* by the individual in potentially upsetting situations, so thinking rationally probably has minimal therapeutic impact if it is not employed when clients are experiencing anxiety. Although many individuals can put upsetting events into realistic perspective at a later point in time, this most crucial phase in the therapeutic procedure involves using the client's hindsight ability to enable them to reevaluate situations rationally before or during the situations themselves. A convenient way for providing clients with practice in using rational reevaluation as a coping mechanism is via imaginal presentations of anxiety-arousing scenes. In many respects, it parallels self-control desensitization, in that clients maintain the image while attempting to cope. Clients may be instructed to "think aloud," so that the therapist can prompt and otherwise assist them in evaluating and modifying unrealistic assumptions. In addition to imaginal practice during the consultation sessions, clients are urged to apply rational thinking *in vivo*.

Empirical Support

Until very recently, most of the empirical support for the effectiveness of rational-emotive therapy has been based on clinical case reports (Ellis, 1962). Within the past several years, however, the positive findings of several controlled outcome studies have added stronger evidence for the clinical utility of this approach. Research has most typically focused on the reduction of three target problems: speech, test, and interpersonal anxiety.

Speech anxiety. In one of the earliest well-controlled studies on the use of a cognitively oriented approach to the reduction of speech anxiety, Meichenbaum et al. (1971) studied the effectiveness of systematic desensitization, rational-emotive therapy, and a combined desensitization and rational-emotive package, utilizing both attention placebo and waiting list control groups. All therapy was carried out in groups, and rational-emotive therapy primarily consisted of discussions of the irrational self-statements that typically occur in a number of anxiety-provoking interpersonal situations, including public speaking. On the basis of behavioral and subjective estimates of anxiety during an actual speech-giving situation, the authors found that rational-emotive therapy and systematic desensitization were comparably effective, and better than either of the control conditions. These improvement effects were maintained at a three-month follow-up. They also noted that the combined treatment procedure was somewhat less effective than either systematic desensitization or rational-emotive therapy alone, possibly because, in combination, neither of the two procedures could be fully implemented within the eight-session treatment. From a post-hoc analysis, Meichenbaum et al. also present data suggesting that systematic desensitization may be more effective in cases of of circumscribed speech anxiety, while rational-emotive therapy seems to produce greater change when anxiety in public speaking situations is part of a larger network of social-evaluative anxieties.

Trexler and Karst (1972) have similarly used rational-emotive therapy in the group treatment of speech anxiety, and compared its effectiveness with attention placebo and waiting list controls. Participants in the rational-emotive condition discussed the ways in which irrational ideas contributed to their feelings of anxiety in speech-giving and in other interpersonal situations. Although the findings indicated that rational-emotive therapy resulted in improvement on some measures (the Personal Report of Confidence as a Speaker, and the Irrational Beliefs Test), other measures (behavioral indicators of anxiety during a speech) failed to show improvement. This is in contrast to the results of Meichenbaum et al., who found improvement on virtually all of their measures of speech anxiety. A number of factors could explain these discrepant findings, including the fact that Meichenbaum et al. used more experienced therapists and conducted the treatment over eight, as opposed to four, sessions. In addition, because the actual rational-emotive procedures employed in both studies are described in only general terms, it is difficult to determine the extent to which the treatments themselves may have differed in these two reports.

The relative effectiveness of rational restructuring and self-control desensitization was investigated in Casas' (1975) outcome study on the treatment of speech anxiety. The treatment procedures were modeled after those described earlier in this chapter, but were implemented within only four group sessions over a two-week period. Casas used the standard dependent variables employed in outcome research in this area, such as giving a speech before a live audience, subjective measures of anxiety, physiological measures, and a variety of questionnaires. Anxiety reduction was found to be comparable for both treatment groups but not significantly different from a waiting list control, a finding that might very well be attributed to the brevity of the treatment. One interesting post-hoc finding that emerged, however, was that within the rational restructuring group, subjects who scored high on the Fear of Negative Evaluation Scale improved significantly more than those whose scores were low. That this interaction was not obtained within the other two conditions suggests that rational restructuring may be particularly appropriate in instances where individuals manifest excessive concern over the opinions of others.

In an interesting study to determine the feasibility of using peers as therapists, Fremouw and Harmatz (1975) studied the effectiveness of a treatment package that emphasized the use of both rational self-statements and relaxation as coping skills, together with training in public speaking. The four conditions that were compared consisted of helpers (who worked with other speech anxious subjects), helpees (who were trained by the helpers), latent helpers (who received the same training as the helpers, but worked with subjects only after posttesting), and waiting list control subjects. The dependent measures included a speech in front of a live audience, and various paper-and-pencil measures of anxiety. The results indicated that both the helper and helpee groups showed comparably significant improvement, which was maintained at follow-up. Although the latent helpers also improved, the change was not as clear-cut at posttest. However, after they worked with the waiting list subjects, improvement of latent helpers matched up to that obtained by the helper and helpee conditions. These findings suggest that even though the latent helpers had the coping skills in their repertoire, these skills were not as effective until they were given adequate opportunity to apply them.

Test Anxiety. Based on the assumption that test anxiety may be comprised of both "worry" and "emotionality" components (Liebert & Morris, 1967; Mandler & Watson, 1966; Marlett & Watson, 1968; Morris & Liebert, 1970), Meichenbaum (1972) developed an eight-session group treatment package involving cognitive restructuring and a modified systematic desensitization. Specifically, test-anxious subjects were given relaxation training, discussed potential irrational thoughts underlying test anxiety, and then were provided with imaginal practice in coping with anxiety in test-related situations by means of relaxation and self-instructions to focus on only the test itself. Compared with traditional systematic desensitization, this cognitive modification treatment package produced greater pre-post reductions in test anxiety, as determined by subjective anxiety, performance in an analog test situation, and grade-point average.

A recent study by Goldfried, Linehan, and Smith (in press) investigated the effects of rational restructuring alone in the reduction of test anxiety. Because of the difficulties associated with obtaining a sufficiently large number of subjects, this study was first done at Stony Brook and then replicated at Catholic University. The same assessment procedures were used in both settings, and to insure standardization of treatment, therapy manuals were utilized and tape recordings of pilot therapy groups were exchanged by the two therapists as cross-checks on consistency of the therapy program. The subjects, undergraduates who responded to various announcements describing the test anxiety program, were assigned to either rational restructuring, prolonged exposure, or a waiting-list control. The two treatment conditions consisted of six group therapy sessions.

In the rational restructuring condition, the subjects were exposed to a 15-item standardized hierarchy, which was based on a preliminary analysis of their scores on the Suinn Test Anxiety Behavior Scale (Suinn, 1969). Prior to the actual implementation of rational restructuring, the therapist served as a model, by imagining that he or she was in a test situation while "thinking aloud," following the process of rational reevaluation. Each hierarchy item was then presented for a total of four one-minute exposures, during which subjects were asked to imaginally "remain" in the scene and to attempt to reevaluate their reactions using a rational perspective. Following each trial, subjects recorded their thoughts and feelings on a special in-session record form, and discussed their experiences during the imaginal situations as a group after the fourth trial presentation.

The prolonged exposure condition served as a control for exposure to the test-anxiety hierarchy items, as well as any nonspecific factors associated with receiving treatment. The rationale presented to the subjects in this condition emphasized the importance of habituation and extinction in the reduction of anxiety. The same hierarchy was used for subjects in the rational restructuring and prolonged exposure conditions. Subjects in this condition, however, were instructed only to focus on their emotional reactions during each of the four one-minute exposures. Following the final presentation of each item, a group discussion was carried out so that group members could share their experiences.

The data analysis revealed a consistent pattern: On the basis of various questionnaire measures of test anxiety (e.g., S-R Inventory of Anxiousness, Suinn Test Anxiety Behavior scale), greater pre-post anxiety reduction was found for subjects in the rational restructuring condition, followed by those having undergone prolonged exposure of the same hierarchy items, with no changes emerging on the pre- and posttesting for the waiting list control. These findings were maintained at follow-up. Further, only subjects in the rational restructuring condition reported a decrease in subjective anxiety (e.g., State Anxiety Inventory) when placed in an analogue test taking situation. Although the rational restructuring procedure was generally found to be consistently superior to prolonged exposure, it is of considerable interest that exposure alone also produced significant anxiety reduction. We have observed this same finding in the case of speech anxiety described earlier (Goldfried & Goldfried, in press), thereby adding to the finding of a number of other studies that suggest that prolonged exposure is a viable therapeutic manipulation—although not as effective as exposure together with some active coping procedure.

In reevaluating Meichenbaum's (1972) study on test anxiety, the Goldfried et al. (1976) findings raise the question of whether the simple presence of a cognitive restructuring component, and not the combined cognitive and relaxation aspects of the treatment, might have been responsible for the observed anxiety reduction. This question was investigated directly by Osarchuk (1974) in an outcome study evaluating the relative effectiveness of rational restructuring and self-control desensitization in the treatment of test anxiety.

Subjects for Osarchuk's study were selected from college student volunteers who responded to announcements describing a test anxiety program. The therapy was carried out in group settings over a six-week period. The four treatment procedures consisted of self-control desensitization, rational restructuring, self-control desensitization plus rational restructuring, and prolonged exposure. The self-control desensitization procedure was based on the guidelines outlined in the earlier portion of this chapter. The 12-item hierarchy was the same as that used in the study by Goldfried et al. (in press). All four treatment groups used this same hierarchy. The subjects assigned to rational restructuring, instead of imagining themselves in test-taking situations and relaxing, were taught to rationally reevaluate these situations. The combined desensitization and rational restructuring procedure involved training in the use of both relaxation and rational restructuring. These subjects were given practice in relaxing away their experienced anxiety and then placing the test-taking situation into a more realistic perspective. Subjects in the prolonged exposure condition were told that therapy would help them habituate to test-taking situations, and that they would learn to bring about extinction by focusing on their anxiety while remaining in the situation. They received imaginal exposure to the hierarchy items and were instructed in the use of focused attention of their feelings of tensions.

The pretest, posttest, and two-month follow-up assessment battery was the same as employed in the Goldfried et al. (in press) study. Although no differences were found in the analogue test-taking situations, various subjective measures revealed that the self-control desensitization, rational restructuring, and combined desensitization and rational restructuring were equally effective; all were superior to the prolonged exposure. That these differences were due to the nature of the treatment procedures themselves is supported by the finding that the credibility of therapy and the confidence and ability of therapists were rated comparably across the four conditions.

Results somewhat discrepant from these were obtained by Holroyd (1976), who similarly attempted to dismantle the cognitive and relaxation components of Meichenbaum's (1972) cognitive modification treatment package for test anxiety. The four conditions, each of which was carried out over seven group sessions, consisted of cognitive therapy (getting subjects to rationally reevaluate anxiety-arousing self-statements, and then to focus on the task at hand), group desensitization, a combined cognitive therapy and desensitization, and an attention placebo control. On the basis of several measures (e.g., performance and anxiety in an analogue testing situation, grade point average), the cognitive therapy procedure was more effective than the other methods. The relative inferiority of the combined treatment package, similarly noted by Meichenbaum et al. (1971) in the case of speech anxiety, may be due to the difficulty of implementing both treatment procedures within the time allotted, or to the difficulties subjects may have in utilizing the two coping procedures in any given situation.

An important distinction between the Osarchuk and Holroyd studies consists of the framework within which the desensitization and cognitive procedures were presented to subjects. Although Osarchuk provided all subjects with a coping orientation (i.e., they were going to learn a procedure for actively and independently reducing their anxiety), Holroyd provided this orientation *only* to subjects undergoing cognitive therapy. Subjects in the desensitization condition were provided with the standard rationale. In a relevant factorial study by May (1975) on the relationship between treatment procedure and therapeutic orientation, she found cognitive and relaxation procedures to be comparably effective in the group treatment of test anxiety. However, subjects provided with a coping orientation to the therapeutic intervention improved more than subjects for whom the therapy was described within more of a passive framework. These same findings were obtained by Denney and Rupert (1976).

Taken together, the studies on test anxiety suggest that a combined therapy program using both cognitive procedures and self-control desensitization is no more effective than a therapeutic intervention program that deals primarily with either of these two components separately. The finding by Meichenbaum (1972) that a combined treatment package was more effective than desensitization may have been more a function of the "coping" emphasis inherent in his treatment package than a function of the fact that it contained relaxation and cognitive components. Holroyd's finding that a cognitive approach was superior to desensitization similarly must be interpreted in light of the coping emphasis given to subjects in this condition.

Interpersonal Anxiety. The relevance of rational restructuring for interpersonal anxiety is frequently observed within clinical settings, where clients' complaints of anxiety in social situations are often accompanied by excessive concern about the reactions of others. Empirical support for the contention that irrational self-statements may mediate various forms of social-evaluative anxiety comes from Goldfried and Sobocinski (1975), who found that the tendency to hold irrational beliefs was positively correlated with paper-and-pencil measures of social anxiety. Goldfried and Sobocinski further found that individuals who unrealistically expected approval from others experienced greater emotional upset when imagining themselves in social situations that might be interpreted as involving rejection by others than did individuals who had fewer such expectations.

Considering this evidence, an approach to anxiety reduction that teaches clients to rationally reevaluate the consequences of their behavior in various situations would seem to be particularly relevant when anxiety primarily centers around social-evaluative interactions. This point received peripheral support from the post-hoc analysis conducted by Meichenbaum et al. (1971) which indicated that rational-emotive therapy was more effective than desensitization when clients' speech anxiety was accompanied by anxiety in other interpersonal situations.

One of the earliest outcome studies to directly focus on this issue was conducted by DiLoreto (1971), who investigated the effectiveness of rational-emotive therapy in the treatment of interpersonal anxiety. Using undergraduates who volunteered for a program on the reduction of interpersonal anxiety, rational-emotive therapy was compared with systematic desensitization, client-centered therapy, an attention-placebo discussion group, and a waiting-list control. Each of the therapy conditions was conducted within a group setting, and carried out over a nine-week period. DiLoreto also studied the interaction between type of client and effectiveness of treatment, and assigned introverts and extroverts to each of the five conditions. On the basis of a variety of measures (e.g., questionnaire measures of social anxiety, behavioral signs of anxiety during an actual social interaction, as well as questionnaire measures of general anxiety), the results indicated that the three treatment procedures produced significantly greater reductions in anxiety than either the placebo or waiting-list controls. For the most part, however, the desensitization procedure was superior to the other two. Although systematic desensitization was comparably effective for extroverts and introverts, the rational-emotive therapy was found to be effective for only the introverted, but not extroverted subjects. When one looks only at the results for introverts, rational-emotive therapy turns out to be just as effective as the desensitization. Although there are undoubtedly a number of ways to interpret these data (e.g., introverted subjects may be more susceptible to attitude change than extroverted individuals), a close inspection of DiLoreto's data reveals that introverted subjects were more interpersonally anxious. This is a particularly relevant consideration, especially in light of the subject population used in the study. That is, out of a class of 600 undergraduates, no less than 100 qualified as being "socially anxious." In looking at the data for only the more anxious subjects, then, the rational-emotive condition produced just as much change as did desensitization.

In a further test of the effectiveness of cognitive therapy for interpersonal anxiety, Kanter and Goldfried (1976) also evaluated the possibility that individuals experiencing high levels of anxiety might encounter difficulties in applying a cognitive restructuring procedure. In clinical contexts, highly anxious clients frequently report that they are "too anxious to think straight." This is consistent with the experimental evidence indicating that subjects typically find it difficult to use complex mental processes when experiencing high levels of anxiety (Gaudry & Spielberger, 1971; Lazarus, 1966; Spielberger, 1966). Highly anxious subjects might therefore require preliminary relaxation training before rational restructuring could prove to be effective, whereas a treatment package involving both relaxation and rational restructuring should be no more effective than rational restructuring alone in the case of individuals for whom social anxiety was less severe.

The study employed a 2 × 4 design, where anxiety level (high vs. moderate) was crossed with treatment procedure (rational restructuring, self-control desensitization, rational restructuring plus self-control desensitization, or waiting-list control). The distinction between high vs. moderate anxiety level was based on a median split of the scores obtained on the Social Avoidance and Distress scale (Watson & Friend, 1969). The subjects in this study were community residents who responded to newspaper announcements of a therapy program focusing on the reduction of interpersonal anxiety. The therapy was carried out in a group setting over seven weekly sessions of approximately one and one half hours each.

Pre-post within group changes were analyzed for 19 dependent variables, including pulse-rate, behavioral signs of anxiety and subjective anxiety during an actual social interaction, as well as various questionnaire measures of social (e.g., S-R Inventory, Social Avoidance and Distress) and general (e.g., Trait Anxiety Inventory) anxiety. Significantly, anxiety reduction was found in 16 variables for the rational restructuring condition, 10 variables for the desensitization procedure, 16 variables for combined procedure, and three variables for the waiting list control. No interaction occurred between effectiveness of treatment procedures and level of anxiety. Between-group individual comparisons revealed that the rational restructuring and rational restructuring plus self-control desensitization conditions were consistently more effective than the waiting list control, and with some measures, more effective than the desensitization procedure. Although follow-up assessment revealed that anxiety reduction continued two months after termination for all three treatment conditions, the rational restructuring procedure was found to be superior to the other two procedures at this point in time. These data are consistent with the results obtained by Meichenbaum et al. (1971) and Holroyd (1976), who also found rational therapy to be more effective than a combination of desensitization and rational therapy. Some trends were also found for greater generalization of anxiety reduction among subjects who had gone through either of the two cognitively oriented therapies.

Another form of interpersonal anxiety that has been the target of cognitive procedures consists of unassertive behavior. Although the absence of assertive behavior has typically been construed in the behavior therapy literature as reflecting a skill deficit—that is, the appropriate behaviors do not exist in the individual's response repertoire—there is abundant anecdotal evidence that clients frequently show dramatic increases in assertive behavior after having carefully considered the consequences of engaging in such behavior. In these instances, the clients' assertion problems appear to be maintained by an unrealistic concern over the possible reactions of others (e.g., disapproval), and not by an actual inability to emit the assertive response itself. If this clinical observation is, in fact, true, then a lack of assertive behavior may be more appropriately construed as a reflection of social-evaluative anxiety than a behavioral deficit. This hypothesis was directly investigated by Linehan, Goldfried and Goldfried, who also addressed the issue of whether the sex of the therapist plays an important role in the effectiveness of therapeutic intervention with women. Although the argument is often informally made that female clients are more likely to show therapeutic progress with female as opposed to male therapists, we hypothesized that this would be less likely to occur with behaviorally oriented intervention procedures based on structured learning experiences.

This large-scale clinical outcome study, the preliminary findings of which have been described by Linehan and Goldfried (1975), was carried out to test the above-mentioned questions. In light of the large number of subjects involved (N = 79), the study was carried out in sequential waves, and at both Catholic University and Stony Brook. A 2 × 3 factorial design was employed, where sex of therapist (female vs. male) was crossed with treatment procedure (behavior rehearsal, rational restructuring, behavioral rehearsal plus rational restructuring, attention placebo, and waiting-list control). The subjects in the study, all of whom were women over the age of 21, responded to announcements advertising an Assertion Training Program.

Each client in the treatment conditions was seen for a total of eight individual therapy sessions. A total of eight different therapists were used (four male and four female), who were either advanced clinical psychology graduate students or postdoctoral fellows. Detailed therapy manuals were drawn up for each procedure, and consistency in implementing the procedures across therapists was maintained by means of training tapes, role-playing, and detailed supervision of sessions. The behavior rehearsal, rational restructuring, and behavior rehearsal plus rational restructuring procedures employed the same hypothetical assertion situations for training purposes, and made use of therapist modeling, coaching, feedback, and between-session homework assignments. The primary focus within the behavior rehearsal condition consisted of training in various behavioral components of assertiveness, such as adequate eye contact, content of assertive responses, and verbal style. In the rational restructuring condition, the training focused solely on learning to more rationally anticipate the consequences of an assertive response, and not on the behavior itself. In the combined condition, subjects were taught to rationally reevaluate the possible consequences of assertion, and then to practice the actual assertive response. The attention-placebo condition was based on a modified version of client-centered therapy, and consisted of reflection of feeling, clarification and questioning, thereby controlling for any nonspecific factors (i.e., nonspecific vis-à-vis our behavioral procedures) associated with receiving treatment. All waiting list subjects received group assertion training (employing a combination of the above procedures) following the completion of the posttesting.

The assessment procedures employed a laboratory role-playing interaction, a quasi-unobtrusive situation test of assertiveness (i.e., having to assert oneself to a confederate interfering with the participant's performance on a task), and a questionnaire battery containing self-report measures of assertiveness, social anxiety, and anxiety specific to assertion situations. The questionnaire findings revealed the following: No significant differences were found as a function of sex of therapist, either as a main effect or as an interaction with specific treatment procedure. A comparison among the different treatment conditions revealed that the most effective procedure was the combined behavior rehearsal plus rational restructuring, followed by rational restructuring and behavior rehearsal, which were no different from each other; next followed the attention-placebo, and finally the waiting-list control. At the time of this writing, further analyses are in progress.

Other recent studies have similarly supported the clinical effectiveness of the use of rational self-statements in what are commonly considered to be "skill deficit" problems. Thorpe (1975) pitted rational therapy against behavior rehearsal, desensitization, and placebo conditions in the treatment of unassertive behavior. He found that training subjects to rationally reevaluate the consequences of their assertive behavior was as effective as skill training procedures. A further interesting finding was that the self-instruction procedure was more effective than desensitization, which is consistent with the results reported by Kanter and Goldfried (1976) for social anxiety. In a related study, Wolfe and Fodor (in

press) compared a skill acquisition program entailing modelling and behavior rehearsal with a procedure that additionally made use of rational-
emotive therapy. Although the skill acquisition and acquisition plus rational-emotive therapy programs produced comparable improvements on a
role-playing assessment measure, each of these procedures was significantly
better than either a consciousness-raising or waiting list control. Interestingly enough, however, only the condition incorporating rational-emotive
therapy resulted in significant decrements in subjective anxiety during
role-playing. An outcome study by Glass, Gottman and Shmurak (1976)
with heterosexually shy college males found that a treatment procedure
emphasizing the use of rational self-statements was significantly more
effective in improving heterosexual interaction than an intervention procedure emphasizing skill training.

The results of these various outcome studies comparing the effectiveness
of different techniques for facilitating assertive behavior cast serious doubt
on the contention that unassertive behavior is best construed as a skill
deficit. Training individuals to rationally reevaluate the potential consequences of behaving assertively may at times be just as effective as skill
training procedures. These findings are consistent with the results of
Schwartz and Gottman (1976), who found that most unassertive subjects
know what to say in certain situations, but are inhibited from emitting
this response themselves when placed in a situation calling for assertive
behavior. Schwartz and Gottman also report data that this inhibition may
be the result of negative self-statements, typically reflecting concern over
the reaction of others (e.g., "I was very worried about what the other
person would think of me"). In light of these other outcome studies on
assertion training, it may be more appropriate to view unassertive behavior as a form of social-evaluative anxiety, amenable to some sort of intervention procedure designed to reduce this form of anxiety.

SUMMARY AND CONCLUSIONS

This chapter has reviewed some of the theoretical and research foundations, clinical procedures, and outcome data associated with the use of
relaxation and rational restructuring as skills for coping with anxiety.
The results of a variety of studies suggest that relaxation training may
be used as an effective clinical procedure when presented as an active
coping skill. This may be accomplished by simply encouraging clients to
actively employ their ability to relax when confronted with anxiety-

provoking situations *in vivo*, or may be presented within the broader context of self-control desensitization. However, there seem to be limits to the effectiveness of this approach to anxiety-reduction, and some findings imply that the effects of anxiety-reduction interventions may reflect an interaction between target problem and therapeutic procedure. Although the precise nature of this interaction is far from clear, available evidence suggests that rational restructuring may be more appropriate in cases of pervasive anxiety, or instances where the anxiety is mediated by concerns regarding the evaluation of others. In the case of social anxiety, including lack of interpersonal assertiveness, training clients to realistically reevaluate the consequences of their behavior may be more effective than focusing on the use of relaxation skills, and just as successful as an approach promoting the acquisition of more effective overt behaviors. In the case of more focal target problems, such as speech anxiety or test anxiety, relaxation and rational restructuring seem to be comparably effective.

Further investigation into the nature of the interaction between treatment procedure and target behavior is clearly in order. Bandura (1969) has suggested that techniques for the reduction of anxiety should differ, depending on whether the emotional response is directly evoked by conditioned aversive stimuli, or is maintained by self-generated symbolic activities. Davidson and Schwartz (1976) have similarly argued that self-regulatory coping procedures in the treatment of anxiety are likely to vary, depending upon whether the anxiety is comprised of cognitive or somatic components. The likelihood that important interactions exist with the maintenance and reduction of other emotional responses should be investigated as well; Beck's (1976) work on coping with depression and Novaco's (1975) research on the control of anger represent important beginnings in this direction.

Another potentially fruitful future direction involves collaborative outcome research with investigators at other settings. Such collaborative efforts are indeed possible, provided that close coordination and appropriate methodological precautions are taken, such as the standardization of treatment procedures, comparability of subjects, and equivalency of outcome measures. Our experiences are consistent with conclusions drawn by Bergin and Strupp (1970), who suggest that with appropriate standardization and close coordination, collaborative outcome studies are feasible, and indeed should be encouraged in the area of clinical outcome research.

REFERENCES

APONTE, J. F. and APONTE, C. E.: Group preprogrammed systematic desensitization in alleviating test anxiety in college students. *Journal of Abnormal Psychology*, 1971, 77, 282-289.

BANDURA, A.: *Principles of Behavior Modification*. New York: Holt, Rinehart, & Winston, 1969.

BARRETT, C. L.: Systematic desensitization versus implosive therapy. *Journal of Abnormal Psychology*, 1969, 74, 587-592.

BECK, A. T.: *Cognitive Therapy and the Emotional Disorders*. New York: International Universities Press, 1976.

BERGIN, A. E. and STRUPP, H. H.: New directions in psychotherapy research. *Journal of Abnormal Psychology*, 1970, 76, 13-26.

BOOTZIN, R. R. and KAZDIN, A. E.: A comparison of systematic desensitization with systematic habituation for fear of heights. Paper presented at the Midwestern Psychological Association, 1972.

BREGER, L. and McGAUGH, J. L.: Critique and reformulation of "learning theory" approaches to psychotherapy and neurosis. *Psychological Bulletin*, 1965, 63, 338-358.

CALEF, R. A. and MACLEAN, G. D.: A comparison of reciprocal inhibition and reactive inhibition therapies in the treatment of speech anxiety. *Behavior Therapy*, 1970, 1, 51-58.

CASAS, J. M.: A comparison of two mediational self-control techniques for the treatment of speech anxiety. Unpublished doctoral dissertation, Stanford University, 1975.

CHANG-LIANG, R. and DENNEY, D. R.: Applied relaxation as training in self-control. *Journal of Counseling Psychology*, 1976, 23, 183-189.

DAVIDSON, R. J. and SCHWARTZ, G. E.: The psychobiology of relaxation and related states: A multi-process theory. In D. I. Mostovsky (Ed.), *Behavior Control and the Modification of Physiological Activity*. Englewood Cliffs, N.J.: Prentice-Hall, 1976.

DAVISON, G. C.: Relative contributions of differential relaxation and graded exposure to *in vivo* desensitization of a neurotic fear. *Proceedings of the 73rd Annual Convention of the American Psychological Association*, 1965, 1, 209-210.

DAVISON, G. C.: Anxiety under total curarization: Implications for the role of muscular relaxation in the desensitization of neurotic fears. *Journal of Nervous and Mental Disease*, 1966, 143, 443-448.

DAVISON, G. C.: Systematic desensitization as a counterconditioning process. *Journal of Abnormal Psychology*, 1968, 73, 91-99.

DAVISON, G. C., TSUJIMOTO, R. N., and GLAROS, A. G.: Attribution and the maintenance of behavior change in falling asleep. *Journal of Abnormal Psychology*, 1973, 82, 124-133.

DENNEY, D. R. and RUPERT, P. A.: Desensitization and self-control in the treatment of test anxiety. Unpublished manuscript, University of Kansas, 1976.

DiLORETO, A. O.: *Comparative Psychotherapy: An Experimental Analysis*. Chicago: Aldine-Atherton, Inc., 1971.

DOLLARD, J. and MILLER, N. E.: *Personality and Psychotherapy*. New York: McGraw-Hill, 1950.

D'ZURILLA, T. J., WILSON, G. T., and NELSON, R.: A preliminary study of the effectiveness of graduated prolonged exposure in the treatment of irrational fears. *Behavior Therapy*, 1973, 4, 672-685.

ELLIS, A.: *Reason and Emotion in Psychotherapy.* New York: Lyle Stuart, 1962.

ENDLER, N. S., HUNT, J. McV., and ROSENSTEIN, A. J.: An S-R inventory of anxiousness. *Psychological Monographs*, 1962, 76, 1-33.

FREMOUW, W. J. and HARMATZ, M. G.: A helper model for behavioral treatment of speech anxiety. *Journal of Consulting and Clinical Psychology*, 1975, 43, 652-660.

GAUDRY, E. and SPIELBERGER, C. D.: *Anxiety and Educational Achievement.* New York: Wiley, 1971.

GLASS, C. R., GOTTMAN, J. M., and SHMURAK, S. H.: Response acquisition and cognitive self-statement modification approaches to dating skills training. *Journal of Counseling Psychology*, 1976, 23, 520-526.

GOLDFRIED, M. R.: Systematic desensitization as training in self-control. *Journal of Consulting and Clinical Psychology*, 1971, 37, 228-234.

GOLDFRIED, M. R.: *Behavioral Management of Anxiety: A Clinician's Guide.* Audiocassette tape-T44A. New York: BioMonitoring Applications, 1976.

GOLDFRIED, M. R.: Reduction of generalized anxiety through a variant of systematic desensitization. In M. R. Goldfried & M. Merbaum (Eds.), *Behavior Change through Self-Control.* New York: Holt, Rinehart, and Winston, 1973.

GOLDFRIED, M. R. and DAVISON, G. C.: *Clinical Behavior Therapy.* New York: Holt, Rinehart, and Winston, 1976.

GOLDFRIED, M. R., DECENTECEO, E. T., and WEINBERG, L.: Systematic rational restructuring as a self-control technique. *Behavior Therapy*, 1974, 5, 247-254.

GOLDFRIED, M. R. and GOLDFRIED, A. P.: Cognitive change methods. In F. H. Kanfer and A. P. Goldstein (Eds.), *Helping People Change.* New York: Pergamon, 1975.

GOLDFRIED, M. R., and GOLDFRIED, A. P.: Importance of hierarchy content in the self-control of anxiety. *Journal of Consulting and Clinical Psychology*, 1977, 45, 124-134.

GOLDFRIED, M. R., LINEHAN, M. M., and SMITH, J. L.: The reduction of test anxiety through rational restructuring. *Journal of Consulting and Clinical Psychology*, in press.

GOLDFRIED, M. R. and MERBAUM, M. (Eds.): *Behavior Change through Self-Control.* New York: Holt, Rinehart, and Winston, 1973.

GOLDFRIED, M. R. and SOBOCINSKI, D.: The effect of irrational beliefs on emotional arousal. *Journal of Consulting and Clinical Psychology*, 1975, 43, 504-510.

GOLDFRIED, M. R. and SPRAFKIN, J. N.: Behavioral personality assessment. In J. T. Spence, R. C. Carson, J. W. Thibaut (Eds.), *Behavioral Approaches to Therapy.* Morristown, N.J.: General Learning Press, 1976.

GOLDFRIED, M. R. and TRIER, C. S.: Effectiveness of relaxation as an active coping skill. *Journal of Abnormal Psychology*, 1974, 83, 348-355.

GRAY, B. B., ENGLAND, G., and MAHONEY, J. L.: Treatment of benign vocal nodules by reciprocal inhibition. *Behaviour Research and Therapy*, 1965, 3, 187-193.

HOLROYD, K. A.: Cognition and desensitization in the group treatment of test anxiety. *Journal of Consulting and Clinical Psychology*, 1976, 44, 991-1001.

JACKS, R. N.: Systematic desensitization versus a self-control technique for the reduction of acrophobia. Unpublished doctoral dissertation. Stanford University, 1972.

JACOBSON, E.: *Progressive Relaxation.* Chicago: University of Chicago Press, 1929.

JACOBSON, E.: *Progressive Relaxation.* Chicago: University of Chicago Press, 1938. (2nd edition.)

JANIS, I. L. and KING, B. T.: The influence of role playing on opinion change. *Journal of Abnormal and Social Psychology*, 1954, 49, 211-218.

JONES, R. G.: A factored measure of Ellis' irrational belief system, with personality and maladjustment correlates. Unpublished doctoral dissertation, Texas Technological College, 1968.

KANFER, F. H. and PHILLIPS, J. S.: A survey of current behavior therapies and a proposal for classification. In C. M. Franks (Ed.), *Behavior Therapy: Appraisal and Status*. New York: McGraw-Hill, 1969.

KANTER, N. J. and GOLDFRIED, M. R.: Relative effectiveness of rational restructuring and self-control desensitization for the reduction of interpersonal anxiety. Unpublished manuscript, State University of New York at Stony Brook, 1976.

KING, B. T. and JANIS, I. L.: Comparison of the effectiveness of improvised versus non-improvised role-playing in producing opinion change. *Human Relations*, 1956, 9, 177-186.

LANG, P. J., LAZOVIK, A. D., and REYNOLDS, D. J.: Desensitization, suggestibility, and pseudotherapy. *Journal of Abnormal Psychology*, 1965, 70, 395-402.

LAZARUS, A. A.: Some clinical applications of autohypnosis. *Medical Proceedings, South Africa*, 1958, 4, 848-850.

LAZARUS, R. S.: *Psychological Stress and the Coping Process*. New York: McGraw-Hill, 1966.

LIEBERT, R. M. and MORRIS, L. W.: Cognitive and emotional components of test anxiety: A distinction and some initial data. *Psychological Reports*, 1967, 20, 975-978.

LINEHAN, M. M. and GOLDFRIED, M. R.: Assertion training for women: A comparison of behavior rehearsal and cognitive restructuring. Paper presented at the Ninth Annual Convention of AABT, December, 1975.

MAHONEY, M. J.: *Cognition and Behavior Modification*. Cambridge: Ballinger, 1974.

MALLESON, N.: Panic and phobia: A possible method of treatment. *Lancet*, 1959, 1, 225-227.

MANDLER, G. and WATSON, D.: Anxiety and the interruption of behavior. In C. D. Spielberger (Ed.), *Anxiety and Behavior*. New York: Academic Press, 1966.

MARLETT, N. and WATSON, D.: Test anxiety and immediate or delayed feedback in a test-like avoidance task. *Journal of Personality and Social Psychology*, 1968, 8, 200-203.

MAY, R. L.: The treatment of test anxiety by cognitive modification: An examination of treatment components. Unpublished doctoral dissertation, University of Kansas, 1975.

MAY, J. R. and JOHNSON, H. J.: Physiological activity to internally elicited arousal and inhibitory thoughts. *Journal of Abnormal Psychology*, 1973, 82, 239-245.

McGLYNN, F. D.: Graded imagination and relaxation as components of experimental desensitization. *The Journal of Nervous and Mental Disease*, 1973, 156, 377-385.

MEICHENBAUM, D. H.: Cognitive modification of test anxious college students. *Journal of Consulting and Clinical Psychology*, 1972, 39, 370-380.

MEICHENBAUM, D. H., GILMORE, J. B., and FEDORAVICIOUS, A.: Group insight versus group desensitization in treating speech anxiety. *Journal of Consulting and Clinical Psychology*, 1971, 36, 410-421.

MEICHENBAUM, D. H. and TURK, D.: The cognitive-behavioral management of anxiety, anger, and pain. In P. Davidson (Ed.), *Behavioral Management of Anxiety, Depression, and Pain*. New York: Brunner/Mazel, 1976.

MISCHEL, W.: *Personality and Assessment*. New York: Wiley, 1968.

MORRIS, L. W. and LIEBERT, R. M.: Relationship of cognitive and emotional components of test anxiety to physiological arousal and academic performance. *Journal of Consulting and Clinical Psychology*, 1970, 35, 332-337.

MYLAR, J. L. and CLEMENT, P. W.: Prediction and comparison of outcome in systematic desensitization and implosion. *Behaviour Research and Therapy*, 1972, 10, 235-246.

NOVACO, R.: *Anger Control: The Development and Evaluation of an Experimental Treatment*. Lexington, Mass.: Lexington Books, 1975.

OSARCHUK, M.: A comparison of a cognitive, a behavior therapy and a cognitive plus behavior therapy treatment of test anxious college students. Unpublished doctoral dissertation, Adelphi University, 1974.

PAUL, G. L.: *Insight versus Desensitization in Psychotherapy*. Stanford: Stanford University Press, 1966.

PAUL, G. L.: Physiological effects of relaxation training and hypnotic suggestion. *Journal of Abnormal Psychology*, 1969, 74, 425-437.

PAUL, G. L. and SHANNON, D. T.: Treatment of anxiety through systematic desensitization in therapy groups. *Journal of Abnormal Psychology*, 1966, 71, 124-135.

PETERSON, D. R.: *The Clinical Study of Social Behavior*. New York: Appleton-Century-Crofts, 1968.

RACHMAN, S.: Studies in desensitization—I: The separate effects of relaxation and desensitization. *Behaviour Research and Therapy*, 1965, 3, 245-251.

RAIMY, V.: *Misunderstandings of the Self*. San Francisco: Jossey-Bass, 1975.

RIMM, D. C. and LITVAK, S. B.: Self-verbalization and emotional arousal. *Journal of Abnormal Psychology*, 1969, 32, 565-574.

RUSSELL, P. L. and BRANDSMA, J. M.: A theoretical and empirical integration of the rational-emotive and classical conditioning theories. *Journal of Consulting and Clinical Psychology*, 1974, 42, 389-397.

SCHILL, T., EVANS, R., MONROE, S., and RAMANAIAH, N. V.: The effects of self-verbalizations on performance: A test of the rational-emotive position. Unpublished manuscript, Southern Illinois University of Carbondale, 1976.

SCHWARTZ, R. and GOTTMAN, J. M.: Toward a task analysis of assertive behavior. *Journal of Consulting and Clinical Psychology*, 1976, 44, 910-920.

SHERMAN, A. R.: Real-life exposure as a primary therapeutic factor in the desensitization treatment of fear. *Journal of Abnormal Psychology*, 1972, 79, 19-28.

SNIDER, J. G. and OETTING, E. R.: Autogenic training and the treatment of examination anxiety in students. *Journal of Clinical Psychology*, 1966, 22, 111-114.

SPIEGLER, M. D., COOLEY, E. J., MARSHALL, G. J., PRINCE II, H. T., PUCKETT, S. P., and SKENAZY, J. A.: A self-control versus a counter-conditioning paradigm for systematic desensitization: An experimental comparison. *Journal of Counseling Psychology*, 1976, 23, 83-86.

SPIELBERGER, C. D. (Ed.): *Anxiety and Behavior*. New York: Academic Press, 1966.

SPIELBERGER, C. D., GORSUCH, R. L., and LUSHENE, R. E.: *The State-trait Anxiety Inventory (STAI) Test Manual for Form X*. Palo Alto, California: Consulting Psychologists Press, 1970.

SUINN, R. M.: The STABS, a measure of test anxiety for behavior therapy: Normative data. *Behaviour Research and Therapy*, 1969, 7, 335-339.

SUINN, R. M. and RICHARDSON, F.: Anxiety management training: A nonspecific behavior therapy program for anxiety control. *Behavior Therapy*, 1971, 2, 498-510.

THORPE, G. L.: Desensitization, behavior rehearsal, self-instructional training and placebo effects on assertive-refusal behavior. *European Journal of Behavioural Analysis and Modification*, 1975, 1, 30-44.

TREXLER, L. D. and KARST, T. O.: Rational-emotive therapy, placebo, and no-treatments effects on public-speaking anxiety. *Journal of Abnormal Psychology*, 1972, 79, 60-67.

TUNNER, W., OELKERS, C., FERSTL, R., and BIRBAUMER, N.: Systematic desensitization and self-control training in the treatment of speech anxiety. Unpublished manuscript, University of Munich, 1973.

VELTEN, E., JR.: A laboratory task for induction of mood states. *Behaviour Research and Therapy*, 1968, 6, 473-482.

WATSON, D. and FRIEND, R.: Measurement of social-evaluative anxiety. *Journal of Consulting and Clinical Psychology*, 1969, 33, 448-457.

WEIL, G. and GOLDFRIED, M. R.: Treatment of insomnia in an eleven-year-old child through self-relaxation. *Behavior Therapy*, 1973, 4, 282-284.

WILSON, G. T. and DAVISON, G. C.: Processes of fear reduction in systematic desensitization: Animal studies. *Psychological Bulletin*, 1971, 76, 1-14.

WOLFE, J. L. and FODOR, I. G.: Modifying assertive behavior in women: A comparison of three approaches. *Behavior Therapy*, in press.

WOLPE, J.: *Psychotherapy by Reciprocal Inhibition.* Stanford: Stanford University Press, 1958.

ZEMORE, R.: Systematic desensitization as a method of teaching a general anxiety-reducing skill. *Journal of Consulting and Clinical Psychology*, 1975, 43, 157-161.

ZUCKERMAN, M. and LUBIN, B.: *Manual for the Multiple Affect Adjective Checklist.* San Diego: Educational and Industrial Testing Service, 1965.

5

Meditation, Self-Control and Alcohol Use

G. ALAN MARLATT

and

JANICE K. MARQUES

In the past five years, there has been an explosion of public interest in the practice of meditation. This interest has been stimulated by the wide publicity given to one particular approach to meditation, Transcendental Meditation (TM). A browse through the paperback racks in the neighborhood supermarket, drugstore, or hotel lobby provides ample evidence of this expanding interest. At the time of this writing (February, 1976), no less than three books related to meditation are on the best-selling list: *TM: Discovering Inner Energy and Overcoming Stress* (Bloomfield, Cain, Jaffe & Kory, 1975); *The TM Book* (Denniston & McWilliams, 1975), and Benson's *The Relaxation Response* (1975). A myriad of other books are competing for the top slots, many of them paperback editions which look as though they have been written or edited within a ninety-day period.

The number of individuals initiated into the TM movement is growing at an exponential rate. According to a recent article in the *Washington Post* (reprinted as Appendix II in White, 1976), well over half a million Americans have now learned TM, a considerable increase over the total of 25,000 reported a few years earlier. The article reports that approximately 30,000 newcomers are initiated each month. At the current fee of $125.00 for each adult, the 6,000 or so teachers of TM in the United States alone are bringing in a lot of money for the movement's coffers (over $20 million in 1974 alone), all of it tax exempt. Much of this money has been ploughed back into the TM program, including the establishment of training centers, a four-year college (Maharishi International University in Fairfield, Iowa), an international research center (Maharishi European Research University in Weggis, Switzerland), a large publishing operation (MIU Press), and a TM-oriented television station (KSCI in Los Angeles), the first of seven such stations planned for the United States by the end of this decade. A lot has happened since the Maharishi first introduced TM into this country in 1959. If the decade of the sixties has been called the "Age of Anxiety," the seventies might well be labeled as the "Search for Serenity" decade.

In the present chapter, meditation will be described as a self-control strategy deserving of study by behaviorally-oriented researchers and therapists. Various forms of meditation will be described, with an emphasis on TM as the most widely-practiced technique. Similarities between meditation and certain procedures in the field of behavior therapy, notably desensitization and strategies of self-control, will be discussed in an attempt to isolate the potential "active ingredients" of meditation as a treatment technique.

Meditation has sometimes been advocated as a treatment procedure for the problems of drug abuse and alcoholism. The research bearing on this area of application will be critically reviewed, along with a discussion of some of the difficulties encountered in evaluating the effects of meditation in comparative outcome studies. A theoretical model will be presented which shows how meditation may be an effective treatment procedure with problem drinkers and alcoholics. The final section of the chapter will present the results of a controlled outcome study evaluating the effects of meditation and other relaxation procedures upon drinking behavior.

WHAT IS MEDITATION?

It is easier to define meditation in terms of the process or procedures of meditating, rather than attempting to describe the experience of the meditative state itself. Although there are a number of different meditation techniques or procedures, each of them is directed toward a common goal: to "quiet" the mind by entering a state of consciousness which goes beyond or "transcends" normal thought processes. Instead of concentrating on active thoughts, perceptions, and ideas, the meditator uses a technique to shut down the "cognitive computer" and enter a state of mental "blankness" or non-thought. Although the experience of non-thought is difficult to describe (words are inadequate descriptors of non-verbal states), meditators often claim that this state is one of deep relaxation and calm, coupled with an attitude of passivity and detachment.

The development of contemporary meditation procedures is rooted in ancient religious writings, stemming back to the sacred Hindu texts known as the Vedas (1000-500 B.C.). The Sanskrit Vedas served as the source for several religious doctrines in India, including the Vedanta, Sankhya, and Yoga. In many of the Eastern religious traditions, including Yoga and various forms of Buddhism, meditative practices are used as steps towards the attainment of spiritual union with God (enlightenment, cosmic consciousness, satori, etc.). From a Western perspective, however, the religious overtones associated with meditation are often downplayed or ignored.

The most popular form of contemporary meditation, TM, is not described officially as a religious practice. For example, in a recent bestselling book on TM, it is stated that: "This technique does not, however, have any connection with the present fashionable cultivation of Eastern philosophy or culture. In fact, the correct practice of the TM technique does not depend on any cultural orientation, but only upon the inherent abilities of the nervous system" (Bloomfield et al., 1975, p. 32). It seems clear that meditation can be studied from a scientific perspective, despite controversy concerning its religious associations.

There are a number of meditation techniques in addition to TM. Ornstein (1972) has attempted to classify these into two major categories: 1) concentrative and 2) "opening up" forms of meditation. Most techniques fall into the first category, *concentrative* meditation. Common to these procedures is the practice of limiting one's awareness to a single, unchanging source of stimulation for a fixed period of time. By "concentrating" on a single stimulus, the meditator is able to clear his mind from distractions stemming from the normal stream of ideation and imagery. Here, the choice of the meditation stimulus differs from one form of practice to another.

In Zen Buddhism, for example, the meditator may concentrate on his breathing, first counting each breath from one to ten over and over again, and then moving on to directing his attention to the process of breathing itself. Another form of Zen meditation (Rinzai Zen) requires concentration on a mental riddle or paradox (koan) for long periods of time (e.g., "What is the sound of one hand clapping?"). TM, on the other hand (!), is a form of Yoga meditation in which the stimulus is a word or sound called a mantra (technically, the singular form is mantram). A Sanskrit word, mantra has the literal meaning of "mind control" (man = mind; tra = control). In this form of meditation, the mantra is repeated silently over and over again throughout the exercise. Other Yoga meditative practices involve the concentration of attention on a visual stimulus, such as a mandala or a candle flame, or on a repetitive auditory stimulus (e.g., the sound of one's heartbeat or the dripping of water). In Transcendental Meditation, the mantra is used to "transcend" normal waking consciousness to achieve a pleasant state of deep relaxation and rest.

In contrast to the concentrative forms of meditation, the *"opening up"* category described by Ornstein includes those exercises in which the individual assumes a passive, open attitude towards normal physical activities (as in the Zen practice of "shikan-taza" or "just sitting"). Attention is focused simply on what is happening in the here and now, with no attempt made to focus one's thoughts in any particular direction. This type of meditation takes the form of a mental "attitude" towards life, such as that described in Pirsig's recent book, *Zen and the Art of Motorcycle Maintenance* (1974), or in Carlos Casteneda's series of books about the teaching of Don Juan.

BASIC MECHANISMS OF MEDITATION

There have been a number of theories proposed to explain how meditation works. Since much of the research has dealt with the physiological effects of TM and other forms of meditation, many of these theories posit psychophysiological mechanisms as central concepts. A complete review of these theoretical positions is beyond the scope of this chapter, but a sampling of viewpoints provides some sense of their direction. Based on their early experimental findings, Wallace and Benson (1972) argued that meditation produced a unique state of consciousness which they termed a "wakeful hypometabolic" state, which could be differentiated physiologically from the three major states of consciousness—waking, sleeping and dreaming. During meditation, the individual drops into a deep state of relaxation as arousal in the sympathetic nervous system decreases, as indicated by various physiological measures (skin resistance, heart rate, respiration, oxygen consumption, blood-lactate level, etc.). At the same time, brain wave records show an increase in alpha rhythm amplitude, some increase in theta activity, and possible synchronization effects in brain wave activity (e.g., Banquet, 1973). Although these physiological signs indicate a deep state of physical relaxation similar to the early stages of sleep, meditators report that they are mentally alert and aware during meditation.

How does the process of meditating produce this restful state? Here the speculations become more diverse and the data sparse. Repetition of the mantra has been suggested as the key to the process. Rhythmic repetitions of a single stimulus have been found to elicit perceptual and neural habituation, and the euphonics of a pleasant-sounding mantra may be a particularly good stimulus to produce a state of relaxation (cf., Schwartz, 1974). Glueck and Stroebel (1975) have argued that the mantra acts as a "driving mechanism" to dampen limbic system activity, which in turn may serve to inhibit cortical activation. Ornstein (1972) has suggested that the meditative experience may inhibit dominant or left-hemisphere brain activity, allowing the operations of the nondominant right-hemisphere to gain ascendance. As a result, the meditator shifts from the linear, logical-verbal mode of consciousness to a more "intuitive" level of awareness, similar to what the TM literature describes as "pure awareness" and "creative intelligence." Benson (1975) claims that any number of relaxation techniques (including TM and other forms of meditation) elicit what he calls the "relaxation response," defined physiologically as a state of parasympathetic dominance. Benson, who has since split ranks with Wallace (currently the president of Maharishi International University) over claims that TM is the most effective form of meditation, has described a simple meditative-relaxation exercise which combines the effects of deep muscle relaxation with the repetition of the word "one." This technique will be described in more detail in a later section.

MEDITATION AND BEHAVIOR THERAPY

Despite the incomplete and sometimes conflicting evidence concerning the physiological effects, much of which can only be settled by future research, there are several features of meditation which are of interest to behavior therapists. In a discussion of some of the similarities between behavior therapy and TM, Bloomfield et al. (1975) suggest that the two approaches might be combined:

> Behavior therapy has been criticized as superficial and applicable only to a narrow range of problems. If it were combined with the TM program we would anticipate deeper and more durable results. Behavior therapy deals quickly and effectively with incapacitating sources of stress such as fear of highway driving, lack of assertiveness or sexual dysfunction, whereas the TM program promotes comprehensive psychological integration (p. 141).

What are some of these similarities? Several recent reviews (e.g., Bloomfield et al., 1975; Carrington & Ephron, 1975) have noted that meditation is similar in some ways to systematic desensitization. The first psychologist to note this parallel was Goleman (1971). In describing meditation as a form of meta-therapy, he stated:

> The whole contents of the mind compose the meditator's "desensitization hierarchy." The contents of this hierarchy are organic to the life concerns of the meditator. . . . As in the desensitization paradigm, the "hierarchy" is presented coupled with the deep relaxation of deep meditation. Unlike the therapy, desensitization is not limited to those items which therapist and patient have identified as problematic, though those are certainly included, but extends to all phases of experience. . . . It is natural, global self-desensitization (p. 5).

In the special language of TM, the desensitization effects are alluded to in the concepts of "unstressing" and "detachment." During the practice of meditation, the subject is in a deep state of physical relaxation. During the meditative session, it is usual to experience a number of thoughts, feelings, and images which tend to "compete" with the mantra. Many of these ideas have an affective or emotional valence. It is natural to expect that by sitting quietly with eyes closed for two time periods each day, one's mind would begin to wander and ponder on the events to come during the day (morning meditation), or on the things which have happened during the day and might be forthcoming for the evening (evening meditation). Many of these ideas may relate to things that are bothering us or that we are worried about. This phenomenon has been noted by Glueck and Stroebel (1975) in their report of treating psychiatric patients with TM:

> The weakening of the repression barrier that occurs in sleep and in other altered states of consciousness, such as free association during

the process of psychoanalytic therapy, *may* be produced in a relatively simple fashion during TM meditation. This would offer an explanation of a phenomenon that has been reported by a number of investigators, and which we have seen repeatedly in our patients. During meditation, thoughts and ideas may appear that are ordinarily repressed, such as intense hostile-aggressive drives, murderous impulses, and occasionally, libidinal ideation (p. 315).

TM advocates would define this as the process of "unstressing" or "normalization" of the nervous system.

As in desensitization, the meditator is instructed to react with passive detachment to these thoughts and feelings, returning to the repetition of the mantra as conveniently as possible. The state of deep relaxation associated with the mantra repetition may come to serve as a "reciprocal inhibitor" of anxiety, much as muscle relaxation serves this purpose in desensitization. In the latter procedure, the subject signals the therapist at the first sign of any tension or anxiety while visualizing the feared stimulus scene, and is then told to "stop visualizing the scene" and concentrate on the relaxed state of his muscles. Muscles or mantra? The similarity between meditation and desensitization as reciprocal inhibitors of anxiety has also been noted by Boudreau (1972).

The potential overlap between meditation and desensitization may help explain the cumulative effects attributed to TM. From this perspective, meditation is not simply a "time-out" procedure or a "rest break" from the day's normal activities. Rather, the meditator may be gradually desensitizing many of his fears and anxieties, perhaps facilitating his approach to otherwise stressful situations in the environment. During meditation itself, the thought-processes which mediate anxiety may lose their potency as conditioned stimuli for emotional reactions. While meditation is certainly less structured or programmatic than desensitization, it may offer an advantage in that a wide variety of fear-related thoughts are reacted to in a relaxed and passive attitude—a kind of global, "whatever-is-on-one's-mind" hierarchy of items.

From this vantage point, meditation can be viewed as a general self-control coping strategy, much in the same way as desensitization has been so described (Goldfried, 1971). Although progressive muscle relaxation has been found to be particularly effective when practiced *just prior* to an impending stressful situation, the effects of meditation as a coping strategy in specific situations have yet to be studied.

It seems clear that anxiety and fear are often augmented by our thoughts and self-statements about ongoing and impending events. Meichenbaum (1975), for example, has argued that clients should be trained in self-instructional techniques which act as coping mechanisms to deal effectively with stress. Rather than catastrophizing about possible traumatic outcomes in a feared situation, the client is told to "talk to himself" in a more constructive manner, evaluating the specifics of the situation and providing instructions to elicit adequate coping strategies. While this treatment method has proved to be effective with a number of clinical problems, it is based on the assumption that coping is facilitated by exchanging one set of thought-processes for another. If thoughts and ideation do indeed mediate anxiety, it might be better to encourage the client to *stop thinking altogether.* Meditation may be effective as a self-control technique because it severs the link between thought and action, between conditioned fear stimuli and conditioned emotional responses. This is the essence of "detachment," one of the principal goals of meditation:

> A story is told of a man who came to Buddha with offerings of flowers in both hands. The Buddha said, "Drop it!" So he dropped the flowers in his left hand. The Buddha said again, "Drop it!" He dropped the flowers in his right hand. And the Buddha said, "Drop that which you have neither in the right nor in the left, but in the middle!" And the man was instantly enlightened. (Watts, 1974, p. 35).

THE EFFECTS OF MEDITATION ON DRINKING BEHAVIOR

In a behavioral approach to drinking behavior and alcoholism (Marlatt & Nathan, 1977), considerable attention is paid to the possible reinforcing effects of alcohol. For the past several decades, the primary guiding assumption in the behavioral literature has been that alcohol is reinforcing because it acts to reduce tension or anxiety (cf. Conger, 1956). A frequently stated corollary of this "tension-reduction hypothesis" is that the probability of drinking will increase under conditions of tension or stress. Data from recent studies have challenged the validity of the tension-reduction hypothesis, however, as indicated in recent reviews by Cappell (1975), Cappell and Herman (1972) and Marlatt (1976). Despite these criticisms of the tension-reduction model, there is some evidence suggesting that alcohol consumption does increase as a response to stress in human subjects, particularly when the stress arises from social or interpersonal sources (Higgins & Marlatt, 1975; Miller, Hersen, Eisler & Hilsman, 1974).

Rather than acting as a kind of tranquilizer for tension or anxiety in these stressful situations, alcohol is reinforcing because it increases the drinker's sense of perceived *control.*

In a review of the literature supporting this contention, the following hypothesis was advanced:

> The notion that alcohol produces an increase in both physiological arousal and fantasies of personal power or control suggests the possibility that drinking will increase in situations in which the drinker feels deprived of personal control. Such a situation has been defined as *stressful* by Sells (1970), who suggests that if an individual is called upon to respond in a stressful situation, and has no adequate response available, s/he will experience the stress as a loss of personal control particularly if the consequences of not responding are important in some way to the person involved. The relationship between stress and personal control has also been noted by Averill (1973) and Mandler and Watson (1966). With this definition of stress in mind, the hypothesis which emerges is that the probability of drinking will vary in a particular situation as a function of a) the degree of perceived stress in the situation, b) the degree of perceived personal control the individual experiences, c) the availability of an "adequate" coping response to the stressful situation and the availability of alcohol; and d) the individual's expectations about the effectiveness of alcohol as an alternative coping response in the situation. If the drinker experiences a loss of personal control in a stressful situation (and has no other adequate coping response available), the probability of drinking will increase. Alcohol consumption, under these conditions, serves to restore the individual's sense of personal control because of its enhancing effects on arousal and thoughts of "personal power" or control (Marlatt, 1976, p. 291).

In one test of this hypothesis, it was demonstrated that if social drinkers who took part in an interpersonally stressful situation (exposure to the criticism and anger of a confederate subject) were given an opportunity to engage in an alternative coping response (retaliation against the confederate subject), they showed a significant decrease in alcohol consumption in an analogue drinking task (Marlatt, Kosturn & Lang, 1975). Similarly, meditation may also serve as an alternative coping response to drinking, if it could be shown that the practice of this technique was associated with an increased ability to cope with stress.

There is accumulating evidence to suggest that meditation may lead to increased personal control, as perceived by the meditator. Several possible mechanisms through which meditation leads to stress control were discussed above. To these can be added another: It may increase the individual's "perceived control." That is, along Rotter's (1966) continuum from internal to external control, the individual may perceive himself to be in control to the extent that he adopts an internal orientation (Phares, 1976). Hjelle (1974) demonstrated this type of control among experienced TM meditators (mean of 22.6 months of meditation) compared with a control group of subjects who were about to be initiated. He administered several personality tests to both groups, including Rotter's Internal-External Locus of Control Scale (1966) and Shostrom's (1966) Personal Orientation Inventory. The experienced meditators were found to be significantly more "internal" on the I-E Scale $(M=6.26)$ than the naive control subjects $(M=10.91; p<.001)$. On the Shostrom inventory, meditators were found to score significantly higher on the "inner directed" and "self-regard" scales (among others), compared to the control group. These results replicate similar findings obtained with meditators who filled out the Personal Orientation Inventory (Nidich, Seeman & Dreskin, 1973; Seeman, Nidich & Banta, 1972). It might be argued that persons interested in beginning meditation might be more internally-controlled than persons not interested in meditation, suggesting a self-selection bias. In one test of this hypothesis, however, Stek and Bass (1973) found no significant differences on the I-E Scale or the POI for subjects who had attended the TM introductory lectures (prior to initiation) compared to subjects reporting no interest in learning to meditate.

If meditation does increase one's perception of control or "inner-directedness" as suggested by the above studies, and if drinking decreases as a function of increased personal control, then it follows that the practice of meditation should be associated with reduced alcohol consumption. Preliminary survey studies provide some support for this hypothesis. In the first major survey of this type, Benson and Wallace (1972) analyzed questionnaire data returned from 1,862 subjects who had practiced TM for periods of time ranging from 3 to 33 months. The majority of respondents reported a sizeable decrease in alcohol and other drug use after beginning regular practice of meditation. The percentage of subjects describing themselves as "heavy drinkers," for example, dropped from 2.7% of the sample, prior to beginning TM, to 0.4% after 22 to 33 months of practice (Benson, 1974). In a more recent study, Shafii, Lavely, and Jaffe (1975) presented the results of a questionnaire study comparing the frequency of alcohol use for subjects who had practiced TM for periods up to 39 months with a non-meditating control group. Most of the subjects (N=216) were young adults, with a college-level education. All subjects were asked to give retrospective accounts of their drinking behavior, dating back to the year preceding initiation into TM for the meditators, or an equivalent time period for the control subjects. The authors report that 40% of the subjects who had been meditating for more than two years said that they had discontinued the use of wine and beer in the first six months following initiation; none of the control subjects reported this effect during an equivalent time period. In addition, 54% of the meditating group had stopped drinking hard liquor, compared to only 1% of the controls.

There are numerous methodological problems with these two studies. In the Benson and Wallace (1972) study, all subjects were training to become teachers of TM, a nonrepresentative and highly motivated group. No control group of nonmeditators (or any other control procedure) was employed. While the Shafii et al. (1975) study did employ a control group of nonmeditators, this group was selected by having each member of the meditation group select his own control subject.

These methodological criticisms are not limited to studies which have assessed the effects of meditation on drinking behavior. Most of the studies to date which have investigated the psychological or behavioral effects of meditation have been poorly designed and executed. In a recent review of studies which have assessed the psychotherapeutic effects of meditation, Smith (1975) describes five of these methodological weaknesses. First, in many of the questionnaire studies, meditators are asked to report about the beneficial effects of the procedure, leading to glowing testimonial responses. As Smith states, "A meditator asked to participate in a study investigating the beneficial effects of meditation might view this as a calling or opportunity to 'step forth for meditation' somewhat analogous to the evangelist's call to 'step forth for Jesus.'" (Smith, 1975, p. 559). Second, studies comparing a group of mediators with a group of nonmeditators often fail to control for the possibility that the meditators, because of their interest in learning meditation, show a motivation for self-improvement not demonstrated by the nonmeditator control subjects. To correct for this deficiency, the experimenter must assign subjects on a random basis to either the meditation or control groups, and apply measures both before and after the treatment period. The third weakness noted by Smith is that some studies with TM compared experienced meditators with subjects who have indicated a desire to learn the technique, but have not yet been initiated (i.e., subjects drawn from the introductory lectures). While this may be an adequate control for initial motivation level in a single-shot assessment procedure, it may be difficult to use these subjects as a waiting-list control group for longer treatment outcome studies because of the "disappointment" subjects feel in not receiving immediate instruction in TM (see, too, Glueck & Stroebel, 1975). Fourth, most studies do not employ a group which controls for the effects of just sitting quietly for periods of time equivalent to the time spent meditating by the experimental subjects. Finally, most importantly, few if any studies employ an attention-placebo group to control for expectation effects. This is particularly important when the treatment being investigated is TM, since the whole initiation procedure into TM, including the hype of the introductory lectures, the persuasion of the teachers, the mutual enthusiasm of the group of initiates, the semi-religious initiation ceremony itself with its secret mantra, the relatively high fee, and the post-initiation checking sessions, has the cumulative effect of building up tremendous positive expectancies for the effects of meditation. Given the wide-ranging publicity currently surrounding TM in America, it is doubtful whether the strong positive expectancy effects could ever be adequately matched through the use of an attention-placebo control group.

In addition to these criticisms and design problems, the available studies investigating the effects of meditation on alcohol and other drug use suffer from other problems. The data are typically based on retrospective, self-report accounts, in which the subject is asked to make a global rating of drug use for a lengthy time period. For example, in the study reported by Shafii et al. (1975), control subjects were asked to "indicate the frequency of their use of wine and beer and/or hard liquor for the preceding 4 years (p. 943)." To date no prospective study testing the effects of meditation on drug use has appeared in the literature. As an alternative, the studies might include objective measures or indices of alcohol or drug use, such as behavioral samplings or performance in analogue drinking tasks. In addition, follow-up data are not usually reported in these studies. Furthermore, subjects who drop out or discontinue the practice of meditation are not accounted for. According to some published accounts, for example, about 30% of individuals who are initiated into TM stop practicing the technique within a relatively short period of time (Glueck & Stroebel, 1975; Shafii et al., 1975). These "drop-outs" may or may not include a disproportionate number of treatment failures. Finally, personality measures which may mediate the effects of meditation upon drug and alcohol use are not administered.

MEDITATION AND SOCIAL DRINKING

Our own study (Marlatt, Pagano, Rose & Marques, 1976) was designed as an attempt to provide a controlled investigation of the effects of meditation on alcohol consumption, employing a design which would be relatively free from these methodological weaknesses. We decided not to use TM as our meditation treatment procedure. Instead we chose Benson's (1975) alternative procedure, which is similar in many respects to TM with the following exceptions: a) There is no "secret" mantra (the subject is given the mantra "one" instead); b) no fee or elaborate semi-religious initiation ceremony is involved. Thus, the Benson procedure is a relatively "pure" meditative exercise, with few of the positive expectancy effects associated with TM. Our study compared the effects of the Benson procedure with Jacobson's (1938) progressive muscle relaxation and included two control groups: an attention-placebo group and a no-treatment group. Volunteer subjects were assigned randomly to each of these four groups, and were paid for their participation in the study.

The subjects in our study were male college students, classified as heavy social drinkers. We chose heavy drinkers instead of problem drinkers or alcoholics as our subjects because we wanted. to determine if meditation or our comparison procedures would lead to a change in alcohol consumption in individuals who had expressed no particular desire to cut down or stop their drinking. In this preliminary investigation, therefore, we chose to assess the "pure" effects of meditation on drinking in subjects who were relatively free from the motivation to alter their drinking behavior with the belief that if the results of our study showed that meditation did lead to a decrease in alcohol consumption, then the use of the technique as a potential treatment procedure for alcoholism would appear even more feasible.

We recruited potential subjects by administering the Drinking Habits Questionnaire to 1200 undergraduates at the University of Washington. This questionnaire, adapted from Cahalan's national drinking habits survey (Cahalan, Cisin & Crossley, 1969), is a computer-scored, multiple choice instrument, which classifies respondents according to the quantity, frequency, and variability of alcoholic beverages consumed. The Volume Variability index (Cahalan & Room, 1974) was used to select high volume drinkers (averaging at least one and a half drinks per day) for the experiment. The 130 males between 21 and 35 years of age who qualified as high volume drinkers were invited to attend a meeting at which the procedures and purpose of the experiment were presented. It was described as an exploratory study of the effects of practicing relaxation techniques on drinking alcoholic beverages. Care was taken to emphasize our uncertainty about what those effects would be, to avoid creating an expectation or demand that drinking would decrease after relaxation training. Potential subjects who were currently practicing relaxation procedures or receiving treatment for drinking problems were excused. A total of 44 qualified heavy drinkers agreed to participate, four of whom described themselves as "problem drinkers." Forty-one subjects (93%) completed the treatment phase of the study; their mean age was 23.5 years.

The study was divided into three distinct phases: a *baseline* period (two weeks), a *treatment* period (six weeks), and a *follow-up* period (seven weeks). During baseline, all subjects reported their daily alcohol consumption on detailed recording forms. At the end of this period, each subject was scheduled for a laboratory session in which he completed the pretreatment personality measures and then participated in a taste-rating task as a further measure of his alcohol consumption rate. Following these tests, we divided the subjects into four groups, matched on their consumption during the first week of the baseline period. Each group contained one of the subjects who described himself as a problem drinker. The four groups were: 1) meditation, 2) progressive relaxation, 3) attention-placebo control (bibliotherapy), and 4) no-treatment control.

Subjects in the first three groups were each taught a relaxation technique, and were instructed to practice it twice daily during the six-week period. Daily records of the time spent in relaxation sessions and the subjective level of relaxation experienced after each session were completed by these subjects throughout the treatment period. All groups, including the no-treatment control group, continued to keep daily records of alcohol consumption. At the end of the treatment period, the personality measures and taste-rating task were again administered.

During the follow-up period, the daily self-monitoring procedures were continued, but practice of the relaxation techniques was optional for the trained subjects. At the end of this period, subjects were asked to complete a follow-up questionnaire, which assessed their personal observations and conclusions about the study. A $4.00 weekly payment was made to each subject throughout the study, contingent upon receipt of his daily records of alcohol consumption. Confidentiality was maximized by having all subjects identify their records with a randomly assigned code number.

We included four treatment conditions in order to compare meditation with another established relaxation procedure, and to insure adequate controls. We were especially interested in how the effects of a *cognitive* relaxation technique (meditation) differ from those of a procedure which focuses on physical sensations and muscular relaxation. Since we also wanted to know whether any observed changes in drinking were the result of the specific "active ingredients" in these procedures, we designed an attention-placebo control condition to assess the nonspecific effects of training and daily relaxation sessions. This was done by using the following standard training conditions and instructions concerning daily practice for the meditation, progressive relaxation, and attention-placebo control groups: 1) subjects in each of these three conditions were trained as a group in a one-hour session with a male experimenter who was a faculty member in the department of psychology; 2) they were told to practice their respective techniques for two 20-minute periods each day, once in the morning before breakfast and once in the late afternoon before dinner; 3) after the training meeting, each subject was contacted by his trainer, who checked to see that the subject was following the instructions, and to answer questions about the procedure. In addition to the relaxation groups, a no-treatment control group was included in our design. This fourth group was especially important in controlling for the possible reactivity of the self-monitoring procedures used. More detailed descriptions of the four experimental conditions are presented below.

Meditation (N = 10)

This group received instruction in the meditative technique developed by Benson (Beary and Benson, 1974) as an analogue to Transcendental Meditation. As in TM, the basic components of Benson's technique are: a) subvocal repetition of a constant sound; b) a passive attitude; c) decreased muscle tonus; and d) regular practice. During the training session, the components of the procedure were explained, specific instructions were given, and a trial session was conducted by the trainer. The instructions used were taken from those published by Benson, Rosner, Marzetta, and Klemchuk (1974):

1. Sit quietly in a comfortable position.

2. Close your eyes.

3. Deeply relax all your muscles, beginning at your feet and progressing up to your face. Keep them deeply relaxed.

4. Breathe through your nose. Become aware of your breathing. As you breathe out, say the word "one" silently to yourself—e.g., breathe in . . . out, "one"; in . . . out, "one"; and so on.

5. Continue for 20 minutes. Occasionally open your eyes to check the time. When you finish, sit quietly for several minutes at first with closed eyes and later with opened eyes.

6. Do not worry about whether you are successfully achieving a deep level of relaxation. Maintain a passive attitude and permit relaxation to occur at its own pace. When distracting thoughts occur, ignore them and continue repeating "one." With practice, the response should come with little effort. Practice the technique twice daily, and not within two hours after any meal, since the digestive processes seem to interfere with the elicitation of anticipated changes.

Subjects were further advised to practice the technique in a straight-backed chair, in a quiet, dimly lit room. When interruptions occurred, such as the telephone ringing or a knock at the door, they were instructed not to respond, except in emergencies. They were told instead to attend to the distracting sound "lightly and passively," returning their awareness to their breathing and the word "one" when the sound ended.

Progressive Relaxation (N = 8)

Subjects in this condition were trained in a relaxation technique similar to that developed by Jacobson (1938) as a method for reducing muscular tension. In this procedure, the subject initially practices muscle relaxation while lying down in a quiet room. By alternatively tensing and relaxing selected muscle groups, he learns to recognize the sensations associated with muscular tension and practices eliminating any tension. In daily sessions, the subject practices making the discrimination of muscle tension and reducing that tension, as he cycles through about 15 different muscle groups. Over time, a progressively larger portion of each session is spent relaxing the muscle groups, rather than discriminating tension in them. Finally, the subject practices progressive relaxation while sitting and then attempts to incorporate his skill, as appropriate, into his daily activities. The trainer introduced the technique as a skill the subjects could teach themselves by following a systematic program. After the basic steps in the progressive relaxation program were described, the subjects participated in a practice session while listening to an audiotape containing standard instructions for tensing and relaxing selected muscle groups. A programmed text for progressive relaxation training, taken from Rosen's (1976a) manual for self-administered systematic desensitization, was then given to each subject to follow during the treatment period.

Attention-Placebo Control (N = 9)

This group was included to control for nonspecific effects of relaxation training, such as those due to: a) contact with the experimenters during training; b) demand characteristics; c) expectations of subjects about the effects of relaxation on drinking; d) daily periods of rest or quiet activities; and e) daily monitoring of relaxation levels (completion of relaxation records). A technique was chosen which could be credible to the subjects as a relaxation procedure and would involve sitting quietly for two periods a day, but which had not been shown to produce the specific relaxation effects (e.g., physiological changes) associated with the other two relaxation techniques. The procedure selected was called "bibliotherapy," and involved having the subjects engage in quiet, restful reading activities twice a day. The trainer, an experienced clinician, presented the following rationale during the training session:

> People often complain that they have no time to engage in "recreational" reading, because of the flow of normal obligations and commitments. The opportunity to engage in quiet reading of material the person has chosen for its restful and relaxing effect is thought to produce a state of quietness and calmness which is very relaxing in its overall effects. There is a sense of, "I am doing *what I want to do* during these reading periods," rather than the sense of obligation one feels in reading assigned materials.

The subjects were instructed to select a quiet room and a comfortable chair, away from other people and any distractions, for their reading sessions. They were asked to choose reading material which was "relaxing" to them, either fiction or reading associated with a hobby or special interest, and to avoid newspapers, news magazines, class assignments, and accounts of violence or eroticism.

No-Treatment Control (N = 14)

This group participated in the pretreatment and posttreatment assessment procedures (personality measures and taste-rating task), and recorded their daily alcohol consumption throughout the study. This condition was included to assess the effects of: a) self-monitoring of alcohol consumption; b) repeated administration of the assessment procedures; and c) environmental influences on alcohol consumption (particularly the effects of the academic schedule, such as examination periods).

The dependent measures used in our study were designed to assess two classes of variables: a) the drinking behavior of the subjects; and b) other variables which might mediate the effects of relaxation on drinking behavior. In the first class, we included two measures of alcohol consumption (consumption diaries and a taste-rating task); in the second class, we included measures of anxiety and locus of control, ratings of relaxation, and a follow-up questionnaire. These measures are described below:

Consumption Diaries

These self-monitoring forms were distributed weekly to all subjects, with instructions to supply on a daily basis the following information: a) exact type and brand of alcoholic beverage consumed ("proof" or per cent alcohol, if known); b) amount consumed (exact number and size of glasses or bottles, ratios of mixers: alcoholic beverages in mixed drinks); c) the period of time spent drinking; d) drinking situation (location and presence of others); and e) total cost of the alcoholic beverages consumed that day. Subjects were also instructed to indicate any extenuating circumstances, particularly illness, which may have affected their consumption that day. When subjects were unable to supply all of the information requested (e.g., exact size of a pitcher at a bar), efforts were made to obtain it from the establishment; in other cases, standard estimates were used (e.g., for mixed drinks in private settings). The consumption diary data were transformed into standard units of consumption (ml of ethanol), and a weekly score recorded as the subject's mean daily consumption.

Taste-Rating Task

This task is a standardized laboratory procedure developed by Marlatt et al. (1973) as an unobtrusive measure of alcohol consumption. Subjects were given individual laboratory appointments for a "wine-tasing test," with the following explanation:

> The overall purpose of this study is to investigate the effects of practicing a relaxation technique on the drinking of alcoholic beverages. In addition to possible changes in daily drinking habits, we are interested in whether relaxation training affects other aspects of drinking behavior, such as the perception of alcoholic beverages. In the wine-tasting sessions, we will be measuring your ability to discriminate taste differences among several wines before and after the 6-week period of relaxation practice.

The task instructions read to the subjects were similar to those described in previous papers (Marlatt, Demming & Reid, 1973; Higgins & Marlatt, 1975). Each subject was given three 700-ml. decanters of wine and was told to sample as much as he needed to rate and compare the beverages on a list of adjectives appearing one at a time on a memory drum. At the end of the 15-minute task period, the amount of wine consumed by the subject was measured.

Personality Measures

Two self-report personality measures were administered pre- and post-treatment to determine whether regular practice of the relaxation procedures affected the levels of anxiety and perceived locus of control in our subjects. The Spielberger State-Trait Anxiety Inventory (STAI) contains two separate scales, one measuring transitory levels of anxiety (A-State), and one yielding a dispositional measure of anxiety proneness (A-Trait) (Spielberger, Gorsuch & Lushene, 1970). The Locus of Control scale developed by Rotter (1966) was administered to assess individual differences in the perception of personal control. Individuals who score higher on the internal control dimension of this scale tend to perceive events as being consequences of their own behavior, while those higher on the external dimension view events as being the result of luck, fate, or the behavior of others.

Relaxation Records

These recording forms were distributed to subjects in the three relaxation groups during the treatment and follow-up periods. The subject was instructed to indicate, immediately after each relaxation session, the period of time spent in the session, and his rating of the level of relaxation achieved. These subjective ratings were based on a seven-point scale, extending from "very tense" (—3) to "very relaxed" (+3). The subject was told to consider the "0" point on the scale equal to the level of relaxation he normally experiences while just sitting quietly. A weekly mean relaxation score was computed by dividing the sum of the subjects' ratings by the number of sessions recorded.

Follow-Up Questionnaire

This instrument, administered at the end of the follow-up period, assessed the subject's personal observations and conclusions about the following topics: a) *drinking patterns* (e.g., his reasons for drinking and changes noted in any drinking habits during the study); b) *purpose of the study* (e.g., his awareness of the hypotheses being tested); and c) *relaxation procedure* (e.g., the relaxation subject's expectations and opinions about his assigned technique).

RESULTS OF THE STUDY

Table 1 presents a summary of our findings on the major dependent measures. From the consumption diary data, changes in alcohol con-

TABLE 1

Group Means on the Major Dependent Measures

		Meditation (n=10)	Progressive Relaxation (n=8)	Attention-Placebo Control (n=9)	No-Treatment Control (n=14)
Daily Ethanol Consumption (ml)	Pre	51.9	39.1	35.9	48.3
	Post	26.6	26.7	23.7	48.6
Taste-Rating Task Consumption (ml. of wine)	Pre	199	115	157	158
	Post	204	129	156	263
Locus of Control	Pre	11.9	11.6	10.8	9.5
	Post	9.9	9.5	7.1	10.2
Trait Anxiety	Pre	34.5	35.5	36.6	34.8
	Post	33.6	35.4	35.6	34.5
State Anxiety	Pre	36.5	34.4	33.9	32.8
	Post	32.1	32.7	33.7	34.2
Relaxation Ratings	Pre	0.80	1.10	.54	—
	Post	1.64	1.41	.66	—

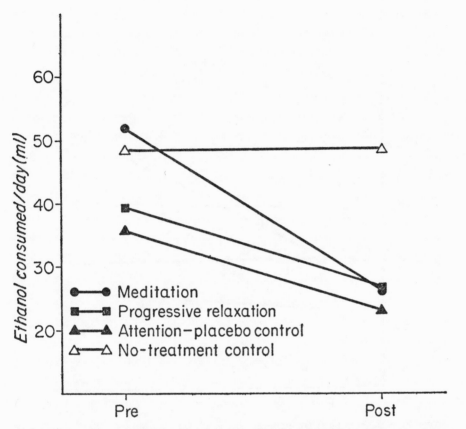

FIGURE 1. Mean daily ethanol consumption in experimental and control groups during the two weeks of baseline ("pre") and the last two weeks of treatment ("post"), reported on consumption diaries.

sumption were determined by comparing the mean daily consumption during the two-week baseline period ("pre"), with that during the last two weeks of the treatment period ("post"). As shown in Figure 1, consumption decreased in the meditation, progressive relaxation, and attention-placebo control groups, but not in the no-treatment control group. The pretreatment consumption means did not differ significantly among the groups, but the posttreatment means for the three relaxation groups were significantly different from that of the no-treatment control group. There were, however, no significant differences in the consumption

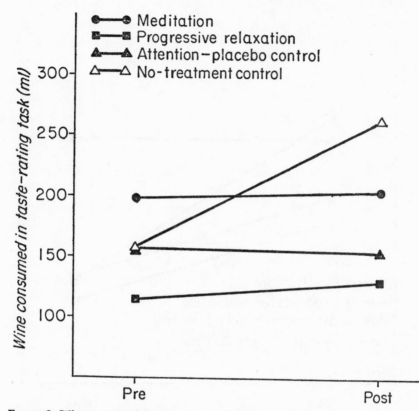

FIGURE 2. Wine consumed by experimental and control groups in pretreatment and posttreatment taste-rating tasks.

changes among the three relaxation groups. In other words, subjects who were regularly practicing a relaxation technique showed decreased alcohol consumption, whether they practiced meditation, progressive relaxation, or the attention-placebo control technique of bibliotherapy.

The results of the taste-rating task, shown in Figure 2, revealed similar group differences. Again, we found no significant differences in consumption among groups in the pretreatment task, but the no-treatment controls showed a significant increase in consumption, compared with no change in the three relaxation groups. In considering this pattern of results, it should be noted that the posttreatment taste-rating task oc-

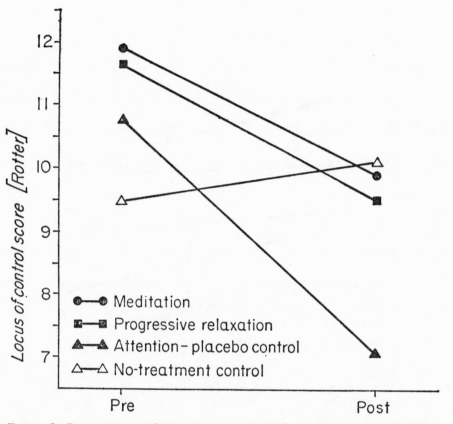

FIGURE 3. Pretreatment and posttreatment scores for experimental and control groups on Rotter's Internal-External Locus of Control Scale. Lower scores indicate a more internal locus of control.

curred just prior to final exam week, typically a period of high stress for students.

Our most interesting results on the personality measures were the changes observed in the locus of control scores (see Figure 3). In this case, decreases in the scores for the meditation and progressive relaxation groups approached significance, while the attention-placebo group showed a significant decrease, and the no-treatment controls showed an insignificant increase. In our study, then, regular practice of a relaxation procedure, including the attention-placebo control procedure, was associated

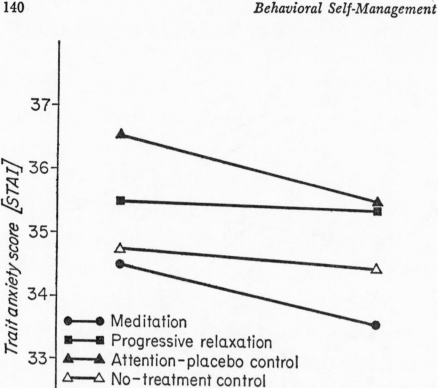

FIGURE 4. Pretreatment and posttreatment scores for experimental and control groups on the A-Trait scale of the Spielberger State-Trait Anxiety Inventory. Lower scores indicate a lower level of trait anxiety.

with shifts toward a more *internal* locus of control, indicated by lower scores on Rotter's measure. Figure 4 shows the pre and post scores on trait anxiety, which did not change significantly for any of the groups. The state anxiety scores (see Figure 5) decreased in the three relaxation groups, but increased in the no-treatment controls. Because of the large within-group variances, however, these differences among the groups did not reach significance.

Data from the daily relaxation records kept by our subjects did reveal some differences among the three relaxation conditions. The group

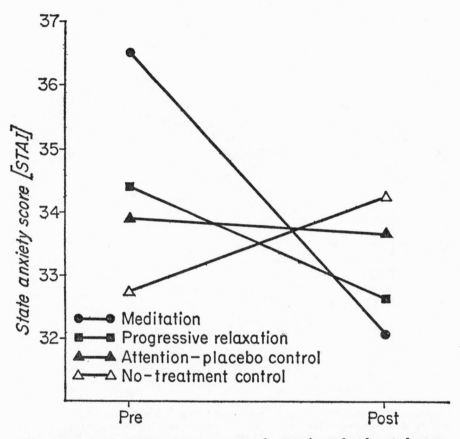

FIGURE 5. Pretreatment and posttreatment scores for experimental and control groups on the A-State scale of the Spielberger State-Trait Anxiety Inventory. Lower scores indicate a lower level of state anxiety.

means for the relaxation ratings during the first and sixth weeks of the treatment period are plotted in Figure 6. These ratings, indicating the subjective level of relaxation perceived by subjects immediately after their sessions, were not significantly different among the groups in the first week of practice. By the end of the treatment period, however, the ratings for the meditation subjects increased significantly (indicating greater relaxation), while those of the other two groups did not. The attention-placebo control subjects consistently reported the lowest levels

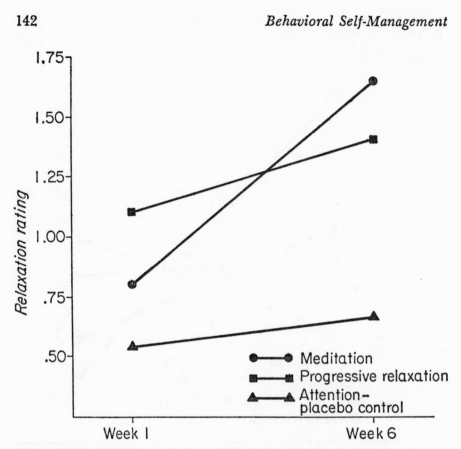

FIGURE 6. Mean relaxation ratings during the first and sixth weeks of treatment in the meditation, progressive relaxation, and attention-placebo control groups, as reported on daily relaxation records. Higher ratings indicate higher levels of relaxation experienced immediately after practicing the technique.

of relaxation throughout the treatment period. The number of relaxation sessions recorded by subjects in the three groups during the six weeks of daily practice differed only slightly; the meditation subjects reported completing 88.2% of their assigned sessions, with the progressive relaxation subjects reporting 92% and the attention-placebo controls 91%.

Eighty-two percent of the subjects who completed the treatment phase of our study also completed the seven-week follow-up phase. We had one drop-out in the meditation group, one in the progressive relaxation

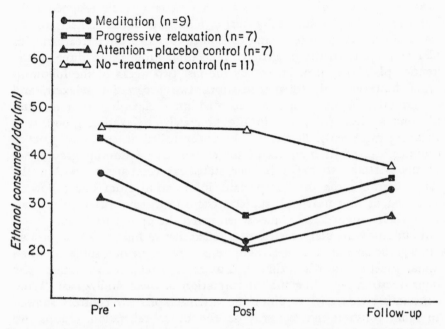

FIGURE 7. Mean daily ethanol consumption in experimental and control groups during the two weeks of baseline ("pre"), the last two weeks of treatment ("post"), and the last two weeks of follow-up, as reported on consumption diaries. Only data from subjects completing the follow-up period are included in the group means.

group, two in the attention-placebo control group, and three in the no-treatment control group. The mean daily consumption at pre- post, and follow-up for subjects completing the entire study is shown in Figure 7. During the last two weeks of the follow-up period, consumption in each of the relaxation groups increased from the posttreatment level, but was still below the pretreatment consumption level. The no-treatment controls showed a decrease in consumption at follow-up, compared with their stable pre and post levels. Although these trends appear fairly clear in Figure 7, none of the groups had a consumption level at follow-up that was significantly different from either its pre or post consumption level. The pre-post changes, however, were still significant for the relaxation groups, even in this reduced sample.

The interpretation of these follow-up data is difficult because of the optional nature of relaxation practice during this period. Most of the relaxation group subjects either stopped practicing their assigned techniques or practiced sporadically during follow-up. Seven subjects in the meditation group reported some continued practice after treatment, as did two subjects in the progressive relaxation groups and three in the attention-placebo control group. By the last two weeks of the follow-up period, however, only three meditators, two progressive relaxers, and two attention-placebo controls recorded any relaxation sessions, and only one subject (who was in the progressive relaxation group) was practicing twice daily. Because of the uncontrolled, intermittent practice schedules and small numbers of subjects in our follow-up groups, we did not attempt to make further statistical comparisons within the groups. Perhaps the most important information from our follow-up data, then, is that nearly all subjects chose to discontinue regular practice of their assigned techniques when given the option to do so.

In our study, regular practice of a relaxation technique was associated with significantly decreased alcohol consumption in our subjects; when regular practice was discontinued, consumption tended to increase. The major question regarding the interpretation of these findings is: "What is mediating this effect?" Since the attention-placebo controls showed the same consumption patterns as the other relaxation groups, we looked first for possible "nonspecific" factors common to all three groups which might answer this question.

We first explored the possibility that expectancy factors accounted for the similar consumption decrements in our meditation, progressive relaxation, and attention-placebo control groups. Although we had attempted to avoid creating an expectation or demand that drinking would decrease after relaxation training, our subjects may have assumed that we were looking for this effect, or may have expected the effect themselves, based on their own experiences or the popular "commonsense" notion that people drink more when tense. Unfortunately, our design did not include a pretreatment assessment of the subjects' expectations, the importance of which Rosen (1976b) has recently discussed. Also unfortunate was our failure to evaluate directly whether our attention-placebo control condition was actually an effective control for placebo effects, e.g., whether the rationale and procedures were as credible as those in the other groups. When faced with a choice between no data and retrospective data on these issues, we chose the latter, including items about expectation and demand factors on our follow-up questionnaire.

TABLE 2

RELATIONSHIP BETWEEN EXPECTATION & CONSUMPTION CHANGE SCORES

	SUBJECTS WITH CHANGE SCORES >MEDIAN (Greater decreases in consumption)	SUBJECTS WITH CHANGE SCORES ≤MEDIAN (Smaller or no decreases in consumption)
EXPECTED RELAXATION TO DECREASE CONSUMPTION	2	3
DID NOT EXPECT RELAXATION TO DECREASE CONSUMPTION	9	9

Since all of the subjects who participated in the follow-up period of our study returned the follow-up questionnaire, we had some data on expectancy factors for all but four of our 27 relaxation subjects. Of these 23 relaxation subjects, only five indicated that they had expected regular practice of their assigned technique to produce decreased alcohol consumption. Three of these five were attention-placebo control subjects; the other two were meditation subjects. Although these data suggest that expectation may have played a greater role in our attention-placebo condition, they do not support the hypothesis that a positive expectation produced the consumption decrements in our groups. In fact, as can be seen in Table 2, we found no evidence for a relationship between subjects' expectations and their consumption change scores.

To assess possible demand characteristics of our study, we asked each subject to indicate what he thought was the purpose of the study, and what results the experimenters were hoping to find. On the basis of their responses to these items, subjects were divided into three levels of awareness: a) "aware" subjects, who indicated that the experimenters were looking for a *decrease* in alcohol consumption after relaxation training; b) "partially aware" subjects, who stated that we were hoping to find *effects* of relaxation on consumption, but who did not indicate the expected direction of these effects; and c) "unaware" subjects, who

TABLE 3

RELATIONSHIP BETWEEN AWARENESS LEVEL & CONSUMPTION CHANGE SCORES

	SUBJECTS WITH CHANGE SCORES >MEDIAN (Greater decreases in consumption)	SUBJECTS WITH CHANGE SCORES <MEDIAN (Smaller or no decreases in consumption)
AWARE	7	6
PARTIALLY AWARE	3	4
UNAWARE	1	2

indicated either that they did not know the purpose of the study, or that we expected drinking to *increase* as a result of relaxation training. The relationship between these awareness levels and consumption change scores is shown in Table 3. Although there is a slight trend toward "aware" subjects showing greater consumption decreases than those who were "partially aware" or "unaware," this relationship is clearly too weak to support the conclusion that demand characteristics alone can account for our consumption results.

We were, of course, unable to conclusively rule out expectancy and demand effects solely on the basis of these retrospective self-report data, but we were encouraged to consider other possible answers to the question of what was mediating the consumption effects of our three relaxation procedures. One such possibility was that the observed consumption decrements were the result of some common "ingredient" in the three procedures. For example, "sitting quietly for 20 minutes twice a day" was a common element in all of the techniques. The relaxation sessions, particularly the evening session, may have simply displaced some drinking activity, or may have disrupted behavioral chains involved in drinking. Alternatively, perhaps all three relaxation techniques produced a type of relaxed state in our subjects, which in turn led to decreased drinking. This hypothesis would predict a relationship between the levels of relaxation experienced by our subjects and their alcohol con-

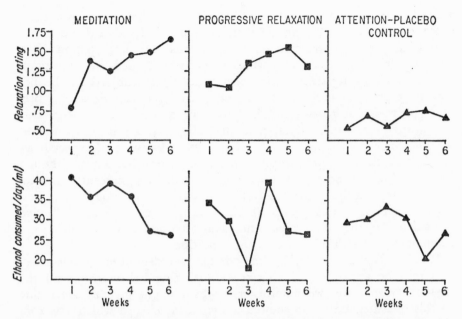

FIGURE 8. Mean relaxation ratings and mean daily ethanol consumption across the six treatment weeks in the meditation, progressive relaxation, and attention-placebo control groups, as reported on daily records.

sumption rates. Figure 8 shows the group means for relaxation ratings and alcohol consumption across the six treatment weeks. Although there is a clear correspondence between weekly levels of relaxation and consumption in the meditation group, this relationship is not so apparent in the other two groups. Within-subject correlations between weekly relaxation ratings and alcohol consumption also failed to provide strong evidence that subjectively-experienced relaxation effects mediated consumption changes in individual subjects. In our study, then, although regular practice of a relaxation technique was associated with significantly decreased alcohol consumption, the relaxation rating data did not help us understand how this effect came about.

SUMMARY AND CONCLUSIONS

The results of our study show that the regular practice of a relaxation technique, whether it is Benson's meditation procedure, progressive relaxation, or just sitting quietly and reading for two short time periods each day, leads to a significant reduction in alcohol consumption for subjects who are heavy social drinkers. The possibility that this decrease is due simply to a reactive effect, stimulated by participation in a study on drinking behavior in which subjects monitored their consumption on an ongoing daily basis, seems unlikely as subjects in the no-treatment group (who also monitored intake and completed the pre- and posttreatment measures) failed to show a similar decrement. Our follow-up questionnaire data, presented above, also call into question whether the obtained effects are mediated solely by subjects' expectancies or response to the experimental demand characteristics. Thus, although the attention-placebo group subjects did not differ significantly in alcohol consumption from the meditation and relaxation groups, it is possible that this control group (bibliotherapy) contained some "active ingredients" (other than expectation and attention factors) which were common to the two other treatment conditions.

What is there about taking time out for two 20-minute periods a day that may be associated with decreased drinking behavior? Of all the personality measures we administered which might give us some clue to this question, only one showed a significant change which was consistent with changes in alcohol consumption shown in three treatment conditions. The locus of control measure (Figure 3) showed that there was a significant shift towards the internal side of the scale for subjects in all three relaxation groups. Subjects in the no-treatment group, on the other hand, actually showed a slight increase in externality on the locus of control scale. It seems unlikely that the shift towards internality in the meditation, progressive relaxation, and bibliotherapy groups was mediated by expectancy or demand effects. How can we then explain the finding that decreased consumption is associated with increased internal control on the I-E scale?

It may be that our three treatment groups practiced techniques which all elicited a common "relaxation response" in our subjects (cf., Benson, 1975). While the exact nature of this response cannot be determined from our findings, the three treatment groups would seem to have the following characteristics in common: a) daily "time-out" periods, in which the subjects sit quietly in a calm and relaxed environment, providing an opportunity for them to reflect on the day's activities (perhaps a form of self-regulated "desensitization"); b) a feeling of taking time out for oneself, to be alone for short periods, uninterrupted by the demands and stresses of daily living (this "doing something for yourself" attitude was also stressed in the bibliotherapy procedure, as subjects were told to choose their own reading materials and avoid reading any assigned materials). It is possible, therefore, that subjects felt an increased sense of personal control as they continued to engage in these procedures over a six-week period. If heavy drinkers use alcohol to increase their sense of perceived control (Marlatt, 1976), these relaxation techniques may have provided an alternative "self-control" procedure which led to a decrease in alcohol consumption. This feeling of increased self-control may have mediated the shift towards internal locus of control on the I-E scale. Similar changes were not observed in our measures of trait or state anxiety, or in the daily ratings of relaxation. It may also be the case, of course, that subjects who are drinking less may describe themselves as having more control over their lives. Our data do not tell us which is cause and which is effect in the relationship between locus of control and alcohol consumption.

Given that all three relaxation procedures were equally effective in terms of reduced alcohol consumption, is there any reason to recommend one procedure over the others? This question assumes considerable significance if any of these techniques are to be applied as treatment procedures for problem drinkers or alcoholics.

In the context of treatment, we would like to recommend a technique which would be readily accepted by our clients, and one that they would continue to practice over long periods of time. It is clear from our own data that although all three techniques were equally effective during the six-week treatment period, the majority of subjects discontinued their practice of the technique during the follow-up period. There is, however, some reason to believe that the meditation group subjects were more "hooked" on the technique than subjects in the other two conditions. As reported earlier, more meditation subjects continued some practice of the procedure of their own volition during follow-up than in any other group. Secondly, as is evident from inspection of Figure 8, the subjects in the meditation group were the only ones who reported a linear increase in daily relaxation reports over the six-week treatment period (associated with a linear decrease in consumption). These data suggest that the meditation subjects were becoming more and more "relaxed" as the treatment period continued. If these findings are representative of meditation techniques in general, it would appear that this procedure is more intrinsically reinforcing or satisfying than the other techniques we investigated. In support of this hypothesis, Glueck and

Stroebel (1975) have reported that patients who were taught progressive relaxation discontinued practice of the technique soon after instruction because it was considered rather laborious and a more difficult procedure than TM. Based on these observations, meditation may be a more effective self-control technique because it is easy to do and intrinsically more satisfying, and thus would be practiced over a longer period of time than the other relaxation methods.

We included four subjects who described themselves as problem drinkers in our sample. Each of these was assigned to a different treatment condition in our study. Examination of the findings for these few subjects may illustrate the relative effectiveness of the different relaxation techniques as potential treatment procedures for alcoholism. The subject assigned to the meditation condition showed the largest drop in daily consumption of all four subjects: a decrease of 66% in daily consumption (absolute drop of 126 ml of pure alcohol a day, from baseline to the treatment period). The other problem drinkers showed drops of 29% (progressive relaxation), 32% (bibliotherapy), and 34% (no-treatment control). Of these four, the only subjects who continued practice of their technique during the follow-up period were the ones assigned to the meditation and progressive relaxation groups. Although these results are certainly speculative, they suggest that meditation may be the best option for alcoholism treatment among the relaxation procedures we evaluated in our study.

There is one additional reason why meditation may be the relaxation treatment method of choice with problem drinkers or alcoholics. Much of the research literature reviewed earlier in this paper strongly suggests that meditation does produce an altered state of consciousness which is qualitatively different from other conscious states, although recent studies have questioned this finding (e.g., Pagano et al., 1976). Numerous reports from meditators describe this altered state as a kind of "high" or pleasant affective experience. It is also clear that most problem drinkers consume alcohol to alter their own consciousness, to get "stoned" or "high" on booze. In the search for alternatives to alcohol, meditation seems to offer the drinker a non-drug "high" which offers none of the drawbacks of excessive drinking. Some alcoholics may, in fact, be searching for a sense of new meaning in their lives by altering their consciousness through ingestion of a drug: the "spirits" in the bottle. The fact that Alcoholics Anonymous is so effective with many alcoholics may be due, in part, to the spiritual orientation and underpinnings of the A.A. philosophy. Meditation may offer a similar experience.

Which form of meditation to recommend? While research may eventually show that the various forms are equivalent in terms of their overall effectiveness, at this stage of development it would seem that TM has the most to offer the problem drinker. The nonspecific effects of TM, which we tried to control for in our own design by employing the relatively neutral Benson technique, may serve to increase the likelihood that the alcoholic would benefit from the meditation experience. The positive expectancies engendered by the introductory lectures and the initiation ceremony, the commitment incurred by paying the course fee, the mutual enthusiasm and group support which the TM instruction offers (not unlike the enthusiasm and social reinforcement which characterize A.A.), and the availability of follow-up and "checking" provided, all combine to increase the probability that the alcoholic will continue the practice of the technique. Whether or not this form of meditation will prove itself to be an effective substitute for drinking remains to be empirically demonstrated.

REFERENCES

AVERILL, J. R.: Personal control over aversive stimuli and its relationship to stress. *Psychological Bulletin,* 1973, 80, 286-303.

BANQUET, J. P.: Spectral analysis of the EEG in meditation. *EEG and Clinical Neurophysiology,* 1973, 35, 143-151.

BEARY, J. F. and BENSON, H.: A simple psychophysiologic technique which elicits the hypometabolic changes of the relaxation response. *Psychosomatic Medicine,* 1974, 36, 115-120.

BENSON, H.: Decreased alcohol intake associated with the practice of meditation: A retrospective investigation. *Annals of the New York Academy of Sciences,* 1974, 233, 174-177.

BENSON, H.: *The Relaxation Response.* New York: William Morrow & Co., 1975.

BENSON, H., ROSNER, B. A., MARZETTA, B. R., and KLEMCHUK, H. M.: Decreased blood pressure in pharmacologically treated hypertensive patients who regularly elicited the relaxation response. *Lancet,* 1974, i, 289-291.

BENSON, H. and WALLACE, R. K.: Decreased drug abuse with Transcendental Meditation: A study of 1,862 subjects. In C. J. D. Zarafonetis (Ed.), *Drug Abuse: Proceedings of the International Conference.* Philadelphia, Pa.: Lea and Febiger, 1972.

BLOOMFIELD, H. H., CAIN, M. P., JAFFE, D. T., and KORY, R.B.: *TM: Discovering Inner Energy and Overcoming Stress.* New York: Dell, 1975.

BOUDREAU, L.: Transcendental Meditation and Yoga as reciprocal inhibitors. *Journal of Behavioral Therapy and Experimental Psychiatry,* 1972, 3, 97-98.

CAHALAN, D., CISIN, I. H., and CROSSLEY, H. M.: *American Drinking Practices: A Na-*

tional Study of Drinking Behavior and Patterns. New Brunswick, N.J.: Rutgers Center of Alcohol Studies, Monograph No. 6, 1969.

CAHALAN, D. and ROOM, R.: *Problem Drinking Among American Men.* New Brunswick, N.J.: Rutgers Center of Alcohol Studies, Monograph No. 7, 1974.

CAPPELL, H.: An evaluation of tension models of alcohol consumption. In R. J. Gibbins, Y. Israel, H. Kalant, R. E. Popham, W. Schmidt, and R. G. Smart (Eds.), *Research Advances in Alcohol and Drug Problems* (Vol. 2). New York: Wiley, 1975.

CAPPELL, H. and HERMAN, C. P.: Alcohol and tension reduction: A review. *Quarterly Journal of Studies on Alcohol,* 1972, 33, 33-64.

CARRINGTON, P. and EPHRON, H. S.: Meditation as an adjunct to psychotherapy. In S. Arieti (Ed.), *New Dimensions in Psychiatry: A World View.* New York: Wiley, 1975.

CONGER, J. J.: Alcoholism: Theory, problem and challenge. II. Reinforcement theory and the dynamics of alcoholism. *Quarterly Journal of Studies on Alcohol,* 1956, 17, 296-305.

DENNISTON, D. and McWILLIAMS, P.: *The TM Book.* New York: Warner Books, 1975.

GLUECK, B. C. and STROEBEL, C. F.: Biofeedback and meditation in the treatment of psychiatric illness. *Comprehensive Psychiatry,* 1975, 16, 303-321.

GOLDFRIED, M. R.: Systematic desensitization as training in self-control. *Journal of Consulting and Clinical Psychology,* 1971, 37, 228-235.

GOLEMAN, D.: Meditation as meta-therapy: Hypotheses toward a proposed fifth state of consciousness. *Journal of Transpersonal Psychology,* 1971, 3, 1-25.

HIGGINS, R. L. and MARLATT, G. A.: Fear of interpersonal evaluation as a determinant of alcohol consumption in male social drinkers. *Journal of Abnormal Psychology,* 1975, 84, 664-651.

HJELLE, L. A.: Transcendental Meditation and psychological health. *Perceptual and Motor Skills,* 1974, 39, 623-628.

JACOBSON, E.: *Progressive Relaxation.* Chicago: University of Chicago Press, 1938.

MANDLER, G. and WATSON, D. L.: Anxiety and the interruption of behavior. In C. D. Spielberger (Ed.), *Anxiety and Behavior.* New York: Academic Press, 1966.

MARLATT, G. A.: Alcohol, stress, and cognitive control. In I. G. Sarason and C. D. Spielberger (Eds.), *Stress and Anxiety* (Vol. 3). Washington, D.C.: Hemisphere Publishing Co., 1976.

MARLATT, G. A., DEMMING, B., and REID, J. B.: Loss of control drinking in alcoholics: An experimental analogue. *Journal of Abnormal Psychology,* 1973, 81, 233-241.

MARLATT, G. A., KOSTURN, C. F. and LANG, A. R.: Provocation to anger and opportunity for retaliation as determinants of alcohol consumption in social drinkers. *Journal of Abnormal Psychology,* 1975, 34, 652-659.

MARLATT, G. A. and NATHAN, P. E. (Eds.), *Behavioral Approaches to the Assessment and Treatment of Alcoholism.* New Brunswick, N.J.: Center of Alcohol Studies, Rutgers University, 1977.

MARLATT, G. A., PAGANO, R. R., ROSE, R. M., and MARQUES, J. K.: The effects of meditation and relaxation upon alcohol consumption in male social drinkers. Unpublished research, University of Washington, 1976.

MEICHENBAUM, D.: Self-instructional methods. In F. H. Kanfer and A. P. Goldstein (Eds.), *Helping People Change.* New York: Pergamon, 1975.

MILLER, P. M., HERSEN, M., EISLER, R. M., and HILSMAN, G.: Effects of social stress on operant drinking of alcoholics and social drinkers. *Behavior Research and Therapy,* 1974, 12, 67-72.

NIDICH, S., SEEMAN, W., and DRESKIN, T.: Influence of Transcendental Meditation:

A replication. *Journal of Counseling Psychology,* 1973, 20, 656-666.

ORNSTEIN, R. E.: *The Psychology of Consciousness.* New York: Viking, 1972.

PAGANO, R. R., ROSE, R. M., STEVENS, R. M., and WARRENBURG, S.: Sleep during Transcendental Meditation. *Science,* 1976, 191, 308-309.

PHARES, E. J.: *Locus of Control in Personality.* Morristown, N.J.: General Learning Press, 1976.

PIRSIG, R. M.: *Zen and the Art of Motorcycle Maintenance.* New York: William Morrow & Co., 1974.

ROSEN, G. M.: A manual for self-administered progressive relaxation. In J. P. Flanders (Ed.), *Practical Psychology.* New York: Harper & Row, 1976. (a)

ROSEN, G. M.: Subjects' initial therapeutic expectancies and subjects' awareness of therapeutic goals in systematic desensitization: A review. *Behavior Therapy,* 1976, 7, 14-27. (b)

ROTTER, J. B.: Generalized expectancies for internal versus external control of reinforcement. *Psychological Monographs,* 1966, 80, No. 1 (Whole No. 609).

SCHWARTZ, G. E.: TM relaxes some people and makes them feel better. *Psychology Today,* 1974, 7, 39-44.

SEEMAN, W., NIDICH, S., and BANTA, T.: Influence of Transcendental Meditation on a measure of self-actualization. *Journal of Counseling Psychology,* 1972, 19, 184-187.

SELLS, S. B.: On the nature of stress. In J. E. McGrath (Ed.), *Social and Psychological Factors in Stress.* New York: Holt, Rinehart & Winston, 1970.

SHAFII, M., LAVELY, R., and JAFFE, R.: Meditation and the prevention of alcohol abuse. *American Journal of Psychiatry,* 1975, 132, 942-945.

SHOSTROM, E. L.: *Personal Orientation Inventory: An Inventory for the Measurement of Self-Actualization.* San Diego: Educational and Industrial Testing Service, 1966.

SMITH, A.: *Powers of Mind.* New York: Random House, 1975.

SMITH, J. C.: Meditation as psychotherapy: A review of the literature. *Psychological Bulletin,* 1975, 82, 558-564.

SPIELBERGER, C. D., GORSUCH, R. L., and LUSHENE, R. E.: *Manual for the State-Trait Anxiety Inventory.* Palo Alto, Ca.: Consulting Psychologist Press, 1970.

STEK, R. J. and BASS, B. A.: Personal adjustment and perceived locus of control among students interested in meditation. *Psychological Reports,* 1973, 32, 1019-1022.

WALLACE, R. K. and BENSON, H.: The physiology of meditation. *Scientific American,* 1972, 226, 85-90.

WATTS, A.: The art of meditation. In J. White (Ed.), *What Is Meditation?* Garden City, N.Y.: Anchor Books, 1974.

WHITE, J.: *Everything You Wanted to Know about TM Including How to Do It.* New York: Pocket Books, 1976.

6
Behavioral Self-Control Training in the Treatment of Problem Drinkers

WILLIAM R. MILLER

For the past 30 years the treatment of problem drinkers has been guided primarily by a single model: the so-called "disease concept" of alcoholism (Alcoholics Anonymous, 1955; Jellinek, 1960). Although interpretations of this model have varied, its proponents have almost universally endorsed two basic assumptions: a) that alcoholism involves an irreversible disease-like progression of symptoms; and b) that total abstinence is the only acceptable goal of treatment because alcoholics are incapable of regaining (or maintaining) control over drinking (Gitlow, 1973; Zwerling & Rosenbaum, 1959).

There are, to be sure, medical aspects of alcohol abuse. The toll taken by excessive drinking upon the human body and brain is becoming increasingly clear. The phenomenon of pharmacological addiction to alcohol is unquestionable. The physical effects of alcohol may even follow a fairly predictable sequence, as in progressive damage to the liver and brain (Miller, 1976a; Miller & Orr, 1976). This sequence is not to be confused with the behavioral progression predicted by the traditional disease model, however, and does not necessarily validate the assumptions of irreversibility and inevitability of loss of control. A large and growing body of research, reviewed elsewhere, has seriously questioned the general applicability of a unitary disease model (Armor, Polich, & Stambul, 1976; Lloyd & Salzberg, 1975; Miller, 1976a, 1976b; Pattison, Sobell, & Sobell, in press; Sobell & Sobell, 1974, 1975; Miller &

154

Caddy, in press). This research has amply demonstrated a) that at least some diagnosed alcoholics do not manifest loss of control or craving when given alcohol under experimental or surreptitious conditions; b) that varying percentages of "alcoholics" drink moderately and without problems following treatment; and c) that improvement on life adjustment measures is not limited to abstinent cases, and may be unrelated to abstinence in some populations.

These findings suggest at least the possibility of controlled drinking as an explicit goal for treatment. The feasibility of this approach has been further supported by the apparent success of early treatment efforts to inculcate controlled drinking (e.g., Lovibond & Caddy, 1970; Sobell & Sobell, 1973, 1976). Several recent reviews have enumerated and discussed a variety of proposed methods for the reduction and control of alcohol use (Briddell & Nathan, 1975; Hamburg, 1975; Lloyd & Salzberg, 1975; P. M. Miller, in press; Miller, 1976b; Nathan, 1976). Although still experimental, these therapeutic methods show considerable promise and some possible advantages. Problem drinkers may, for example, be willing to enter a control-oriented program at a much earlier stage than if abstinence were the only available goal, thus improving prognosis. Controlled drinking therapies may also be beneficial to clients who repeatedly fail to attain abstinence, and may even indirectly help to convince other clients that abstinence is the only possible course for them (Miller & Caddy, in press).

Three studies exploring the outcome of various controlled drinking therapies will be described. Our first study (Miller, 1976c) compared the effectiveness of three procedures for teaching self-control to problem drinkers. A second study (Miller, Gribskov, & Mortell, 1976) evaluated the effectiveness of a self-help manual with and without the assistance of a therapist. The third study (Miller, Pechacek, & Hamburg, 1976) explored the feasibility of a group treatment program based upon a revised self-control manual for problem drinkers (Miller & Muñoz, 1976).

STUDY 1

Although a number of treatment procedures have been proposed for the control of overdrinking (Miller, 1976b), little is known about their relative effectiveness and few guidelines have been provided for selecting among these modalities. Our first study was designed to provide information about the relative efficacy of three therapeutic approaches to controlled drinking:

1) *Aversive Counterconditioning (AC)*, consisting of ten weekly half-hour sessions of shock aversion. These sessions were conducted in a simulated bar setting, where the client self-administered finger shocks (0-5 ma) on a partial punishment schedule. A session included 40-50 shocks paired with holding and sniffing (but not tasting) favorite beverages. A therapist supervised all sessions.

2) *Behavioral Self-Control Training (BT)*, which involved detailed record keeping by clients of all drinks consumed. These records were discussed during ten weekly half-hour sessions designed to a) identify stimulus antecedents of drinking; b) teach specific rate control methods for slowing drinking; and c) identify desired effects of alcohol and find alternative methods for achieving these effects (Miller & Muñoz, 1976).

3) *Controlled Drinking Composite (CD)*, an extensive and expensive treatment package consisting of ten weekly sessions of two to three hours each. The CD program included a) discriminated aversive counterconditioning (Lovibond & Caddy, 1970); b) training in the estimation of blood alcohol concentration through the use of external cues (Huber, Karlin, & Nathan, 1976; Miller & Muñoz, 1976); c) in-session drinking with directed practice and avoidance learning of rate control (Sobell & Sobell, 1973); and d) behavioral self-control training similar to that offered to BT clients.

All three treatments were conducted by trained paraprofessional therapists. Clients in all three groups kept daily record cards as a source of outcome data, although no use was made of these within AC sessions. Further details regarding treatment procedures and the training of therapists are reported by Miller (1976c).

A total of 46 persons were treated in this first study, conducted at the University of Oregon. Twenty-nine were self-referred clients with an average age of 37.3, who had been having problems related to drinking for 10.7 years. The other 17 clients were selected referrals from the courts (following conviction of driving while intoxicated), with a mean age of 35.8 and a mean problem drinking history of 7.7 years. Fifteen clients were women. All clients were randomly assigned to treatment groups and to therapists.

Outcome

The primary dependent variables for assessing alcohol consumption were obtained from three sources: a) clients' self-reports during assessment interviews; b) reports of significant others; and c) clients' daily

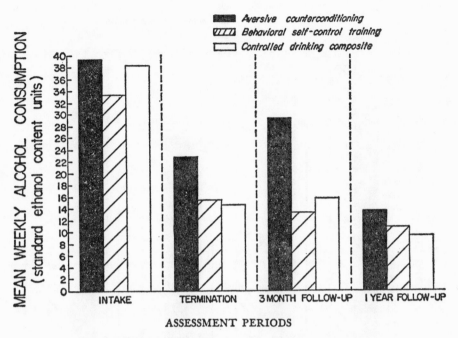

FIGURE 1. Mean self-report of weekly alcohol consumption.

record cards. Information from all of these sources was translated into a standardized unit of alcohol consumption, the Standard Ethanol Content (SEC). One SEC is that amount of any beverage containing one-half ounce (15 ml) of pure ethanol. This is equal to approximately 12 ounces (360 ml) of beer (4% ethanol), or 4 ounces (120 ml) of table wine (12% ethanol), or 2½ ounces (75 ml) of fortified wine (20% ethanol), or 1 ounce (30 ml) of 100 proof distilled spirits (50% ethanol).

Clients' self-reports of alcohol consumption at intake, termination, a three-month and a one-year follow-up are reported in Figure 1. A repeated measures analysis of variance showed a significant decrease in the drinking of all groups over the course of treatment and follow-up, as well as a significant difference among treatment methods. Thus, although all groups showed decreased alcohol consumption, the greatest initial improvement was evidenced by clients in the BT and CD groups, and least improved were clients in the AC group. By the one-year follow-up, however, the AC group had shown improvement comparable to that

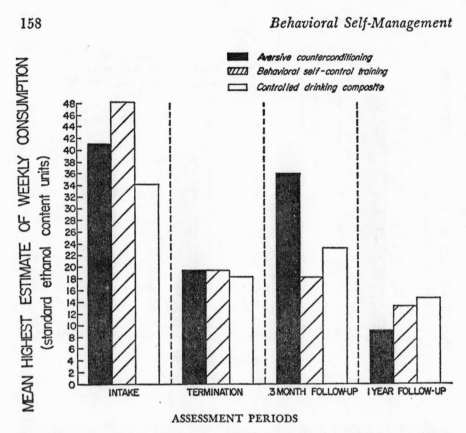

FIGURE 2. Mean highest estimate from significant others of clients' weekly alcohol consumption.

of BT and CD groups. As will be seen, this general pattern of findings extends across measures of outcome.

The *reports of significant others* provided corroborative information. When estimates of drinking rate were available from more than one significant other (we tried to reach three in each case), the highest estimate was used. These highest estimates by significant others were reported in Figure 2. The pattern is similar to that of self-report, although significant others consistently reported higher consumption rates than did the clients themselves. This discrepancy was larger by far among court-referred clients.

Further indices of drinking were obtained from a more detailed source, the *daily record cards*. These cards provided a drink-by-drink narrative

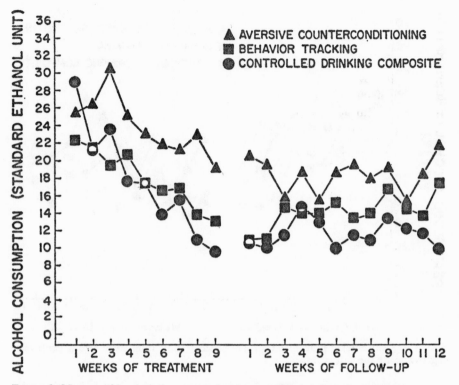

FIGURE 3. Mean weekly alcohol consumption from daily record cards during treatment and follow-up.

of at least 22 consecutive weeks of treatment and follow-up. From these cards it was possible to determine weekly alcohol consumption (in SECs) and to estimate the highest Blood Alcohol Concentration (BAC) point reached during each week (for calculation procedures see Miller & Muñoz, 1976). Graphic representations of these two variables are presented in Figures 3 and 4, respectively. These data were submitted both to analysis of variance and to time-series analysis. These analyses revealed significant decreases in the weekly consumption and BAC of each and all groups, but no significant differences among treatment groups.

Improvement ratings were devised to provide a convenient, if somewhat oversimplified, condensation of these complex results. The criteria for ratings are reported by Miller (1976a) and included consideration of a) percent reduction in drinking; b) consistency among data sources; and

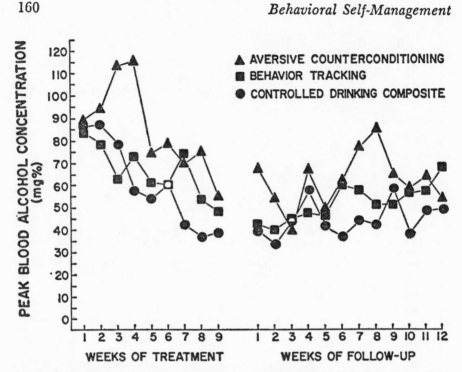

FIGURE 4. Mean weekly peak blood alcohol concentration from daily record cards during treatment and follow-up.

c) conformity of consumption pattern with a controlled style of drinking. Because nine clients (eight of whom had been court-referred) met the criteria for "controlled drinking" *before* treatment began, two special categories of "controlled-improved" and "controlled-no change" were included. The remaining 37 clients, problem drinkers at intake, were rated as considerably, moderately, slightly, or not improved. Abstaining clients are reported separately but are regarded as "considerably improved." Improvement ratings of all clients available for assessment at termination, three-month and one-year follow-ups are reported in Table 1. Consistent with other measures of outcome, these data show AC to have been least effective initially, with BT and CD demonstrating approximately equal effectiveness throughout the study.

A variety of other measures, not reported in detail here, were used to assess *general psychological functioning*. These measures supported the overall pattern described above for indices of drinking. All groups showed

TABLE 1

Number and Percentage of Clients Assigned to Each Improvement Rating at Termination and Follow-Ups

Improvement Rating	At Termination			At 3-month Follow-Up			At 1-year Follow-Up		
	AC	BT	CD	AC	BT	CD	AC	BT	CD
Problem Drinkers at Intake									
Abstinent	0	0	2 (15%)	0	1 (07%)	2 (15%)	2 (20%)	1 (07%)	1 (08%)
Considerably Improved	4 (40%)	8 (57%)	8 (62%)	3 (30%)	9 (64%)	4 (31%)	3 (30%)	7 (50%)	5 (38%)
Moderately Improved	3 (30%)	3 (21%)	3 (23%)	2 (20%)	3 (21%)	3 (23%)	2 (20%)	3 (21%)	1 (08%)
Slightly Improved	0	2 (14%)	0	1 (10%)	0	0	0	1 (07%)	1 (08%)
Not improved	3 (30%)	1 (07%)	0	4 (40%)	1 (07%)	2 (15%)	1 (10%)	0	1 (08%)
Insufficient Data	0	0	0	0	0	2 (15%)	2 (20%)	2 (14%)	4 (31%)
Controlled Drinkers at Intake									
Improved	2	2	1	1	1	1	0	0	1
No Change	2	1	1	3	2	1	4	3	1

AC = Aversive Counterconditioning
BT = Behavioral Self-Control Training
CD = Control Drinking Composite

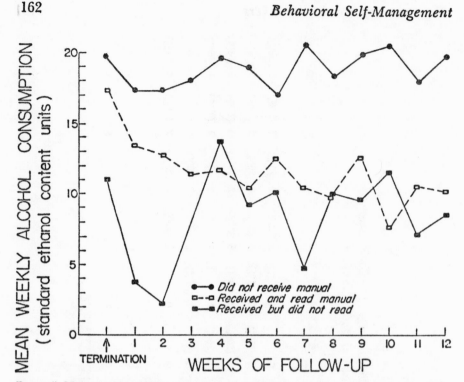

FIGURE 5. Mean weekly alcohol consumption during follow-up of clients with and without the self-help maintenance manual.

significant improvement on five of six subscales of the Profile of Mood States (POMS) (McNair, Lorr, & Droppelman, 1971) and on eight of the ten clinical subscales of the Minnesota Multiphasic Personality Inventory (Hathaway & McKinley, 1943). All three groups also showed a significant change in the "internal" direction on Rotter's (1966) Locus of Control Scale following treatment. Without exception, the AC group showed least improvement on these variables. Particularly curious was the finding that, although all three groups showed improvement on the POMS over the course of treatment, the AC group had "relapsed" to baseline levels by the three-month follow-up whereas BT and CD groups showed continued improvement in mood states.

Evaluation of a Manual Designed to Improve Maintenance

A 61-page self-help manual (Miller & Muñoz, 1975) was designed to improve maintenance of treatment gains by a) reviewing self-control procedures relevant to drinking; and b) elaborating upon alternatives to the use of alcohol (e.g., progressive relaxation training). For each client a random decision (coin toss) was made to determine whether or not he or she would receive a copy of the manual at termination. The relative maintenance of manual vs. no-manual clients was then assessed during the three-month follow-up period. Clients who did not receive the manual at termination were given copies following their three-month follow-up interviews.

At termination 26 clients were given the manual and 20 were not. Of those who received the manual, 17 indicated at follow-up that they had read all or parts of it, and the nine others indicated that they had not read it or had only skimmed it. The mean weekly alcohol consumption of these three groups over the course of follow-up is shown in Figure 5.

Statistical comparisons were made between clients who read the manual and clients who did not receive it, recognizing that non-random selection processes contributed to the membership of the former group. Analyses of variance revealed no difference between groups at the beginning of the follow-up period (when manuals were distributed). At the end of the three-month follow-up, however, significant differences were reflected in two-way ($p < .05$) and in repeated measures ($p < .001$) analyses of variance. Similar results obtained for estimated weekly peak BAC. Thus, the maintenance manual appears to have been somewhat helpful to clients in continuing a controlled style of drinking. Although the effect was a small one, the use of a self-control manual is a very economical procedure, and may thus be justifiable for even small increments in improvement and maintenance (Christensen, Miller, & Muñoz, in press).

A somewhat surprising aspect of these data is the low level of alcohol use displayed by clients who received but did not read the manual. One might expect these to have been "less motivated" and perhaps less successful clients. It appears, however, that clients who "did not bother" to read the manual were those who had already achieved a considerable degree of self-control by the time of termination. The low mean drinking level is particularly noteworthy because this group includes no abstainers.

Discussion

The pattern of outcome for our three treatment groups was quite consistent across measures. All groups showed significant reduction in alcohol use, but the AC group was consistently least improved of the three prior to the one-year follow-up. The BT and CD groups were approximately equal in effectiveness throughout the study. This pattern also obtained on indices of psychological functioning. These findings argue against the use of aversion therapy alone in the treatment of problem drinking.

These data provide no basis for choosing between BT and CD with regard to effectiveness. There are, however, important differences in the pragmatics of these two treatment methods that argue for the use of BT, all else being equal. The CD program as we offered it required six times the amount of therapist contact, expensive equipment, an experimental bar setting, the use of electric shock, and the consumption of alcohol within the treatment setting. The BT mode requires no special equipment or setting, and is more amenable to a variety of delivery modes including group therapy, classroom and media presentation, and self-instruction. Although the difference in effectiveness is small, the contrast in cost-effectiveness is substantial. The lack of difference between BT and CD modes is also noteworthy because the latter included virtually all of the components of the former. Apparently the additional components in CD (e.g., aversion therapy, rate-control practice with in-session drinking and avoidance learning) added little to the basic self-control training program.

STUDY 2

Study 1 encouraged us to continue the development of a behavioral self-control training program for problem drinkers. Self-control procedures similar to those employed in the BT group have been included in several effective "broad spectrum" treatment programs (Hamburg, 1975; Lloyd & Salzberg, 1975; Miller, 1976b). Our own findings and those of Caddy and Lovibond (1976) suggested to us that the self-control training methods might be a critical nucleus in such multimodal programs. Our interest in replicating the effectiveness of self-control training alone, and the limited success of our first self-help manual suggested a second study. Could a self-control manual effectively teach clients both the principles needed to reduce drinking and the skills to maintain controlled drinking? How much advantage would there be in learning self-control from a therapist instead of from a self-help manual? We addressed these questions in Study 2 by randomly assigning self-referred clients to one of two treatment conditions:

1) *Manual Only*. The 16 clients in this group were interviewed and were then provided with a copy of the manual and a supply of self-monitoring cards. Each week for ten weeks the clients returned their record cards in mailers we provided. After ten weeks they were contacted by mail and asked to complete several questionnaires. The mail contact was repeated after another three months had elapsed. Significant others were telephoned at each assessment point for corroborative information.

2) *Manual Plus Therapist*. The 15 clients in this group received the same interview, manual, and self-monitoring cards. In addition they were assigned to a paraprofessional therapist with whom they met for 30 minutes each week for 10 weeks. Treatment closely paralleled the BT therapy of Study 1. Assessment times and instruments were identical to those for the Manual Only group. The paraprofessionals were two women who had been trained and had served as therapists during Study 1. (Four other clients assigned to this group failed to complete more than one treatment and were excluded from analyses.)

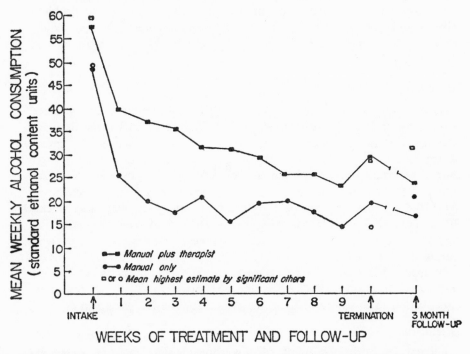

FIGURE 6. Mean weekly alcohol consumption of clients with and without therapist contact.

TABLE 2

Number and Percentage of Clients Assigned to Each Improvement
Rating at Termination and Follow-up

Improvement Rating	At Termination		At 3-Month Follow-Up	
	Manual Only	Therapist	Manual Only	Therapist
Problem Drinkers at Intake				
Abstinent	2 (17%)	2 (14%)	3 (25%)	1 (07%)
Considerably Improved	4 (33%)	5 (36%)	5 (42%)	6 (43%)
Moderately Improved	3 (25%)	5 (36%)	2 (17%)	4 (29%)
Slightly Improved	1 (08%)	2 (14%)	1 (08%)	1 (07%)
Not Improved	0	0	1 (08%)	1 (07%)
Insufficient Data	2 (17%)	0	0	1 (07%)
Controlled Drinkers Intake				
Improved	1	1	1	0
No Change	3	0	3	1

The average age of clients in this study was 40.4, with a mean problem
drinking history of 9.3 years. Eight clients were women. Further details
regarding the design of Study 2 are reported by Miller, Gribskov, and
Mortell (1976).

Outcome

As in Study 1, separate indices of drinking behavior were obtained
from self-report, significant others, and daily records. All three domains
reflected a significant decrease in alcohol consumption over the course
of treatment and follow-up. Alcohol consumption data from all three
sources are graphically displayed in Figure 6. Analyses of variance yielded
significant repeated measures effects for self-report of alcohol consumption
($p < .001$), highest report of significant others ($p < .001$), and weekly
SECs reported on self-monitoring cards ($p < .025$) over the course of
treatment. No significant differences between treatment groups were
found.

Improvement ratings were assigned to each client, following the criteria used in Study 1. These ratings, reported in Table 2, reflect an
effectiveness rate comparable to that found for the BT group in Study 1.

Discussion

Clients in both treatment groups showed significant improvement
in weekly alcohol consumption across three measurement domains. No

significant differences between the Manual Only and Manual Plus Therapist groups were found on any measure of outcome. Differences that did exist between the two groups tended to favor the Manual Only treatment. Thus, the consultation of a paraprofessional therapist provided no apparent gains beyond those obtainable from use of the manual alone.

STUDY 3

Our first study encouraged us that behavioral self-control training is a feasible and effective method for helping at least some problem drinkers to attain and maintain moderation. This was further supported by Study 2, which indicated that a self-control manual can be effectively used in a self-help program and by paraprofessional therapists as the basis for individual consultation. A third possible format for self-management training would be presentation in a group or classroom setting, where consultation is available but only minimal therapist contact is required. Group presentation would seem to be an efficient use of therapist time, and modeling and vicarious learning from other group members may promote additional gains. The utility of group self-control training for problem drinkers was explored in our third study (Miller, Pechacek, & Hamburg, 1976).

An experimental class in the self-control of alcohol use was announced through news media in Palo Alto and San Jose, California. The class was described as being for people "who are having life problems related to drinking but who have not yet reached a point of no return." A total of 35 persons inquired about the class, completed an initial assessment interview, and entered the program. No applicants were excluded from the program. Applicants were assigned to one of four classes, determined by proximity of the date of intake and the starting date of a class. The enrollment of each class was limited to ten students, plus significant others who wished to attend. Classes began sequentially (one each month for four months) and were led by clinical psychology interns (Ph.D. level) at the Palo Alto Veterans Administration Hospital. The author conducted the first group and supervised the progress of subsequent groups.

All students completed an initial one-hour interview, attended a group orientation meeting, kept two weeks of baseline data on daily record cards, and provided the names of two significant others who could provide corroborative information. Following these prerequisites, students began the ten-session class.

Class meetings were held in the lounge of a local community center that sponsors an ongoing program of adult education. The "textbook" for the course was an enlarged and revised version of the self-control manual used in our first two studies (Miller & Muñoz, 1976). The class meetings, which followed the organization of the textbook, covered the following topics:

Session 1: Overview of the course and goal-setting
Session 2: Rate control training
Session 3: Training in self-reinforcement
Session 4: Introduction to stimulus control principles
Session 5: Functional analysis of drinking
Session 6: Individual consultations regarding present self-control
Session 7: Introduction to alternatives to drinking
Session 8: Alternatives—Progressive relaxation training
Session 9: Alternatives—Assertiveness and communication
Session 10: Final assessment and course evaluation.

All sessions lasted for 90 minutes. The entire treatment program requires less than two hours of therapist time per student.

Seven of the original 35 applicants failed to attend more than two class sessions, and were not included in the data reported here. The average age of the 28 clients considered "treated" was 44.8, with a mean problem drinking history of 8.6 years. Ten clients were women.

Outcome

Alcohol use was assessed by measures identical to those employed in Study 2. Students' mean weekly alcohol consumption, according to self-report, reports of significant others, and daily record cards, is presented in Figure 7. The improvement ratings of students at termination and at three-month follow-up are provided in Table 3. On the whole, improvement appears comparable to that observed in our first two studies, indicating that a group presentation format is feasible.

DISCUSSION

Three studies have been presented, encompassing the treatment of 105 individuals within five separate behavioral modalities. Taken together these studies support the feasibility of controlled drinking in

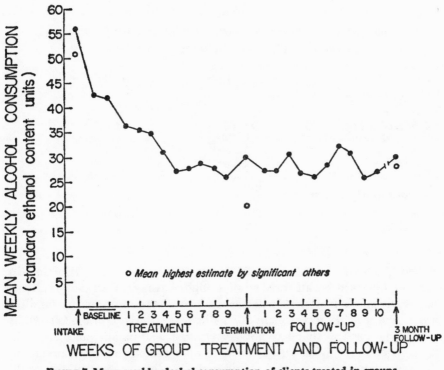

FIGURE 7. Mean weekly alcohol consumption of clients treated in groups.

general, and of behavioral self-control training in particular in the treatment of problem drinkers. Our findings converge with those of other researchers (e.g., Bellack, Rozencsky & Schwartz, 1974; Caddy & Lovibond, 1976; McFall & Hamman, 1971; Stuart, 1967) to support the utility of self-monitoring and of functional analysis training as basic elements within a self-management program for behavioral excesses. Certainly this approach is deserving of further study as a treatment method for problem drinkers. A relatively economical procedure oriented toward control rather than abstinence, it offers considerable promise as an *early* intervention method.

Methodological Problems

Several problems with the above-discussed research should be noted. First all three studies were essentially uncontrolled, providing no un-

TABLE 3

Number and Percentage of Clients Assigned to Each Improvement
Rating at Termination and Follow-Up

Improvement Rating	At Termination	At 3-Month Follow-Up
Problem Drinkers at Intake		
Abstinent	0	0
Considerably Improved	11 (41%)	13 (48%)
Moderately Improved	8 (30%)	6 (22%)
Slightly Improved	5 (19%)	2 (07%)
Not Improved	2 (07%)	4 (15%)
Insufficient Data	1 (04%)	2 (07%)
Controlled Drinkers at Intake		
Improved	0	0
No Change	1	1

treated groups for comparison. It is conceivable that the reduction in
drinking observed on all three studies might have occurred even if clients
had received no treatment whatsoever. Here we encounter the familiar
Scylla of withholding treatment from clients seeking it, and the Charybdis
of offering therapy that has not been tested against adequate controls.
My own choice, obviously, has been to offer some form of treatment to
all clients requesting it. I had considered a waiting-list control, but could
not justify the three- to four-month delay it would have required. It has
been my experience that problem drinkers are often at a critical point
when asking for help, and that they frequently refuse treatment if its
onset is delayed by more than a few weeks (seldom because of spontaneous improvement). Still our need for adequate controls remains.
One alternative is to conduct *comparative* outcome research, as in
Studies 1 and 2, pitting treatment modalities against each other. A
"minimal" therapy such as a self-help manual, rather than no treatment
at all, may be used as a criterion against which to judge effectiveness
(Rosen, 1976; Christensen, Miller, & Muñoz, in press). Emrick (1974, 1975)
has provided an exhaustive review of alcoholism treatment effectiveness,
approximating the average improvement rate achieved by abstinence-
oriented therapies. As research on controlled drinking therapies accum-
ulates, a similar review may establish success rates with which to compare
the effectiveness of novel programs. Finally, careful research into the
natural history of alcohol use in untreated problem drinkers may help

us to judge whether our improvement rates exceed what might be expected from spontaneous remission.

A second common problem present in our research is its reliance upon self-report. We obtained both verbal report and daily record cards, but both involve self-presentation. Corroborative information from significant others, though difficult to obtain, did generally confirm the accuracy of clients' self-reports. The use of less reactive measures would be desirable. Among the possibilities would be the use of random *in vivo* breath alcohol tests (P. M. Miller, Hersen, Eisler, & Watts, 1974), behavioral assessment methods such as a "taste rating" task (Miller, 1973; P. M. Miller, Hersen, Eisler, & Elkin, 1974; Marlatt, 1973a), or unobtrusive observational measures (Reid, in press).

A third caution relates to the period of follow-up reported for the above studies. In Studies 2 and 3, in particular, the follow-up period of three months after termination might be regarded as too brief to judge actual effectiveness. Long-range maintenance of self-control is certainly more important than immediate behavior change (Christensen, Miller, & Muñoz, in press). On the other hand, evidence is beginning to suggest that success rates among problem drinkers may not vary substantially after a three-month follow-up (Sobell & Sobell, 1976; Marlatt, 1973b). Further evidence for this is provided by the long-range follow-up data of Study 1.

Future Directions

Several directions for future research are suggested by the present studies. One pressing need, as new therapeutic approaches are developed, is for information regarding the differential response of clients to treatment modalities. Traditional diagnostic criteria focusing upon an alcoholic/nonalcoholic dichotomy are of questionable validity (Miller, 1976a) and may provide little assistance in the determination of optimal treatment modes. Successful clients in our studies ranged in age from 22 to 69; in alcohol consumption from less than 20 to more than 120 drinks per week; in Michigan Alcoholism Screening Test scores from 2 to 43. They represented a broad range of personality and intellectual characteristics. Predictors of differential outcome are needed, and are likely to be determined through the accumulation of findings from many studies of relatively small treatment samples.

A second direction would be to determine the optimal combinations of treatment components for the control of overdrinking. Self-monitoring and functional analysis training seem to have earned their places as basic elements. Other promising procedures include a) training in the estimation of blood alcohol concentration through extrinsic cues; b) instruction in rate-control procedures; c) training in principles of self-reinforcement; d) basic education regarding the short- and long-term effects of alcohol use; and e) training in alternatives to drinking (e.g., desensitization, assertiveness training). Such additional methods may assist initial behavior change or may improve the maintenance of gains made during treatment. The utility of these specific components remains to be demonstrated, however, and our research argues against the assumption that additional components necessarily improve effectiveness.

A third direction would be the application of self-control procedures to new populations. It is likely that present methods will require substantial revision to be applicable within different racial, cultural, and socioeconomic groups.

Finally, self-control training would seem to hold considerable potential for the primary and secondary prevention of problem drinking (Muñoz, 1976). Our research group at the University of Oregon, under the leadership of Dr. Edward Lichtenstein, has developed a high-school-level curriculum on alcohol and responsible drinking, and is in the process of preliminary evaluations of its effectiveness within the public schools of Eugene. The secondary prevention potential of self-control methods may be enhanced by their appeal to problem drinkers at a much earlier stage in the development of problems. The large majority of clients treated in our three studies had not received previous treatment, and had not been publicly identified as alcoholics. To the extent that effective self-help methods can be developed, such persons may attain self-control before problems reach a point where they must seek professional assistance. The marked and immediate suppressing effect of self-monitoring observed in all three studies is promising for the possibilities of self-help, as is our initial moderate success with self-control manuals. Hopefully, future prevention and self-help materials will be accompanied by critical evaluative research (Rosen, 1976).

Whatever the future directions of controlled drinking therapies, it will be essential that they be integrated into an existing structure of service delivery if they are to have an impact upon the general public. Agencies offering an integrated program of abstinence- and control-oriented treatments would seem to have the best potential for reaching a wide variety of problem drinkers, and for reaching them earlier (Miller & Caddy, in press). This integration may represent the greatest challenge for controlled drinking therapies over the next ten years.

REFERENCES

ALCOHOLICS ANONYMOUS: *Alcoholics Anonymous: The Story of How Many Thousands of Men and Women Have Recovered from Alcoholism.* New York: A. A. Publishing, 1955.

ARMOR, D. J., POLICH, J. M. and STAMBUL, H. B.: *Alcoholism and Treatment.* Santa Monica, Calif.: The Rand Corporation, 1976.

BELLACK, A. S., ROZENCSKY, R. and SCHWARTZ, J.: A comparison of two forms of self-monitoring in a behavioral weight reduction program. *Behavior Therapy,* 1974, 5, 523-530.

BRIDDELL, D. W. and NATHAN, P. E.: Behavior assessment and modification with alcoholics: Current status and future trends. In M. Hersen, R. M. Eisler, and P. M. Miller (Eds.), *Progress in Behavior Modification.* New York: Academic Press, 1975.

CADDY, G. R. and LOVIBOND, S. H.: Self-regulation and discriminated aversive conditioning in the modification of alcoholics' drinking behavior. *Behavior Therapy,* 1976, 7, 223-230.

CHRISTENSEN, A., MILLER, W. R. and MUÑOZ, R. F.: Paraprofessionals, partners, peers, paraphernalia, and print: A model for the use of therapeutic adjuncts in prevention, treatment, and maintenance. *Professional Psychology,* in press.

EMRICK, C. D.: A review of psychologically oriented treatment of alcoholism. I. The use and interrelationships of outcome criteria and drinking behavior following treatment. *Quarterly Journal of Studies on Alcohol,* 1974, 35, 523-549.

EMRICK, C. D.: A review of psychologically oriented treatment of alcoholism. II. The relative effectiveness of different treatment approaches and the effectiveness of treatment versus no treatment. *Journal of Studies on Alcohol,* 1975, 36, 88-108.

GITLOW, S. E.: Alcoholism: A disease. In P. G. Bourne and R. Fox (Eds.,), *Alcoholism: Progress in Research and Treatment.* New York: Academic Press, 1973.

HAMBURG, S.: Behavior therapy in alcoholism: A critical review of broad-spectrum approaches. *Journal of Studies on Alcohol,* 1975, 36, 69-87.

HATHAWAY, S. R. and McKINLEY, J. C.: *The Minnesota Multiphasic Personality Inventory.* New York: The Psychological Corporation, 1943.

HUBER, H., KARLIN, R. and NATHAN, P. E.: Blood alcohol level discrimination by nonalcoholics: The role of internal and external cues. *Journal of Studies on Alcohol,* 1976, 37, 27-39.

JELLINEK, E. M.: *The Disease Concept of Alcoholism.* Highland Park, N. J.: Hillhouse Press, 1960.

LLOYD, R. W., JR. and SALZBERG, H. C.: Controlled social drinking: An alternative to abstinence as a treatment goal for some alcohol abusers. *Psychological Bulletin,* 1975, 82, 815-842.

LOVIBOND, S. H. and CADDY, G.: Discriminated aversive control in the moderation of alcoholics' drinking behavior. *Behavior Therapy,* 1970, 1, 437-444.

MARLATT, G. A.: Determinants of alcohol consumption in a laboratory taste-rating task: Implications for controlled drinking. Paper presented at the annual meeting of the American Psychological Association, Montreal, August, 1973. (a)

MARLATT, G. A.: A comparison of aversive conditioning procedures in the treatment of alcoholism. Paper presented at the annual meeting of the Western Psychological Association, Anaheim, California, April, 1973. (b)

McFALL, R. and HAMMAN, C.: Motivation, structure and self-monitoring: Role of non-specific factors in smoking reduction. *Journal of Consulting and Clinical Psychology*, 1971, 37, 80-86.

McNAIR, D. M., LORR, M., & DROPPELMAN, L. F.: *Manual for the Profile of Mood States*. San Diego, CA: Educational and Industrial Testing Service, 1971.

MILLER, P. M.: Behavioral assessment in alcoholism research and treatment: Current techniques. *International Journal of the Addictions*, 1973, 8, 831-837.

MILLER, P. M.: Assessment of addictive behaviors. In A. R. Ciminero, K. S. Calhoun, and H. E. Adams (Eds.), *Handbook of Behavioral Assessment*. New York: John Wiley & Sons, in press.

MILLER, P. M., HERSEN, M., EISLER, R. M. and ELKIN, T. E.: A retrospective analysis of alcohol consumption on laboratory tasks as related to therapeutic outcome. *Behaviour Research and Therapy*, 1974, 12, 73-78.

MILLER, P. M., HERSEN, M., EISLER, R. M. and WATTS, J. G.: Contingent reinforcement of lowered blood alcohol levels in an outpatient chronic alcoholic. *Behaviour Research and Therapy*, 1974, 12, 261-263.

MILLER, W. R.: Alcoholism scales and objective assessment methods: A review. *Psychological Bulletin*, 1976, 83, 649-674. (a)

MILLER, W. R.: Controlled drinking therapies: A review. In W. R. Miller & R. F. Muñoz, *How to Control Your Drinking*. Englewood Cliffs, N. J.: Prentice-Hall, 1976. (b)

MILLER, W. R.: Behavioral treatment of problem drinkers: A comparative outcome study of three controlled drinking therapies. Unpublished doctoral dissertation, University of Oregon, 1976. (c)

MILLER, W. R. and CADDY, G. R.: Abstinence and controlled drinking in the treatment of problem drinkers. *Journal of Studies on Alcohol*, in press.

MILLER, W. R., GRIBSKOV, C. and MORTELL, R.: The effectiveness of a self-control manual for problem drinkers with and without therapist contact. Unpublished manuscript, University of Oregon, 1976.

MILLER, W. R. and MUÑOZ, R. F.: Control over drinking: A self-help manual. Unpublished manuscript, University of Oregon, 1975.

MILLER, W. R. and MUÑOZ, R. F.: *How to Control Your Drinking*. Englewood Cliffs, N. J.: Prentice-Hall, 1976.

MILLER, W. R. and ORR, J.: The nature and sequence of neuropsychological deficits in alcoholics. Unpublished manuscript, Palo Alto Veterans Administration Hospital, 1976.

MILLER, W. R., PECHACEK, T. F. and HAMBURG, S.: A minimal-therapist-contact behavioral treatment for problem drinking. Unpublished manuscript, Palo Alto Veterans Administration Hospital, 1976.

MUÑOZ, R. F.: The prevention of problem drinking. In W. R. Miller and R. F. Muñoz, *How to Control Your Drinking*. Englewood Cliffs, N. J.: Prentice-Hall, 1976.

NATHAN, P. E.: Alcoholism. In H. Leitenberg (Ed.), *Handbook of Behavior Modification*. Englewood Cliffs, N. J.: Prentice-Hall, 1976.

PATTISON, E. M., SOBELL, M. B. and SOBELL, L. C. (Eds.), *Emerging Concepts of Alcohol Dependence*. New York: Springer, in press.

REID, J. B.: Observational studies of alcohol consumption in natural settings. In G. A. Marlatt and P. E. Nathan (Eds.), *Behavioral Approaches to the Assessment and Treatment of Alcoholism*. New Brunswick, N. J.: Center of Alcohol Studies, in press.

ROSEN, G. M.: The development and use of nonprescription behavior therapies. *American Psychologist*, 1976, 31, 139-141.

ROTTER, J. B.: Generalized expectancies for internal versus external control of reinforcement. *Psychological Monographs*, 1966, 80 (Whole No. 609).

SOBELL, M. B. and SOBELL, L. C.: Individualized behavior therapy for alcoholics. *Behavior Therapy*, 1973, 4, 49-72.

SOBELL, M. B. and SOBELL, L. C.: Alternatives to abstinence: Time to acknowledge reality. *Addictions*, 1974, 21, 2-29.

SOBELL, M. B. and SOBELL, L. C.: The need for realism, relevance, and operational assumptions in the study of substance dependence. In H. D. Cappell and A. E. LeBlanc (Eds.), *Proceedings of the International Symposia on Alcohol and Drug Research: No. 6, Biological and Behavioral Approaches to Drug Dependence.* Toronto: Addiction Research Foundation, 1975.

SOBELL, M. B. and SOBELL, L. C.: Second year treatment outcome of alcoholics treated by individualized behavior therapy: Results. *Behaviour Research and Therapy*, 1976, 14, 195-215.

STUART, R. B.: Behavioral control of overeating. *Behaviour Research and Therapy*, 1967, 5, 357-365.

ZWERLING, I. and ROSENBAUM, M.: Alcoholic addiction and personality (non-psychotic conditions). In S. Arieti (Ed.), *American Handbook of Psychiatry.* New York: Basic Books, 1959.

7

Effects of Self-Control Procedures for Insomnia

RICHARD R. BOOTZIN

Almost everyone suffers from an occasional sleepless night, and a surprisingly large number of people identify themselves as insomniacs. Epidemiological surveys indicate that between 10% and 15% of the population state that they have frequent or severe insomnia and another 10% to 15% state that they have mild insomnia (Kales, Bixler, Leo, Healy & Slye, 1974; Montgomery, Perkin & Wise, 1975). Therefore, as many as one out of every four people may seek relief from sleeping difficulties at one time or another.

Although many people claim to have bouts of insomnia, this is a rather subjective judgment. There is great individual variability on measures such as time to fall asleep, number and duration of awakenings, and total amount of sleep. Insomnia is generally believed to occur when more than 30 minutes is needed to fall asleep, when awakenings during the night total more than 30 minutes, and when less than six and a half hours of total sleep occurs nightly (e.g., Dement & Guilleminault, 1973). Although these cutoffs may be useful for identifying what is an average sleeping pattern, they do not define insomnia in any clinical or functional sense.

Some people identify themselves as insomniacs if they are not getting seven or eight hours of sleep a night. Although most people will get more than six and a half hours of sleep a night, if someone gets less than that and shows no aftereffects the next day (i.e., the person is not

176

irritable or tired and is energetic), then he or she is getting as much sleep as he personally needs. There is no magic number of hours of sleep required. There are documented cases of people who have slept for only two or three hours a night for years with no harmful effects (e.g., Jones & Oswald, 1968). Under most circumstances the body will get the amount of sleep that it requires.

Others identify themselves as insomniacs because they are unaware that sleeping patterns change with aging. As a person gets older, sleep is neither as long nor as deep as it was when younger. A man of 65 is just not going to sleep as well as he did when he was 25. Early morning awakening, in particular, seems to be associated with aging.

Insomnia is not a unitary construct. There are many different patterns of sleep disturbance and different causes. A common descriptive taxonomy divides sleeping difficulties into three major types: sleep onset insomnia, early morning awakening, and frequent awakenings throughout the night. These categories are by no means incompatible with one another and severe insomniacs may experience difficulty in more than one dimension. Among chronic, severe insomniacs, however, there is considerable variability on sleep measures. Dement and Guilleminault (1973), in a sleep lab study of 55 chronic insomniacs, found that only about 5% on any one night were beyond the insomnia cut-off on all the three sleep measures (time to fall asleep, total duration of awakenings, and total amount of sleep). As many as 20% on any one night failed to meet the insomnia criterion for even one of the measures. Sleep onset insomnia is the most frequent complaint and most self-control procedures for treating insomnia focus on problems in falling asleep. Consequently, the focus of this paper will be primarily on treatments for sleep-onset insomnia.

CAUSES OF INSOMNIA

Disturbed sleeping has many different causes. It can be caused by a physical disorder. For example, there is a rare breathing disorder, sleep apnea, in which the person essentially stops breathing for a fraction of a second and wakes himself up (Guilleminault, Eldridge & Dement, 1973). This may happen often enough throughout the night so that the person never gets very much deep continuous sleep. Another rare physical condition causes the person to have leg twitches throughout the night (e.g., Frankel, Patten & Gillin, 1974). This, too, can result in disrupted sleep. Insomnia may also be caused by physical illness. This can be either because the discomfort from the illness (such as gastric pain from duodenal ulcers) disrupts sleeping or more directly because disrupted sleep is caused by the disease process itself (as would be the case in some central nervous system disorders).

Drug use is another cause of insomnia. Caffeine, for example, is a more potent arousal drug than most people realize. Over-the-counter products sold to help people stay awake (such as No-Doz) are almost entirely caffeine. Cocoa, coffee, tea, and colas all have caffeine in them. Although some people have a cup of coffee or a cup of cocoa every night before going to sleep and never have any difficulty, others are extremely sensitive to even small amounts of caffeine.

Prescription drugs for medical problems, even those unrelated to insomnia, should be evaluated as to whether they might be affecting sleep as a side-effect. Some medication for asthma contains adrenalin which causes arousal. If taken at night, it would interfere with falling asleep. Thus, insomnia may be the inadvertent consequence of taking medication for other problems.

Insomnia may also be caused by drugs taken to relieve insomnia. In fact, this is a frequent and almost inevitable consequence of taking sleeping pills over a long period of time and is called drug-dependent insomnia. The problem is that most sleeping pills lose their effectiveness within two weeks of continuous use (Kales, Allen, Scharf & Kales, 1970). The body builds a tolerance to them rapidly, larger and larger doses are required to have any effect, and, finally, continuous use results in less deep sleep and more light, fitful sleep. Drug-dependent insomnia is a very serious problem which will be discussed in more detail in the section on common remedies for insomnia.

Another possible cause of insomnia is stress and emotional disturbance. Sometimes the stress is temporary and the sleeping difficulty disappears when the stress does. For example, a soldier will sleep better away from the front lines than he did at the front lines, a student will sleep better after that crucial exam than before the exam, and a person with money problems will sleep better after the paycheck arrives. However, sometimes the stress is not temporary. Then a vicious cycle begins. The stress causes insomnia and the resulting lack of sleep makes it less likely that the person will have the resources to deal with those very factors causing the stress.

The obvious way to treat stress-induced insomnia would be to help the person deal with the stress. This could be done in a variety of ways.

The person could be taught more appropriate coping skills, alternatives could be analyzed, or it might require a somewhat longer commitment to therapy. Although it may be useful to acquire more appropriate coping skills and eventually it may result in better sleep, this process is time consuming. And during all of this time, the insomniac still may not be sleeping better. Thus, the promise of directly treating insomnia is that it might be possible to help a person sleep better irrespective of the amount of stress in his life. If it can be done, it would provide additional resources to the person to help deal with other problems.

Another cause of insomnia is the possibility that the person has learned poor sleep habits. One part of this problem may be that the person never allows himself to acquire a consistent sleep rhythm. Everyone does this to some extent. People seldom go to sleep on weekends at the same time that they go to sleep during the week. Some people, because of their job or interests (such as watching late night TV), put exceptional strain on their natural sleep rhythm. It is to be expected that this constant disruption in sleep rhythm would result in disturbed sleep.

Another possibility is that the person engages in activities at bedtime which are incompatible with sleep. Many insomniacs make their bed and bedroom the focus of their entire existence. The TV, books, crossword puzzles, and food all are readily available. And the insomniac may spend many waking hours in bed. The result is that the bed is no longer just a cue for sleeping, it is also a cue for many other activities.

One common habit is that many insomniacs use bedtime as an occasion to rehash the day's events and to worry about the next day. They may have been too busy during the day to think about what was happening. The first quiet time available for reflection may be in bed. If this happens regularly, the bed becomes a cue for worrying rather than a cue for sleeping.

Poor sleeping habits may help maintain insomnia even if the sleeping difficulties were initially caused by physical illness or situational stress. For the chronic insomniac, sleeping difficulties have usually continued long after the initial causes have disappeared.

In summary, there are many possible causes for insomnia. A thorough evaluation of an insomniac's sleeping pattern will lead to a more accurate diagnosis of possible causes. Knowledge of the cause of the problem would also suggest particular treatments. Unfortunately, it is often impossible to identify with certainty the cause of an insomniac's difficulty, and sometimes even knowing the cause will not suggest a treatment. In fact, most treatments and remedies for insomnia seem to have been generated quite independently of possible causes.

COMMON REMEDIES

There have been many famous insomniacs and a long list of recommended remedies for insomnia. Charles Dickens suggested that one would sleep better if the bed faced north, thus taking advantage of the magnetic pull from the North Pole. Another famous insomniac, Benjamin Franklin, suggested that a fresh cold bed was sleep inducing. He recommended that the insomniac should get out of bed, remake the bed so that it would be cold and fresh, walk around the bedroom nude until cold, and then return to bed. If the insomniac followed his suggestions, Franklin guaranteed a sound sleep.

More typical solutions for insomnia include eye shades, ear plugs, recordings of the surf, special hard mattresses, special soft mattresses, warm baths, cold baths, and many specially constructed devices. The sleep industry is a multi-million dollar industry ready to cater to every imaginable whim.

By far the most common self-management technique for insomnia is the taking of some drug. In a survey in Florida (Karacan, Warkeit, Thornly & Schwab, 1973), 26% of those surveyed reported using "sleeping pills" to help them get to sleep. This figure combines both prescription and nonprescription drugs. As recently as 1965, 800 thousand pounds of barbiturates were being sold in the United States each year (Sharpless, 1965). That is enough to make six billion 60 mg capsules. In 1975, over 60 million dollars were spent on drugstore prescriptions for hypnotics and sedatives in the United States (Wykert, 1976); that figure does not include hospital dispensed hypnotics or over-the-counter formulations.

Despite this heavy reliance on sleeping medication, there are a number of problems associated with drug dependence, not least of which is that sleeping pills are not effective over the long run. As pointed out earlier, most hypnotics (barbiturate and nonbarbiturate) lose their effectiveness within two weeks of continuous use.

Still another problem is that most hypnotics deprive the person of REM (rapid eye movement sleep—the stage of sleep associated with dreaming). The person who has been taking sleeping pills will experience an REM rebound when he does not take pills. Rebound nights are miserable. The night will be most likely spent in restless dreaming, nightmares and very fitful sleep. Thus, even though hypnotics are not helping the insomniac to fall asleep, the insomniac may conclude that he needs them because of what occurs when he does not take them.

In this discussion, I have not differentiated between barbiturates, non-barbiturate sedatives, and tranquilizers. Barbiturates have the most serious side-effects and the most potential for addiction, accidental overdose, and drug abuse. During a five-year period in New York City alone, there were more than 8,000 cases of barbiturate overdose (Sharpless, 1965).

The effects on sleep of nonbarbiturate sedatives is similar to that of barbiturates; that is, with continuous use, they lose their effectiveness, they result in less deep sleep, and many are REM depriving. For short-term or occasional sleeping disturbances, nonbarbiturate sedatives would be preferred to barbiturates. The side-effects are not as dangerous and they are as effective. In fact, only a nonbarbiturate hypnotic, flurazepam (Dalmane), has been found to retain its effectiveness throughout one month of continuous use (Kales, Kales, Bixler & Scharf, 1975).

The problems associated with hypnotics hold as well for alcohol and tranquilizers. Like barbiturates, alcohol is REM depriving. In addition, heavy drinking results in fragmented sleep with frequent awakening throughout the night. Withdrawal produces the same type of REM rebound as produced by barbiturates with fitful sleep and nightmares. As regards tranquilizers and other psychotropic drugs, the effects are complicated. There are many different drugs; some are REM depriving and some are not. However, there is no evidence that any of them provide an effective treatment for the chronic, severe insomniac.

What about over-the-counter medication such as Nytol, Sleep-Eze, Compoz, and Sominex? The active ingredient in most over-the-counter sleep medication is an antihistamine. Antihistamines often make people drowsy, but there is no evidence that they will effectively induce sleep for insomniacs. Some over-the-counter medications also contain a mild sedative called scopolamine. However, the dose is too small to be an effective sedative. In a study comparing Sominex (which contains an antihistamine and scopolamine) with a placebo, Sominex was found to be no more effective than the placebo which was itself ineffective (Kales, Tan, Swearingen & Kales, 1971).

Although over-the-counter medications are no more effective for insomnia than a placebo, they are not harmless. They have potent side-effects: Scopolamine, which is contained in Compoz, Sleep-Eze, and Sominex, can cause dry mouth, blurred vision, increased pressure in the eyes, and difficulty in urinating. Prolonged or high doses can lead to mental confusion and delirium. In a study comparing Compoz, librium, aspirin and a placebo for their effectiveness in reducing anxiety, Compoz (which contains two antihistamines and scopolamine) produced both the most side-effects and the most severe side-effects. In addition, Compoz was no more effective than aspirin or the placebo in reducing anxiety (Rickels & Hesbacher, 1973).

Another set of popular remedies has to do with eating or drinking particular foods. There may be some basis in fact for the popular suggestion to have a glass of warm milk before going to sleep. It has been discovered that a certain amino acid, tryptophan, found in dairy products and other high protein foods is sleep inducing. Thus, it is not the warmth of the milk that is important but the fact that it is a high protein food. Other high protein foods would do as well.

BEHAVIORAL SELF-HELP PROCEDURES

Relaxation Training

The most commonly recommended alternative to drugs is some type of relaxation training. This would include procedures as informal as imagining each part of your body falling asleep in sequence (for example, my toes are asleep, my feet are asleep, etc.) or more formal training procedures such as yoga, progressive relaxation training, transcendental meditation, hypnosis, and biofeedback. As treatments for insomnia, all of these procedures are based on the same premise: If people can learn to be relaxed at bedtime, they will fall asleep faster.

This premise derives some support from the sleep research literature. First, muscle relaxation is associated with the onset of sleep and some researchers have held that muscle relaxation induces sleep (e.g., Kleitman, 1963). One form of evidence for this conclusion is that people deprived of sleep for more than 24 hours are unable to stay awake while completely relaxed (Murray, 1965). Since one might consider insomniacs, in some sense, deprived of sleep, then it follows that if they can be taught to completely relax while in bed, sleep should come naturally.

Another reason that relaxation training may be a promising approach is that most insomniacs are very aroused and anxious. A number of studies examining personality characteristics of insomniacs and normal sleepers have typically found that insomniacs are much higher than normals on self-report measures of anxiety, depression, and on symptom checklists (Monroe, 1967; Nicassio & Bootzin, 1974; Coursey, Buchsbaum & Frankel, 1975). For these people relaxation could be used as a general coping skill, hopefully reducing anxiety and arousal throughout the day. Thus, there might be a double benefit from a relaxation treatment—first, providing a means of inducing sleep and second, providing a means of coping more adequately with the stresses of the day.

Over the years, there have been many case studies reporting the effectiveness of one or another relaxation training procedure as a treatment for insomnia (e.g., Jacobson, 1964; Schultz & Luthe, 1959). It has only been during the past few years, however, that systematic controlled research comparing different relaxation procedures has been conducted. Borkovec and Fowles (1973) is the first study reported in the literature to include control groups within their study. Subjects were randomly assigned to one of four treatment conditions: progressive relaxation, hypnotic relaxation instructions, a type of minimally instructed self-relaxation, and a no-treatment control. They found that although progressive relaxation and hypnotic relaxation instructions produced more improvement than did no treatment, relaxation instructions were no more effective than self-relaxation. However, the Borkovec and Fowles' subjects had only moderate sleeping difficulties, as they were students recruited from an introductory psychology course.

At about the same time, Perry Nicassio and I were executing a similar study (Nicassio & Bootzin, 1974). We recruited severe, chronic insomniacs through newspaper stories published in the Chicago area. All potential subjects were interviewed about the history and duration of their problem, agreed to stay off sleep medication (with their physician's approval) for the duration of the study, and took seven days of baseline sleep diary records. The 30 insomniacs whose average time to fall asleep exceeded 30 minutes were retained for the study. They were chronic insomniacs who averaged about two hours a night to fall asleep.

A major methodological problem for studies of insomnia is the measurement of sleep. An effective treatment is one which decreases the amount of time to fall asleep when the patient is *at home in his own bed*. Most reliable measures of onset of sleep are both reactive and impractical outside of a sleep laboratory. Measures taken while the client is in a sleep lab may not be representative of those taken at home. Because of this, studies investigating behavioral treatments for insomnia (see Knapp, Downs & Alperson, 1976) have relied on the client's self-report. Such reports, however, are vulnerable to both intentional and unintentional sources of bias. Nevertheless, the client's report is an important measure. It was his verbal complaint of insomnia which initiated treatment, so his verbal statements of improvement should not be dismissed lightly. In addition, not all verbal reports are susceptible to the same degree of bias. Biased reporting can be reduced by making the client's task more specific and less ambiguous. Daily logs are likely to be less biased than global reports of improvement. Reports of household members (roommates and spouses) can provide an independent and convergent measure of improvement.

Subjects in our evaluations kept daily records throughout the treatment period and made global assessments of their status at the end of treatment. Convergent information was obtained from household members where possible. Subjects were randomly assigned to one of four treatment conditions: autogenic training, progressive relaxation, self-relaxation, and no treatment.

"Autogenic training" was developed by Johannes Schultz and Wolfgang Luthe (1959) and is widely used in Europe for a variety of disorders. The Schultz and Luthe technique was developed after observing that people seemed to be able to induce physiological changes in themselves during hypnosis. The suggestion under hypnosis that an arm is getting heavy often elicits changes in muscle potential indicating that the person's arm is becoming very relaxed. Schultz speculated that a person could use language to elicit physiological changes without hypnosis. To accomplish this, the person is told to suggest to himself that an arm is heavy. He practices this suggestion repeatedly, saying, "My arm is heavy, I am at peace, my arm is heavy"; each trial lasts from 30 to 60 seconds. According to Schultz and Luthe, it takes from three to six weeks for a person to become accomplished at being able to relax any part of the body in this way. After a person is able to make his whole body "heavy," similar procedures are followed for inducing warmth. Whereas the self-instruction of heaviness seems to elicit muscular relaxation, the self-instruction of warmth seems to elicit vasodilation. In the complete procedure, following training in heaviness and warmth, the person practices controlling heart rate, respiration, abdominal warmth, and cooling of the forehead. In our evaluation of autogenic training as a treatment for insomnia, we limited the procedure to training in heaviness and warmth which each person practiced twice a day for 15 to 20 minutes. One of the two times was to be in bed at bedtime before falling asleep.

Progressive relaxation was developed by Edmund Jacobson (1938, 1964) in this country. Rather than relying upon self-suggestions of peace, heaviness, and warmth, Jacobson had people practice muscle relaxation directly by first discriminating tension and stress in various muscle groups, and then relaxing these groups. For example, an early instruction to a person would be to bend the left hand as far back as possible and to notice the pattern of strain in the back of the hand and up the arm. After maintaining that position for one to two minutes, the person would be told to let the hand completely relax (Jacobson calls this "going negative") and to notice the difference in sensation at the points where previously strain had been felt. The object of the training program is to teach the person what relaxation of each muscle group feels like and to provide practice at achieving more relaxation. A person able to discriminate the patterns of tension in a muscle group is no longer told to tense before relaxing. Rather, he just relaxes the muscles from whatever level of tension they are at already.

Ordinarily, the training program proceeds slowly over a period of months. There is considerable evidence, however, to indicate that abbreviated training procedures are quite effective (e.g., Paul, 1969; Paul & Trimble, 1970). In our evaluation, we employed an abbreviated form of progressive relaxation which each person practiced twice every day, once in bed before bedtime.

Relaxation treatments may be effective, not because of the specific training, but because they require people to schedule time to relax. Threfore, insomniacs in the self-relaxation condition received no actual training in relaxation, but as in the other conditions were told to schedule time to relax for 15 to 20 minutes twice a day, once in bed before going to sleep.

Subjects in the no-treatment condition kept extensive sleep records but did not receive any treatment for the duration of the evaluation. After the evaluation was completed they were offered relaxation training.

The results of the study were that daily practice of either progressive relaxation or autogenic training produced about 50% improvement in time to fall asleep within one month. Improvement was substantiated by reports from household members; and treatment gains were maintained at a six-month follow-up (see Figure 1). Subjects receiving no treatment had improved slightly by the end of the month, but not significantly. The subjects who scheduled time to relax but were not given training showed the most variable results. As a group, they did not

FIGURE 1

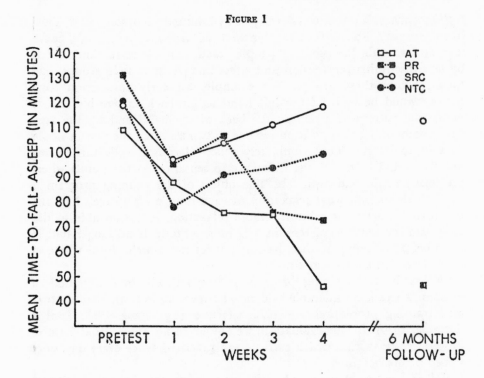

improve. However, the standard deviation of sleep latency scores for the self-relaxation subjects was over twice as large as the standard deviation for the other experimental groups. One self-relaxation subject improved dramatically while others actually got worse. In our study it appeared that severe, chronic insomniacs require training in relaxation to obtain some benefit. Just scheduling time to relax is not sufficient.

Other studies evaluating relaxation procedures have found results similar to ours. No particular relaxation procedure has been consistently more effective than others (see Knapp, Downs & Alperson, 1976 for a review of relevant studies). The mean improvement in sleep latency across different studies is between 40% and 50%. Almost everyone benefits some from relaxation training, and it is useful as a general coping skill; however, it is seldom a sufficient treatment for insomnia.

Biofeedback should be mentioned as one variation of relaxation training. Most investigators have evaluated the effects of frontalis EMG bio-feedback (tension from the forehead) as a means of inducing general deep relaxation. Subjects are required to practice relaxation daily at home without the aid of the biofeedback equipment. The results of this biofeedback treatment have been variable. Hauri and Good (1975) found such training to be ineffective for chronic insomniacs while Freedman and Papsdorf (1976) produced a 70% improvement in sleep onset in their subjects. Nevertheless, even in the Freedman and Papsdorf study, biofeedback was not significantly more effective than progressive re-laxation.

Other biofeedback researchers (Stoyva & Budzynski, 1972) have sug-gested either combining frontalis EMG with theta EEG biofeedback or providing biofeedback for a completely different EEG pattern, the sensory-motor rhythm or SMR (Feinstein, Sterman & MacDonald, in press). There have been promising case studies in support of both of these suggestions, but as yet there have been no systematic, controlled evaluations. At present, biofeedback must be grouped with other relaxa-tion training procedures. There is no evidence to support a claim that biofeedback is superior to them.

Stimulus Control Instructions

If relaxation training is not sufficient as a treatment for insomnia, what else is available? During the past five years I have developed and evalu-ated a set of stimulus control instructions derived essentially from an operant analysis of sleep and insomnia. In this analysis, falling asleep is conceptualized as an instrumental act emitted to produce sleep. Thus, stimuli associated with sleep become discriminative stimuli for the occur-rence of sleep which functions as a reinforcer. Difficulty in falling asleep, then, may be due to inadequate stimulus control. Strong discriminative stimuli for sleep may not have been established and/or discriminative stimuli for activities incompatible with sleep may be present.

If falling asleep is an emitted response, then it should be possible to increase its frequency by reinforcing it. Wyrwicka and Sterman (1968) were able to increase the frequency of brain wave patterns which are characteristically seen at the onset of sleep by reinforcing them in food-deprived cats with milk. In addition to increasing the frequency of sleep by altering the consequences, it should also be possible to bring sleep under the control of discriminative stimuli. Wilcox (1970) was able to train a rat to fall asleep when a tone was presented in order to obtain food when it woke up. These sleep bouts usually only lasted a few seconds. Suggestive results also have been described in a study of children by Boynton and Goodenough (1930). They found that children who assumed a particular posture when going to bed fell asleep faster. The stereotyped posture may have been a discriminative stimulus which facilitated the onset of sleep.

Just as a particular sleep ritual may facilitate falling asleep, other behaviors may interfere with sleep onset. In that case, the bed and bedtime may become cues for behaviors that are incompatible with falling asleep. As mentioned earlier, this includes a variety of activities such as watching TV, reading, eating, and worrying. Such activities are usually begun in order to distract the insomniac from his primary concern—being unable to fall asleep. For the insomniac, bed at bedtime becomes a cue for all the anxiety and frustration associated with *trying* to fall asleep. As a result, insomniacs often find themselves fighting the bed—they dread going to bed because they anticipate still another night of misery. Because of this, insomniacs often can sleep any place other than bed. They can fall asleep in an easy chair or on a couch, and they often have no trouble sleeping when away from home on a trip. But in their own bed, they just cannot fall asleep. Their bed has become a cue for behavior incompatible with sleep onset.

In contrast, people who have no difficulty falling asleep in their own bed often have difficulty in strange surroundings. For them, there are strong cues for sleep associated with their bed and it is only when these cues are not available that they have difficulty.

This analysis suggests that it might be possible to develop a treatment for insomnia that separates the cues for falling asleep from the cues for other activities. Similar stimulus control treatments have been effectively employed to alter a variety of problems such as studying (Fox, 1962; Goldiamond, 1965), overeating (Ferster, Nurnberger & Levitt, 1962; Stuart, 1967) and marital difficulties (Goldiamond, 1965).

The goals of the stimulus control instructions for insomnia are to help the insomniac acquire a consistent sleep rhythm, to strengthen the bed as a cue for sleep and to weaken it as a cue for activities which might interfere with sleep. The following rules are offered to clients as a means of developing new permanent sleeping habits. Thus, they are to be followed even the insomniac is falling asleep faster and sleeping better.

1. Lie down intending to go to sleep *only* when you are sleepy.

2. Do not use your bed for anything except sleep; that is, do not read, watch television, eat, or worry in bed. Sexual activity is the only exception to this rule. On such occasions, the instructions are to be followed afterwards when you intend to go to sleep.

3. If you find yourself unable to fall asleep, get up and go into another room. Stay up as long as you wish and then return to the bedroom to sleep. Although we do not want you to watch the clock, we want you to get out of bed if you do not fall asleep immediately. Remember the goal is to associate your bed with falling asleep *quickly!* If you are in bed more than about 10 minutes without falling asleep and have not gotten up, you are not following this instruction.

4. If you still cannot fall asleep, repeat step 3. Do this as often as is necessary throughout the night.

5. Set your alarm and get up at the same time every morning irrespective of how much sleep you got during the night. This will help your body acquire a consistent sleep rhythm.

6. Do not nap during the day.

Based upon successful pilot work with one client (Bootzin, 1972), 78 clients were offered various sleep induction treatments as follows: stimulus control instructions (18), progressive relaxation training (28), self-relaxation (18), and no treatment (14) (Bootzin, 1973).

Before treatment, subjects averaged over 90 minutes a night to fall asleep and were sleeping 5.5 hours a night. From the baseline week to the last week of treatment (four weeks later), stimulus control subjects improved an average of 74 minutes as compared to improvement of 38 minutes for progressive relaxation, 15 minutes for self-relaxation and 24 minutes for no treatment. At the end of treatment, subjects receiving either stimulus control instructions or progressive relaxation training were falling asleep significantly faster than subjects in the other two groups; in addition, subjects receiving stimulus control instructions were falling asleep significantly faster than subjects receiving progressive relaxation. Sixty-one percent of subjects receiving stimulus control instructions were averaging less than 20 minutes a night to fall asleep during the last week of treatment. In comparison only 14% of those receiving progressive relaxation, 28% of those in the self-relaxation condition, and 7% of the no-treatment subjects met this criterion.

Other results were that both stimulus control and progressive relaxation subjects averaged an hour more of sleep after treatment than subjects in the control groups, and, at the end of treatment, stimulus control subjects rated themselves as feeling better upon awakening than subjects in the other groups.

In summary, stimulus control instructions were very effective in reducing insomnia across measures of time-to-fall-asleep, number of hours slept, and feeling upon awakening. Relaxation training produced some improvement but did not match the degree of effectiveness produced by stimulus control.

Evaluations of stimulus control instructions in other laboratories have confirmed our findings. Successful case studies have been reported by Hauri (1974) and Haynes, Price and Simons (1975). Impressive controlled evaluations have been conducted by Tokarz and Lawrence (1974) and Slama (1975).

Slama (1975) found that stimulus control instructions produced dramatic improvement even during a counterdemand condition in which subjects were told they would not improve. From baseline to the end of treatment, subjects receiving stimulus control instructions improved in time to fall asleep on the average 72%.

Tokarz and Lawrence (1974) evaluated the different components of the stimulus control instructions. They separated the instructions focused on regularizing the sleeping pattern (temporal control) from those focused on making the bed and bedroom a more powerful cue for falling asleep (stimulus control). They found that both types of instructions were more effective than self-relaxation or no treatment. The combined instructions constituted the most effective treatment but this was not significantly better than either component alone. Subjects receiving the combined stimulus control instructions improved 88% on the average in time to fall asleep.

The mean improvement in sleep latency as a result of stimulus control instructions across different studies is about 75%. This is considerably better than the results from relaxation training. These two treatment approaches are not incompatible with one another, however. It is possible that combining relaxation training with stimulus control instructions would provide a treatment package more effective than either treatment by itself.

EFFECTS OF MISATTRIBUTION AND SUGGESTION

Recently there has been considerable interest in the clinical applications of attribution theory (e.g., Valins & Nisbett, 1971). It may have particular relevance for the treatment of insomnia.

The misattribution hypothesis is derived from Schachter and Singer's (1962) theory of emotions, which proposes that nondifferentiated physiological arousal is associated with many different emotions. Emotions are experienced as different, one from the other, not because of different patterns of arousal but because of different situational contexts. It is as if the person notices that he is physiologically aroused and then looks around to see what cues are available for interpreting his arousal. If the cues suggest anger, he concludes that he is angry; if they suggest joy, he concludes that he is euphoric.

In a test fo the clinical utility of this hypothesis, Storms and Nisbett (1970) attempted to induce insomniacs to misattribute their arousal at bedtime to an external source. To do this insomniacs, recruited on the Yale campus for a study on dreaming, were given pills to take for two nights and were told that these pills would cause arousal. Subjects were told that the investigators were studying the effect of arousal on dreaming. The pills were placebos. The hypothesis was that since subjects would attribute any arousal experienced to the pills, they would fall asleep faster.

Another group of subjects were given pills and told that they would cause relaxation. The hypothesis for these subjects was that if their arousal remained unaffected despite the ingestion of a relaxation pill, they would infer that their real arousal level was particularly intense. They should, thus, worry more and, consequently, take longer to fall asleep. There was also a no-instruction control group.

The results of the study confirmed the authors' hypotheses. Insomniacs receiving the arousal pill fell asleep faster on pill nights than they did the two nights before. Insomniacs receiving the relaxation pill took longer to fall asleep, and the control group did not change from pretest to experimental nights. Unfortunately there were a number of methodological problems with the study which precluded unequivocal conclusions.

There were substantial differences between the three groups at pretest and the group that had the most severe insomnia on pretest nights was the arousal pill group for whom an improvement was hypothesized.

Since arousal pill subjects only improved enough at posttest to bring them back to the mean of the control group, it is impossible to determine whether that improvement was due to misattribution or was due to regression to the mean because of the relative unreliability of the pretest. Also, since subjects recorded their time to fall asleep for four consecutive nights, those having the worst times to fall asleep on the first two nights (the pretest) might be expected to show improvement because of fatigue on the next two nights (the pill nights).

The results of this study, although equivocal, seemed to challenge the conventional wisdom of the strength of placebo effects. Why did subjects not respond with a direct suggestion effect; that is, why did arousal pill subjects not take longer to fall asleep and relaxation pill subjects not take less time to fall asleep?

A possibility that occurred to us was that instructions for placebo effects usually refer directly to the behavior to be changed; i.e., this pill will keep you awake or this pill will help you fall asleep faster. Storms and Nisbett referred indirectly to the person's arousal and studiously avoided any overt implication on how the pill would affect falling asleep.

Given this difference, we (Bootzin, Herman & Nicassio, 1976) attempted to replicate and extend Storms and Nisbett's study. To accomplish this, subjects were told either that the pills would affect their arousal in some way (as in Storms and Nisbett's study) or that the pills would have a direct effect on falling asleep. In addition, we attempted to correct some of the methodological inadequacies by separating pretest and experimental nights by a full week and by having subjects fill out both pretest and experimental measures immediately upon arising (Storms and Nisbett's pretest data were retrospective, often over 36 hours after arising).

Our results failed to replicate the misattribution or reverse placebo effect in any respect. There was instead only a direct suggestion effect in that subjects instructed that the pill would either produce relaxation or help them fall asleep faster did in fact fall asleep faster on experimental nights than on pretest nights. They also fell asleep faster than subjects told that the pills would arouse them or interfere with falling asleep. The latter subjects stayed about the same from pretest to experimental nights; they did not get significantly worse.

The results of another study attempting to replicate Storms and Nisbett (Kellogg & Baron, 1975) complement our findings. They found that subjects in an arousal condition took significantly longer to fall asleep. The

Kellogg and Baron study and our study did not simply fail to replicate the misattribution effect, both found a significant direct suggestion or placebo effect. These studies call into question the current enthusiasm for clinical applications of the misattribution effect. Until misattribution effects can be reliably induced, treatment interventions for insomnia based on misattribution seem as likely to exacerbate symptoms as to reduce them.

How strong are placebo effects? Earlier, it was pointed out that over-the-counter medication is no more effective than a placebo. Placebos, however, may be reasonably effective. In the Kales et al. (1971) study evaluating over-the-counter medication, the placebo was ineffective. In Bootzin, Herman, & Nicassio (1976) the placebo, when combined with direct suggestion instructions, produced an average of 26% improvement in sleep latency. The average improvement produced by placebo across different studies is about 25%.

To summarize, the average effectiveness of the different types of interventions on sleep latency are: no treatment produces about 6% improvement, self-relaxation about 21%, placebo about 25%, relaxation training about 45%, and stimulus control instructions about 75%.

REFERENCES

BOOTZIN, R. R.: A stimulus control treatment for insomnia. *Proceedings of the American Psychological Association*, 1972, 395-396.

BOOTZIN, R. R.: A stimulus control treatment of insomnia. In: P. Hauri (Chr.), *The Treatment of Sleep Disorders*. Symposium presented at the American Psychological Association Convention, Montreal, 1973.

BOOTZIN, R. R., HERMAN, C. P., and NICASSIO, P.: The power of suggestion: Another examination of misattribution and insomnia. *Journal of Personality and Social Psychology*, 1976, 34, 673-679.

BORKOVEC, T. D. and FOWLES, D. C.: Controlled investigation of the effects of progressive and hypnotic relaxation on insomnia. *Journal of Abnormal Psychology*, 1973, 82, 153-158.

BOYNTON, M. A. and GOODENOUGH, F. L.: The posture of nursery school children during sleep. *American Journal of Psychology*, 1930, 42, 270-278.

COURSEY, R. D., BUCHSBAUM, M., and FRANKEL, B. L.: Personality measures and evoked responses in chronic insomniacs. *Journal of Abnormal Psychology*, 1975, 84, 239-250.

DEMENT, W. C. and GUILLEMINAULT, C.: Sleep disorders: The state of the art. *Hospital Practice*, 1973, 8, 57-71.

FEINSTEIN, B., STERMAN, M. B., and MACDONALD, L. R.: Effects on sleep of EEG biofeedback training of sensorimotor cortical rhythms. *Biofeedback and Self-Regulation*, in press.

FERSTER, C. B., NURNBERGER, J. I., and LEVITT, E. B.: The control of eating. *Journal of Mathetics*, 1962, 1, 87-110.

FOX, L.: Effecting the use of efficient study habits. *Journal of Mathetics*, 1962, 1, 75-86.

FRANKEL, B. L., PATTEN, B. M., and GILLIN, J. C.: Restless legs syndrome: Sleep-electroencephalographic and neurologic findings. *Journal of the American Medical Association*, 1974, 230, 1302-1303.

FREEDMAN, R. and PAPSDORF, J. D.: Biofeedback and progressive relaxation treatment of sleep-onset insomnia: A controlled, all-night investigation. *Biofeedback and Self-Regulation*, 1976, 1, 253-271.

GOLDIAMOND, I.: Self-control procedures in personal behavior problems. *Psychological Reports*, 1965, 17, 851-868.

GUILLEMINAULT, C., ELDRIDGE, F. L., and DEMENT, W. C.: Insomnia with sleep apnea: A new syndrome. *Science*, 1973, 181, 856-858.

HAURI, P.: Personal communication, 1974.

HAURI, P. and GOOD, R.: Frontalis muscle tension and sleep-onset. Paper presented at the 15th Annual Meeting of the Association for the Psychophysiological Study of Sleep, Edinburgh, 1975.

HAYNES, S. N., PRICE, M. G., and SIMONS, J. B.: Stimulus control treatment of insomnia. *Journal of Behavior Therapy & Experimental Psychiatry*, 1975, 6, 279-282.

JACOBSON, E.: *Progressive Relaxation*. Chicago: University of Chicago Press, 1938.

JACOBSON, E.: *Anxiety and Tension Control*. Philadelphia: Lippincott, 1964.

JONES, H. S. and OSWALD, I.: Two cases of healthy insomnia. *Electroencephalography and Clinical Neurophysiology*, 1968, 24, 378-380.

KALES, A., ALLEN, W. C., JR., SCHARF, M. B., and KALES, J. D.: Hypnotic drugs and their effectiveness: All-night EEG studies of insomniac subjects. *Archives of General Psychiatry*, 1970, 23, 226-232.

KALES, A., BIXLER, E. O., LEO, L. A., HEALY, S., and SLYE, E.: Incidence of insomnia in The Los Angeles Metropolitan area. *Sleep Research*, 1974, 4, 139.

KALES, A., BIXLER, E. O., TAN, T. L., SCHARF, M. B., and KALES, J. D.: Chronic hypnotic use: Ineffectiveness, drug withdrawal insomnia, and hypnotic drug dependence. *Journal of the American Medical Association*, 1974, 227, 513-517.

KALES, A., KALES, J. D., BIXLER, E. O., and SCHARF, M. B.: Methodology of sleep laboratory drug evaluations: Further considerations. In: F. Kagan, T. Harwood, K. Rickels, A. D. Rudzik, & H. Sorer (Eds.), *Hypnotics: Methods of Development and Evaluation*. New York: Spectrum, 1975.

KALES, J., TAN, T. L., SWEARINGEN, C., and KALES, A.: Are over-the-counter sleep medications effective? All-night EEG studies. *Current Therapeutic Research*, 1971, 13, 143-151.

KARACAN, I., WARKEIT, G., THORNLY, J., and SCHWAB, J.: Oral presentation. Association for the Psychophysiological Study of Sleep, San Diego, 1973 as reported by F. Kagan, Introduction to Brook Lodge Symposium on hypnotics. In F. Kagan, T. Harwood, K. Rickels, A. D. Rudzik, and H. Sorer (Eds.), *Hypnotics: Methods of Development and Evaluation*. New York: Spectrum, 1975.

KELLOGG, R. and BARON, R. S.: Attribution theory, insomnia, and the reverse placebo effect: A reversal of Storms and Nisbett's findings. *Journal of Personality and Social Psychology*, 1975, 32, 231-256.

KLEITMAN, N.: *Sleep and Wakefulness*. Chicago: University of Chicago Press, 1963.

KNAPP, T. J., DOWNS, D. L., and ALPERSON, J. R.: Behavior therapy for insomnia: A review. *Behavior Therapy*, 1976, 7, 614-625.

MONROE, L. J.: Psychological and physiological differences between good and poor sleepers. *Journal of Abnormal Psychology*, 1967, 72, 255-264.

MONTGOMERY, I., PERKIN, G., and WISE, D.: A review of behavioral treatments for insomnia. *Journal of Behavior Therapy & Experimental Psychiatry*, 1975, 6, 93-100.

MURRAY, E. J.: *Sleep, Dreams, and Arousal*. New York: Appleton-Century-Crofts, 1965.

NICASSIO, P. and BOOTZIN, R.: A comparison of progressive relaxation and autogenic training as treatments for insomnia. *Journal of Abnormal Psychology*, 1974, 83, 253-260.

PAUL, G. L.: Physiological effects of relaxation training and hypnotic suggestion. *Journal of Abnormal Psychology*, 1969, 74, 425-437.

PAUL, G. L. and TRIMBLE, R. W.: Recorder vs. "live" relaxation training and hypnotic suggestions: Comparative effectiveness for reducing physiological arousal and inhibiting stress response. *Behavior Therapy*, 1970, 1, 285-302.

RICKELS, K. and HESBACHER, P. T.: Over-the-counter day time sedatives: A controlled study. *Journal of the American Medical Association*, 1973, 223, 29-33.

SCHACHTER, S. and SINGER, J. E.: Cognitive, social and physiological determinants of emotional state. *Psychological Review*, 1962, 69, 379-399.

SCHULTZ, J. H. and LUTHE, W.: *Autogenic Training*. New York: Grune & Stratton, 1959.

SHARPLESS, S. K.: Hypnotics and sedatives. In L. S. Goodman and A. Gilman (Eds.), *The Pharmacological Basis of Therapeutics*. New York: Macmillan, 1965.

SLAMA, K.: Unpublished Master's Thesis, University of Iowa, 1975.

STORMS, M. D. and NISBETT, R. E.: Insomnia and the attribution process. *Journal of Personality and Social Psychology*, 1970, 16, 319-328.

STOYVA, J. and BUDZYNSKI, T.: Biofeedback training in the self-induction of sleep. Progress Report to the San Diego State College Foundation, 1972.

STUART, R. B.: Behavioral control of overeating. *Behaviour Research and Therapy*, 1967, 5, 357-365.

TOKARZ, T. P. and LAWRENCE, P. S.: An analysis of temporal and stimulus factors in the treatment of insomnia. Paper presented at the 8th Annual Meeting of the Association for the Advancement of Behavior Therapy, Chicago, 1974.

VALINS, S. and NISBETT, R. E.: *Attribution Processes in the Development and Treatment of Emotional Disorders*. Morristown, N. J.: General Learning Press, 1971.

WILCOX, R. H.: Sleep as a behavior: A review. Unpublished paper, University of Chicago, 1970.

WYKERT, J.: Why sleeping pills are keeping you awake. *New York Magazine*, May 24, 1976, 33-38.

WYRWICKA, W. and STERMAN, M. B.: Instrumental conditioning of sensorimotor cortex EEG spindles in the waking cat. *Physiology and Behavior*, 1968, 3, 273-277.

8

Parameters of Self-Monitoring

RICHARD M. McFALL

"Self-monitoring," or SM, refers to the act of systematically observing or recording one's own behavior. In recent years, behavior therapists have shown considerable interest in SM, both as a promising behavioral assessment method and as a possible component for inclusion in their therapy programs. In this paper, I will examine both the assessment and treatment utility of SM, in general, and will explore the special significance of SM procedures for self-management approaches to behavior modification. Since excellent, up-to-date literature reviews on SM are available elsewhere (Kazdin, 1974a; Nelson, 1977). I will not attempt to provide yet another comprehensive review; rather, I will attempt to provide an overview of the key issues, a conceptual integration of the available evidence, and a discussion of the clinical implications of this conceptualization.

SELF-MONITORING IN ASSESSMENT

What to Monitor?

When SM is used for assessment purposes, clients or subjects are asked to collect data on their own behavior and to report the results to the therapist or investigator. The data typically are used either to help explore the nature of specific behavioral problems or to evaluate the effects of specific interventions. The use of SM methods for assessment purposes is consistent with the increasingly common practice among behavioral

196

assessors of enlisting the aid of their clients as active collaborators in the data-collection process. This practice stems from the behaviorist's stress on the importance of situational determinants of behavior and on the importance of obtaining naturalistic samples of target behaviors. An incomplete list of the target behaviors that have been assessed via SM methods to date would include the following: cigarette smoking, food and caloric intake, alcohol consumption, face touching, use of habit phrases (e.g., "you know"), contributions to classroom discussions, hallucinations, eye blinks, use of personal pronouns, various study behaviors, participation in pleasurable activities, feelings of depression, tics, dating behaviors, sexual activities, use of drugs, time spent by phobic patients in fearful situations, mothers' responses to positive and negative child behaviors, nail biting, swimming, room cleaning, use of praise, speech dysfluencies, respiration, sleep patterns, hand gestures, and successfully resisted urges to engage in undesirable acts. As this list suggests, there seems to be almost no limit to the behaviors with which SM methods may be employed for assessment purposes.

How to Monitor?

The particular method by which subjects monitor particular behaviors may vary along a number of general dimensions: It can range from a very *informal* and unstructured operation, as when subjects are asked to make mental notes of any event that seems related to mood changes, to something fairly *formal* and structured, as when subjects are asked to fill out a mood-rating sheet according to a time-sampling schedule. It can be fairly *simple*, as when subjects are asked to keep track of how many cigarettes they smoke in a given time period; or it can be *complex* and time-consuming, as when they are asked to record not only how many cigarettes they smoke, but also the time, place, circumstances, and affective response associated with lighting each cigarette. It can be a relatively *objective* matter, as when counting the calories consumed each day; or it can be a very *subjective* matter, as when recording the number of instances each day when they successfully resist the temptation to eat sweets. A *single*, discrete target behavior might be monitored, like the number of textbook pages read per day; or *several* target behaviors might be monitored concurrently, like the number of pages read, classes attended, assignments completed, hours spent in the library, contributions made to class discussions, and grades received—all seen as related elements in the general category of effective study behavior. The *timing* of the SM act also can vary: For example, it is possible for subjects to record caloric intake immediately prior to eating, immediately after, or retrospectively at bedtime.

Numerous recording devices and methods have been developed to assist subjects in the collection of SM data. The following list is not exhaustive; it merely illustrates the range of possibilities:

1) *Record booklets, checklists, forms.* Compact, inexpensive, easily transported, and simple to use, these paper-and-pencil devices are useful for collecting nominal data over time (e.g., hour-by-hour cigarette consumption).

2) *Counters.* These devices can be fairly simple or sophisticated (e.g., a wrist counter designed to keep track of golf scores; an abacus-like bracelet [Mahoney, 1974]). They are useful whenever the timing of target behaviors is not considered especially important, and when simple frequency counts are sufficient.

3) *Timers.* When it is important to collect data on the timing of target behaviors, then clocks and timers can function as SM devices (e.g., stopwatches to measure time elapsed since last response; parking-meter timers to monitor response rate over a predetermined period).

4) *Meters, measures, and scales.* These devices enable subjects to play a more passive role in monitoring their behavior (e.g., a water meter might provide an indirect measure of obsessive-compulsive hand washing; a weight scale provides an indirect measure of caloric intake).

5) *Residual records.* Another potential source of passively-collected SM data is found in the residual artifacts or byproducts of our consumatory behaviors (see Webb et al., 1966). In some instances, the target behavior results in an accretion of artifacts (e.g., cigarette butts, empty bottles); in other instances, it is associated with an erosion of resources (e.g., decreased supplies; wear and tear).

6) *Archival records.* Many behaviors are recorded in the normal course of events by existing monitoring systems (e.g., checkbooks, charge accounts, appointment books, telephone records). These also can be exploited as sources of SM data.

7) *Diaries.* A subject's written account of the subjective feelings and objective events associated with one or more target behaviors represents the richest, most comprehensive, and most personal of all SM data sources. On the other hand, a diary tends to produce less systematic data, to be more time-consuming, and to require greater

subject cooperation than some other SM methods. Some of these disadvantages can be overcome by asking subjects to use hand-held cassette recorders to make oral diaries; the major drawback of this approach, however, is the cost of equipment and of transcribing data from the tapes.

Why Use Self-Monitoring?

Behavior therapists are attracted to self-monitoring as a data-collection procedure for several reasons. First, most SM methods tend to be cost-efficient. That is, they are less costly than, for example, employing trained, paid observers. Second, due to practical and ethical considerations, SM sometimes is the only feasible method of obtaining naturalistic data on certain classes of sensitive, private, or inaccessible behaviors, such as sexual thoughts and activities. Third, SM provides a means of minimizing the possibility of unwanted effects occurring as a result of the obtrusive presence of observers. Fourth, SM can yield a behavioral record characterized by a thoroughness and density of coverage that few other methods can equal. Finally, there is reason to believe that, in general, the predictive validity of behavioral self-report data, although imperfect, is surpassed only by the validity of data obtained via direct observation (Mischel, 1968). That is, the best way to predict an individual's future behavior in a particular situation is to observe his past behavior in that same situation, but the next best way is simply to ask the person how he typically behaves in that situation. A systematic use of SM methods seems to stand midway between these two methods: While it may lack some of the objectivity of independent behavioral observations, it probably is more objective than informal retrospective self-reports. This is because it prompts subjects to use a formal structure for their self-observation and reporting. In effect, each subject plays the dual roles of actor and observer.

What Are the Limitations of SM?

As an assessment method, self-monitoring is not without its faults. There is good reason to be concerned, for example, about the quality of the data it yields. To the extent that its data are not reliable and valid, then SM methods will be of limited value for assessment purposes. There are two major questions concerning the quality of SM data: First, how accurately do subjects observe, record, and report on their own behavior? Second, how reactive are SM methods?

Accuracy of SM data. The research evidence on the accuracy of SM data is mixed. Where it has been possible to compare SM data against the data of independent, unobtrusive observers, the results have ranged from poor (agreement below 40%) to excellent (agreement over 95%). These inconsistent results suggest that the most appropriate experimental question at this point is, "What are the important factors that affect the accuracy of SM data?" Until very recently, there had been almost no research specifically addressed to this question. In the absence of solid evidence, we can only speculate as to what some of the more influential factors might be. The following is a partial list of some possible factors:

1) *Training.* It is only reasonable to expect that training subjects in the correct use of SM methods should result in increased accuracy. Nelson, Lipinski, and Boykin (in press), for example, recently reported that in one study the accuracy of SM data provided by trained subjects was .91; for untrained subjects it was .78.

2) *Systematic methods.* The more systematic the SM method used, the more reliable and accurate it is likely to be. This is basically a matter of common sense and sound scientific practice. Studies explicitly examining this factor in relation to the accuracy of SM data are needed.

3) *Monitoring devices as aids and prompts.* SM methods that simplify the subject's data-collection task and are less dependent on the subjects' memory should yield more accurate data. For example, it may be that smoking data recorded on a form attached to the cigarette pack would be more accurate than data recorded on a form kept in the subject's pocket. This is another factor that needs careful study.

4) *Timing.* Evidence suggests that the closer in time the monitoring act is to the actual target behavior, the more likely it is that it will yield accurate data. Frederiksen, Epstein, and Kosevsky (1975), for example, found that subjects were more accurate if they immediately recorded each cigarette they smoked (93%) than if they recorded at the end of each day (85%) or at the end of each week (87%).

5) *Response competition.* When concurrent responses compete for the subject's attention, this interference may decrease the accuracy of SM data. This was demonstrated in two studies by Epstein, Webster, and Miller (1975). Subjects showed a significant increase in their percentage of errors in an SM task when required to perform a concurrent operant task. The increase in monitoring errors oc-

curred even when subjects were given monetary incentives for SM accuracy. Interestingly, performance in the operant task was not detrimentally affected by SM.

6) *Response effort.* The more demanding an SM method, in terms of the subject's time and energy, the less accurate it is likely to be. Direct evidence concerning the effects of effort on SM accuracy are not yet available; however, it seems unlikely that subjects will faithfully carry out SM methods that are tiring, tedious, or cumbersome. Decreased compliance, in turn, should lead to decreased accuracy.

7) *Reinforcement contingencies.* If positive reinforcers are contingent on the production of accurate SM data, this should increase the level of accuracy. Conversely, if accurate data are consequated negatively, this should result in decreased accuracy. Lipinski, Black, Nelson, and Ciminero (1975) differentially reinforced college students for accurate self-reports of face touching and found an increase in accuracy from a baseline of .67 to a new level of .84. A second group, reinforced for decreases in face touching rather than for accuracy, subsequently increased their accuracy only slightly (to .72).

8) *Attention to accuracy.* If a subject is made aware that SM accuracy is being assessed, this should result in increased accuracy. This factor was illustrated in a study by Nelson, Lipinski, and Black (1975), where there was a dramatic increase in the accuracy of SM data for face touching (from .55 to .81) when subjects were made aware that their reports were being checked for accuracy.

9) *Target behaviors.* Certain target behaviors, by their very nature, may be monitored more accurately than others. Behaviors that are more salient, more easily discriminated, or more memorable are more likely to be recorded more accurately. Verbal behaviors, for example, have been monitored with relatively low levels of accuracy (e.g., Cavior & Marabotto, 1976); in contrast, higher levels of accuracy have been reported for motor behaviors, such as face touching (e.g., Lipinski & Nelson, 1974). Positively valued behaviors also may be recorded more accurately than negatively valued behaviors (Nelson, Hay, Hay, & Carstens, 1976).

10) *Subject characteristics.* Although there has been little or no research bearing directly on this factor, it seems reasonable to hypothesize that some subjects may be more accurate monitors than others. For example, children, hospitalized psychiatric patients, and involuntary research subjects might be expected to provide less accurate SM data than college student volunteers (Kazdin, 1974a).

By controlling the various factors listed above, it may be possible to develop SM assessment methods that yield maximally accurate data.

However, the necessary research aimed specifically at enhancing the fidelity of SM reports has been undertaken only recently (e.g., Bornstein et al., 1975). Much more work needs to be done along this line.

Reactivity. The second potential shortcoming of SM as an assessment method is that it sometimes proves to be a reactive procedure. That is, the very act of observing and recording one's own behavior sometimes exerts an unintended and unwanted influence on that behavior. To the extent that SM methods are reactive, this reduces the representativeness of the behavioral samples it produces and limits the generality of any conclusions based on such data. Thus, the potential reactivity of SM methods is an especially significant concern to those who are attempting to assess the true base rates of naturalistic behaviors.

To date the greatest share of published research on SM has been addressed to this question of its potential reactivity. Unfortunately, the question has not always been clearly stated, and this has tended only to confuse matters rather than clarify them. Some of the earlier studies were devoted to seeking a categorical answer to the question: "Is SM reactive?" In a similar spirit, early reviews of the SM literature took a "box-score" approach toward evaluating the research evidence. They sorted the available studies into two columns—studies providing evidence *for* reactivity versus those providing evidence *against* it—and then simply totaled the scores to see which side won ("six *for*, seven *against*—guess it isn't reactive after all").

It has been only recently that investigators have addressed the reactivity issue in a more sensible and informative manner. Instead of asking whether or not SM is reactive, they have been asking: "What effects occur, as a function of what SM procedures, under what conditions, in what behaviors, with what subjects?" Consistent with this more analytic approach, Nelson (in preparation) has provided an excellent comprehensive review of the available research in which she has identified eight variables that seem to influence the occurrence, magnitude, or direction of reactive effects associated with SM methods. Briefly, these eight variables are as follows:

1) *Motivation.* Subjects who are already motivated to alter their behavior—such as volunteer subjects in a smoking cessation study—are more likely to show reactive effects when they monitor their behavior. This was demonstrated in a recent study by Lipinski, Black, Nelson, and Ciminero (1975). Subjects who were motivated to quit smoking showed a decrease in smoking when asked to moni-

tor their smoking frequency. Subjects who were not motivated to quit failed to show a similar reactivity to SM.

2) *Valence.* The valence of the target behavior appears to determine the direction of SM effects. Positively valued behaviors are likely to increase, negatively valued behaviors are likely to decrease, and neutral behaviors are not likely to change. For example, when Cavior and Marabotto (1976) asked subjects to select and monitor a verbal behavior which they regarded either as positive or negative, the frequency of the positive behaviors increased whereas the frequency of the negative behaviors decreased.

3) *Target behaviors.* The specific nature of the target behavior selected for monitoring also may influence the reactivity of SM methods. Romanczyk (1974) found that it was more reactive for subjects in a weight-control study to monitor both their daily weight and calorie intake than to monitor only their daily weight. McFall (1970) instructed some subjects to monitor their urges to smoke and other subjects to monitor their actual instances of smoking; the former instructions resulted in decreased smoking, while the latter led to increased smoking.

4) *Goals, reinforcement, and feedback.* The presence of performance goals and the availability of performance feedback or reinforcement tend to promote reactivity, especially as the discrepancy between the goals and the actual behavior increases. The effects of goals and feedback were demonstrated by Kazdin (1974b): Subjects given a performance goal in an experimental task showed greater reactivity to SM than subjects not given such a goal. Reactivity was also enhanced when subjects were provided with feedback via a digital counter about the frequency of their target behavior. In a study by Lipinski, Black, Nelson, and Ciminero (1975), subjects showed greater reactivity to SM when they were given monetary reinforcement for decreases in face touching than when they simply monitored without such reinforcement.

5) *Timing.* The timing of the SM act, relative to the target behavior, also can influence the reactivity of SM. For example, Bellack, Rozensky, and Schwartz (1974) conducted a weight-loss study in which subjects recorded their food intake either prior to eating or after eating. Subjects who recorded prior to eating lost the most weight.

6) *SM devices.* Some recording devices seem to be more prone to reactivity than others. In general, the more obtrusive the device, the more reactive it tends to be. For example, Nelson, Lipinski, and Boykin (in press) reported that when subjects held a counter in their hand it exerted a stronger influence on their target behavior than when they kept the counter in their pocket.

7) *Number of target behaviors.* There is some evidence that reactivity may decrease, or become diffused, as the number of target behaviors monitored concurrently increases (Hayes & Cavior, in press).

8) *Schedule of SM.* There also is suggestive evidence that the frequency or schedule of SM may affect its reactivity. Mahoney, Moore, Wade, and Moura (1973), for example, found that continuous recording of correct answers in a learning task resulted in more persistence at the task than an intermittent schedule of recording every third correct answer.

Many of the variables which Nelson identified as possible factors in SM's reactivity were extracted post hoc from studies involving SM methods of all sorts; thus, these variables are in need of more careful and controlled experimental study. Unfortunately, there have been few such experiments. One exception has been the programmatic research of Nelson and her colleagues, as evidenced by the studies cited above. Another exception was a series of three studies by Kazdin (1974b). These were controlled laboratory experiments involving a Taffel-type sentence construction task in which the frequency of sentences starting with "I" or "We" was the target behavior for SM and also was the dependent variable. The first experiment revealed that the direction of SM effects was systematically related to variations in the target behavior's perceived social desirability. When a positive valence was attached to the target behavior, it increased in frequency. A negative valence, however, led to a decrease, and the absence of a specific valence produced no change. These valence effects were most evident when subjects were instructed to keep a formal count of their target behavior, but also were present to a lesser extent when subjects were simply aware that their behavior was being recorded by the experimenter. The second experiment demonstrated that both the reactivity of SM and the directional influence of response valence tended to be enhanced when subjects were given a performance standard against which to compare their own behavior. The third experiment revealed that visual feedback in the form of a digital counter displaying the target behavior's frequency also enhanced the reactivity of SM.

Quite independently of Kazdin's studies, Sieck and McFall (1976) conducted a controlled laboratory study of some of the same parameters of SM's reactivity. For several reasons, the eye blink response was selected as the target behavior: a) it occurs with regularity and reasonable frequency; b) it is a neutral response that readily can be assigned positive or negative values via simple instructional manipulations; c) it is a discrete, easily counted behavior that can be unobtrusively recorded electromechanically; and d) it is a response that subjects can control, although it ordinarily occurs without their awareness.

The experimental hypotheses examined were: a) that the direction of reactive effects is a function of the perceived valence of the target behavior; b) that neither the behavior's valence nor SM alone is sufficient to produce significant reactive effects, but that both are necessary; c) that *self*-monitoring is more reactive than monitoring by the *experimenter*, and that a *combination* of self- and experimenter-monitoring is at least as reactive as self-monitoring alone; d) that multiple reports of monitored data are more reactive than a single overall report of monitored data; and e) that SM effects are not due simply to attending to the target behavior, but are a function of the explicit monitoring act itself.

Eighty undergraduate subjects were randomly assigned to one of ten experimental groups, with a limit of eight subjects per condition. Subjects were seen individually for a single session that was divided into four five-minute experimental periods: baseline, value-induction, monitoring, and return-to-baseline. All subjects were led to believe that the purpose of the study was to gather normative physiological data, and electrodes were attached for the ostensible purpose of measuring heart rate, EEG, and palmer sweat. Actually, the electrodes measured eye blinks by bone conduction. Subjects were seated alone in an experimental room and received all instructions via prerecorded tapes equated for length.

Six of the subject groups were employed in a 3 x 2 design aimed at assessing the effects of three levels of target-behavior valence (positive, neutral, and negative) and two levels of monitoring (self-monitoring versus no monitoring) on eye-blink rates. A baseline period of unobtrusively recorded eye-blink rates was followed by the value-induction period, which began with subjects receiving information designed to attribute either a positive, neutral, or negative valence to the eye blink response; subjects still were unaware, however, that their eye blinks were actually being measured. In the third period, half of the subjects in each valence condition counted their eye blinks, and half received no such monitoring instructions.

As expected, analyses of subjects' percent change in blink rates (blinks per minute) across experimental periods revealed that neither the value-induction nor the self-monitoring manipulations alone were sufficient to produce reactive effects. When these two factors were combined, however, significant changes in blink rates were obtained. Monitoring of positively valued behavior resulted in increased blinking (monitor vs. no monitor, $p = .025$), while monitoring of negatively valued behavior produced a marginally significant decrease (monitor vs. no monitor, $p = .065$). These reactive effects disappeared when subjects stopped monitoring in the return-to-baseline period.

Two of the remaining subject groups, along with the self-monitoring, positive-value group described above, were compared in another part of the experimental design. This comparison provided an assessment of the relative reactivity of *self-*, *experimenter-*, and *combined*-monitoring. All three groups received positive value-induction instructions; they differed only in terms of who performed the monitoring act during the crucial third period. For subjects in the experimenter-and combined-monitoring conditions, curtains covering a one-way window were opened at the beginning of the monitoring period and then were closed again at the end of that period.

The experimenter-monitoring group showed an inexplicable increase in blink rate during the value-induction period. This near-significant change occurred *prior* to the introduction of differential monitoring instructions—that is, at a point where all three groups still had experienced identical treatments. They showed no such increase during the monitoring period, however. The self- and combined-monitoring groups, in contrast, tended to increase their blink rates between the value-induction and monitoring periods only, as expected ($p = .045$ & $.065$, respectively).

Also included in the design was a positive-value self-monitoring group that was instructed to provide multiple reports of SM data (10 reports over a five-minute period) instead of the usual single report at the end of the monitoring period. The effect of multiple reporting seemed contrary to predictions; subjects in this condition actually showed a slight *decrease* in their blink rates, whereas single report subjects had increased theirs. This difference between the two groups approached significance ($p = .065$).

In general, the various results of this study tended to support the basic hypotheses concerning some of the main factors responsible for the occurrence, direction, and magnitude of reactive SM effects. One noteworthy finding deserving further study was the unexpected failure of multiple reporting to show any evidence of reactivity. It had been hypothesized that multiple reporting would be even more reactive than single reporting.

Clearly, far more research along the lines of the laboratory studies described above must be conducted before we can say with confidence that we understand the major determinants of SM's reactivity. Unless we know what the determinants are, we cannot reasonably hope to control unwanted reactivity. And if we cannot minimize such reactivity, then the practical utility of SM methods for purposes of behavioral assessment is seriously limited.

SELF-MONITORING AS A TREATMENT COMPONENT

The same questions that were raised about the use of SM in assessment can also be raised about the use of SM in therapy: What to monitor? How to monitor? Why monitor? And why not monitor (accuracy and reactivity)? To the extent that the objectives of assessment and treatment differ, however, their respective answers to these questions are also likely to differ. To avoid unnecessary repetition, only the important differences implied by the use of SM in treatment will be presented here. Also—for reasons that should become apparent—the order of the questions to be considered will be rearranged.

Reactivity

The most significant difference between assessment and treatment perspectives is on the issue of SM's potential reactivity. Here, the two perspectives are diametrically opposed to one another; that is, the therapeutic potential and assessment utility of a given SM procedure tend to be inversely related to one another. The more reactive an SM procedure is, the less suitable it is for assessment purposes, but the more attractive it becomes as a potential treatment component. Conversely, the less reactive it is, the better it is for assessment, but the less potential it has as a treatment component. Basic research into the determinants of SM's reactivity, therefore, has implications for both assessment and treatment: The research results can be used either to help develop methods of minimizing and controlling reactivity for assessment, or to help find ways of maximizing and exploiting reactivity for treatment.

It is important to note that not *all* reactivity is therapeutically desirable; it is desirable only to the extent that it can be harnessed and used constructively to foster positive behavioral changes. Thus, to be of real value in designing interventions, the previously presented list of factors contributing to reactivity should be elaborated further in terms of the particular effect we might expect with each factor. The available evidence, though far from complete, suggests that SM is most likely to produce positive behavioral changes when change-motivated subjects continuously monitor a limited number of discrete, positively-valued target behaviors; when performance feedback and goals or standards are made available and are unambiguous; and when the monitoring act is both salient and closely related in time to the target behaviors. Positive changes also seem likely, however, when a negatively-valued habitual response is monitored by an obtrusive method, with the recording act preceding the target behavior. Some of the research evidence supporting these assertions was listed previously in the section on reactivity in assessment, and will not be repeated here. It should be noted, however, that much of the evidence is indirect and highly inferential. Far more research is necessary before we will have an adequate understanding of how best to maximize and exploit SM's reactivity.

Accuracy

Accurate data are the *sine qua non* of SM's use in assessment. In treatment, however, there is no intrinsic necessity for such accuracy. Regardless of whether or not subjects monitor their target behaviors accurately, if the monitoring act somehow fosters the desired behavior change, then this is all that is important from a treatment perspective. (Of course, if subjects are instructed to engage in SM for the dual purposes of promoting change and gathering data to reflect that change, then accuracy is important, but only for the assessment function.)

As with many of the other issues considered in this paper, there is too little evidence at present to allow us to draw firm conclusions. Nevertheless, the available research seems to suggest that, indeed, very inaccurate monitoring sometimes may have therapeutically valuable effects (e.g., Broden, Hall, & Mitts, 1971). Nelson (in press) has suggested, however, that perhaps a minimum level of accuracy is required before reactive effects are possible. Future research is needed to clarify this issue. Most likely, the accuracy requirements for therapeutic effects will vary as a function of the particular problem being treated and the specific contribution that SM is expected to make to the overall change process.

How to Monitor?

From a treatment perspective, the choice of monitoring methods or devices is essentially a pragmatic affair: The best method or device is the one that contributes most significantly to achieving the desired treatment outcome. This is in sharp contrast to the choice of SM methods in assessment, where the best method is the one that collects the highest quality data. In treatment, SM methods are actually therapeutic interventions, and should be selected and evaluated on the basis of the same criteria as any other therapy component. Only when two or more methods are shown to be equally effective treatments is it reasonable to choose on the basis of secondary considerations, like economy, efficiency, or elegance.

Again, there is insufficient research evidence, at this point, to allow us to choose intelligently from among the available SM methods and devices. There is a growing body of studies demonstrating that specific SM methods can contribute significantly to behavioral change with specific problems, such as weight control (Bellack et al., 1974). But studies comparing the relative contributions of different SM methods to the same treatment program are virtually nonexistent. This is yet another area in which we must await further investigation before we can confidently draw any conclusions.

What to Monitor?

In assessment, the aim of SM is to collect high-quality data on specific dependent variables; thus, the target behaviors chosen for monitoring must be directly related to the dependent variables of interest. In treatment, however, the SM procedure serves as an independent variable; thus, the target behaviors selected for monitoring need not be directly related to the dependent variables and, in fact, may be quite dissimilar from them. For example, from a treatment perspective, clients suffering from migraine headaches might be instructed to monitor the skin temperature of their hands according to some predetermined schedule; from an assessment perspective, these same clients probably would be instructed to monitor the frequency, duration, and intensity of their headaches. When SM is used as a treatment component, the choice of target behaviors, like the choice of monitoring methods and devices, is essentially a pragmatic matter to be decided empirically. The best target behavior is simply the one that contributes most significantly to producing the desired treatment effects.

Unfortunately, few studies have systematically compared the relative effects of monitoring different target behaviors as part of the treatment for specific behavioral problems. One exception was a weight-control study (Romanczyk, 1974) in which some subjects monitored their daily body weight while other subjects monitored both their daily body weight and caloric intake. The results suggested that significant weight loss occurred only when calories were counted. In another study (Gottman & McFall, 1972), students in a class for "potential high school dropouts" were instructed to monitor either the frequency of their oral class participation or the frequency of their failure to participate when they wished to do so. There were two subject groups and four experimental periods: a baseline, two monitoring periods with a cross-over of treatments, and a return-to-baseline. An independent observer recorded actual frequencies of participation over the four periods. There was a clear relationship between the frequency of oral participation and the particular target behaviors monitored. When students monitored *talk* behavior, their talking increased, and when they monitored *no-talk* behavior, their talking tended to decrease. Furthermore there seemed to be an order effect, with *talk*-monitoring showing the greatest increase when it followed a *no-talk*-monitoring period; this suggests a possible rebound effect.

These two studies, one on weight control and one on class participation, illustrate the importance of carefully selecting the target behavior when using SM in treatment. It is not entirely clear from these studies, however, why some target behaviors are better than others, or how we might go about identifying the best target behaviors for the treatment of specific behavioral problems.

EXPLANATIONS OF SELF-MONITORING EFFECTS

This review of SM's use in assessment and treatment has pointed repeatedly to the need for additional systematic research into the parameters of SM. It would greatly facilitate such research if there were a general theoretical model of the processes underlying SM's effects. Such a conception not only should be capable of integrating the available evidence, but also should be of heuristic value, providing hypotheses to be explored in future studies. Until we develop a better general understanding of *why* SM sometimes results in systematic behavioral changes, we cannot hope to control such effects either for assessment or treatment purposes.

To date, two explanatory models for SM effects have been proposed. The first, and most detailed, is based on Kanfer's (1970; Kanfer & Phillips, 1970) feedback model of self-regulation. In brief, this model proposes that a self-regulatory sequence is set in motion when an individual responds to a stimulus situation and then observes the results of his performance. The individual compares his performance results against a personal performance standard, goal, or norm, and then self-administers either positive reinforcement or punishment, depending on the direction and magnitude of the discrepancy between his observed performance and his standard. The self-administered reinforcements, in turn, modify or regulate his subsequent performance in the same situation. The primary function of SM in this model is to promote self-observation and evaluation of performance. Of course, persons engage in self-observation even when they are not subjects in SM experiments, but the SM procedure tends to enhance the ongoing self-regulatory process by focusing the subject's attention on his performance in a more explicit and systematic way than might otherwise be the case. There is another possible function for SM, according to this model. The monitoring act also can serve a cueing function for subsequent behavior; in this capacity, it exerts a more direct regulatory influence by modifying the stimulus environment, which alters the response requirements. Generally, the explanatory model seems promising. It is consistent with much of the available research evidence, and it has provided fruitful hypotheses for some of the better SM experiments to date.

A second explanatory model of SM effects is based on an operant conditioning formulation (see Kazdin, 1974a). This model, which is similar to Kanfer's, places greater emphasis on the importance of SM responses as controlling stimuli. Monitoring one's own behavior may produce a change by increasing the salience of remote response consequences, both positive and negative. The monitoring act itself (e.g., recording the incidence of positively or negatively valued behaviors) may acquire positively reinforcing or aversive properties. Monitoring also may serve either as a discriminative stimulus for thoughts about response consequences or as a cue for engaging in learned alternative responses. In general, the effect of SM in this model is to alter behaviors by rearranging the cueing and consequating stimuli that control such behaviors.

Both of these explanatory models seem capable of subsuming much of the available research, but neither is capable of encompassing all of it. Neither model, for example, provides a satisfactory explanation of how it is possible that behavioral changes sometimes occur even when subjects fail to monitor their behavior accurately. In general, both models seem to place too much confidence in the validity of their subjects' perceptual processes. Even under the best of circumstances, human subjects tend to be faulty observers. Research has shown, for example, that the average human observer is likely to commit a number of specific perceptual and judgmental errors, like perceiving the existence of correlations among events when no such correlations actually exist (Chapman & Chapman, 1969).

It seems likely that not one, but several mechanisms are responsible for the various kinds of SM effects that have been reported. In fact, it may be that one of the mechanisms underlying SM effects is essentially perceptual in nature; that is, the monitoring process may cause changes in subjects' perceptions of events, which in turn may effect changes in their responses to these perceived events. It should be noted that the altered perceptions need not be any more or less veridical than the ones they replaced; almost any change in perceptual set would be accompanied by an altered response set. From this perspective, the tendency for SM to cause behavioral changes would simply be a function of the extent to which the monitoring act resulted in new perceptual sets that were discrepant from those held by the subject prior to monitoring.

Clearly, there is a need for more research into the specific parameters of SM. As stated previously, such research should be addressed to the complex question: What effects occur in what behaviors as a function of what SM procedures being administered to what subjects under what conditions? The accumulation of additional evidence should lead to improved theories of SM effects; in turn, such theories should enable us to ask even better experimental questions. Ultimately, the aim is to increase our understanding of and control over the processes involved in SM. Only then can we take full advantage of SM's apparent potential for assessment and treatment.

REFERENCES

BELLACK, A. S., ROZENSKY, R. and SCHWARTZ, J.: A comparison of two forms of self-monitoring in a behavioral weight reduction program. *Behavior Therapy*, 1974, 5, 523-530.

BORNSTEIN, P. H., HAMILTON, S. B., CARMODY, T. P., RYCHTARIK, R. G. and VERALDI, D. M.: Reliability enhancement: Increasing the accuracy of self-report. Unpublished manuscript, University of Montana, 1975.

BRODEN, M., HALL, R. V. and MITTS, B.: The effect of self-recording on the classroom behavior of two eighth-grade students. *Journal of Applied Behavior Analysis*, 1971, 4, 191-199.

CAVIOR, N. and MARABOTTO, C. M.: Monitoring verbal behaviors in a dyadic interaction: Valence of target behaviors, type, timing, and reactivity of monitoring. *Journal of Consulting and Clinical Psychology*, 1976, 44, 68-76.

CHAPMAN, L. J. and CHAPMAN, J. P.: Illusory correlation as an obstacle to the use of valid psycho-diagnostic signs. *Journal of Abnormal Psychology*, 1969, 74, 271-280.

EPSTEIN, L. H., WEBSTER, J. S. and MILLER, P. M.: Accuracy and controlling effects of self-monitoring as a function of concurrent responding and reinforcement. *Behavior Therapy*, 1975, 6, 654-666.

FREDERIKSEN, L. W., EPSTEIN, L. H. and KOSEVSKY, B. P. Reliability and controlling effects of three procedures for self-monitoring smoking. *The Psychological Record*, 1975, 25, 255-264.

GOTTMAN, J. M. and McFALL, R. M.: Self-monitoring effects in a program for potential high school dropouts: A time-series analysis. *Journal of Consulting and Clinical Psychology*, 1972, 39, 273-281.

HAYES, S. C. and CAVIOR, N.: Effects of multiple tracking and target difficulty on the reactivity of self-monitoring: I. Negative behaviors. *Behavior Therapy*, in press.

KANFER, F. H.: Self-monitoring: Methodological limitations and clinical applications. *Journal of Consulting and Clinical Psychology*, 1970, 35, 148-152.

KANFER, F. H. and PHILLIPS, J. S. *Learning Foundations of Behavior Therapy*. N. Y.: Wiley, 1970.

KAZDIN, A. E.: Self-monitoring and behavior change. In M. J. Mahoney and C. E. Thoresen (Eds.), *Self-Control: Power to the Person*. Monterey, Ca.: Brooks-Cole, 1974. (a)

KAZDIN, A. E.: Reactive self-monitoring: The effects of response desirability, goal setting, and feedback. *Journal of Consulting and Clinical Psychology*, 1974, 42, 704-716. (b)

LIPINSKI, D. P., BLACK, J. L., NELSON, R. O. and CIMINERO, A. R.: The influence of motivational variables on the reactivity and reliability of self-recording. *Journal of Consulting and Clinical Psychology*, 1975, 43, 637-646.

LIPINSKI, D. P. and NELSON, R. O.: The reactivity and unreliability of self-recording. *Journal of Consulting and Clinical Psychology*, 1974, 42, 118-123.

MAHONEY, K. Count on it: A simple self-monitoring device. *Behavior Therapy*, 1974, 5, 701-703.

MAHONEY, M. J., MOORE, B. S., WADE, T. C. and MOURA, N. G. M.: The effects of continuous and intermittent self-monitoring on academic behavior. *Journal of Consulting and Clinical Psychology*, 1973, 41, 65-69.

McFALL, R. M.: Effects of self-monitoring on normal smoking behavior. *Journal of Consulting and Clinical Psychology*, 1970, 35, 135-142.

MISCHEL, W.: *Personality and Assessment*. N. Y.: Wiley, 1968.

NELSON, R. O.: Methodological issues in assessment via self-monitoring. In J. D. Cone and R. P. Hawkins (Eds.), *Behavioral Assessment: New Directions in Clinical Psychology*. N. Y.: Brunner/Mazel, 1977.

NELSON, R. O., HAY, L. R., HAY, W. M. and CARSTENS, C. B.: The reactivity and reliability of teachers' self-monitoring of positive and negative classroom verbalizations. Paper presented at the Association for the Advancement of Behavior Therapy meetings, New York, December, 1976.

NELSON, R. O., LIPINSKI, D. P. and BOYKIN, R. A.: The effects of self-recorders' training and the obtrusiveness of the self-recording device on the accuracy and reactivity of self-monitoring. *Behavior Therapy*, in press.

ROMANCZYK, R. G.: Self-monitoring in the treatment of obesity: Parameters of reactivity. *Behavior Therapy*, 1974, 5, 531-540.

SIECK, W. A. and McFALL, R. M.: Some determinants of self-monitoring effects. *Journal of Consulting and Clinical Psychology*, 1976, 44, 958-965.

WEBB, E. J., CAMPBELL, D. T., SCHWARTZ, R. D. and SECHREST, L.: Unobtrusive measures. Chicago: Rand McNally, 1966.

9

Development and Evaluation of Weight Reduction Procedures in a Health Maintenance Organization

CAROL LANDAU HECKERMAN
and
JAMES O. PROCHASKA

Obesity plagues between 25% and 45% of American adults (U.S. Public Health Service, 1966). Many others who are not obese still are concerned with their weight. One prominent researcher has called this "the age of caloric anxiety" (Van Itallie, 1973). This anxiety is reflected in the "revolutionary" diets and new types of dietetic foods and beverages which are frequently advertised in the mass media.

A recent review of the literature (Heckerman, 1974) revealed that although several behavioral paradigms have had some success in the treatment of obesity, the mixed model of self-control procedures as originally described by Ferster et al. (1962) and developed by Stuart (1967) had produced the most convincing research demonstrating effective treatment (Heckerman, 1974).

This article is based upon a dissertation by the senior author under the direction of the junior author at the University of Rhode Island. Gratitude is expressed to other dissertation committee members, Allan Berman, Thomas A. Gunning and Wayne Velicer, and also to Robert G. Rosenberg, Medical Director of the Rhode Island Group Health Association.

Additional tables and appendices are available from the senior author at Brown University/Butler Hospital, 345 Blackstone Blvd., Providence, Rhode Island 02906.

215

The self-control techniques focus on both the stimuli which lead to overeating and inactivity, and on the individual's responses. Stimulus control techniques manipulate the antecedents of unhealthy eating. Reinforcement for weight loss and for healthy eating habits increases the probability of these responses. These programs have been successful with obese college students (Harris, 1969; Wollersheim, 1970) and have been shown to be more effective than traditional group therapy, diet therapy, and self-help groups (Stuart, 1971; Penick, Filion, Fox, & Stunkard, 1971).

Several research questions remain unanswered. First, can the self-control procedures be used effectively with people who are not from university population? Most of the previous studies have dealt with a university or private practice population. Hall, Hall, Nandon and Borden (1974) and Levitz and Stunkard (1974) treated subjects who were older and more obese than subjects in earlier studies, but they did not report educational level or socioeconomic status. Could these treatment programs be offered through a new delivery system—the health maintenance organization? By using such a system, subjects of various ages, socioeconomic levels and educational levels could be treated in a convenient facility. In addition, the cooperation of the subjects' medical treatment team could be encouraged.

Can the self-control procedures for weight reduction be improved? Theoretically, adding one of two possible factors could provide even more effective treatment of obesity. Self-control procedures consist primarily of self-monitoring and of stimulus control techniques. They are not necessarily, as the name might suggest, internally controlled procedures. However, the self-control procedures can be modified in order to provide more internal control. Likewise, adding a reinforcement system to the treatment package can make the program more externally controlled. Thus the self-control procedures can be modified and presented with more internal control, or be modified in a different way and presented with more external control.

Adding external control should theoretically improve the effectiveness of the self-control techniques. The work of Schacter and his associates suggested that obese subjects' eating behavior is controlled by the external stimuli in the environment (Schachter, & Gross, 1968; Nisbett, 1968; Schacter, 1971). More external control could be added by the use of contingency contracting. No controlled studies have specifically combined self-control procedures with contingency contracting.

An approach opposite to maximizing the external control of obese subjects' behavior would be to modify that externality to one of internal control of eating behavior. Instead of adding external controls, an attempt can be made to heighten internal control.

Mahoney and Thoreson (1974) have referred to self-control as "power to the person." They stated that behavior therapy techniques, specifically self-control procedures, can be used for individual development and growth—a humanistic end. By becoming aware of his/her internal state, and by manipulating the environment, the person can gain greater freedom.

Stunkard (1972) suggested that the use of self-control in the treatment of obesity can lead to weight loss and a more inner-directed life. By gaining control of eating behavior (rather than being controlled by eating) the subject can gain a sense of mastery. Some support for Stunkard's view was found by Jeffrey (1974), who reported that subjects in a self-control group became significantly less external as measured by the Rotter Internal-External Scale.

Rodin (1974) suggested that psychologists must learn to treat the externality, not the obesity of obese people. Thus, an exploratory attempt was made to emphasize self-control by focusing on internal control. If successful, such a treatment method would presumably lead to long-term weight loss.

METHOD

Treatment Setting

The weight reduction program was offered to all members of a health maintenance organization. The program was announced in a newsletter, and by posters in the health maintenance center. The program was also described to staff members during their clinical meetings.

Subjects

Subjects were 43 members (34 females, 9 males) who were prescreened for any medical contraindications to weight reduction. Subjects were at least 10% overweight according to Metropolitan Life Insurance Height and Weight Tables (1959).

Subjects ranged in age from 17-60 years, with a mean age of 37 years. The mean weight was 192.9 pounds and the mean percentage overweight

64.15. Socioeconomic status, as measured by the Hollingshead scale, was 3.39 or middle-class (Hollingshead, 1957). The mean educational level was 13 years indicating one year of post-secondary education, usually in a technical school. Many of the subjects, 58%, did not volunteer for the program, but were referred to the program by their physicians. These subjects often had medical problems such as hypertension or edema, or they were surgical risks because of their obesity. Their non-volunteer status make some of these subjects quite different from those included in earlier studies.

Experimenter

The experimenter was a third-year female graduate student in clinical psychology.

Procedure

All subjects agreed to pay a $25.00 deposit. Ten dollars of the deposit were refunded at the end of treatment for all groups, except the contingency contracting group, which had a specific refund rate. Since the subjects were unaware of the refund, all subjects were equally prescreened for this motivational factor.

Subjects were randomly assigned to one of four groups: 1) standard self-control (SC); 2) self-control plus external control via contingency contracting (SC-EC); 3) self-control plus internal control (SC-IC); or 4) a no-treatment group.

All subjects were weighed and categorized by percentage overweight. All subjects completed Rotter's Internal-External Control Scale (Rotter, 1966) and a medical problem checklist before and after the experimental period.

Treatment Groups

The three treatment groups met once a week for approximately one and a half hours for 12 consecutive weeks. Subjects in all groups began each treatment session by being weighed in privately by the experimenter.

All subjects were given *Slim Chance in a Fat World* (Stuart and Davis, 1972) as a textbook. All experimental groups spent an equal amount of time outside of the group doing homework assignments. All subjects were assigned the task of describing self-control procedures in their own words in order to determine whether the procedures were understood. Other assignments varied according to the group.

Standard Self-Control (SC)

This treatment package was modeled after that of Stuart and Davis (1972). The program consisted of nutritional information and behavioral principles including self-monitoring, stimulus control, self-reinforcement and social reinforcement.

Subjects were assisted in developing a specific behavioral plan which identified the specific problematic stimuli and responses in their lives. Sessions were spent discussing and reviewing the techniques. Any specific problems were analyzed from a behavioral, self-control perspective.

Homework assignments included description of specific personal self-control plans, and essays on personal responses to these plans.

Self-Control Plus More External Control Via Contingency Contracting (SC-EC)

This group began with the same treatment package as the SC group. However, this group also included an external reinforcement system, by adding a contingency contract. Each subject contracted to lose at least one pound per week. After each weigh-in, the subject received two dollars of the deposit if one or more pounds had been lost. If there were no weight loss, or if the subject failed to attend the meeting, then the subject lost two dollars of the deposit. Thus, if treatment were effective, each subject in this group would lose at least 12 pounds, and all but one dollar of the deposit could have been refunded.

Homework assignments included personal descriptions of self-control plans, and essays on individual reactions to the contingency contract.

Self-Control Plus More Internal Control (SC-IC)

This group also began with the same treatment package as the SC group. In addition, an attempt was made to increase subjects' internal control of their eating behavior.

The philosophy of this group was to be one of increased awareness of alternatives and of choices leading to individual, internal control. Subjects were presented with the philosophy that they could gain control over their eating behavior. They were taught to analyze the antecedents and consequences of their eating behavior, with respect to how they could change their lives. The fact that they could choose to overeat or to create new alternatives to overeating was emphasized. Such new alternatives included hobbies, social activities, and relaxation training. The same alternatives were discussed with other groups. In this group, however, much emphasis was placed on the individual's choice and ability to control his/her behavior.

Internal control was also encouraged by changing self-statements. Meichenbaum and Cameron (1974) found that what subjects say to themselves can lead to clinical improvement. This modification of "thinking aloud" can also be used with obese subjects.

Subjects were told to substitute statements such as "I won't" for involuntary statements like "I can't." Similarly, when confronted by a tempting food, subjects were encouraged to have a "healthy dialogue" with themselves. Too often, obese subjects tend to say inwardly, "Why not? One piece of pie won't hurt." Subjects rehearsed stopping at this point, and replying, "Because if I eat it, I choose to be fat."

Similarly, errors were discussed. Frequently, when an obese person breaks his diet, he continues to overeat because "It's too late now." Rehearsals included replying, "Even if I slip up, I can choose to regain control now."

This is an exploratory area. However, Meichenbaum and Cameron (1974) have reported success in treating impulsive children, phobics, and test-anxious college students with this technique.

No-Treatment Control Group

Subjects in the no-treatment group were told that it was not possible for them to be scheduled for treatment at this time. They were offered treatment at the end of the 12-week treatment period. They were weighed at the beginning and end of the 12 weeks.

Follow-Up

Three months after the treatment program ended, follow-up weights were recorded for all 43 subjects, either by the subject being weighed by the experimenter or by the subject being weighed by his/her physician during an office visit.

Follow-Up After One Year

One year after the end of treatment, a follow-up weight was obtained from each subject's medical record. The weights of 29 subjects were available. This was a nonobtrusive measure, to which the subjects consented at the beginning of the program. It was therefore possible to monitor the subjects' weights without their knowing the precise time of the follow-up. This prevented crash dieting and was a more valid measure of the subjects' progress.

RESULTS

Of the 43 original subjects, four subjects attended less than 50% of the sessions, and were considered to be dropouts. This was an overall attrition rate of 9%. The four subjects were unavailable for being weighed at posttreatment. The attrition rate for the experimental groups were 10% (one subject), 17% (three subjects), and 0% (no subjects) for the SC, SC-IC and SC-EC groups respectively. In order to achieve equal n, two subjects from the SC-EC group and one subject from the no-treatment group were dropped from the analysis. The complete data are presented in Tables 1 and 2.

Analyses of covariance on the Rotter Scores and the problem checklist at posttreatment with the pretreatment scores as covariates revealed no significant differences.

The one-way analysis of covariance on the post-experimental weights with the pretreatment weights as covariates resulted in a significant difference between the four groups $(F (3,31) = p < .01)$. Mean weight losses were 11.73, 9.86 and 10.75 pounds for the SC, SC-IC and SC-EC groups respectively. The no-treatment group showed a gain of 1.67 pounds. Newman-Keulls analyses on the adjusted weights at posttreatment revealed a significant difference between each of the three experimental groups as compared to the no-treatment group, but no significant differences among the three experimental groups. These significant differences remained at both the three-month $(F (3,31) = 4.15; p < .01)$ and the one-year $(F (3,24) = 3.15; p < .05)$ follow-up assessment periods. After one year, mean weight losses were 10.06, 12.00 and 13.42 pounds for the SC, SC-IC and SC-EC groups respectively.

Results of Questionnaire

At posttreatment a questionnaire concerning the subjects' attitudes, expectations, and behavior during treatment was given to all 27 subjects in the experimental groups. Twenty-four questionnaires were returned. A principal components analysis was performed on the correlations be-

TABLE 1

Weight Losses for Individual Subjects

	Pretreatment Weight	Posttreatment Weight	3-Month Follow-up Weight	Change at Three Months	One-year Follow-up Weight	Change at One Year
SC						
Female	170.00	151.50	152.25	—17.75	153.00	—17.00
Female	138.50	131.25	128.00	—10.50	137.00	— 1.50
Female	176.50	156.25	158.00	—18.50	169.50	—16.00
Female	222.00	213.00	215.00	— 7.00	223.00	1.00
Female	202.50	193.00	192.25	—10.25	195.00	— 7.50
Female	188.50	185.00	177.00	—11.50	.....	.....
Female	312.25	298.50	302.00	—10.25	305.00	— 7.25
Male	156.75	139.50	134.00	—22.75	185.00	—21.75
Female	234.50	228.00	227.25	— 7.25	224.00	—10.50
Mean	200.17	188.44	187.30	—12.87	191.56	—10.06
SC-IC						
Female	225.75	225.00	228.50	2.75	224.00	— 1.75
Male	219.50	191.25	190.50	—29.00	205.00	—14.50
Female	244.50	239.50	247.50	3.00	239.75	— 4.75
Male	328.00	319.50	307.00	—21.00	302.50	—25.50
Female	191.00	188.50	196.50	5.50	.....	.....
Female	217.00	210.00	214.00	— 3.00	215.00	— 2.00
Female	208.50	211.75	188.75	—19.75	196.50	—12.00
Female	149.50	127.50	124.00	—25.50	126.00	—23.50
Female	223.50	205.50	207.50	—16.00	.....	.....
Mean	223.03	213.17	211.58	—11.45	215.54	—12.00

TABLE 1 (continued)

	Pretreatment Weight	Posttreatment Weight	3-Month Follow-up Weight	Change at Three Months	One-year Follow-up Weight	Change at One Year
SC-EC						
Female	207.50	206.00	202.00	— 5.50	210.75	3.25
Female	170.75	159.00	153.00	—17.75	161.00	— 9.75
Female	179.25	184.50	185.00	5.75	.....	....
Female	145.00	124.00	124.00	—21.00	128.00	—17.00
Female	170.75	146.50	133.00	—37.75	126.50	—44.25
Female	192.75	181.00	182.00	—10.75	179.50	—13.25
Female	176.75	162.75	155.00	—21.75	166.00	—10.75
Female	144.50	135.75	140.00	— 4.50	.....	....
Male	274.25	265.25	270.25	— 4.00	272.00	— 2.25
Mean	184.61	173.86	171.58	—13.03	177.68	—13.42
No Treatment						
Female	205.25	202.25	200.00	— 5.25	202.00	— 3.25
Female	197.00	197.00	195.00	— 2.00	198.00	1.00
Female	140.00	135.00	140.00	0.00	140.00	0.00
Male	255.00	265.00	252.00	— 3.00	250.25	— 4.75
Female	199.50	194.00	197.00	— 2.50	.....	....
Female	234.75	249.75	250.00	15.25	.....	....
Female	185.50	185.00	186.00	0.50	184.00	— 1.50
Female	160.00	165.00	164.25	4.25	162.00	2.00
Male	173.25	172.25	175.75	2.50	176.00	2.75
Mean	194.47	196.14	195.56	1.09	187.46	— 0.54

TABLE 2

Means and Standard Deviations of Weight for Experimental
and Control Groups

	Pretreatment	Posttreatment	3-Month Follow-up	One-year Follow-up
SC				
Mean	200.17	188.44	187.31	191.56
SD	51.86	52.89	54.88	54.26
N	9	9	9	8
SC-IC				
Mean	223.03	213.17	211.58	215.54
SD	47.67	50.79	49.46	48.84
N	9	9	9	7
SC-EC				
Mean	184.61	173.86	171.58	177.68
SD	39.18	42.69	45.17	47.04
N	9	9	9	7
No Treatment				
Mean	194.47	196.14	195.56	187.46
SD	35.57	47.18	36.61	32.34
N	9	9	9	7

tween the 14 items on the questionnaire using Velicer's method for determining the number of components to extract (Velicer, 1976). One component was extracted. Eight of the 14 items had loadings of .40 or above (see Table 3). This component was identified as a compliance and involvement measure. All the items in the component deal with the extent to which the subjects reported that they did homework assignments and made the suggested changes in their eating behavior.

A scaled score was calculated for each subject for this component by taking the sum of the scores for the eight items loading on the component. A one-way analysis of variance on the scaled compliance scores of the three groups revealed no significant differences among the groups.

The correlations between the scaled compliance scores and weight loss were calculated, resulting in an overall correlation of $r = .64$ ($p < .05$). It should be noted that the correlations between the scaled compliance scores and weight loss were .51, .41 and .78 for the SC, SC-IC and SC-EC groups, respectively. Because of the extremely small sample

TABLE 3

Loadings of Questionnaire Items on Component I

Question No.	Question	Loading
06	Did you read the book?	0.5647
07	Did you understand the specific steps in the book?	0.7416
08	How many of the steps did you try?	0.7784
09-B	How important were the specific ideas and steps on how to lose weight?	0.7194
09-C	How important was your personal commitment to losing weight?	0.7595
09-E	How important was being weighed once a week?	0.7711
09-F	How important was the involvement of other members of your family?	0.6810
10	Please rate the usefulness of the program to you in losing weight.	0.7695

size, however, these correlations did not significantly differ from each other.

DISCUSSION

This study demonstrated that self-control procedures are effective in treating obese subjects from a non-university, non-volunteer population. These data are particularly significant considering Hall and Hall's (1974) and Levitz and Stunkard's (1974) earlier comments that studies where subjects have not been university students have produced less successful results than studies with a university population. In this study, each of the treatment groups lost significantly more weight than a no-treatment group.

The three groups also demonstrated maintenance of the weight loss at three-month and one-year follow-up periods. However, subjects did not continue to lose weight. Although a significant weight loss continued to exist in each of the experimental groups, the need for long-term follow-up is reemphasized by these data.

The follow-up questionnaire also revealed important data. Mahoney (1975) pointed out that, although behavioral programs for weight reduction such as the self-control procedures are more effective than non-behavioral programs, it has not been demonstrated that subjects have actually adopted the recommended changes. Yet, the significant correlation between compliance and weight loss suggests that subjects who do report actually following the steps of the program are more successful in losing weight than those who do not.

There were no significant differences in weight loss among the three treatment groups. There are several possible explanations of why neither the addition of the philosophy of internal control nor the addition of contingency contracting contributed significantly to the treatment package.

With respect to contingency contracting, there are several possible explanations. It is possible that contingency contracting does not add to the basic self-control package. A second possibility is that the amount and rate of reinforcement used in the contract were inadequate to control eating. Several subjects stated that once they had made the decision to part with the initial deposit of $25.00, the return of $2.00 per week was not a powerful reinforcer; thus, the rate of $2.00 per week may not have been potent enough. It should be noted, however, that none of the subjects in this group dropped out of treatment. The contingency contract, then, may have improved the attendance rate without producing greater weight loss.

With respect to the addition of the philosophy of internal control, it appears that this did not significantly add to treatment. Subjects in this group resisted the idea of internal control, and some subjects stated flatly that they had no internal control. The dropout rate of 17% may have been due to the subjects' increased anxiety over responsibility for their obesity.

It is possible that, indeed, the subjects might not have had internal control and were unable to develop such control. It might also take a more intensive or a longer program in order to change their attitudes toward their own potential for choice and for change. Finally, additional written materials might have made this additional component more potent.

It might have been more appropriate to test this innovative addition to weight reduction treatment with a university population. University students might be more familiar with ideas concerning consciousness and choice, and might be more comfortable with these concepts which are based on an existential philosophy.

The results of this study, then, compare favorably with earlier weight reduction studies. Yet, one must challenge the standard criteria for success. The rate of one pound per week was suggested by Ferster (1962) and accepted by Stuart (1967). Yet, in many of the studies, the treatment period is less than ten weeks, and there is frequently a regaining of weight during the follow-up period. In many studies, if there is no regaining of weight, there is still no continued weight loss, as one would expect from a "self-control" procedure. Thus, what is reported as "successful treatment" may involve subjects who have lost a total of less than ten pounds. For few subjects does such a weight loss make a significant impact on their weight problem. Thus, new techniques should be explored which would make the package more powerful and which would lead to greater maintenance of weight loss.

One addition to the self-control package is that described above as internal control. Subjects must implement the self-control procedures themselves. If they do not continue to lose weight after the initial treatment period, the program cannot be seen as successful. By changing the overweight subjects' philosophy and emphasizing their ability to gain internal control of their eating behavior, perhaps a truly self-controlled program can be maintained.

As it stands now, it is a misnomer to call the present package "self-control," since the subjects do not adequately control their eating behavior after treatment. If it were indeed self-control, subjects should continue to lose weight until they reached their ideal weights. However, in neither this study nor in most of the other studies using so-called self-control have subjects continued to lose weight once the regular contact with the experimenter and with the group has ended. Weight loss *only* while seeing a therapist or attending group meetings can hardly be called self-control.

If social control is the critical variable, then ongoing group treatment until the ideal weight is reached and continued contact for maintenance is a logical form of treatment. Perhaps obesity is a disorder similar to alcoholism—one which requires, according to some sources, long-term, ongoing treatment. Self-help groups such as Overeaters Anonymous and TOPS and commercial groups such as Diet Workshop and Weight Watchers could provide relatively inexpensive and continued treatment. Family involvement could also increase external control and lead to greater weight loss (Brownell, Heckerman, & Westlake, in preparation).

Health maintenance organizations can also provide long-term treatment for obesity. Health maintenance organizations provide ideal facilities for the development and evaluation of weight reduction programs for several reasons. Subjects can be taught self-control procedures for weight reduction and for other health-related problems (e.g., smoking, alcohol abuse) within the context of health education and self-care Nurses, health aides and other staff can be trained in behavioral techniques. The weights and medical condition of subjects can be followed nonobtrusively over long periods of time. Finally, through health maintenance organizations, subjects who are marginally overweight can be treated. These subjects (5-10% overweight) are usually omitted from weight reduction groups. They miss the opportunity to learn techniques which could prevent the development of a serious weight problem. This area of prevention should be another focus of future research.

REFERENCES

BROWNELL, K., HECKERMAN, C. L. and WESTLAKE, R. J.: Effects of couples training and partner cooperativeness in the behavioral treatment of obesity. Submitted for publication.

FERSTER, C. B., NURNBERGER, J. L. and LEVITT, E. B.: The control of eating. *Journal of Mathetics*, 1962, 1, 87-109.

HALL, S. M. and HALL, R. G.: Outcome and methodological considerations in behavioral treatment of obesity. *Behavior Therapy*, 1974, 5, 352-364.

HALL, S. M., HALL, R. G., NANDON, R. W. and BORDEN, B. L.: Permanence of two self-managed treatments of overweight in university and community populations. *Journal of Consulting and Clinical Psychology*, 1974, 42, 781-786.

HARRIS, M. B.: Self-directed program for weight control. A pilot study. *Journal of Abnormal Psychology*, 1969, 74, 263-270.

HECKERMAN, C. L.: The behavior therapy of obesity. Unpublished manuscript, U. of Rhode Island, 1974.

HOLLINGSHEAD, A. B.: *Two Factor Index of Social Position*. New Haven: A. B. Hollingshead, Yale Station, 1957.

JEFFREY, D. B.: A comparison of the effects of external control and self-control on the modification and maintenance of weight. *Journal of Abnormal Psychology*, 1974, 83, 404-410.

LEVITZ, L. S. and STUNKARD, A. J.: A therapeutic coalition for obesity: Behavior modification and patient self-help. *American Journal of Psychiatry*, 1974, 131, 423-427.

MAHONEY, M. J.: The obese eating style: Bites, beliefs, and behavior modification. *Addictive Behaviors*, 1975, 1, 47-53.

MAHONEY, M. J. and THORESON, C. E. (Eds.): *Self-Control: Power to the Person*. Monterey, California: Brooks/Cole, 1974.

MEICHENBAUM, D. and CAMERON, R.: The clinical potential of modifying what clients say to themselves. In M. J. Mahoney and C. E. Thoreson (Eds.), *Self-Control: Power to the Person*. Monterey, California: Brooks/Cole, 1974.

METROPOLITAN LIFE INSURANCE COMPANY: New weight standards for men and women. *Statistical Bulletin*, 1959, 40, 1-4.

NISBETT, R. E.: Taste, deprivation, and weight determination of eating behavior. *Journal of Personality and Social Psychology*, 1968, 10, 107-116.

PENICK, S. B., FILION, R., FOX, S. and STUNKARD, A.: Behavior modification in the treatment of obesity. *Psychosomatic Medicine,* 1971, 33, 49-55.

RODIN, J.: Colloquium given at University of Rhode Island, 1974.

ROTTER, J. B. Generalized expectancies for internal vs. external control of reinforcement. *Psychological Monographs,* 1966, 80 (1, Whole No. 609).

SCHACTER, S.: *Emotions, Obesity, and Crime.* New York: Academic Press, 1971.

SCHACTER, S. and GROSS, L. P.: Manipulated time and eating behavior. *Journal of Personality and Social Psychology,* 1968, 10, 98-106.

STUART, R. B.: Behavioral control of overeating. *Behavior Research and Therapy,* 1967, 5, 357-365.

STUART, R. B.: A three dimensional program for the treatment of obesity. *Behavior Research and Therapy,* 1971, 9, 177-186.

STUART, R. B. and DAVIS, B.: *Slim Chance in a Fat World.* Champaign: Research Press, 1972.

STUNKARD, A. J.: Foreword in R. B. Stuart and B. Davis, *Slim Chance in a Fat World.* Champaign: Research Press, 1972.

U.S. PUBLIC HEALTH SERVICE: Definitions of obesity and methods of assessment. In U.S. Public Health Service Publication No. 1485. *Obesity and Health: A Sourcebook of Current Information for Professional Health Personnel.* Washington, D. C.: U.S. Government Printing Office, 1966.

VAN ITALLIE, T.: Quoted in "Dietmania." *Newsweek,* September 10, 1973, 74-80.

VELICER, W.: Determining the number of components from the matrix of partial correlations. *Psychometrika,* 1976, 41:321-327.

WOLLERSHEIM, J. P.: Effectiveness of group therapy based upon learning principles in the treatment of overweight women. *Journal of Abnormal Psychology,* 1970, 76, 462-474.

10

Using Environmental Restriction to Initiate Long-Term Behavior Change

PETER SUEDFELD

HISTORICAL INTRODUCTION

The first documented use of reduced sensory stimulation in psychotherapy occurred several thousand years ago: Both at Delphi and at Trophonius, the oracle was approached by entering a cave in which the supplicant was isolated and sensorially deprived. ·While the major purpose for consulting the oracle was to divine the future, there apparently were instances of psychological problems being treated (Kouretas, 1967; Papageorgiou, 1975). A number of non-Western cultures have also used sensory deprivation in connection with psychotherapy. Among such methods are the rituals of healers in sub-Saharan Africa (Margetts, 1968) and the Northwest coast of America (Jilek, in press). In addition, modern therapeutic practices that have grown out of national traditions have, in some cases, incorporated this technique (e.g., Morita therapy; see Doi, 1962).

The research described in this paper was made possible by the help of numerous research assistants and colleagues (who are individually named in the original publications), and by financial support from the NIH Biomedical Sciences Support Program, the Canada Council, the Medical Research Council, and the Research Committees of The University of British Columbia and Rutgers—The State University.

230

When sensory deprivation became a popular research technique among Western psychologists in the early 1950s, among the earliest suggested applications was its use in a therapeutic context. A team of researchers at Allan Memorial Institute, in Montreal, found schizophrenic, depressive, and neurotic patients exhibiting improvement after several days of sensory deprivation (Azima & Cramer-Azima, 1956, 1957). One review (Suedfeld, 1975a) cites reports of successful treatment using this technique in cases of schizophrenia, childhood autism, and anorexia nervosa; further, treatments closely related to sensory deprivation are commonly used in the treatment of manic and depressed patients (Fitzgerald & Long, 1973), acting-out children (Pendergrass, 1971) and infantile colic (Wilcox, 1957, and personal communication, 1974). In addition, various investigators, besides those already mentioned, have found that sensory deprivation, either by itself or in conjunction with appropriate messages, resulted in improved scores on measures of such characteristics as state anxiety (Antista & Jones, 1975), ego strength (Gibby, Adams & Carrera, 1960; Kammerman, 1977; Antista & Jones, 1975), and various clinical scales of the MMPI (Kammerman, 1977).

My own involvement in the use of sensory deprivation in behavior change settings grew out of research on attitude change. It was clear from the studies reported that subjects undergoing stimulus reduction did become more persuasible, and that this change occurred in relation to a wide variety of external suggestions, ranging from simple things like increased body sway to quite elaborate, persuasive message presentations (see Suedfeld, 1969, for a review).

I had done several studies in this general paradigm, and had successfully changed the attitudes of some uninterested college students about the politics and people of Turkey. Like many other experimental social psychologists, I then became infected by a growing dissatisfaction with the attitude area in general. In the late 1960s, it was becoming obvious that a high proportion of the literature in this field concerned itself with either artificially induced attitudes or extremely peripheral ones in which the subjects had no real interest. Moreover, the fashion was to use trivial, or at least weak, manipulations, hoping to obtain changes on reactive and purely verbal dependent measures. The whole controversy on the relationship of attitudinal change to behavioral change, one of the oldest and most enduring arguments, reflects this point: Obviously, if the manipulations were really strong, attitude-behavior discrepancies would be quite small.

Being a good experimental psychologist, I was somewhat ambivalent about strong manipulations; not only were there some possible ethical questions involved in experimentally changing attitudes about important issues by a powerful technique, but to do so seemed crass in light of the genteel norms of laboratory research. Also, I had a vague feeling, later put into words by a graduate student in one of my seminars, that, "Social psychology is a lot of fun, but social psychology that works is frightening." However, after a lot of soul-searching, I decided that sensory deprivation probably would not be social psychology that works anyway. While it seemed to be an interesting experimental technique, perhaps somewhat more powerful than many of the standard laboratory procedures, it was, most likely, not strong enough to have serious impact on "real" attitudes.

STUDIES ON SMOKING CESSATION

Method

To demonstrate the weakness of the technique, some colleagues and I set up an experiment (Suedfeld, Landon, Pargament & Epstein, 1972). From a group of volunteers signing up to participate in an unspecified experiment using sensory deprivation, we selected 40 who had indicated that they were habitual smokers. They were randomly assigned to one of four groups, with sensory deprivation and an anti-smoking message being varied factorially. We wrote and tape-recorded a brief message, lasting less than two minutes, which summarized some of the major health hazards of smoking as they had been presented to the public some time before in the Surgeon General's report. We carefully made the wording and the tone of voice as undramatic as possible. In other words, we stacked the cards against ourselves fairly carefully: Our subjects were not people who came to us to get help quitting, they did not know what the experiment was about, and the treatment was a thoroughly unimpressive one. A brief, banal message at the end of 24 hours of sensory deprivation, under these circumstances, was not really likely to change anybody's attitudes or behavior in relation to a fixed habit.

The 24-hour period of sensory deprivation was spent in our usual chamber. This is a prefabricated model, one of a number produced by Industrial Acoustics Inc. of New York. The one that I currently use measures about 6 ft. x 8 ft., is completely light-proof, and quite sound-reducing within the usual frequency ranges. The procedural details below remained constant in all of the studies that I am going to describe.

When a subject reports to the laboratory, he is instructed to lie on the bed as quietly as possible, although not so still as to become uncomfortable; the only time he may get off the the bed is to use the chemical toilet which is located in the room. Water and a bland tasting liquid diet food are available through plastic tubes which are pinned to the pillow, so that the subject need only turn his head in order to drink. The chamber is kept completely dark and silent throughout the experimental session. The subject is told that a monitor will be present in the room next door at all times, and will listen over the intercom occasionally to make sure that everything is all right and that the instructions to remain quiet are being followed. The orientation emphasizes that most participants find the situation quite tolerable, or even pleasant; but the subject is informed that a few people find it so aversive that they do not wish to continue for the entire scheduled duration. It is made clear that an aversive reaction does not in any way imply that there is anything wrong with the person, since one's response to sensory deprivation is purely a matter of individual taste. The door is not locked: If the subject should find the situation unpleasant, he is free to get off the bed and walk out of the room at any time. However, once out, he may not change his mind and go back in, so he should be sure that he wants to quit before leaving.

In the few cases where the subject does leave the experimental situation, the monitor is trained to be very supportive and in no way critical. A debriefing is held; a senior member of the research staff is on call if the subject seems unusually upset (so far, in about 12 years of research, this provision only had to be used once). Otherwise, the subject is shown where to wash, he empties the chemical toilet if he has used it, replaces the bed linens, and is then free to go home. These latter steps are also followed upon the end of the experimental session by the subjects who have completed the scheduled time. In the research that I am going to describe, the rate of early attrition was well under 10%.

Since we did not expect significant changes in behavior, we were careful to take measures of any possible change in attitude. In particular, we measured the stability of beliefs about smoking, using the random incomplete blocks method (Koslin & Pargament, 1969). This technique asks the subject to rank a number of statements on the basis of what they imply for a particular opinion; stability is then measured as a function of the degree to which their ratings are transitive. This has been proposed as an operational measure of the attitude "unfreezing" process (Lewin, 1958). We also administered an attitude scale about the effects and desirability of smoking. Both of these measures were given after the subject had emerged from the sensory deprivation room.

Results

We were not surprised to find that, among the 20 nonconfined subjects, those who had heard the message showed more negative attitudes toward smoking and greater belief instability than those who had not heard the message. This, after all, is what one would expect as the result of a persuasive message. Among the sensorially deprived subjects, however, the pattern was quite different. As expected, deprived subjects who had heard the message had an instability level equal to that of control subjects who had heard it, that is, significantly more instability than un-treated controls. However, sensory deprivation subjects who did not hear the message had an even higher level of instability. This was quite sur-prising, since one would expect that the two treatments would summate in reducing the clarity and firmness of the subject's belief structure. Furthermore, while there was in both conditions a positive relationship between the degree of instability and the amount of agreement with anti-smoking opinion statements, the diverging patterns on the former led to the finding that the message had contradictory effects as a function of the environment in which it was given. In the normal condition, the message resulted in greater agreement with anti-smoking evaluations; in sensory deprivation, the opposite was the case. One last important finding was that subjects in sensory deprivation did not indicate that they had missed smoking during the 24-hours any more than did the control sub-jects, who in fact had not been deprived of cigarettes. In other words, the unavailability of cigarettes in the low-stimulus setting did not result in any feeling of deprivation.

Obviously, some of these data require explanation. Unfortunately, my explanations are not terribly firm, so that the word speculation may be more appropriate. It appears clear that both the message and sensory de-privation acted as cognitive unfreezers, in that they induced substantial instability in the belief structure. However, when the message was presented at the end of sensory deprivation, this effect was diminished. One may hypothesize that the subjects had been able to reorganize their attitudes because the presentation served as an informational stimulus, thus reducing the general uncertainty and need for information generated by sensory deprivation. This may have resulted in an approach-avoidance reaction to the message, which in turn led the deprived subjects to reject many of the attitude items; we found that not only did they express disagreement with the anti-smoking statements on the post-experimental questionnaire, but they also disagreed with the pro-smoking statements. It may well be that the combined treatments had evoked a reactance response (Brehm, 1966). We, and other researchers, had found in several previous studies that intelligent subjects receiving sensory deprivation and a blatantly persuasive message sometimes reacted against the propositions presented to them, exhibiting a boomerang effect. All of these data are fairly interesting as they related to the general body of sensory deprivation literature, but obviously are less impressive as regards the usefulness of the technique as a therapeutic tool.

A few months after the experiment, while writing a report on the project, I thought it would be interesting to get in touch with the subjects and see whether their behavor had changed. I had a research assistant telephone each subject, without identifying himself as being connected with the sensory deprivation laboratory, and collect the relevant data under the guise of taking a survey on the smoking habits of college students. We were slightly unhappy to discover that, because it was now summer vacation, only 28 of the 40 subjects could be reached; but the guardian angel of researchers ensured that there were seven accessible subjects in each of the four groups. We got the first dramatic surprise of the study when we looked at the pattern of changes from pre-experimental baseline (see Table 1).

The first thing we needed to explain was the large increase in the number of cigarettes smoked by those in the unconfined, no message control group. Looking at the individual data, this was easy enough to understand: One subject had increased his smoking rate by 400%. After eliminating the datum from this individual, we found that the control group had exhibited essentially no change. This left us with the striking data from the two sensory deprivation groups, which had two extremely interesting aspects. The first was that the rather undramatic conditions of the experiment had resulted in such a large change; the second, that there was no difference as a function of whether the message had been presented or not. In retrospect, I suppose it makes sense that so weak a message did not affect the behavioral outcome; the surprising thing then is that sensory deprivation did do so, and to such an extent.

In general, we were quite encouraged by the findings, which gave us both theoretical and applied ideas. For example, they supported the hypo-

TABLE 1

Changes in Smoking Behavior: Three-Month Follow-Up*

Group	Mean No. Cigarettes per Day	Mean % Change from Baseline
Sensory Deprivation/Message	10.6	—38%
Sensory Deprivation/No Message	11.5	—38%
Nonconfined/Message	12.4	—23%
Untreated Control	18.6	+44%

* Suedfeld et al., 1972.

thesis that sensory deprivation is an attitude unfreezer, and our theoretical standpoint that this is one aspect of its potency as a cognitive disorganizer (Suedfeld, 1972). Among other interesting results were: the interaction between environmental conditions and the persuasive message, on both belief instability and actual attitude; the unexpected reduction in smoking behavior as a function of sensory deprivation, but with the intriguing twist that the people who had not heard the message changed just as much as those who had; and the fact that confined subjects whose cigarettes had been taken away from them did not suffer as a result. One possible explanation for this is that at the same time that they were removed from the possibility of smoking, they were also removed from external smoking cues; whether or not this is the whole answer is still doubtful. At any rate, we wondered about the pattern of effects, and in particular about the nonadditivity of sensory deprivation and the message.

There had been plenty of evidence previously that sensory deprivation makes the individual more open to new information, and perhaps more willing to accept it. Presumably, the attitude and belief stability measures, presented immediately after the end of the experiment, had made salient to our subjects the topic of the procedures, so that even those who had not heard the message were faced with the need to think about their status as habitual smokers. I think it is clear that this was not some kind of over-whelming attitude bulldozer, and that in fact the changes occurred because sensory deprivation made the subjects aware of the problem, and they themselves during the subsequent three months responded to that awareness.

I must admit that this is to some extent hindsight; at the time, we were still thinking in terms of externally induced changes in attitudes and behavior, and we designed the next step accordingly (Suedfeld & Ikard, 1973). This was to develop a more elaborate and powerful set of messages, with an eye to increasing the usefulness of the technique. In order to do this, I had to engage in an activity that I had not bothered to pursue previously, since I was convinced of the hopelessness of trying to "cure" smokers—that is, reading the research available in this area.

From a large amount of reading, I emerged with a deep sense of pessimism and a lot of information to be put into the next set of messages. In their final form, these consisted of 18 brief presentations. They included several items about the health hazards caused by smoking (put in much more graphic terms than before); a deep breathing exercise which the subject was urged to do instead of reaching for a cigarette; a message taken from Spiegel (1970) concerning the need to protect his body from poisons such as those contained in cigarettes; and ways of coping with problems that might arise from renouncing cigarettes. In addition, there were four brief reinforcement messages of the format "Congratulations, you have now gone—hours without a cigarette. You're doing fine." This or a similar reinforcer was played after 4, 10, 16 and 22 hours of deprivation.

To try out these messages, we found five people, all of whom smoked quite heavily and had been smoking for a long time, and all of whom scored as being addictive smokers on the Tomkins-Ikard Smoking Scale (Ikard & Tomkins, 1973). This test measures the degree to which the individual falls into one of several categories of smokers. The categories are defined in terms of the functions that smoking serves for the person, but they can also be arranged in rough order of the difficulty with which smoking can be abandoned by the individual. Psychologically addicted smokers represent a category where there is always strong awareness when the individual is not smoking, a craving to be doing so, and fear at the possibility that cigarettes might not be easily available. This is the most difficult category of all to treat successfully.

All of our subjects were people who had tried to stop before and had always failed; they now volunteered specifically because they had been told that there was a possibility that this new treatment might be helpful. Three of them wanted desperately to quit, primarily because of medical reasons; of the others, one was mostly interested in the sensory deprivation experience itself and the other had been taking so much harassment from her teenage children about her smoking that she came to us in order to quiet them down. Our feeling was that for her, this technique was going to be like her previous attempts to quit—that is, another opportunity to show her children that she was really trying to stop smoking but was unable to do so.

This experiment marked a real change of approach in my line of research. To begin with, it was the first study that was deliberately therapeutic, with individuals being recruited essentially as clients rather than purely as experimental subjects. It also marked a change in emphasis as to the target variable on which we hoped to demonstrate the effect. The series of studies of which it was a part was entitled "Attitude Manipulation in Restricted Environments"; it would have been appropriate (although I did not do it) to change at this point to something like "Using Restricted Environments to Initiate Changes in Behavior." In this study, as in the next one on smoking, we dispensed with attitude measures completely, concentrating purely on smoking behavior and self-reports of some related emotions.

Once again, the subjects underwent 24 hours of sensory deprivation, with the messages interspersed at regular intervals. Much to their surprise, our subjects found that while in the chamber they were not particularly stressed by the unavailability of cigarettes. This did not surprise me, since it was a phenomenon that we had observed before, and that we had heard in anecdotes from other researchers in the area. What was unexpected was that all five of the subjects gave up their addicted smoking after emerging from the experiment. Of course, anyone who knows the smoking literature could have expected that, and could also predict the aftermath. Complete abstinence did not last long; in fact, four of the five subjects resumed smoking again. These included the two subjects with relatively low motivation. The other two recidivists requested a "booster shot" of sensory deprivation, and two months after their initial participation were put back into the chamber for eight hours each and a repetition of six of the messages. At the end of a three-month follow-up, all three highly motivated subjects were completely abstinent, while the other two were smoking at their original baseline levels.

This study was only a pilot project for the next piece of research in this area (Suedfeld & Ikard, 1974). We felt that the technique needed a large-scale test for proper evaluation, and the next study was designed to provide this. Due to the interest of the mass media in anything that seems to be successful as a smoking cure, a large number of local newspapers in New Jersey carried articles about our research, emphasizing that the technique was in the experimental stage and that we were looking for subjects to find out whether in fact the approach was worthwhile. Many hundreds of volunteers wrote or called our laboratory at Rutgers in response to these articles. Each of these was sent a form, containing biographical and demographical questions, and a copy of the Tomkins-Ikard scale. We made the test a difficult one, so that we accepted only subjects who had been smoking for a long time, and who scored as either addicted or negative affect pre-addicted smokers on the scale. The meaning of the addicted category has already been discussed; negative affect pre-addicted smokers are those who reach for a cigarette whenever they are experiencing negative affects such as anxiety, tension, anger, or sadness, and who have moved in the direction of feeling general negative affect whenever they are not smoking. These are the two categories which, according to Tomkins' theory (1968), exhibit the greatest resistance to any kind of intervention or change designed to eliminate smoking.

The design was the same as in the first study, with sensory deprivation-nonconfinement and messages-no messages being varied factorially. Non-confined message subjects heard the material over the telephone. Untreated controls were told, truthfully, that we could not accommodate them at that time. They were given the address of the American Health Foundation as an alternate source of help with their problem, and were also encouraged to try other smoking clinics. Because some of our subjects in the second study had indicated that there were too many messages, we reduced the number to a dozen, keeping those that either our previous subjects or we ourselves thought were the most pertinent and useful. We also kept the brief reinforcement statements.

Follow-ups were made monthly for a year after the session, and then again at the end of the second year. All of the instructions emphasized the need for accurate feedback, to prevent smokers and therapists from either abandoning the technique if it was actually helpful or wasting time, effort, money, and hope if it was really ineffective. These exhortations led to responses that in many cases included quite detailed comments and suggestions, not merely offhand reports of smoking rates. Our belief that the feedback was given truthfully and with careful thought was further bolstered by cross-checks. Several of our subjects spontaneously informed us that other participants whom they knew personally had or had not benefited from the treatment; also, some subjects were acquaintances of students or colleagues who also commented on the apparent degree of success of the technique.

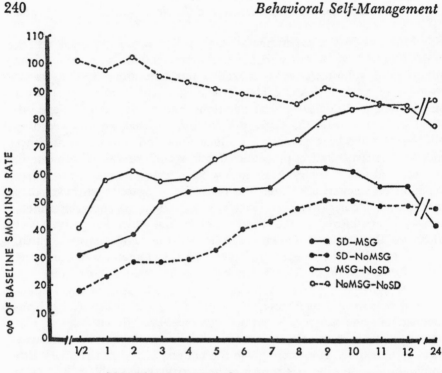

FIGURE 1. Changes in Smoking During 24-Month Follow-up (Suedfeld & Ikard, 1975)

The results of this study are shown in Figure 1. As can be seen, sensory deprivation, again regardless of presentation of messages, had a significant and long-lasting effect on smoking. The results at the end of one year, and on a somewhat reduced sample at the end of two, were quite impressive. Not only were approximately a quarter of the sensory deprivation subjects totally abstinent, but there was a very unusual finding that many of those who had not quit completely were maintaining consumption rates considerably below their pre-session baselines. Typically, smoking clinics find that their clients either remain abstinent or quickly regain their original smoking rates; so far, we have found no reason as to why ours seems to be somewhat different in this regard.

OTHER STUDIES

Several other studies using sensory deprivation as a therapeutic technique have been run in the laboratory, including two on the reduction of fear of snakes and a current one in which sensory deprivation and the smoking messages are preceded by a satiation smoking session. The study is being done in conjunction with Allan Best, who has been running a successful research and clinical program at The University of British Columbia using the satiation technique. A fairly thorough study combining satiation and sensory deprivation is currently under way; with the few pilot subjects run so far, we have found good results and even some unexpected beneficial side-effects (Suedfeld & Best, in press). For example, one subject not only stopped smoking, but also stopped drinking her usual 30 cups of coffee a day, went on a diet, began a course of exercises, and got divorced! Another, who had a supervisory position in which he was quite ineffective because of his shy and retiring behavior, unexpectedly blossomed forth as an assertive and decisive individual. Not only did he get much better ratings on the job, but his intolerably disrespectful teenage son was suddenly reformed. Our subject's personality change was so marked that one of his acquaintances, who had really liked this gentle and modest man, remarked that he had certainly become a pain in the neck since his sensory deprivation session.

Another current project is a dissertation by Roderick Borrie (in preparation), in which the same basic design is being applied to help grossly obese women, at least 25% overweight and referred to us by their physicians, to maintain their diets. In this case, the messages are quite elaborate. They include a deep relaxation exercise which the subjects are taught in detail and are encouraged to practice during their session, as well as messages designed to teach them to pay attention to internal hunger cues rather than external stimuli as initiators of eating. Some passages deal directly with situations that are critical for our particular subjects—e.g., the problem of sampling what one is cooking. Still others prepare the subject for participation in a program of self-maintained diet and exercise (Stuart & Davis, 1972). We are collecting weight loss and skinfold measures. Preliminary weight loss data (Figure 2) indicate that the technique again looks effective. It is noteworthy that subjects in the two nonconfined groups have already begun to regain the weight they lost originally, while the two deprived groups are still reducing.

I should mention that the follow-up data are adversely influenced by an uncontrolled variable that probably affects many obesity studies— Christmas. Possibly some research on attitude change toward turkey (as opposed to Turkey) is advisable after all. However, even this major occasion for relapses seems to have been overcome successfully by many partici-

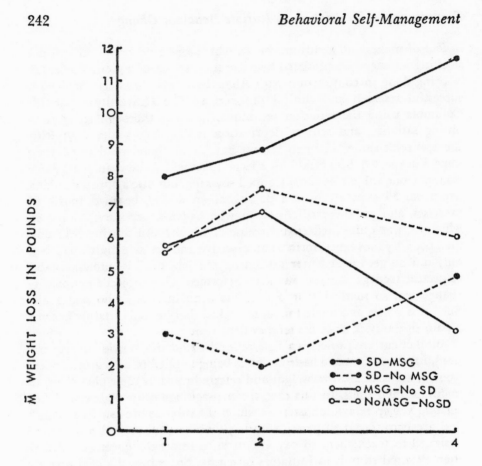

FIGURE 2. Weight Loss: Four-Month Follow-ups (Borrie, in preparation)

pants in the experiment. Eight of the ten sensory deprivation-message
subjects have lost a minimum of 1 lb. a week since their session, the same
number as in the three other groups combined. Clearly, in this study the
very detailed and highly focused set of messages, devised with the help
of Dr. Richard Stuart, seems to have an incremental effect beyond that of
sensory deprivation by itself.

DISCUSSION

Why should sensory deprivation have these effects? I think there are
many reasons, some of which are more or less environmental while others

are more intrapersonal. Among the environmental ones are the facts that the subject is removed from the cues that normally lead him to smoke, such as an argument, or a cup of coffee, or seeing someone else light a cigarette. As mentioned previously, the sensory deprivation subject does not miss the absence of cigarettes and thus for the first time realizes that he can go for as long as 24 hours without having a cigarette and without really needing one. I cannot say why this should be so. Possible reasons include the absence of smoking cues, and the fact that many people find the details of the sensory deprivation experience interesting enough to concentrate on at the expense of other topics, at least for some proportion of their session. Quite a few subjects also spend considerable time either sleeping or drifting in and out of shallow naps, which may reduce the craving for a cigarette.

Another factor is that sensory deprivation appears to induce unfreezing of the attitude structure, thus making it more responsive to counter-attitudinal messages. In fact, the term unfreezing, taken from Kurt Lewin's (1958) analysis of the stages of persuasion, may provide a critical explanatory concept. According to Lewin, a successful persuasion consists of the unfreezing of the existing attitude structure, followed by changing as new information and arguments are assimilated, and then a refreezing in the newly developed pattern. Sensory deprivation by itself is an unfreezer, a modifier of the way beliefs are organized (Tetlock & Suedfeld, 1976), and this may be its major role in the process of modifying attitudes and behaviors. As another aspect of this increased openness, several of our participants have reported that the experience has enabled them to probe beneath the surface habit patterns of their lives and to think deeply about issues that they had become accustomed to ignoring.

Changing must come either from the messages or other cues as to the target topic. It may be that the subject's own desire to modify an undesirable habit or characteristic can serve as the change input once the unfreezing has been accomplished. If this were to be true, no messages or any other sort of treatment would be necessary, although they might be helpful. We do know that sensory deprivation subjects sometimes spend a great deal of time in introspecting about problems and plans; this is probably an extremely important component of the total impact of the technique. Such self-searching increases the effectiveness of relevant messages and sets the stage for a change in behavior. This implies that sensory deprivation can be thought of as a very rapid, environmentally produced meditation-like state. It surely seems to produce some of the same effects as are found with more traditional internally generated meditation conditions.

Refreezing, in my opinion, must come about after the subject leaves the chamber. Contributing to it may be factors such as the person's own willpower, social support from significant others and from group norms, consonant information, and possibly further treatments either with sensory deprivation or with other methods. This stage is crucial for the new attitude-behavior pattern to become permanent—in this context, to prevent backsliding. The problem of refreezing or maintenance of change is the next crucial concern.

At any rate, it is clear that sensory deprivation is *not* a brainwashing manipulation that somehow magically alters the subject's desires, opinions, and actions. Rather, it makes it possible for the individual to weaken existing habits that he considers to be undesirable, makes the problems resulting from these habits more salient, removes the person from the pressures and cues that maintain his undesired patterns, and thus frees him to change himself in the direction that he wants to go.

GENERAL USEFULNESS OF THE METHOD

How generally useful could the sensory deprivation technique be in therapeutic settings? One obvious question is that of economics. There is little doubt that on this criterion sensory deprivation is an extremely acceptable methodology. While the commercially made sensory deprivation chambers are fairly high in cost (at this time, almost $5,400 for the model that I use), I do not believe that they are necessary. An inside room, or one with the windows completely blocked, can be soundproofed quite well and equipped appropriately at minimal cost. I know of one psychiatrist who is currently constructing such a therapy room in his own office, and almost any private house could have a quiet room of this sort at minimal expense.

But the real economic advantages lie in more elaborate or even institutional setups. One control room, with a technician monitor who checks up to make sure that the subjects are all right, and with the stimulus presentations and response recording automated, can handle an essentially infinite number of chambers as long as intercommunications systems, tape recorders, slide projectors and the like are available as needed. The original installations in these cases may be relatively expensive, but the saving in the time of highly trained professional personnel is staggering.

The saving to the client, in time as well as in money, is also an attractive feature. There has even been a facetious suggestion that a franchise system be set up, where the potential client can go to his neighborhood sensory deprivation emporium, insert his credit card, punch a button identifying his problem, and then enter the chamber and have the appropriate messages presented automatically. At the moment, I am trying to think of a catchy title for this magnificent chain of installations (Suedfeld, in press)!

Aside from economics, there is some concern about the appropriateness of sensory deprivation as a widely applied therapeutic tool. While the technique obviously has its limitations, one would think that the magnitude of available evidence would have made it a widely used and thoroughly tested approach in the past 20 years or so. Unfortunately, this has not been the case. We are still at the stage where, for many practitioners, the idea of using reduced environmental stimulation in therapy is relatively new. For others, it is not merely novel, but shocking.

For a considerable time, the profession has been bombarded with information that sensory deprivation is detrimental. A number of learned papers and books, and their popularized counterparts, have told us that sensory deprivation and social isolation can lead to insanity, unpredictable swings of mood, hallucinations, and emotional breakdowns. In part, this emphasis may be the result of the fact that psychologists and psychiatrists tend to do their training and work in environments of high population density and high general stimulation. Being well adapted to such conditions, they find it unpleasant to think about situations where the individual is isolated and removed from an incessant supply of stimuli. Popular writers may share these preferences, and are further oriented toward the dramatic and even bizarre.

The exaggeratedly negative view of sensory deprivation effects is based, I think, on two mistaken ideas. The first is that sensory deprivation is in itself an extremely stressful experience, where subjects suffer various degrees and forms of psychological breakdown. I shall address myself to this concept later; for the moment, I would merely like to point out that one must be careful to distinguish between the outcomes of relatively brief deprivation sessions using adult human beings as opposed to the uniformly adverse effects of insufficient stimulation on young organisms during significant portions of their development (Riesen, 1975). The second misconception is that the technique subordinates the will of the subject (or perhaps victim) to that of some external agent, eliminating the possibility of resistance. I hope I have convinced you that sensory deprivation is not a form of coercive control (see London, 1969; Stuart, 1972). It is, in fact, a method of informational control at the individual level.

One digression may be appropriate here, related to the idea that sensory deprivation is a significant component of coercive conversion techniques. In fact, as demonstrated in a large number of studies and reports, these techniques rely to a great extent on physical abuse, deprivation and threat; on the weakening of the victim's existing loyalties and emotional ties; and on the recognition that the captor has fate control over the prisoner, which he will exercise with leniency or with extreme severity depending on satisfaction with the progress of conversion. Farber, Harlow and West (1957) have described the major components of brainwashing as "debility, dependency and dread." In many historical instances, the prisoner has been sick and wounded, starved, cold, badly clothed and sheltered, and deprived of needed medical aid, completely dependent upon his indoctrinators for material sustenance as well as for social support, and aware of the fact that the captors have not only the power but the determination to degrade, injure, or even kill him whenever they decide that this might be desirable.

To these three components, which have been found in all brainwashing situations in recent history, we may add a fourth, "disorientation." This refers to a state of thoroughgoing confusion, in which the victim is brought to question his self-concept, his basic beliefs, and his relationship to the world in general and to his indoctrinators in particular. Disorientation is accomplished through the complete control of information by the institutional authority. The most frequently used techniques of intensive persuasion have involved continual interrogation by teams of experts, coupled with sleep deprivation, lack of privacy, intense glaring light, and insistent repetition of the persuader's point of view (Conquest, 1968). In the Chinese version, a peer group of prisoners who are more "advanced" than the focal victim takes a major role, engaging in indoctrination, criticism and self-criticism, and the administration of rewards and punishments depending upon the subject's responsiveness (Lifton, 1961). Depriving the subject of information that would bolster his original position or counteract the messages that the persuader wants him to accept is a logical part of the disorientation process (Schein, 1961). One way to accomplish this is to keep the subject in solitary confinement, thus preventing prisoners from reinforcing each other's resistance and from receiving support from visitors, as well as increasing the feeling of dependency and of dread. The use of sensory deprivation per se as a component of the brainwashing process has been rare.

In spite of these facts, novelists and television script writers have repeatedly used situations in which one or another experimental sensory deprivation technique was invoked to explain coercive conversion. Even less justifiably, some supposedly nonfictional publications have perpetuated the myth. For example, a recent article discussing the treatment of detainees in Ulster argued "for more stringent editorial control of papers on sensory deprivation to reduce the chances of an Orwellian use of psychology" (Shallice, 1972, p. 385). As one might expect, the actual interrogation technique fails to justify the recommendation. The prisoners were forced to stand against the wall in a very uncomfortable position for up to 16 hours at a time, were bombarded with constant and extremely loud noise, were intensely interrogated by teams of questioners, were deprived of sleep for up to three days at a time, were restricted to bread and water, were kept in uncertainty as to the length of their detention and their eventual fate, and in some cases apparently. were physically assaulted. An ex-detainee, John McGuffin (1974), similarly excoriates sensory deprivation research, and then makes clear that his definition of the technique includes overcrowding, poor ventilation, lack of medical attention, beatings, constant interrogation, the use of hallucinogenic drugs, humiliation, and so on.

It is, I think, obvious to even the most casual observer that a confusion of this magnitude cannot be due to mere inattention or ignorance. Shallice and McGuffin both make political attacks on what they perceive to be the role of the behavioral sciences in Western society; why they pick sensory deprivation as the scapegoat is difficult to establish, except for its general aura of being mysterious, stressful, and historically related to interest in coercive persuasion techniques. I would encourage Shallice or anyone else who would like to test the validity of his accusations to subject himself to both versions of the treatment for a few days, and then decide whether the term "sensory deprivation" has any relevance to the intensive interrogation technique. Most interrogation victims would no doubt find that a few days in real sensory deprivation would provide an extremely welcome period of physical and psychological rest and recuperation.

The most stimulus-reducing feature of the Ulster procedure, a black cloth hood covering the prisoner's head, probably had little to do with ideas of sensory deprivation. It serves the much more obvious function of depersonalizing the prisoner and maintaining the anonymity of the interrogator (Zimbardo, 1969). Furthermore, its use can hardly be blamed on inferences from sensory deprivation research—the hooded detainees were antedated by the Man in the Iron Mask and by the captured conspirators involved in Abraham Lincoln's assassination, among others.

THE STRESSFULNESS OF SENSORY DEPRIVATION

The general impression that sensory deprivation is an extremely unpleasant experience is consonant with our culture-bound biases. As mentioned above, most individuals writing about the phenomenon are adapted to a society which is probably higher in chronic stimulation levels than any previous human environment, or than any other contemporary one. The extremely high stimulation afforded to inhabitants of Western technological civilization includes both diverse, high-intensity stimuli at any given period of time, and rapid alteration in the specific components of the stimulus pattern. It is also probable that, even among the citizens of this high-stimulation culture, the urbanized, highly educated, scientifically oriented professional may be more favorably oriented towards stimulation than the average. It has been 15 years since John Lilly, one of the pioneer investigators in sensory deprivation and the first researcher to use the water immersion technique, made the argument that negative expectations brought about negative results and that negative expectations themselves were an outgrowth of social bias (e.g., Lilly & Shurley, 1961). These comments have been largely ignored in the subsequent debate.

Interestingly, the past few years have seen an exponential growth in the number of publications that focus on the problems that may result from excessively high stimulation (e.g., Glass & Singer, 1972; Lipowski, 1975; Toffler, 1970). This literature, and the growth of interest in stimulus-reducing techniques ranging from meditation to the return to nature movement, obviously deserve major attention both as general cultural phenomena and as topics for more scientific investigation. At the same time, one would have thought that this new emphasis might have led to a more objective evaluation of sensory deprivation as a time-out from overstimulation.

In spite of these considerations, it appears that the general attitude toward sensory deprivation held by workers in psychiatry, psychology, criminology, social work, and related fields has not been ameliorated by the knowledge that high levels of stimulation are aversive and harmful, nor by the fact that an increasing number of people are seeking at least occasional periods of reduced stimulation in order to restore some kind of psychological balance. Similarly, there has been very little change as a result of the wider availability of historical and anthropological studies demonstrating the universality of isolation and stimulus reduction as religious or curative techniques. A beginning may be made by considering these points in combination with the growing literature in experimental and therapeutic contexts indicating that the stressfulness of sensory deprivation has been greatly exaggerated and its usefulness largely ignored (Suedfeld, 1975b).

Early studies of stimulus reduction tended to support the bias with which many investigators probably approached the area. The fact that perhaps the most widely cited article in the field even now, although it was published almost 20 years ago, is entitled "The Pathology of Boredom" (Heron, 1957), is indicative of the fortuitous compatibility between data and expectations. There is little point in a detailed reexamination of the literature; a brief summary shall suffice. Participants in sensory deprivation studies have reported unpleasant experiences, in some cases extremely unpleasant ones. Also, subjects not infrequently have requested to terminate the experiment before its scheduled end (see, for example, Myers, 1969). It is also clear that some aspects of psychological and behavioral functioning are temporarily impaired by severe stimulus reduction (see Zubek, 1969).

Many of these findings were confounded to some now unknown extent by the use of stress-inducing manipulations ancillary to sensory deprivation, as well as by the authors' understandable tendency to emphasize dramatic reactions. For example, in my own first contact with the field, as a naive subject, the first two things I was faced with when reporting to laboratory were a "panic button" in the chamber and a daunting form for signing away my right to sue the university in case I suffered physical or psychological damage as a result of my participation. Before reporting for the experiment, it had never entered my mind that I would be likely to panic, nor that I would be taking a chance on being damaged. Needless to say, these two aspects of the experimental procedure significantly changed my expectations of and probably my responses to the experiment.

Given this kind of experimental procedure, in which frightening manipulations were superimposed on an already rather strange and unusual environment, it is no wonder that many subjects were uncomfortable. But that is hardly the point. The real issue is twofold: whether there is more to the problem than unpleasantness (that is, whether actual damage to the subjects is likely to occur); and to what extent adverse effects can be eliminated if the sensory deprivation experience is presented in a more positive fashion.

As to the first of these questions, once again the popular mythology is quite inaccurate. Citing reports of hallucinations, mood swings, changes in body image, and the like (most of which came early in the history of the field), some people concluded that sensory deprivation causes psychotic or pseudo-psychotic reactions. In actuality, the occurrence of hallucinations that a clinician might recognize as such is extremely rare in sensory deprivation (Suedfeld & Vernon, 1964; Zuckerman, 1969). The other bizarre effects are also relatively rare, and probably include misinterpreted reports of vivid dreams, hypnagogic images, and daydreams.

When one turns to reports of low endurance times, once again the picture is not nearly as bad as is generally thought. While endurance times in water immersion are in fact low, this is a very strange and in itself frightening experience except perhaps for experienced scuba divers. The relative roles of the knowledge that one is underwater and dependent on an air hose cannot be separated from stimulus deprivation. Incidentally, I have recently read a book (Smith, 1975), in which even this environment is presented as not excessively stressful. In examining the effects of more commonly used methods, we find that in experiments using room confinement the completion rate in shorter studies (up to 24 hours) is frequently in the 90% range. In studies lasting six or seven days or longer, successful completers typically represent over half or two-thirds of the sample.

Most subjects going into sensory deprivation tend to expect some unpleasantness (Myers, 1964), and since expectations strongly influence the experience of the subject in sensory deprivation (Jackson & Pollard, 1966; Orne & Scheibe, 1964; Suedfeld et al., 1971), it is no surprise that some stress is, in fact, experienced. However, some colleagues are quite surprised to see the relatively low level found in many studies, where not too many unpleasant experiences are reported and various affect scales and measures indicate only slight if any negativeness. For example, in our own recent research the mean responses of sensory deprivation and nonconfined control groups on the Subjective Stress Scale (Berkun, Bialek, Kern & Yagi, 1962) have been so close as to be statistically indistinguishable, clustering around the statements "It didn't bother me" or "I was indifferent."

To determine whether there is a serious danger of substantial adverse effects, I have conducted a survey in which questionnaires were sent to representatives of all of the leading programs in this area, past and present. More than 20 individuals have now responded, from seven countries, reporting on over 3,300 subjects in sensory deprivation using various techniques. The results of this survey are presented in Table 2.

As the table indicates, there have been very few problems indeed with previously nonpathological subjects, although there have been some psychiatric patients who reacted badly to the sensory deprivation experience. Among those laboratories that did not reply to the survey, we found three additional cases of adverse effects with obsessive neurotics, and a few individuals who reported unpleasant experiences but without the necessity for intervening beyond a standard or, at the most, a somewhat extended post-experimental and follow-up debriefing (e.g., Bressler, Silverman, Cohen & Shmavonian, 1959). There has only been one reported case of an individual who, not previously a psychiatric patient, required actual psychotherapy after a sensory deprivation experiment (Curtis & Zuckerman, 1968). The symptoms reported by this individual included delusions for several days and anxiety and depression lasting several weeks. The symptoms disappeared after therapeutic intervention.

In brief, then, the proportion of adequately functioning subjects who had serious psychological aftereffects of significant duration and requiring psychotherapy as a result of sensory deprivation is about 3/100 of 1% of the population covered by reports from the major research programs in the field. It would be informative to establish the comparable trauma rates for other types of experiments in medicine and psychology, or as far as that goes, for any sort of common activity in modern life. Given that our survey covers an extremely wide variety of specific techniques, orientation procedures, and a very diverse subject pool (including, for example, both volunteers and nonvolunteers; occupational backgrounds ranging all the way from high level professional people to laborers and conscripts; and citizens not only of North America but Eastern and Western Europe, Japan, and Australia), with recruitment from elite liberal arts colleges on the one hand to advertisements in wide-circulation newspapers on the other, and so on, it seems fairly safe to say that the dangers of going through a sensory deprivation experiment have been grossly exaggerated. Unfortunately, some people still persist in bandying

TABLE 2
Adverse Effects Reported

Laboratory	Years Active	Techniques Used	Duration of Session	Aprox. No. of Subjects	Major Subject Population	Serious Adverse Effects	Other Relevant Observations
1	1958-70	Darkness, silence.	Up to 2 wks.	100	Eye operation patients	0	Some instances of "acting out": exhibitionism, masturbation
2	1963-74	Darkness, silence.	8-72 hrs.	400	Volunteers	0	Early termination rate: 5-10%.
3	1965-69	Darkness, silence.	4 hrs.	150	College students	0	Early termination rate: 10%.
4	1956-72	Darkness, silence.	12 to 48 hrs.	370	Servicemen	0	Some subjects observed overnight after release: no problems.
5	1972-74	Darkness, silence.	6 hrs.	20	Psychiatric patients	0	1 subject required ½ hr. interview after session.
6	1971-74	Darkness, diffuse noise.	5 hrs.	40	Volunteers	0	
7	1958-69	Darkness, silence.	Up to 2 wks.	500	College students	1	1 other subject required "reassurance."
8	1964-67	Diff. light, silence.	24-48 hrs.	36	Volunteers	0	
9	1963-70	Darkness, silence; water immersion; diff. light & noise.	Up to 2 days	75	College students	0	3-4 immersed subjects required conversation, shower, and meal to regain poise.

TABLE 2 (continued)

#	Dates	Condition	Duration	Subjects	N	Early termination	Notes
10	1961-72	Diff. light & noise.	3-48 hrs.	College students	100	0	Early termination rate: 3%.
11	1951-58, 1969-73	Diff. light & noise.	Up to 1 wk.	College students	45	0	
12	1955-74	Water immersion.	Up to 8 hrs.	Volunteers	300	0	
13	1969-73	Darkness, silence.	Up to 6 hrs.	Psychiatric patients	155	0	Some subjects showed increased symptoms; most decreased.
14	1959-74	Darkness, silence; diff. light & noise; variations.	Up to 3 wks.	College students	614	0	
15	1963-67	Darkness, silence.	Up to 1 day	Volunteers	75	0	
16	1961-65	Diff. light & noise.	Up to 2 days	College students	55	0	
17	1958-62	Darkness, silence.	Up to 3 days	College students	55	0	
18	1955-66	Water immersion; diff. light & noise.	Up to 8 hrs.	College students, patients, actors, etc.	100	1	Severely obsessive-compulsive subject developed paranoid symptoms.
19	1958-63	Diff. light & noise.	Up to 8 hrs.	College students	162	0	1 subject reported emotional problems a year after participating; no connection with experiment was established.

about phrases like "sensory deprivation psychosis," but the weight of the evidence strongly supports the conclusion that, "In spite of the numerous studies in experimental sensory deprivation, no specific psychiatric syndrome has been delineated in adults in which deprivation is customarily implicated in etiology" (Tarjan, 1970, p. 71).

Perhaps I should also mention the existence of many subjects who in fact greatly enjoy sensory deprivation. This shows up not only on rating scales and post-session interviews, but also on the disappointment of some individuals to find that the experiment is over, and their eagerness to continue or to volunteer for repeated sessions. A considerable number of people do find sensory deprivation to be a relaxing, peaceful, and refreshing experience; I have noted that as I discuss the topic with people who are not professional psychologists, an increasing number sigh that a day or two in the dark, quiet room by themselves seems like a dream come true. And mothers of small children tend to identify the prospect with Paradise!

CONCLUSION

In summary, sensory deprivation appears to be a situation that, by unfreezing the belief structure, removing the individual from his normal life experiences and cues, and enabling him to think seriously about his problem, greatly facilitates the first step in self-managed change. This first step is a firm decision to make a permanent alteration in behavior, and at the same time the realization that such a change can be made without unbearable stress. Given appropriate message inputs during the session, and supportive follow-up treatments either formal or informal, the effectiveness of any behavior modification technique might be improved if the practitioner included a period of stimulus reduction early in his procedures. Obviously, the technique is not a panacea, but it certainly deserves a wider and more intensive trial than it has ever received in the past.

REFERENCES

ANTISTA, B. and JONES, A.: Some beneficial consequences of brief sensory deprivation. Paper read at the 1975 meeting of the Western Psychological Association.
AZIMA, H. and CRAMER-AZIMA, F. J.: Effects of partial isolation in mentally disturbed individuals. *Diseases of the Nervous System*, 1956, 17, 117-122.
AZIMA, H. and CRAMER-AZIMA, F. J.: Studies on perceptual isolation. *Diseases of the Nervous System* (Monograph Supplement), 1957, 18, 80-85.

BERKUN, M. M., BIALEK, H. M., KERN, R. P., and YAGI, K.: Experimental studies of psychological stress in man. *Psychological Monographs*, 1962, 76 (15, Whole No. 534).

BORRIE, R. A.: The use of sensory deprivation and relaxation training in the initiation and maintenance of weight loss. Ph.D. dissertation, The University of British Columbia, in preparation.

BREHM, J. W.: *A Theory of Psychological Reactance.* New York: Academic Press, 1966.

BRESSLER, B., SILVERMAN, H. A., COHEN, S. I., and SHMAVONIAN, B.: Research in human subjects and the artificial traumatic neurosis: Where does our responsibility lie? *American Journal of Psychiatry*, 1959, 116, 522-526.

CONQUEST, R.: *The Great Terror.* New York: Macmillan, 1968.

CURTIS, G. C. and ZUCKERMAN, M.: A psychopathological reaction precipitated by sensory deprivation. *American Journal of Psychiatry*, 1968, 125, 255-260.

DOI, L. T.: Morita therapy and psychoanalysis. *Psychologia*, 1962, 5, 117-123.

FARBER, I. E., HARLOW, H. F., and WEST, L. J.: Brainwashing, conditioning and DDD (debility, dependency and dread). *Sociometry*, 1957, 20, 271-285.

FITZGERALD, R. G. and LONG, I.: Seclusion in the treatment and management of severely manic and depressed patients. *Perspectives in Psychiatric Care*, 1973, 11, 59-64.

GIBBY, K. G., ADAMS, H. B., and CARRERA, R. N.: Therapeutic changes in psychiatric patients following partial sensory deprivation. *Archives of General Psychiatry*, 1960, 3, 57-64.

GLASS, D. C. and SINGER, J. E.: *Urban Stress: Experiments on Noise and Social Stressors.* New York: Academic Press, 1972.

IKARD, F. F. and TOMKINS, S. S.: The experience of affect as a determinant of smoking behavior: A series of validity studies. *Journal of Abnormal Psychology*, 1973, 81, 172-181.

JACKSON, C. W., JR. and POLLARD, J. C.: Some nondeprivation variables which influence the "effects" of experimental sensory deprivation. *Journal of Abnormal Psychology*, 1966, 71, 383-388.

JILEK, W. G.: Brainwashing as therapeutic technique in contemporary Canadian Indian spirit dancing. In J. Westermeyer (Ed.), *Anthropology and Mental Health: Setting a Fresh Course.* The Hague: Mouton, in press.

KAMMERMAN, M.: Personality changes resulting from water-suspension sensory isolation. In M. Kammerman (Ed.), *Sensory Isolation and Personality Change.* Springfield, Ill.: Charles C Thomas, 1977.

KOSLIN, B. L. and PARGAMENT, R.: Effects of attitude on the discrimination of opinion statements. *Journal of Experimental and Social Psychology*, 1969, 5, 244-264.

KOURETAS, D.: The oracle of Trophonius: a kind of shock treatment associated with sensory deprivation in ancient Greece. *British Journal of Psychiatry*, 1967, 113, 1441-1446.

LEWIN, K.: Group decision and social change. In E. E. Maccoby, T. M. Newcomb, and E. L. Hartley (Eds.), *Readings in Social Psychology* (3rd ed.). New York: Holt, 1958. Pp. 197-211.

LIFTON, R. J.: *Thought Reform and the Psychology of Totalism.* New York: Norton, 1961.

LILLY, J. C. and SHURLEY, J. T.: Experiments in solitude, in maximum achievable Flaherty (Ed.), *Psychophysiological Aspects of Space Flight.* New York: Columphysical isolation with water suspension, of healthy intact persons. In B. E. bia University Press, 1961. Pp. 238-247.

LIPOWSKI, A. J.: Sensory and information inputs overload: Behavioral effects. *Comprehensive Psychiatry*, 1975, 16, 199-221.

LONDON, P.: *Behavior Control.* New York: Harper & Row, 1969.
McGUFFIN, J.: *The Guineapigs.* Harmondsworth, England: Penguin, 1974.
MARGETTS, B. L.: African ethnopsychiatry in the field. *Canadian Psychiatric Association Journal,* 1968, 13, 521-538.
MYERS, T. I.: Some further data from the Subjective Stress Scale (SSS). Paper read at the meeting of the Eastern Psychological Association, 1964.
MYERS, T. I.: Tolerance for sensory and perceptual deprivation. In J. P. Zubek (Ed.), *Sensory Deprivation: Fifteen Years of Research.* New York: Appleton-Century-Crofts, 1969, Pp. 289-331.
ORNE, M. T. and SCHEIBE, K. E.: The contribution of non-deprivation factors in the production of sensory deprivation effects: The psychology of the panic button. *Journal of Abnormal and Social Psychology,* 1964, 68, 3-14.
PAPAGEORGIOU, M. G.: Incubation as a form of psychotherapy in the care of patients in ancient and modern Greece. *Psychotherapy and Psychosomatics,* 1975, 26, 35-38.
PENDERGRASS, V. E.: Effects of length of time-out from positive reinforcement and schedule of application in suppression of aggressive behavior. *Psychological Record,* 1971, 21, 75-80.
RIESEN, A.: *The Developmental Neurophysiology of Sensory Deprivation.* New York: Academic Press, 1975.
SCHEIN, E. H.: *Coercive Persuasion.* New York: Norton, 1961.
SHALLICE, T.: The Ulster depth interrogation techniques and their relation to sensory deprivation research. *Cognition,* 1972, 1, 385-405.
SMITH, A.: *Powers of Mind.* New York: Random House, 1975.
SPIEGEL, H.: A single-treatment method to stop smoking using ancillary self-hypnosis. *International Journal of Clinical and Experimental Hypnosis,* 1970, 18, 235-350.
STUART, R. B.: The role of social work education in innovative human services. In F. W. Clark, D. R. Evans & L. A. Hamerlynck (Eds.), *Implementing Behavioral Programmes for Schools and Clinics. Proceedings of the 3rd Banff International Conference on Behaviour Modification.* Champaign, Ill.: Research Press, 1972. Pp. 3-39.
STUART, R. B. and DAVIS, B.: *Slim Chance in a Fat World.* Champaign, Ill.: Research Press, 1972.
SUEDFELD, P.: Theoretical formulations; II. In J. P. Zubek (Ed.), *Sensory Deprivation: Fifteen Years of Research.* New York: Appleton-Century-Crofts, 1969. Pp. 433-448.
SUEDFELD, P.: Attitude manipulation in restricted environments: V. Theory and research. Symposium paper read at XXth International Congress of Psychology, Tokyo, 1972.
SUEDFELD, P.: The clinical relevance of reduced sensory stimulation. *Canadian Psychological Review,* 1975, 16, 88-103 (a).
SUEDFELD, P.: The benefits of boredom: Sensory deprivation reconsidered. *American Scientist,* 1975, 63, 60-69 (b).
SUEDFELD, P.: The use of sensory deprivation in the treatment of claustrophobia: Another study in the development of a panacea. *Worm Runner's Digest,* in press.
SUEDFELD, P. and BEST, J. A.: Satiation and sensory deprivation combined in smoking therapy: Some case studies and unexpected side-effects. *International Journal of the Addictions,* in press.
SUEDFELD, P. and IKARD, F. F.: Attitude manipulation in restricted environments: IV. Psychologically addicted smokers treated in sensory deprivation. *British Journal of Addiction,* 1973, 68, 170-176.
SUEDFELD, P. and IKARD, F. F.: The use of sensory deprivation in facilitating the re-

duction of cigarette smoking. *Journal of Consulting and Clinical Psychology,* 1974, 42, 888-895.

SUEDFELD, P., LANDON, P. B., EPSTEIN, Y. M., and PARGAMENT, R.: The role of experimenter and subject expectations in sensory deprivation. *Representative Research in Social Psychology,* 1971, 2, 21-27.

SUEDFELD, P., LANDON, P. B., PARGAMENT, R., and EPSTEIN, Y. M.: An experimental attack on smoking (Attitude manipulation in restricted environments, III). *International Journal of the Addictions,* 1972, 7, 721-733.

SUEDFELD, P. and VERNON, J.: Visual hallucinations in sensory deprivation: A problem of criteria. *Science,* 1964, 145, 412-413.

TARJAN, G.: Sensory deprivation and mental retardation. In L. Madow and L. H. Snow (Eds.), *The Psychodynamic Implications of Physiological Studies on Sensory Deprivation.* Springfield, Ill.: Charles C Thomas, 1970. Pp. 70-89.

TETLOCK, P. E. and SUEDFELD, P.: Inducing belief instability without a persuasive message: The roles of attitude centrality, individual cognitive differences, and sensory deprivation. *Canadian Journal of Behavioural Sciences,* 1976, 8, 324-333.

TOFFLER, A.: *Future Shock.* New York: Random House, 1970.

TOMKINS, S. S.: A modified model of smoking behavior. In E. Borgatta & R. Evans (Eds.), *Smoking, Health, and Behavior.* Chicago: Aldine, 1968. Pp. 165-186.

WILCOX, J.: A practical approach to treatment of colic. Paper read at the meeting of the Southwestern Pediatric Society, 1957.

ZIMBARDO, P. G.: The human choice: Individuation, reason, and order vs. deindividuation, impulse, and chaos. In W. J. Arnold and D. Levine (Eds.), *Nebraska Symposium on Motivation,* 1969, 17, 237-307.

ZUBEK, J. P. (Ed.): *Sensory Deprivation: Fifteen Years of Research.* New York: Appleton-Century-Crofts, 1969.

ZUCKERMAN, M.: Hallucinations, reported sensations, and images. In J. P. Zubek (Ed.), *Sensory Deprivation: Fifteen Years of Research.* New York: Appleton-Century Crofts, 1969. Pp. 85-125.

11

Development of Women's Self-Help Clinic

LYNN BUHLER
and
RETA MCKAY

INTRODUCTION

The purpose of this paper is to describe the experience of a group of women in Vancouver, British Columbia, who came together in 1971 because of feelings of dissatisfaction regarding their health care. This group eventually formed the Vancouver Women's Health Collective, an umbrella organization encompassing a phone line referral service, health education groups, and a Self-Help Clinic.

Following a discussion of the rationale for use "self-help," a brief history of the Collective and its methods for teaching self-help will be presented. Emphasis will be placed on the Women's Self-Help Clinic as an arena for learning new expectations and behaviors relating to health care. Some research findings carried out by the Collective, under a National Health and Welfare Demonstration Grant, will illustrate the effectiveness of the Self-Help Clinic.

The authors wish to thank the following friends/colleagues who read the draft of this paper and offered criticisms and suggestions: Jutta Mason, Norma Perryman, Darlene Steele, Nancy Kleiber, Barney Eades, Ian McKay, and members of the Vancouver Women's Health Collective. For her assistance with the research, thoughtful reading of our work and comments, a special thanks to Linda Light, one of the researchers with the Collective.

258

BACKGROUND OF THE SELF-HELP APPROACH

At meetings during the late 1960s and early 1970s, women began meeting in order to discuss their common concerns. One of the most frequently expressed concerns focused on what the women perceived as humiliating and unsatisfactory medical experiences. Faced with special needs, such as birth control, pregnancy and recurrent vaginal infections, women who were not actually "sick" were made to feel that they were infringing on the doctor's time. Questions were stifled or not answered and medical attention was brisk and often coupled with unsolicited lectures on moral issues. Experiencing frustration in their efforts to humanize the care which they received, women in several places in North America elected to form their own self-care groups in order to provide services which were elsewhere rendered poorly, if at all.

Self-help is an ideal remedy for this frustrating situation. In the self-help health groups, experts are not regarded as necessary and the women turn to each other to learn. This is not the first time self-help has emerged as a tool for women's movement: In consciousness-raising groups, self-help has been applied to teach one another how to change and/or understand themselves and society. This type of self-help is an exploration into feelings and reasons for everyday situations that caused anger and frustration. With sharing and group support, women learn to relate to each other and themselves.

Thus, it was a natural evolution that women who found it necessary to reject some aspects of the health care system would utilize self-help to learn about, and, in some cases, offer an alternative to, what was taught and experienced in the doctor's office. With the newfound confidence and understanding of their bodies, they attempted to demystify the health care experience. Discussions and presentations by members of the group were on the usual agenda for each meeting. Information found in professional and lay journals, as well as personal experiences, were the main sources; few doctors were requested to give lectures. Many women learned for the first time how the "Pill" prevented pregnancy, and how other methods worked and affected women. Women also learned about abortions, breast self-examination, normal sexual functioning, vaginal infections, menopause, physiology, cervical self-examination and more. The emphasis was on preventing health care problems and learning how to take care of oneself.

Self-help was found to be a highly motivating method for studying health care. When women freely chose to learn about their bodies, they retained much of what was learned. When this learning took place in a group, women had help in exploring the implications of their new knowledge and this helped to strengthen their motivation to apply what they had learned.

Self-help has several prerequisites. First, both the teacher and learner must be open to new knowledge: There can be no closed system. Second, the teacher must respect the learner as an equal and must be prepared to exchange roles often. Third, ample time must be allowed for lengthy explanations, questioning and further explanation. More often than not, professionals operate in comparatively closed systems with fixed definitions. Professionals also tend often to be locked into hierarchical structures which impede flexible interchange with those whom they serve. And professionals tend to work within tight time frames which do not permit the freedom of give-and-take exchanges. Therefore, organizers of the self-help groups elected to draw little from professionals, turning instead to the energetic, inquisitive, informed, flexible members of their own groups.

Within this model, the self-help group adopted the goal of helping women to function as informed, independent individuals. Women are helped to act with self-confidence, responsibility, pride and assertiveness. They are helped to become informed so that they can be intelligent consumers of essential services. They are encouraged to turn to professionals as consultants, recognizing that they, those who are served, have the ultimate responsibility of making decisions about their own health care.

History

The Vancouver Women's Health Collective (VWHC) began quietly. An article was published in a Vancouver feminist newspaper in the fall of 1971 describing one woman's dissatisfaction with her medical care. The article invited other women with similar concerns to join in a discussion of the difficulties which they experienced in obtaining sensitive and competent health care. Weekly meetings were begun where focus was placed upon such issues as:

1) the anger and frustration which the women felt when dealing with male medical professionals who handled pelvic examinations insensitively and who dismissed with embarrassment questions about sexuality;

2) the common difficulty in obtaining adequate information about preventive health practices;

3) inconsistency in the quality and types of care received;

4) frustration with being treated as though they could not understand fundamental aspects of their biological functioning and the care of their bodies.

As these discussions unfolded, women began to realize that many others shared their concerns. They also began to realize that a different style of service could be offered. To prepare for constructive action, the content of the meetings turned to the sharing of basic information on topics ranging from anatomy to birth control, from nutrition to exercise. Women with diverse backgrounds pooled their expertise and struggled to maintain a pattern in which no single woman dominated but rather all shared in decision-making. This required development of means of coping with feelings of jealousy, inferiority, incompetence or the urge to control, all of which could disrupt the orderly process of interchange among women with widely varied skills, experiences and interests.

As group process developed, six of the original 20 women dropped out of the group. The 14 who remained elected to "apprentice" with helpful doctors and clinics in Vancouver during the summer and fall of 1972. During this time, the women became skilled at doing and teaching breast and cervical self-examination, bi-manual examination, simple urine tests, pregnancy tests, and tests for gonorrhea, yeast and trichomonas infections. A visit to the Seattle Self-Help Clinic in the fall of 1972 helped the women to form their own plan to open a self-help clinic in Vancouver.

Discussions and practice sessions with a small group of physicians (male and female) were an integral part of the Collective's development. The opportunity to share ideas about the Collective's approach to women's health, the structure of health care delivery, and the role of female physicians in a primarily male profession, together with the doctors' perceptions of inadequacies in care and their desire for change, led to an exciting working relationship. A stimulating learning environment was thus created for both parties. As the learning process developed, confidence was evident all around.

Members were now ready to share their knowledge and skills with others. On December 1, 1972, the Women's Self-Help Clinic was opened one night per week, in the premises of the Vancouver Free Clinic. A female physician was in attendance each night to serve as a consultant and to verify findings.

The group had discussed its expectations of the physician's role in the Clinic at length. Would she be merely a backup technician without an important interpersonal relationship with clients? Would she become a member of a "team" and function largely as other workers? Some physicians indicated they would not be satisfied with a purely "technical" role. Without a strict prescription of expected behavior but with respect for each other's skills and ideology, physicians and workers at the Clinic seemed to develop a compatible working relationship. Some initial fear that women workers would be criticized by the doctors dissipated when it was learned that the doctors wanted to learn from the Clinic workers (concerning, for example, diaphragm fittings and ways of discussing sexuality). Through shared experiences like this, some of the "mystification" of health care lessened.

The primary responsibility for imparting ideas and for aiding in the experience of self-help came from each team of two lay women who saw a client. Approximately one to one and a half hours was spent with each individual because of the strong educational component. Increased demands for service have not changed this experiential learning focus.

The Clinic has moved its location several times for different reasons. A comfortable old house equipped with overstuffed furniture, the first location, which was shared with the Vancouver Free Clinic, was vacated in March, 1974 when the building was to be demolished for redevelopment. Temporary quarters at the Free Youth Clinic, sponsored by the Metropolitan Board of Health, were utilized until an arrangement at the Seymour Medical Clinic was established in May, 1974.

Doctors at the Seymour Medical Clinic initially agreed to let the Collective use four examining rooms once a week. Some members were excited at the prospect of working in closer proximity with the medical profession, as they hoped that attitudes and knowledge in both groups would change; others feared negative alterations in the Self-Help Clinic as a result of the association. It was hoped that the Self-Help Clinic would refer clients to the doctors when necessary and vice versa, and that the doctors might incorporate some new practices into their services (teaching cervical self-examination, for instance). Concern was expressed by some that the previous clientele would not feel comfortable in the new setting, but other members thought a broader segment of the population would be reached.

The Self-Help Clinic continued to operate one night per week in what was a much more traditional medical environment, attracting a clientele comparable to that using services in the first location. However, after four months, following newspaper reports of statements about the medical system made by members of the Collective at a women's health symposium, the administration of the Seymour Clinic requested a statement of aims and objectives of the Women's Health Collective. A letter replying to the Seymour Clinic doctors stated, in part,

> We are dedicated to the principles of self-help, information sharing and health consciousness-raising through lay participation and education. Our main commitment is to women regaining power over their own bodies through knowledge and support.
> In the community at large there is a growing awareness of the need for change in the health care system. At the recent women's health symposium sponsored by the N.D.P. Women's Subcommittee on Health, representatives from many community groups as well as individual health consumers, nurses, doctors, and lay health workers expressed the need for change, not only on an individual level with one's own doctor, but within the health system as a whole.
> The Vancouver Women's Health Collective is part of this movement for change in the health care system. We are determined to see policies initiated in health care which incorporate our principles.

The reply from the administration of the Seymour Medical Clinic stated, in part,

> Unfortunately, conflict exists between the ideological spectra of our respective groups as to the method of bringing about such changes.

Thus this formal relationship came to an end.

Energy, therefore, was directed towards finding a more compatible clinic setting. Subsequently, in August, 1974, the Self-Help Clinic moved back into the facilities of the Free Youth Clinic. The Women's Self-Help Clinic has continued to operate from that location once a week.

Other aspects of the Collective had been developing concurrently with the Self-Help Clinic. A look at the funding patterns will elaborate on these developments.

FUNDING

Volunteer involvement, along with high energy and interest levels, kept the group together initially. During the spring of 1972, the group acquired its first meeting place at a "Woman's Place." This space was shared by another group of women doing abortion referral and counselling. In the summer of 1972, several women, some of whom had been in the winter health education group, applied for and received an Opportunities for Youth (O.F.Y.) federal grant to do a questionnaire/survey of women's experiences with doctors. The idea was to compile a doctor directory for women in the Vancouver area based on the experience and recommendations of other women. The results of this project were published in the "Green Booklet" and the information was also shared on the phone line.

Funding for two salaries from the Company of Young Canadians, a federal program for community development, was sought in the early stages of the Health Collective development. Successful application meant that first one, then, six months later, two, women were able to work full time on Collective activities. These salaried workers performed similar functions to the volunteer workers answering phones, making abortion referrals and counselling, planning for future development), but were also able to provide a much needed continuity for the mushrooming activities.

Increasing demands for health education groups in the spring and summer of 1973 necessitated the application for three more workers' salaries to respond to this need. The Opportunities for Youth granted these salaries to extend for three months. The women working on these health activities formed themselves into a nonprofit society called the Vancouver Women's Health Collective Society, after which the fundraising began in earnest (July, 1973).

Much effort went into seeking short-term financial support from sources in Vancouver such as United Community Services, Vancouver Foundation, Social Service Committee of City Council and various Church outreach programs. But the great amount of effort and energy required to constantly barrage agencies for even minimal support soon came to be viewed as ineffective (although this activity did serve to educate community services about the aims of the Collective). By this time, more women wanted to be able to work fulltime with the Collective. Therefore, to provide long-term, stable funding for more workers, the Collective decided, in the summer of 1973, to apply for a National Health and Welfare Demonstration Grant, "To demonstrate a lay-participation model of providing preventive health services to women." Much background work went into the preparation of the grant proposal and support was elicited from doctors, members of the Provincial Legislative Assembly and other community leaders.

After several months of waiting, the Collective learned in the fall of 1973 that the grant had been awarded for two salaries for one year, negotiable to three years. The total amount involved in this was $117,000.00 for two and a half years, including the salaries as well as a research component. An important condition of receiving this grant was that approximately one-half of the money be used for the research component. This altered the personnel and activities at the Health Collective because two "outside" researchers were now participating.

This grant, together with help from some workers from the Vancouver Opportunity Program (V.O.P.—a supplement for social assistance recipients), meant additional women could be more intensively involved in the functioning of the Collective. The initial expectation was that every member would participate in all facets of the organization—that is, that she would take one or two phone shifts each week, be a resource person in a health education group and work in the Clinic, rotating through all the roles. However, as the programs have evolved, women have sometimes concentrated in the one area in which they feel more knowledgeable, interested and comfortable. Constant discussion and examination of the generalist/specialist dilemma still occur at the Collective.

ORGANIZATION

The organization of the Collective has altered over time but the organizational principles have remained constant. A hierarchical structure was avoided because of what the group perceived to be the inherent problems: concentration of information and decision-making power in the hands of a few with attendant feelings of alienation and powerlessness in those not privy to the information. Earlier some of these problems did, in fact, arise. However, the strength of the collective, decision-making model enabled the members to discuss these tensions and work towards resolving them.

The consensus model of organization was chosen by the Collective. Everyone had an opportunity to speak her mind on all decisions. If someone felt strongly opposed to a course of action, the responsibility for convincing her lay with the rest of the group.

Weekly meetings have always been an integral part of the Health

Collective organization. When three diverse areas of responsibility developed (Self-Help Clinic, health groups, and phone line), the meetings were an essential means of communication among members. As social and personal relationships within the group developed, a potluck dinner prior to the weekly meetings was established.

At the meetings, open to anyone who considered herself a Collective member, reports were heard from the various areas, efforts were made to solve problems the Collective was experiencing, and complaints and suggestions from members were presented. Members stated that they often left a three-hour meeting feeling exhausted and exhilarated—exhausted because of the energy of a support group, alive with ideas and excitement.

An important aspect of the meetings was criticism and self-criticism; in this way members attempted to arrive at new understandings of their work together. Struggles developed since some women felt on the outside of the hub of activity; however, a sensitivity towards this situation and open communication allowed the group to work through such issues. This working through process was long and tedious on occasions. Individuals would perceive problems others did not consider areas of concern; thus, conflicts of interests would come forth. These differences would usually be resolved by the end of the meeting, but before resolution occurred expressions of deep feelings about the philosophy of the Health Collective would come forth.

When the Collective was at its height of expansion and activity, members instituted "rounds" at the weekly meetings as a way of fostering integration of personal and work experience. "Rounds" was an opportunity for each woman to talk about what had been affecting her life recently. Although this practice became time consuming, integration of experience continues to be explored and incorporated into the Collective organization.

FUNCTIONS OF THE COLLECTIVE

As the Collective developed, five different functions emerged. As these are the channels through which the self-help goals are achieved, each will be described briefly.

Health Education Groups

The Collective offers health groups to women who are interested in learning about their bodies, birth control, and related topics. The subjects discussed at the group meetings depend on the areas of interest to the women in attendance. The groups now consist of eight to 12 women, who meet for four to eight weeks. One or two women from the Health Collective come to the meetings regularly; they act as resource people and initiate group interaction. The response by the women who attend varies: Some groups are highly motivated and explore and discuss many issues; other groups are more passive and want a lecture series to be given them by Health Collective members. The latter type of group is discouraged because this is not self-help; it is not conducive to discussion, nor does it encourage acceptance of the responsibility for one's health. Many members of these groups become involved with other Collective activities, and some maintain themselves as a group after involvement with the Collective ceases.

It is felt by most Health Collective members that involvement in a health group is a necessary step for further activities, for it lays the groundwork for gaining basic knowledge, and teaches the practical philosophy of self-help. In the groups, one learns from non-experts, and one realizes that a doctorate in medicine is not essential for learning about common normal and abnormal bodily functions and treatments. The health groups give the women involved an opportunity to discuss with other women their problems, fears and positive experiences with such topics as birth control, sexuality, abortion, doctors, and living. From these discussions a clearer understanding of the female body develops, and the feelings of passive dependence upon the medical profession begin to change.

Phone Line and Counselling

During the day, and one evening per week, the Health Collective has a telephone line giving whatever help is possible regarding a large variety of health-related problems. Women are the usual callers, and they have questions about abortion, birth control, gynecological problems, doctor referral, and community information. They are given the information requested if it is available, and/or they are referred to the Self-Help Clinic, a doctor, or an appropriate community service when indicated. If a question or problem needs in-depth discussion (for example, a diaphragm fitting), or if resource material can be offered, callers are invited to come to the Collective to look into the matter more fully. In this area the Collective acts as a resource center, and a backup to the Clinic, offering counselling and information so that a woman can make an educated decision about a situation (abortion, for example), or so that she can solve her problem herself. Advice is usually not given: Women are encouraged to make their own decisions.

Recently the Health Collective has started group counselling for women wanting abortions or diaphragms. Group counselling is a very effective method of dispensing health care information, since it enables women to share experiences and discuss various alternatives. It also allows the Health Collective to see more people. Feeling the support of a group at a time of crisis is beneficial and encourages feelings of strength. Learning to relate to other women at a time of crisis or when seeking health information is an alternative to discussing the situation alone, with a doctor, in an office. Peer relations are likely to be more useful because the women can relate to each other, resulting in freer discussion. In this situation, real fears and questions emerge, since many women feel more comfortable talking with other women who are experiencing the same situation. The Collective is continuing to have group counselling for they feel that it is a beneficial way of dealing with crisis and learning situations, and it promotes self-help by relying on the group members for information and support, and not on an individual counsellor.

Self-Help Clinic

At the Women's Self-Help Clinic, clients are given a unique method of care. When they enter, they are asked to fill out a lengthy "herstory" form (medical history) in duplicate with a copy for the woman. Clients are then seen by two lay workers who have knowledge about birth control, pregnancy, abortion, sexual functions, vaginal infections, and some physiology, and who can do speculum examinations, bi-manual examination, fit diaphragms, and take lab tests. The visit begins with a review of the client's past medical "herstory" and inquiries are made about the reason for the visit.

Women usually come to the Self-Help Clinic for birth control, vaginal infections, or because they want to learn self-examination. If the woman requests, for example, birth control, a review of the various methods usually ensues, using special teaching tools (for example, a pelvic model, samples of IUD's). Questions about past experiences and feelings about sexuality are often asked so that an effective and desirable method of birth control can be chosen by the client. If she has a vaginal infection, symptoms are discussed and she is taught about the common types of infection and usual methods of treatment. Breast self-examination is usually taught at some point in the discussion, either individually or in a group.

Following the discussion, a speculum examination is usually done, and an explanation with instructions for self-examination is given unless the woman states that she doesn't want that information. The client is encouraged to insert her own speculum. Lab tests accompany the examinations done on a client with a vaginal infection, and a pap test is done on anyone who has not had one in the last year. The purposes of the tests are explained, and, with the aid of a mirror, the woman is shown her cervix. Following the examination, the client goes to the lab to see any of the few tests that are processed at the Clinic. She then returns to the examining room where diagnosis and treatment are discussed if an infection is present. A doctor is invited to join the group at this point, if she has not already been included in the process. After treatment is decided upon, and the woman has a good understanding of her condition and has no more questions, the visit ends.

If the client has come for birth control, the visit ends after a method has been chosen and after the lay workers are sure that she understands how it works, and how it should be used. If the method chosen is a diaphragm, the woman is invited to return in a few weeks to ask any questions that develop (as they often do). This first visit to the Clinic usually lasts from one to one and a half hours.

From this brief description of the routine visit to the Clinic, it can be seen that self-help is stressed. Information is given, and time is provided so that a woman can truly make her own decisions about her health care and her body.

Clinic Training Groups

After the Clinic had been established for a few months, many Clinic users, excited with the experience of participating in the Clinic's operation, wanted to become more active in passing that experience on to other women, by learning and then teaching about health care and self-examination. What apparently was happening was a profound realization for some users of their right to understand and participate in their health care.

As a result of this interest, Clinic training groups were established at various times, depending on the needs of the workers and the demand. Women who wanted to work in the Clinic went to a health group first, after which they could become involved in a Clinic training group. The major emphasis of this group was on acquiring the knowledge and skills to work in the Clinic. The women practiced speculum exams, lab tests, breast examination, and diaphragm fitting on each other so that they would be skilled and have confidence before meeting new women. It was also important that the women practice on someone that they knew, so that real feedback about skills would occur. Thus, the women helped each other to learn. During the training period, these women would come to the Clinic a few times and would work with an experienced member who would further instruct them and encourage them to use their new skills. This initiation process worked fairly well, so that by the time the 12-week training process was completed, the women could function effectively in the Clinic.

Speaking to Other Groups

It is important to mention that, although it is a small proportion of women who seek out and become involved in the Collective, there are requests from the wider community for speakers on various topics. Members of the Collective have, accordingly, spoken to high school guidance classes on birth control/sexuality/responsibility, talked about self-help at community college courses, and addressed sessions at political party workshops. They now do most of their public speaking at women's health workshops.

However, the increasing demands for this type of involvement were very time- and energy-consuming, and it became obvious that the Collective was being regarded as the "expert" on women's self-help in health. This development was contrary to the basic tenets of self-help; that is, the group came to be viewed as special by virtue of its knowledge and experience. Consequently, the Collective decided to limit involvements to actual demonstration/practice sessions of self-help by teaching breast and cervical self-examination. In this way, others could learn or see the applications of self-help and decide for themselves whether they wanted to develop their interest in women's health.

The Collective hopes to spread the ideology of self-help, rather than limit itself primarily to information sharing. Thus, it is assumed that other groups of women will take responsibility for their own learning, and develop appropriate methods for themselves. Resources at the Collective (books, pamphlets, journals, information sheets, teaching aids) are available to interested people.

CHARACTERISTICS OF COLLECTIVE MEMBERS AND CLINIC USERS

What types of women become actively involved in the Collective? A partial answer to this question is found in the results of research done at the Collective (Kleiber & Light, 1974). During May and June, 1974, interviews were conducted with 26 women who considered themselves members of the Health Collective. The following is a profile using some of the pertinent data. (Since there is a constant change of membership, many present members are not included in these data.)

The age range was from 22 years to 49 years with seven women 25 years or younger, 14 women between 26 and 30 years and 5 women 31 years and over.

The following is a breakdown of the education/training of the members:

High school	3
High school plus some university and/or some further training	11
Bachelor degree	5
Bachelor degree plus work towards Master's or M.D.	3
Master's degree	3
M.D.	1
Total	26

Availability of time and energy to become involved in the Collective is partially indicated by other responsibilities. Fourteen women had no children; 10 had one child; and two women were mothers of two children each.

Members varied in their time commitment to the Collective, per week, as follows:

Less than 8 hours	5
9-20 hours	8
21-30 hours	9
31-40 hours	3
Over 40 hours	1
Total	26

272 Behavioral Self-Management

During the period of research six women were on fulltime salary from the Collective, three on half-salary, one on less than half-salary, three on V.O.P. (welfare supplement), and 13 women received no salary. Many of these women had been active in some aspect of the Women's Movement prior to joining the Collective and wanted to realize a feminist ideology in terms of their health care.

Some characteristics of women attending the Self-Help Clinic are similar to those of the workers in the Collective. This is documented in a study of 61 women using the Clinic.

> The demographic data show that a typical woman's profile is as follows: The woman is between the ages of 25-29 years, single, lives in Vancouver . . . in a communal/cooperative housing set-up, is a professional or technical white collar worker, has a university education. . . . The woman supports herself with her own earnings, has medical insurance and generally seems to be in good health (Steele, 1974).

The two most common reasons given in Steele's study for choosing the Self-Help Clinic were: "I appreciate being seen by women paramedics and doctors" (43 out of a total of 214 responses); and "I find doctors' visits rather rushed and impersonal" (38 responses out of 214). Thus women obviously chose this setting because they seem desirous of a different type of health care experience. They were seeking a more empathetic and personal relationship with a health worker. Steele accordingly reached the following conclusion:

> The results which emerged from the area of women's responses to their health care and self-help experience suggest that women have many health care needs which are not being met in the traditional system of medical services. Some of these unmet health care needs include: the desire for an egalitarian relationship with the health care worker, availability of accurate information about their bodies and health concerns, the right to partake in decisions about their own health care, time and opportunity to ask questions and seek information on areas of concern from the health care worker, an atmosphere which is relaxed, comfortable and caring in which to deal with their concerns, the desire to be seen as sexual beings and the opportunity to share feelings and problems about sexuality with other open and empathetic persons, and the wish to be treated in a respectful, humanistic adult fashion (Steele, 1974).

EVALUATION OF EFFECTIVENESS

The Vancouver Women's Health Collective has affected the lives of thousands of women in British Columbia. Many women throughout the province have read articles about the Collective's activities and written to the group, asking for more information. Hundreds of people have attended talks about self-help given by members to community colleges, YWCA's, schools, university groups, and mothers' groups. Several hundred women have had more active involvement with the Collective as users via the phone line, a health group, or through visiting the Clinic.

It seems an almost impossible task to evaluate the effectiveness of such a far-reaching project. However, it is possible to present some data from the draft of the Clinic Impact Study, done by the researchers on the Demonstration Grants (Light, 1976). This study was done using a qualitative follow-up interview with 43 women who had attended the Self-Help Clinic. This study is one part of a comprehensive research project still in progress. Some information follows:

Forty-three women were interviewed; 28 had been to the Clinic once, 11 had been twice, and 4 had attended more than twice.

Reasons for visiting the Clinic varied, but the majority (37 out of 43) attended with specifically female concerns. The largest number (24) were interested in birth control, either in requesting a specific method (diaphragm (9), pill (6), IUD (2)) or in discussing the alternatives in order to make an informed choice. The other 13 women came with a variety of female concerns. Only two respondents stated "self-examination" as their reason for visiting the Clinic, but it is interesting to note that in a later question, 35 women state that they learned self-examination.

At the time of their last visit to the Self-Help Clinic, 26 women had a regular doctor. At the time of the interview, 32 women had a regular doctor. The main reasons given by the 11 women who did not have a doctor at the time of the interview were: that they didn't need one (5) or they used an alternate facility (5).

Ten women had changed their regular physician since the time of the first visit, seven of these giving as their reason for changing the fact that they were not comfortable with their former doctor.

All women were asked why they had chosen to visit the Self-Help Clinic rather than another clinic or doctor. The answers were as follows:

"More comfortable," "more at ease," "better atmosphere than own doctor"	16
"They take more time," "explain things better," "give more information"	8
"Convenient," "no appointments," "location"	7
"Transient," "no doctor of own"	4
"Wanted another medical opinion"	4
"Didn't want to go to family doctor because wanted privacy"	4
"Thought it would be better to know more, specifically knowledge regarding women's things"	4
"Recommended by friends"	4
"Interest in Clinic," "wanted to find out about it"	3
"Sent by teachers, houseparents"	3
"It's free," "don't have medical insurance"	2
"Wanted to see female doctor"	2
"Own doctor wasn't very helpful"	2

The total number of reasons given exceeds the number of respondents because some women had more than one reason for choosing the Clinic.

Most of the women who attended the Clinic had regular doctors and this number increased between the Clinic visit and time of the interview. Thus, it is clear that, for the majority of women using the Clinic, it is a supplement to, *not* a substitute for, a doctor's care. In fact, the Clinic could be seen as encouraging some women to find a regular doctor.

However, as 10 women changed their doctors following the last Clinic visit, some relation may exist between the Clinic visit and the desire to obtain a different doctor. Many women indicated that they were already somewhat critical of their doctor before their visit to the Clinic (see reasons for choosing self-help).

Women were asked what they had learned at the Clinic. Twenty-six responses indicated learning about birth control, 21 learned how to do a cervical self-exam, and 14 mentioned learning breast self-examination. Eleven women spoke of learning about some aspect of their bodily functioning; nine referred to learning about the Clinic (as an alternative). Three women learned to feel more comfortable with their bodies and two responses indicated learning about the "mystification of the medical profession." Five responses indicated learning regarding specific disease processes or treatment methods (e.g., venereal disease, medication).

The two largest areas of learning involved birth control and cervical self-examination. The first is to be expected as many women attended specifically for birth control information. Although very few women go asking to learn about cervical examination, most women are shown this procedure and report it as something learned. The following comments, given by women who had seen inside their vaginas for the first time, are examples of the responses many women had to the new information they were acquiring.

> . . . they taught me how to examine myself and I was thrilled because they showed me . . . my cervix with a mirror and I really had no idea that my body looked anything the way it did and it was really something.

Another woman spoke of the entire pelvic examination procedure:

> . . . they went to the trouble of telling you exactly what they were going to do; you don't feel like an animal in a test laboratory that just has things done to you without you knowing it and if you ask any questions, well, they either don't tell you or just tell you in very simplistic terms as fast as they can . . . it was a very good educational thing by itself . . . same thing for the pelvic examination.

The next largest area of learning was breast-self-examination which none of the 43 women gave as a reason for attending the Clinic, but which is, nevertheless, taught to nearly all women visiting the Clinic.

The comments about birth control learning stress the importance of an open atmosphere in which thorough discussion can occur. For example:

> . . . I went through a stage where I was deciding between an IUD and the pill and in the end I got a lot of counselling. It helped me make a clearer decision just by talking to them, by finding out what was involved. Not so much the risk and the statistics, those I knew from reading, but more what would be involved in both . . . those were the kinds of things I found out.

Or:

> . . . I learned primarily how to fit a diaphragm and how it should feel and I tried over and over and over again under supervision to put it in properly and to take it out properly and to make sure it was in properly.

Many women commented on the friendly, open atmosphere at the Clinic. The following comment illustrates a common response:

> . . . there, people are talking about all kinds of things that I consider very private and you just don't talk about those things in public, but it seemed that there was an environment there for people to talk about it.

With two exceptions, women who saw a doctor at the Clinic commented favorably on the experience.

The following quotes indicate some of the reactions to the doctors:

> . . . she made me feel I was talking to a friend. . . .

> . . . and you know she took me to the microscope and we looked at it together . . . and it was a learning experience.

Women were asked if their experience at the Self-Help Clinic changed their feelings about or their behavior towards their bodies. Twenty-nine affirmative responses indicated these changes: Seventeen women felt more comfortable and accepting of their bodies; eight women now take "better care" of themselves; seven responded that they feel more knowledgeable about bodily functions. Only one woman stated that her Clinic visit created concern that something was wrong with her body.

Finally, while 16 of the women studied reported that their attitudes toward their doctors were unchanged, many others felt that they had become aware of inadequacies in the type of care which they received as a result of their clinic experience. Because of this awareness, many can be expected to ask for and to receive a better quality of care from their physicians.

Generally, while more exposure to an alternative system tends to increase awareness of how medical practice could be improved, no cause and effect relationship should be assumed. Often the Clinic visit was the result of an already developing critical awareness of doctors and the health care system.

Thirty-five women stated that they had encouraged friends to visit the Self-Help Clinic. Clearly, they want to "spread the word." Of the women who reported a working knowledge of breast self-examination, 20 learned it for the first time at the Self-Help Clinic. A total of 32 women stated that they did breast self-examination, 22 on a regular basis, and 10 on an irregular basis. Nine women reported teaching someone else breast self-examination.

One indication of the effectiveness of the Clinic, as shown in this study, is that many women who attend the Clinic leave with an increased feeling of power to participate in their health care. This is evident in such behavior changes as women seeking out doctors with whom they feel more comfortable, involving themselves with their physicians by asking questions relating to disease process and treatment alternatives, practicing breast self-examination, and encouraging friends to visit the Collective. Thus, many women learned how to help themselves to better health.

Conclusion

Working towards the development of a Women's Self-Help Clinic has taught the women involved many things. A new experience for many was the shared excitement and energy generated by women working together. This feeling of sisterhood, combined with ideas of self-help, was generalized into other aspects of many members' lives, enabling women to continue to search for and to develop more comfortable arrangements in, for example, living situations and interpersonal relationships. Thus, women learned how "to be" with each other and others in new ways.

Members also learned about the process of developing and maintaining a "collective" as an alternative organizational structure. Most certainly this entire experience has promoted a clearer analysis of the present health care system and sparked the determination of some women both to recreate their participation in that system and, concurrently, to work for changes.

These women learned it was possible to become more responsible for their health care by seeking out information, sharing personal experiences, discussing new patterns of behavior, and developing an organization which permitted implementation of the self-help ideal.

REFERENCES

KLEIBER, N. and LIGHT, L.: *Profile of Membership*. National Health Grant No. 610-1020-20, February, 1974.

HERON, W. The pathology of boredom. *Scientific American,* 1957, 196, 52-56.

LIGHT, L.: *Clinic Impact Study*. Rough Draft, National Health Grant No. 610-1020-20, February, 1976.

PETCH, J.: *Women's Attitudes Towards Internal Examinations*. A survey, Vancouver, December, 1974.

STEELE, D.: *A Study of Women Using A Self-Help Clinic*. Thesis, Vancouver, September, 1974.

12

Self-Help Group Approach to Self-Management

RICHARD B. STUART

During the past 20 years there has been an explosion in the number and variety of self-help efforts to meet personal needs. In increasing numbers we are fixing our own leaky faucets and cleaning our dirty carburetors. We are arranging our own marriages and divorces, bearing children with minimal outside help and undertaking the planning of our own estates. We are also making valiant efforts to bring under control our feelings of depression and anxiety and our urges to eat, drink and use drugs to excess. The two most remarkable features of this radical movement are 1) that it has taken place at a time when trade schools and universities are turning out a surfeit of professionals who are trained to do these jobs for us, and 2) that the results achieved by self-helpers surpass those of professional services in many instances.

Because self-help efforts have met with great success, a study of these methods can be very instructive for professionals. Of interest are the three technologies shared by all human services: techniques for changing behavior, for maintaining this change, and for delivering both change and maintenance techniques to clients (Stuart, 1972b). From this study, professionals may find ways to improve their programs. They may also find that, for certain problems at least, professional activities cannot be

The author wishes to acknowledge with thanks the critical reading and helpful suggestions of Mr. Ken Wein.

278

improved to the point at which they equal or surpass the benefit/cost performance of self-help programs.

In this paper, the roots and advantages of the self-help movement will be traced. Then, focusing on services to the overweight, it will be argued that for some problems self-help is the treatment of choice and that an appropriate role for professionals is to contribute to, but not to compete with, the self-help programs.

THE ROOTS OF THE SELF-HELP MOVEMENT

The roots of the self-help movement can be traced to a combination of ideological developments and environmental inadequacies. On the ideological side, the Protestant Ethic preached the virtue of self-reliance, which the Social Darwinists fashioned into a social doctrine, the conceptual cornerstone of which is, "God helps those who help themselves!" On the environmental side, the rigors of frontier life helped to popularize the heroic image of successful individualism. The shortages created by mobilization for both world wars forced families that had depended upon others to take care of many of their own social and material needs. In addition, disenchantment with professional services that proved to be costly, aloof, condescending and ineffective also caused many to turn toward their own efforts to meet life crises.

A CONTINUUM OF SELF-HELP EFFORTS

An intertwining of both ideology and necessity sowed the seeds of the self-help movement, which has spawned a broad continuum of services. At one end of the continuum are the unaided efforts of individuals to "pull themselves up by their bootstraps." Virtually everyone uses a self-directed trial and error means of attempting to meet personal crises before turning outside for help and uses additional help only when his own efforts have failed. A little further along on the continuum are efforts to make use of some of the profusion of manuals for self-management that are now marketed by the thousands each year. For example, there are manuals for weight control (Stuart, in press; Stuart & Davis, 1972), for toilet training (Azrin & Foxx, 1974), for improvement of marital interaction (Stuart & Lederer, in press) for managing non-assertiveness (Fensterheim & Baer, 1975) and for helping develop mentally disabled children to improve intellectual and social skills (Baker, Heifetz & Brightman, 1972), to name but a few.

These manuals contain many instigations for changing behavior in the natural environment. To these instigations can be added the use of support equipment, as has been done with audiotapes as cues for relaxation training (e.g., Denholtz & Mann, 1975; Lang, Melamed & Hart, 1970; Morris & Thomas, 1973). Addition of the instruments moves the user a little further along the self-help continuum.

Up to this point, the individual has self-selected the program to be followed and pursues the program alone. Clearly the program is under *self-direction*. Within the rubric of the self-help approach, however, are also a number of programs that are carried out on a group basis. They are still considered to be self-help activities because participants have an unusual level of control over the kind of service that they receive and because the services are under lay rather than professional direction. Some of these groups are purely *ad hoc,* informal get-togethers by several people who have shared concerns. But the groups may be formalized in regional, state, national or international organizations and they may include professional advisors as full-time contributors to their programs without losing their self-help characteristics.

EFFECTS OF SELF-HELP TREATMENTS

Most of the self-help efforts fall into the category of "nonprescriptive therapies" (Rosen, 1976), because they are self-prescribed and used independently of any outside supervision. Because their development is motivated by both service and commercial interests, the potential for marketing useless or even destructive services is real. For example, it is impossible to thumb through the pages of any woman's magazine without finding invitations to "melt pounds off in hours, inches in days," or to invest five minutes of every day to insure a new personality for life.

Few of the self-help manuals have been evaluated. When evaluations have been undertaken, the results almost always indicate at least some degree of positive change. (Of course, it is possible that studies yielding negative results might not find their way into publications as readily as those for which the outcome is positive.) The first of these evaluations was the work of Hagen (1974), whose subjects lost over one pound per week during the ten weeks that they used the printed material, and then maintained their losses through a brief follow-up period. For example, Hanson et al. (1976) found that a self-instructional manual addressed to overweight adults yielded results comparable to those achieved by members of high contact weight management groups, and that subjects in the manual only condition maintained their losses more effectively than those whose treatment included both the manual and group contact.

In contrast, however, another team (Brownell et al., 1976) found that clients who received standard group treatments significantly outperformed those in a manual only condition at the end of treatment and maintained their advantage during the follow-up period, although their improved performance was no longer statistically significantly better than that of those using the manual only. In the same vein, Bellack, Schwartz and Rozensky (1974) also found that manuals alone were not as effective when used without, as opposed to with, backup instructional contacts. Unfortunately, few studies use the same manual and most studies use their manuals in individual ways so that generalization is impossible at this time. Nevertheless, Glasgow and Rosen (in press) concluded an exhaustive review of the self-help manual literature with the view that "developers of self-help weight reduction manuals have conducted excellent studies in an attempt to validate their programs, and current findings are generally favorable" (p. 11). Unfortunately, their review of manuals in other areas—e.g., fear reduction, smoking cessation, sexual dysfunction—did not come to the same consistently positive conclusion.

Because the results of the use of these self-help manuals cannot be assumed to be positive on an *a priori* basis, some regulation of their publication in a manner similar to that currently governing the publication of psychological tests (American Psychological Association, 1966) or the marketing of drugs as monitored by the Federal Drug Administration is desirable.

Evaluation of the self-help groups is a relatively untouched area, and that research which has been done is generally lacking in experimental rigor. Lundwall and Baekland (1971) have suggested six criteria for these studies, few of which have been met in any of the efforts to date. First, they stress the value of *objective criteria for rating improvement*. Among groups aimed at promoting their members' improved "self-esteem" or "self-understanding," effective criteria are almost totally lacking. In studies of alcohol control programs, disagreement exists as to whether abstinence or a return to normal social drinking should be accepted as the critical outcome measure. For example, Pattison, Headley, Gelsser and Gottschalk (1968) found that social drinkers adjusted well as total abstainers, while Gerard, Saenger and Wile (1962) found that many abstainers were psychologically disturbed. Even in weight control studies in which the ultimate dependent variable is the objective measure of pounds lost, few studies agree in the way in which loss should be measured (Stuart, 1975). Therefore, as a rudimentary condition for effective evaluative research, consensus must be reached regarding an adequately triangulated set of reliable and valid measures of outcome.

As a second methodological criterion, Lundwall and Baekland (1971) suggest that whatever outcome measures are selected, they should be applied by *raters who are uninformed about the treatment received by the individuals whose behavior they are judging.* Thirdly, they suggest that *adequate statistical tests* should be used to evaluate these measured differences. This, in turn, requires often difficult decisions about how to treat change scores with their intrinsic bias of regression toward the mean.

Each of the three foregoing criteria can be met with reasonable effort. The remaining three criteria, however, are all but impossible standards for research on self-help groups and this fact dooms such studies to a quasi-experimental status. Lundwall and Baekland (1971) argue that: 1) treatment and no-treatment groups should be matched on variables known to affect outcome; 2) that clients should be randomly assigned to treatment or no treatment conditions; and 3) that the treatment and control groups should come from comparable populations. These basic criteria for laboratory research cannot be met in the self-help context precisely because self-help clients are self-directed: Those who do choose voluntary attendance by definition have a different motivational structure than those who do not. Even if this type of manipulation were possible, it would constitute, as Bebbington (1976) points out, "an infringement of the patient's liberty of action . . . (and) an ethical impossibility" (p. 574).

As an additional criterion, it should also be suggested that some control or standardization of the intervention methods would be an essential evaluation criterion. However, for organizations, such as Alcoholics Anonymous, where the format but not content is directed by organizational design, this, too, is an impossible standard to meet. On the other hand, for organizations like Weight Watchers with a centrally defined program, greater standardization exists as an asset for evaluative research.

With all of these limitations, it may be impossible to ever arrive at a fully objective assessment of self-help efforts. Those investigations that have been completed have reached the conclusion that self-help groups are more than modestly successful. For example, a recent review of encounter groups (Hartley, Roback & Abramowitz, 1976) concluded that the majority of participants in these groups derive some benefit. On the other side of the coin, they found that approximately one in eight suffered some deterioration attributable to their involvement in the group while Bergin and Garfield (1971) had earlier estimated that only one in ten psychotherapy patients deteriorate in the same way. Elsewhere, Leach (1973) concluded that Alcoholics Anonymous does work and Blum and Blum (1967) viewed Synanon as the best treatment available for drug users.

As a reference point for evaluating the weight management programs that probably reach more self-helpers than any other efforts, it is useful to review the results of medical treatment of this problem. In his Presidential Address before the American Psychosomatic Society in 1974, Stunkard (1975) observed that:

1) Most people do not enter treatment of obesity;
2) Of those who do enter treatment, most will not remain; ...
3) Of those who remain, most will not lose much weight; ...
4) Of those who lose weight, most will regain it; and
5) Many will pay a high price for trying (p. 196).

Particularly disheartening is the fact that Stunkard (1976) found equally dismal results whether the treatment was nutrition education, psychotherapy or pharmacologic. Exemplary of these negative findings is Christakis' (1967) analysis of the experience of the Bureau of Nutrition of the City of New York. Of a total of 2,603 patients, 558 or over 21% dropped out within two weeks. Of those who stayed, only 9.8% of the patients achieved their goal weights and they tended to have much smaller amounts of weight to lose than did the failures. (Successes were 24% overweight at the start of treatment, contrasted to failures, who averaged 41.6% overweight at the same time.) Moreover, the small percentage of the successes who maintained their losses for 12 to 24 months further illustrates the bleak results achieved by professional programs even when they are under the leadership of extremely well informed and competent physicians and dietitians.

Comparisons between self-help and professional treatments of overweight are doomed to be quasi-experimental because it is not possible to randomly assign applicants to one or the other of the treatments.

Nonetheless, comparisons between the results of the two types of programs can be instructive. Recently, Williams and Duncan (1976b) compared the results of patients treated at Australia's Royal Adelaide Hospital with people participating in Weight Watchers classes. Hospital treated patients received individually prescribed diets of 800 to 1200 calories per day. Some were invited to participate in small group sessions of from eight to ten members while others were offered supportive services by both medical officers and dietitians who regularly monitored their weight. Many patients also received either active appetite suppressant drugs or placebos that they believed would reduce their hunger. Weight Watchers members received the standard program that was in effect worldwide in the company's operations at the time.

The average female patient in the hospital program remained 11 weeks and lost just under eight-tenths of a pound per week. The average male also remained 11 weeks and had a loss of one pound per week. In contrast, the average woman attended 17 Weight Watchers classes and lost 1.5 pounds per week, while the average man attended 16 classes and lost 1.4 pounds weekly. The percentage of hospital patients losing 20 or more pounds was half that of Weight Watchers members. These findings led the authors to conclude that:

> . . . the weight loss achieved by admission to hospital is usually regained: this form of treatment is expensive and rarely justified. The results indicate that the major therapeutic effect of the hospital clinic lies in its supportive role. . . . Accepting this, it is . . . highly questionable whether professional resources should be used at all, for the routine treatment of obesity (p. 802).

The same conclusion has been reached by others (e.g., Mann, 1974; Slayen, 1974) and leads to serious questions about whether hospitals in particular, and professional settings in general, are appropriate sites for the treatment of weight management problems.

WHERE PROFESSIONAL SERVICES STOP AND SELF-HELP BEGINS

Weight management probably found its way into medical settings indirectly. First, physicians have been called upon to treat the many health problems associated with obesity (Stuart & Davis, 1972; Stuart, in press). It is only natural for them to seek to treat obesity as well. Second, excess weight is very clearly a corporal phenomenon and the body is clearly the domain of the medical establishment. Third, the fact that the obese were social deviants to some degree may have impelled them to define their problems as originating in the flesh—over which they had no control—rather than in their behavior—which they were expected to control. This would lead them to delegate responsibility for management of their weight to medical professionals.

Four important developments have raised serious questions about the suitability of professional settings for the treatment of problems of weight control. First, of course, is the fact that professional settings have not yielded satisfactory results. Second, it has been shown that prejudices against the overweight are strong in these settings (e.g., Dwyer, Feldman & Mayer, 1970). Third, the situational, as opposed to the intrapersonal factors, linked to obesity have been shown clearly in studies of the ethnic and socioeconomic correlates of obesity (Stunkard, 1975). Finally, recent research has shown that eating is highly responsive to situational changes and that these are the necessary, if not sufficient, conditions for the development of new eating management patterns (Stuart, 1972a). These discoveries have contributed to the development of a technology for the management of overeating that has met with unprecedented results (Stuart, 1975), a technology that is sufficiently straightforward to be applicable in settings not overseen by professionals.

A similar argument can be presented for other kinds of problems, such as problem drinking, drug use, marital interaction and child abuse, to name but a few. In each of these instances, situational factors contribute significantly to the etiology of the problem and problem mastery requires important life-style change by the troubled person. To be sure, each of these behavioral problems can have biological effects that must be the targets of medical care. Some can also have psychological effects that should be the targets of professional services appropriate to these needs. But the primary treatment can and should be the responsibility of self-help groups because these groups have recently demonstrated the skill and resources to produce good results. Indeed, the time has come to consider the self-help approach to be the treatment of choice for programs aimed at helping people to make lasting changes in their patterns of living.

THE INGREDIENTS OF THE SELF-HELP FORMULA

Whether they are *ad hoc* get-togethers or units of a national organization, self-help groups tend to have ten characteristics in common and each of these differentiates them from professional programs.

1) Self-help groups tend to *define their targets of concern as inappropriate behavior,* while many professionals tend to define the same problems as matters of intrapersonal illness (Hurvitz, 1970; Stuart, 1971). This leads self-help groups to have a practical focus in their search for "how" the problem can be overcome in contrast to a more speculative concern with "why" the problem started in the first place. This is important because it has been shown that the more practical the group focus, the more effective the group is in meeting its objectives (Weitz et al., 1975), because most of the time group discussion can be task-oriented and because potentially deteriorating regression can be avoided (e.g., Hartley, Roback and Abramowitz, 1976).

2) Self-help groups also develop a kind of *faith building* morality, despite their practical concerns. Allon (1975) and Bruch (1973) both describe a "revival meeting" flavor in some self-help groups where, for example, a procession of dieters offers their bodies to "totem scales" and then sit in meetings where they "atone for their sins." While perhaps more of a caricature than a reality, meetings do provide opportunities for a certain amount of catharsis and breast beating. This legitimates a level of animation in group meetings which brings a level of humor, pathos and general expressiveness that is rarely, if ever, found in groups that are under the leadership of professionals.

3) As a background for the third advantage of self-help groups, it is important to remember that members tend to join most groups for a combination of short- and long-term objectives (Simmel, 1949). Their short-term objective may be an opportunity to blow off steam, to make friends or perhaps just to have a brief respite from a life of relative social isolation. Their long-term objective could be the opportunity to develop skills that can make problem mastery a reality. Unlike many professional services, self-help groups are often *sufficiently informal to permit the attainment of social objectives at the same time that they are sufficiently task-oriented to permit attainment of the longer range goals.* Interestingly, the two facets of the group interaction feed into each other nicely because it has been noted that groups that do have specific objectives often have greater group cohesion as well (Liberman, 1970, 1971). Because of the greater sense of cohesion, group members are also more likely to express themselves in self-help settings (Johnson, 1975; Johnson & Ridener, 1974) and through this expressiveness they are more likely to offer and to receive constructive feedback about their

own problem solving efforts (Kolb, Winter & Berlew, 1968). All of these factors can contribute significantly to the success of the group.

4) A fourth asset of the self-help group is the fact that its *leader almost always serves as an important role model for all members*. Whereas professional services tend to be rendered by clinicians who strive to maintain a mask of neutrality, self-help groups are under the direction of leaders who rely heavily upon the "power of radical sincerity" (Bumbalo & Young, 1973). While professionals work to conceal all but the most superficial details about their past and present lives, lay group leaders openly discuss many of their relevant life experiences. Whereas professionals are often chosen for leadership roles precisely because they have *not* faced the same life adjustment conflicts as their clients, lay leaders are selected precisely because they *have* faced and mastered these conflicts. Whereas professionals are chosen because of their formal training credentials, lay group leaders are chosen because of their life experience and their self-expressive and persuasive abilities, factors that may be both more relevant and more valid than typical vita entries. Starting at the top—e.g., with A.A.'s "Bill W." and Weight Watchers' Jean Nidetch —and working down to each group leader, members of self-help groups are in constant contact with living and breathing models of the fact that triumph over problem behavior is possible not only in the abstract but for people very much like themselves.

5) Another advantage of self-help groups is the fact that their *members can join and resign from the groups with relative ease*. Applicants for professional services must often complete lengthy applications, undergo one or more interviews and accept a diagnostic label with all of its secondary deviance implications (Lemert, 1967). In contrast, applicants for self-help services are readily accepted if they meet the simple criteria of suffering from the same problem as that faced by other members of the group, and wishing to develop new behaviors. No entries will be made on their records anywhere; they can and often do use pseudonyms. No one will ask them to defend their motivation to change, since members take this motivation as a matter of course. And no strings are tied to joining the group, as evidenced by the fact that missing a meeting is all that one need do to terminate his or her membership.

As a result of the uncomplicated admission process, self-help groups tend to have heterogeneous membership cutting across class, ethnic and racial lines in ways not often paralleled by professional services. Furthermore, because exit from the group is equally uncomplicated, unhappy members do drop out leaving only those who are comparatively well served among the active. This helps to maintain a spirit of optimism in the meetings at all times.

6) The sixth asset of the self-help groups is their success in *helping members to "accept" their problem by viewing it as a "normal" reaction.* This comes about because both the leader and the members acknowledge their own battles with the same urges. Normalization (Warren, 1974) helps members to view their behavior as a logical consequence of their past experiences when viewed in the light of their present environments. This enables them to minimize guilt about past wrong-doing and to take a cooler and more analytic approach to planning present solutions to their problem. It also helps them to feel more confident in the value of planned actions because they can see others who closely resemble them meeting with success in problem mastery.

7) To help in the normalization process and to facilitate personal planning, self-help groups also *develop their own* argot (Allon, 1975; Laslett & Warren, 1975). The existence of labels that are shared not only among members locally but among members of a worldwide organization helps to name the temptation and give it the aura of a universal threat. Words like "legal" and "anniversary" also have the effect of dichotomizing and thereby simplifying choices so that constructive decisions can be reliably reached by anyone willing to use the value-directing language of the group.

8) Attribution theory (Jones & Davis, 1965; Kelley, 1967) offers an explanation of the eighth advantage of the self-help approach. Attribution theory suggests that people will be more likely to seek help with a problem if they attribute their past failures to environmental pressures rather than to personal deficits (Tessler & Schwartz, 1972). The practical orientation of the self-help group does stress external pressures and this contrasts sharply with the intrapersonal explanations offered by many professionalized services (Stuart, 1971). Attribution theory also suggests that those who believe that positive behavioral changes are due to changes in their skills in self-mastery are more likely to be able to sustain these changes over time than are those who attribute their new behaviors to forces that they do not directly control (Davison & Valins, 1969; Cialdini & Mirels, 1976). This may explain the fact that biofeedback and

simple relaxation techniques were found in one study to be more effective than medication in overcoming tension headaches (Cox, Freundlich & Meyer, 1975) as well as the finding that some studies of the effectiveness of self-help manuals show that they can, under some conditions, yield results that surpass group mediated effects over time (e.g., Hanson, Borden & Hall, 1976).

Self-help groups capitalize on this attribution advantage by demystifying treatment. Demystification comes about through their effort to fully explain to members the logic of their methods, through their putting methods in the hands of lay leaders who were former participants, and by giving members a significant role to play in selecting and planning the details of their own treatment. This latter feature also helps to adapt both the goals and methods of service to the members' personal objectives, something which has been shown to have a very positive effect upon treatment outcome (Willer & Miller, 1976).

Because treatment via the self-help route is almost always self-selected and peer-directed, and because its methods are overt and fully explained, successful members are quite likely to take personal credit and pride in their gains. Conversely, the professionally treated client is very likely to attribute to the therapist the power to produce change, if for no other reason than simply to resolve any conflict about having had to reach out and to pay dearly for the service received. Therefore, while professionalized services are more likely to attempt to change the "inner person" through their probative techniques, self-help groups are more likely to accomplish this important task precisely because their techniques are more practical in focus.

9) A ninth advantage of self-help groups is their *utilization of the principles of social marketing* to bring their service to the attention of the public in a manner most likely to trigger positive action (Kotler & Zaltman, 1971).

Marketing success depends upon the operation of several interrelated factors (Wiebe, 1951-52). Before the program exists, potential members must be motivated to act. This motivation depends upon a complex of factors, perhaps the strongest of which are the immediate, perceived consequences of action and nonaction and the implications that each has for the health and happiness of the individual. For example, smoking offers some immediate satisfaction through the impact of the chemical properties of the smoke and the physical experience of lighting and maintaining the cigarette, cigar or pipe. Dryness of throat and shortness of breath are for many smokers very mild prices to pay for the satisfaction of smoking; further, the potential health hazards of smoking are delayed and unpredictable. In contrast, overeating offers the immediate satisfaction associated with the ingestion of food, but its cosmetic effect for chronic overeaters are immediate and real although the health hazards are often delayed as with smoking. In addition, while smoking is still considered to be a symbol of maturity by many, fatness is the badge of dishonor to most. Unlike smoking control programs that must predicate their appeal upon health motives, weight control programs can stress the virtues of looking and feeling good in their efforts to attract members.

The importance of better appearance in the decision to seek weight loss is evidenced by the fact that a survey of the members of Diet Workshop, a commercial weight control organization, found that 90% selected cosmetic concerns as opposed to 56% who selected improved health as important factors in their decision to lose weight (Berman, 1975). A similar study in Weight Watchers, also a commercial group, found that women were three times as likely to choose improved appearance as contrasted with improved health as the *primary* reason for their wishing to lose weight, although men were slightly more likely to attribute their motivation to health rather than cosmetics (Stuart & Jacobson, in press). Commercial groups are much more likely than professional organizations to address their appeals to this "real world" motivation of their prospective clients and for this reason they are likely to be more successful in attracting potential weight losers.

Taking a health action also requires the availability of a mechanism or agency through which the action can become a reality. Professionalized services tend to be offered in institutional settings that are often relegated to only certain parts of the community. Self-help programs, on the other hand, are less cumbersome and can be placed in many available locations in host settings throughout the community. While interested citizens wishing to sponsor a professional service must work through an exhausting decision-making hierarchy, those wishing to underwrite a self-help service can act swiftly and more simply. As a result, self-help services tend to become available when and where needed while professional services lack this flexibility.

For a service to be utilized, prospective clients must also know when and where it is offered and what to expect as potential costs and benefits. Self-help organizations often publicize their programs on a scale that is unknown in professionalized services. As a result, most members of the community are more aware of the existence of self-help, as opposed to professional services. In addition, because the self-help programs tend to attract larger populations than their professional counterparts, more members of the community are available to spread the word through what Friedson (1961) has termed a "lay referral system." This distribution of many people through the community who are informed about the existence and potential benefits of the self-help service can go far toward helping others to move from passive predisposition to action (Richards, 1975).

10) Self-help groups are able to make use of the technology of social marketing because they have the resources to do so, since most self-help organizations either charge fees or request voluntary contributions. While some may consider fee-charging a deterrent to service utilization (e.g., Williams & Duncan, 1976a), it is quite possible that the *fees charged by self-help groups may help to improve the effectiveness of their services* in ways other than providing adequate funds for promotion, service development and service delivery. Torrey (1972) noted that client expectancy is an important predictor of successful treatment and clients in our culture generally place a higher value on things that they pay for than on things that are available without charge. Therefore, the charging of fees that are collected on a weekly basis by many self-help groups, fees that are paid directly by the client and not by a third party, may help to build the expectation of positive results.

As a crude test of this hypothesis, two clinicians contrasted the results of offering their services to nonrandomly selected clients who were and were not charged fees for weight control services. Stanton (1976) offered four sessions of hypnotherapy for problem eating to 20 clients, half of whom were charged no fee. The fee-paying clients lost an average of 19.9 pounds (range 14-30 pounds) in contrast to the non-paying clients who lost an average of 11.1 pounds (range 1-20). Lindner (1976) offered a drug treatment for overweight patients backed up by behavior modification training lasting 10 weeks to 30 individuals: Ten patients were seen without fee (doctors's wives, physicians, teenager whose parents paid, and one "charity case"), 10 paid partial fees (paramedics), and 10 paid full fees. The groups had average starting weights of between 195 and 200 pounds. The non-fee patients lost an average of 9.9 pounds, the partial fee patients averaged a loss of 20.4 pounds. Therefore, it appears as though fee-charging can have a positive therapeutic effect and that it need not deter potential clients from making use of an available service.

Fee charging can have another obvious advantage—providing funds for the development of quality service. Professional fees tend to be much higher than the charges for self-help programs, which are often $4.00 per session or less. But a very large proportion of the professional service dollar is spent on maintaining expensive buildings, large full-time staffs and costly equipment, leaving little for the funding of direct services. In contrast, self-help groups do not have this expensive overhead. They use space that is rented by the hour, often have part-time staffs, and have little, if any, equipment. Those that are national in scope may save further by consolidating services such as accounting, advertising and the keeping of necessary records. Therefore, even though some of their intake may be diverted into profits, a much higher percentage of the self-help dollar is spent on direct service than is true for the professional service dollar. This cost efficiency helps self-help groups to deliver remarkably sophisticated service at comparatively minor cost.

While the self-help formula is not a mystery, professionals seem curiously unable to mix these ten elements into a successful operation. For example, in 1957 the Bureau of Nutrition of the City of New York did attempt to run a weight control program under the direction of lay leaders. However, the program was promptly aborted "after an unsuccessful trial period" (Christakis, 1967, p. 501). However, a few years later Mrs. Jean Nidetch used the Bureau of Nutrition diet and many of its procedures to start Weight Watchers, perhaps the most successful of all nonmedical health care delivery systems.

For whatever reason—perhaps their inflexibility, their insistence upon stereotyped professional behavior or their inability or unwillingness to promote their programs effectively—it would seem that professional agencies are not able to use the self-help formula nearly as effectively as it has been used by lay people. Yet the need exists to deliver professionally discovered technologies to large numbers of people. One way to do this is to put the professionally developed tools of behavioral management into the hands of self-help groups that can bring them effectively to large segments of the population. Two attempts which have been made to achieve this goal in services to the overweight, with somewhat different results, will be discussed in the next section.

ADDING PROFESSIONAL TECHNOLOGIES TO SELF-HELP OFFERINGS

It is natural to think about a marriage between professionally developed strategies of self-management and self-help organizations' capacity for bringing these techniques to those who need them. Dr. Albert Stunkard and his colleagues at the University of Pennsylvania recognized this opportunity in the early 1970s and undertook a trial marriage between a non-profit weight control organization, Take Off Pounds Sensibly (TOPS), and the techniques of behavioral self-management.

The TOPS Experiment

TOPS is the oldest and, apparently, the second largest of the weight management groups. It was founded in Milwaukee, Wisconsin, in 1948 by Mrs. Esther S. Manz, who was herself struggling in a personal battle for weight control. According to its own "Information Sheet" (TOPS, 1974), the organization has "five facets." First, it has a medical orientation requiring that all members consult their personal physicians for goal weights and diet prescriptions. Second, it offers "group therapy" through which members are asked to maintain contact with each other not only during the meetings but through the intervening days as well. Third, it stresses "keen competition in weight loss" with announcements of the names of the most successful losers on an international basis each year. Fourth, it stresses recognition of members' successes in other ways as well—through jewelry awards, membership in a subgroup called Keep Off Pounds Sensibly, and attendance at an annual convention, among other ways. Finally, it is also committed to sponsoring an obesity research program.

TOPS boasted 300,000 members in 1969 (Jordan & Levitz, 1973) and 350,000 in 1972 (Stunkard, 1972), with members drawn from the United States, Canada and 29 other countries.

In 1975, members paid dues of $7.00 annually for the first two years and $5.00 per year thereafter. Groups elect their own leaders who oversee their operations. Members are privately weighed in at each meeting and their weekly weight changes are announced to the group. Losers are recognized with applause, occasional cash prizes and the opportunity to become "Queen" for the week by achieving the greatest loss. Gainers are reprimanded, occasionally fined, or asked to perform embarrassing activities. In addition, they are sometimes labeled "Pig" of the week for recording to a large weight gain. The names of members who register gains for two consecutive weeks are placed on an "emergency list" and they are telephoned by other group members several times each day in order to prompt and to reinforce constructive eating.

Members record the caloric value of the foods eaten through the week. Their experience in attempting to curb their eating through self-discipline occupies much of the remaining time of the meeting. The general format of these sessions is one of loosely organized "cathartic group therapy," although outside lecturers are occasionally invited into the group to speak about weight related nutritional and medical concerns.

According to Stunkard (1972), members of TOPS are women whose average age is 42, whose average initial weight is 188 pounds, or 58% above their average desirable weight of 119 pounds. With wide variability both among and within chapters, the average TOPS member remained active in the organization for 16.5 months during which time she lost an average of 15 pounds or an average of slightly less than one quarter of a pound per week. These results were remarkably constant when sampled in both 1968 and 1970 by Garb and Stunkard (1974), who also found that 53% of the members remained active for one full year while 30% were active for at least two years. By 1974 (TOPS, 1974), the organization boasted that its members lost a total of 1,137 tons of excess weight in one year alone. Unfortunately, data are not available on the extent to which these losses were maintained.

Jordan and Levitz (1973) experimented with the impact of adding behavior modification techniques to the TOPS program. When contacted by the leader of a group of 12 members, they provided him with some books and manuals and met with him eight times in an effort to train him in the techniques. They found that members lost an average of one quarter pound per week through a three-week baseline period and that the addition of behavior modification techniques increased the rate of loss to eight-tenths of a pound weekly. Levitz and Stunkard (1974) then extended this program to a sample of 234 TOPS members. Some of these members received behavior modification instruction through professional leaders (psychiatric residents or graduate students of clinical psychology) who replaced their lay leaders. Others received the techniques through their own leaders, who had participated in 12 training sessions conducted by the investigators. An additional subset of members received more intensive nutritional education than was normally offered during their meetings, and a final group of members underwent the standard TOPS program.

Following 12 weeks of treatment, the members of the professionally led group lost an average of .35 pounds per week, and those in groups led by lay leaders who had received behavior modification training lost an average of .16 pounds weekly, while the members of groups with nutrition education or normal TOPS activities registered either negligible losses or small gains for weekly averages. These differences were statistically significant. Followed over 12 months, the results of the professionally led groups were still superior to the other treatments, averaging losses of slightly over one-tenth pound per week. Unfortunately, however, when contrasted with the average weight losses for TOPS members that were reported earlier (.25 pounds per week over 16.5 months), the results of this experiment are at best a partial vote of confidence in the value of behavior modification techniques.

The best results obtained by Levitz and Stunkard were those for the professionally led groups, and even these did not equal the national norms that these same investigators reported earlier for the TOPS organization. It is quite possible that these, less than exciting, results were a consequence of the novelty of the procedures. When they were introduced, TOPS already had a 14-year history with members and leaders alike fully committed to the five tenets of the organization's program. It is possible that more time would be needed to resocialize members to accept a new technology, no matter how powerful that technology might be.

It is also possible that the positive focus of the behavioral management techniques may have been in conflict with the competitive, and often negative, focus of the TOPS meetings. Dissonance created by this clash could have vitiated the power of the new technology. It is quite posible that the professionals were better able to control the negativism in their group meetings and that, coupled with the courtesy extended to them by members, could explain their improved results. These are, however, only speculations until we examine another opportunity for a similar trial under different conditions.

The Weight Watchers Experiment

The opportunity to explore these speculations arose promptly in the context of the classes sponsored by the Weight Watchers organization. Weight Watchers was established in 1963. It also supports a nonprofit research foundation. It is clearly the largest of the weight control organizations. In 1976, its services were used by 1,655,000 new and rejoining members. Over 400,000 members attended more than 13,000 classes in all 50 states and 25 foreign countries each week.

Anyone over the age of 10 who has 10 pounds or more to lose is eligible to join a Weight Watchers class. Upon joining, members generally pay a registration fee of from *$3 to $5* and then a weekly class fee of around *$3*. Members who reach their goal weight are eligible to attend monthly classes without charge for life so long as they remain within two pounds of their goal weight and do not miss a monthly meeting.

Members are offered one of three nutritionally balanced food plans that were developed under medical supervision. Separate basic plans are available for women, men and youth who eat approximately 1300, 1600 and 1650 calories per day (Abrams, 1976). Those members whose weight remains at a plateau while following the basic plan are temporarily offered a different program intended to help them to resume regular weight loss. Finally, those who do reach their goal weights are offered a weight maintenance plan which allows them to reintroduce into their diet most of the foods that are in common use.

Upon registration, members are weighed privately and assigned a temporary goal weight range based upon actuarial tables of desirable weights. They then take their seats in a classroom to await the start of the meeting. Like the clerk who handled their registration and the weigher who recorded their goal, the lecturer is a person who lost weight through attending Weight Watchers classes.

The class generally begins with the lecturer's self-introduction, including mention of the number of pounds that the lecturer lost and the length of time that this loss has been maintained. The lecturer then presents awards earned by members who have attended class for 16 weeks, reached their goal weight or maintained their goal weight for eight weeks while following a maintenance plan. Both the lecturer's self-introduction and the presentation of awards help to establish positive models for any newly joining members and others who are working to shed their excess weight.

The lecturer then introduces the theme of the class presentation. In the past this theme tended to consist of motivational exhortation and anecdotes with a considerable discussion of the prospect of life as a "civilian" (person of normal weight), of ways of coping with new recipes for "legal" (allowable) foods, and of means of responding to "cheating" or eating foods which are not included in the organization's food plan.

Against this background it was possible to introduce behavior modification technology in the form of the Personal Action Plan. This is a series of "modules" or printed instruction sheets, each of which contains the rationale for several specific steps aimed at self-management, as well as charts for members' recording their own progress in taking these steps. The modules are based upon techniques that have been developed in experimental settings (Stuart & Davis, 1972) and tested thoroughly in many different programs (Stuart, 1975). The 18 modules contain recommendations for steps in coping with mood-triggered eating, for differentiating between hunger and appetite, for arranging environments that potentiate constructive eating and for reprogramming social interactions related to eating, among other topics.

The module program was carefully pretested to determine the optimal length and level of complexity for each module. The relevance and effectiveness of each recommended technique were also evaluated in the light of the experiences of several hundred members who used the program during its early days. When the modules were adequately refined, a full range of training materials was prepared so that lecturers could present this material to their classes with enthusiasm and accuracy. The materials included a detailed explanation of the logic of each module through modeling, audio and videotapes of successful module presentations, and cue cards for lecturers' use in conducting their classes. These materials were and continue to be discussed at regular staff meetings and supervisory sessions in an effort to build lecturers' skills in their use.

During discussion of each module, the lecturer attempts to stimulate the maximum possible interaction among members. This interaction helps the members to explore and to resolve their questions and concerns about the content of the module. Their active involvement in module discussion also helps to build their commitmnt to the recommended steps and to give them opportunities for self-expression in groups, experiences that many members have never had before.

After several months of pilot testing, several counties in one state were selected as a test site because their populations were adequate to generate samples of 2,000 or more members and because the three counties had comparably varied populations.

A quasi-experimental model was used for the evaluation. One area was selected randomly to continue the traditional Weight Watchers pro-

TABLE 1

Characteristics of Members in Each
Intervention Condition

Characteristic	Non-Module (2856)	Condition First Module Cycle (2219)	Second Module Cycle (2548)
Average Age	37.5	36.9	36.5
Percent Female	92.9	93.9	91.7
Percent Married	62.1	72.0	73.5
Percent Employed Out of Homes	56.8	53.7	54.5
Initial Weight	176.4	176.9	178.0
Goal Weight	132.5	132.0	132.9
Percent Overweight	33.1	34.0	33.9

gram during the same 12 weeks that another area was selected for the introduction of the module program. Six months later, the module test was repeated in the original experimental area as a means of assessing the impact of the program when lecturers and members alike were more familiar with it.

The characteristics of the members in the three phases of the test are presented in Table 1. The three groups are similar in all respects except marital status, the traditional or non-module classes having fewer married members. The age and initial weight levels of all three groups were, however, comparable with those of the Weight Watchers population in general (Stuart & Jacobson, in press) and with the members of comparable weight control organizations (e.g., Stunkard, 1972; Berman, 1975).

Because the difference in marital status did distinguish the three groups, it was necessary to study the results for each demographically defined subset of members separately. Table 2 reports the results of this analysis of covariance in which ponderal index was the covariant. There it will be seen that men had greater average weekly weight losses than women, that members under 21 and over 51 were slightly less successful than those in the middle age groups, that those who were divorced, separated or widowed lost slightly less weight than those who were married or single, and that those who were employed out of their homes scored better results than those who were not. Each of these differences was statistically significant except for marital status, the one demographic characteristic that differentiated the groups. Accordingly, it was decided that the groups could be considered to be comparable with respect to their potential for weight loss success.

Because it stands to reason that those attending classes for longer periods of time might gain more from the behavioral technology than those whose attendance is shorter, the results are presented for the entire group and for these two groups separately. Members of the non-module classes lost an average of 1.19 pounds per week during the 12 test weeks while those in both the first and second cycles of module presentations lost an average of 1.34 pounds per week. These differences were statistically significant (F-5.94, $df = 7662$, $p < .01$). When those who attended one to seven classes were studied, it was found that those in traditional classes lost an average of 1.16 pounds per week in contrast to average weekly losses of 1.30 in both the first and second module cycles. Again, these differences were statistically significant (F-7.81, $df = 6144$, $p < .001$). Finally, when the results of members staying for eight to 12 classes were studied, it was found that the traditional class members lost a weekly average of 1.30 pounds, while those in the first cycle of the module lost 1.55 pounds and those in the second cycle lost 1.60 pounds. These differences, too, were statistically significant (F-21.93, df-1518, $p = .001$).

As a further test of the power of the techniques it was possible to identify classes in the test cycle whose members were more or less active in complying with at least one aspect of the behavioral self-management program—recording the rates of their own behavior. Four hundred forty-five members attended the better performing classes in which at least one-fourth of all members completed self-monitoring charts as requested. In contrast, 401 members attended classes in which relatively few members complied with the request. This difference could have been due to the level of lecturers' enthusiasm for the new program at the time of its introduction or it may have been attributable to differences in the attitudes of members in each class. Whatever the explanation, members in the more-likely-to-self-monitor group lost a weekly average of 1.5 pounds while those less-likely-to-self-monitor lost 1.3 pounds weekly. Moreover, in classes where self-recording was strong, weight gains from week to week were less than half as frequent as in the other classes.

TABLE 2

Covariance Analysis of Average Weekly Weight Losses
for Various Demographically Defined
Groups of Members

	N	Average No. Lbs. Lost/Wk	F	Scheffe
Sex				
(a) Male	555	—1.87	21.46	A > B
(b) Female	6499	—1.24	p < .001	
Age				
(a) 21 and younger	744	—1.23		
(b) 22-30	1908	—1.37		B > A, D
(c) 31-40	1649	—1.32	13.41	C > A, D
(d) 41-50	1313	—1.29	p < .001	D > E
(e) 51-65	1029	—1.18		
Marital Status				
(a) Married	3897	—1.30		
(b) Single	1178	—1.31	N.S.	
(c) Divorced, Sep., and/or Widowed	397	—1.19		
Employment				
(a) *Not* out of home	2209	—1.20	6.07	B > A
(b) Out of home	3458	—1.39	p < .01	

Virtually equal percentages of members in the Personal Action Plan
and the traditional groups attended one to seven and eight to 12 classes.
Unfortunately, the 12-week limit on the testing did not permit monitoring either the long-term effect of the behavior modification program upon
members' attendance or the success with which weight losses were maintained. Future evaluations can and must include attendance and maintenance as ultimate criteria of any weight management program.

At least on the basis of short-term data, it is clear that behavior modification techniques can be successfully introduced into a self-help organization and that these techniques can greatly improve the results of lay
groups that already outstripped the effectiveness of their professional counterparts. In this connection, Mann (1974, p. 231) noted that: "it now
appears that the group therapies and the behavior modifications are the

most effective and the most promising means of dealing with obesity." Stunkard (1975, p. 233) then went one step further with this observation that: "private industry may be the most effective vehicle for [the introduction of these] techniques for the widespread control of obesity."

CONCLUSION

The rapid increase in the range and number of self-help efforts is a signal. It reflects a growing disenchantment with the cost and quality of some professional services. It reflects, too, a realization by the public that some problems are more effectively treated through self-directed efforts. By dint of tradition, professionals have claimed for themselves mastery of the most effective techniques for the control of human behavior. Now that claim is being challenged in some areas and it is time for the professionals to self-evaluate in order to determine: 1) in which areas they do have legitimate claim of being able to conceive and offer the most effective services; 2) in which areas their behavior change or maintaining technologies are superior, but means of delivering these services are inferior to those of lay groups; and 3) perhaps most difficult of all, in which areas the professions have neither an effective technology nor an efficient service delivery system that matches the success of the self-help groups.

There are some high technology treatments—those involving surgery and drugs for example—that require professional development and professional delivery. There are other areas of human concern in which professionally developed technologies are better delivered to the general public by laymen as opposed to professionals. The obesity services described here are one example; health maintenance services for women as described in Chapter 11 are another outstanding example. Finally, there are areas in which the technologies developed and delivered by laymen offer many advantages over those rendered by professionals. Activities such as those of the Vancouver Mental Patients Association that are described in the next chapter of this book and of Alcoholics Anonymous are extraordinary examples of the powerful services that can be offered by lay people who recognize a need and use their own experience as a guide for developing means to meet that need. Rather than attempting to co-opt these programs that are partly or fully independent of the professions, a wiser course would be for the professions to concentrate on developing intervention methods in areas in which high technology is essential, borrowing as much as they can from the self-help programs as a means of humanizing the delivery of these services.

This book is far from closed on the effectiveness of self-help groups. Few have been studied experimentally. When research has been conducted, it has frequently fallen short of the standards of rigorous design and execution. Bebbington (1976), for example, recognizes that the published reports about Alcoholics Anonymous are very positive but also notes that the data in support of these claims are often "elusive." Moreover, the ability of members of self-help groups to maintain their changed behavior over time is still in doubt. Nevertheless, such evidence as has been collected to date does clearly indicate that self-help groups have delivered exceptionally effective services in the past and there is no reason to think that they will not continue to do so.

REFERENCES

ABRAMS, B.: Weight Watchers: A total approach to weight control. *Canadian Home Economics Journal*, 1976, 26, 4-10.

ALLON, N.: Fat is a dirty word: Fat as a sociological and social problem. In A. Howard (Ed.), *Recent Advances in Obesity Research: I.* London: Newman Publishing Co., 1975. (a)

ALLON, N.: Latent social services in group dieting. *Social Problems*, 1975, 23, 59-69. (b)

AMERICAN PSYCHOLOGICAL ASSOCIATION: *Standards for Educational and Psychological Tests and Manuals.* Washington, D. C.: American Psychological Association, 1966.

AZRIN, N. H. and FOXX, R. M.: *Toilet Training.* New York: Doubleday, 1974.

BAKER, B. L., HEIFETZ, L. J., and BRIGHTMAN, A. J.: *Parents as Teachers: Manuals for Behavior Modification of the Retarded Child.* Cambridge, Massachusetts: Behavioral Education Project, 1972.

BEBBINGTON, P. E.: The efficacy of Alcoholics Anonymous: The elusiveness of hard data. *British Journal of Psychiatry*, 1976, 128, 572-580.

BELLACK, A. S., SCHWARTZ, J., and ROZENSKY, R. H.: The contribution of external control of self-control in a weight reduction program. *Journal of Behavior Therapy and Experimental Psychiatry*, 1974, 5, 245-249.

BERGIN, A. E. and GARFIELD, S. L. (Eds.): *Handbook of Psychotherapy and Behavior Change: An Empirical Analysis.* New York: John Wiley, 1971.

BERMAN, E. M.: Factors influencing motivations in dieting. *Journal of Nutrition Education*, 1975, 7, 155-159.

BLUM, E. M. and BLUM, R. H.: *Alcoholism, Modern Psychological Approaches to Treatment.* San Francisco: Jossey-Bass, 1967.

BROWNELL, K. D., HECKERMAN, C. L., and WESTLAKE, R. J.: Therapist and group contact as variables in the behavioral treatment of obesity. Paper presented at the annual meeting of the Association for the Advancement of Behavior Therapy, New York, December, 1976.

BRUCH, H.: *Eating Disorders: Obesity, Anorexia Nervosa, and the Person Within.* New York: Basic Books, 1973.

BUMBALO, J. A. and YOUNG, D. E.: The self-help phenomenon. *American Journal of Nursing*, 1973, 73, 1588-1592.

CHRISTAKIS, G.: Community programs for weight reduction: Experience of the Bureau of Nutrition, New York City. *Canadian Journal of Public Health*, 1967, 58, 499-504.

CIALDINI, R. B. and MIRELS, H. L.: Sense of personal control and attributions about yielding and resisting persuasion targets. *Journal of Personality and Social Psychology*, 1976, 33, 395-402.

COX, D. J., FREUNDLICH, A., and MEYER, R. G.: Differential effectiveness of lectromyographic feedback, verbal relaxation instructions and medication placebo with tension headaches. *Journal of Consulting and Clinical Psychology*, 1975, 43, 892-899.

DAVISON, G. C. & VALINS, S.: Maintenance of self-attributed behavior change. *Journal of Personality and Social Psychology*, 1969, 11, 25-33.

DENHOLTZ, M. S. and MANN, E. T.: An automated audiovisual treatment of phobias administered by non-professionals. *Journal of Behavior Therapy and Experimental Psychiatry*, 1975, 6, 111-115.

DWYER, J. T., FELDMAN, J. J., and MAYER, J.: The social psychology of dieting. *Journal of Health and Social Behavior*, 1970, 11, 273-294.

FENSTERHEIM, H. and BAER, J.: *Don't Say Yes When You Want To Say No*. New York: Rawson, 1975.

FRIEDSON, E.: *Patients Views of Medical Practice*. New York: Russel Sage, 1961.

GARB, J. R. and STUNKARD, A. J.: Effectiveness of a self-help group of obesity control: A further assessment. *Archives of Internal Medicine*, 1974, 134, 716-720.

GERARD, D. L., SAENGER, G., and WILE, R.: The abstinent alcoholic. *Archives of General Psychiatry*, 1962, 6, 83-95.

GLASGOW, R. E. and ROSEN, G. M.: Behavioral bibliography: A review of self-help behavior therapy manuals. *Psychological Bulletin*, in press.

HAGEN, R. L.: Group therapy vs. bibliotherapy in weight reduction. *Behavior Therapy*, 1974, 5, 222-234.

HANSON, R. W., et al.: Use of programmed instruction in teaching self-management skills to overweight adults. *Behavior Therapy*, 1976, 7, 366-373.

HARTLEY, D., ROBACK, H. B., and ABRAMOWITZ, S. I.: Deterioration effects in encounter groups. *American Psychologist*, 1976, 31, 247-255.

HURVITZ, N.: Peer self-help psychotherapy groups and their implications for psychotherapy. *Psychotherapy: Theory, Research and Practice*, 1970, 7, 41-49.

JEFFREY, D. B.: Treatment evaluation issues in research on addictive behaviors. *Addictive Behavior*, 1975, 1, 23-36.

JOHNSON, W. G.: Group therapy: A behavioral perspective. *Behavior Therapy*, 1975, 6, 30-38.

JOHNSON, D. L. and RIDENER, L. R.: Self-disclosure, participation, and perceived cohesiveness in small group interaction. *Psychological Reports*, 1974, 35, 361-362.

JONES, E. E. and DAVIS, K. E.: From acts to dispositions: The attribution process in person perception. In L. Berkowitz (Ed.), *Advances in Experimental Social Psychology, Vol. 2*. New York: Academic Press, 1965.

JORDAN, H. A. and LEVITZ, L. S.: Behavior modification in a self-help group. *Journal of the American Dietetic Association*, 1973, 62, 27-29.

KELLEY, H. H.: Attribution theory in social psychology. *Nebraska Symposium on Motivation*, 1967, 15, 192-241.

KOLB, D. A., WINTER, S. K., and BERLEW, D. E.: Self-directed change: Two studies. *Journal of Applied Behavioral Science*, 1968, 4, 453-470.

KOTLER, P. and ZALTMAN, G.: Social marketing: An approach to planned social change. *Journal of Marketing*, 1971, 35, 3-12.

LANG, P. J., MELAMED, B. G., and HART, J.: A psychophysiological analysis of fear modification using an automated desensitization procedure. *Journal of Abnormal Psychology*, 1970, 76, 220-234.

LASLETT, B. and WARREN, C. A. B.: Losing weight: The organizational promotion of behavior change. *Social Problems*, 1975, 23, 70-80.

LEACH, B.: Does Alcoholics Anonymous really work? In P. G. Bourne and R. Foxx (Eds.), *Alcoholism: Progress in Research and Treatment*. New York: Academic Press, 1973.

LEMERT, E.: *Human Deviance, Social Problems and Social Control*. Englewood Cliffs, N. J.: Prentice Hall, 1967.

LEVITZ, L. S. and STUNKARD, A. J.: A therapeutic coalition for obesity: Behavior modification and patient self-help. *American Journal of Psychiatry*, 1974, 131, 423-427.

LIBERMAN, R. A.: Behavioral approach to group dynamics: Reinforcement and prompting of cohesiveness in group therapy. *Behavior Therapy*, 1970, 1, 141-175.

LIBERMAN, R. P.: Behavioral group therapy: A controlled clinical study. *British Journal of Psychiatry*, 1971, 119, 534-544.

LINDNER, P. G.: The professional fee—A therapeutic modality in Bariatrics? *Obesity and Bariatric Medicine*, 1976, 5, 166-167.

LUNDWALL, L. and BAEKLAND, F.: Disulfram treatment of alcoholism: A review. *Journal of Nervous and Mental Disease*, 1971, 153, 381-394.

MANN, G. V.: The influence of obesity on health. *The New England Journal of Medicine*, 1974, 291, 218-232.

MORRIS, L. W. and THOMAS, C. R.: Treatment of phobias by a self-administered desensitization technique. *Journal of Behavior Therapy and Experimental Psychiatry*, 1973, 4, 379-399.

PATTISON, E. M., HEADLEY, E. B., GELSSER, G. C., and GOTTSCHALK, L. A.: Abstinence and abnormal drinking: An assessment of changes in drinking patterns in alcoholics after treatment. *Quarterly Journal of Studies on Alcohol*, 1968, 29, 610-633.

RICHARDS, N. D.: Methods and effectiveness of health education: The past, present and future of social scientific involvement. *Social Science and Medicine*, 1975, 9, 141-156.

ROSEN, G. M.: The development and use of non-prescription behavior therapies. *American Psychologist*, 1976, 31, 139-141.

SIMMEL, G.: The sociology of sociability. *American Journal of Sociology*, 1949, 55, 254-261.

SLAYEN, P. W.: Group participation and behavioral change in dietary habits. *South African Medical Journal*, 1974, 1, 342.

STANTON, H. E.: Fee-paying and weight loss: Evidence for an interesting interaction. *American Journal of Clinical Hypnosis*, 1976, 19, 47-49.

STUART, R. B.: *Trick or Treatment: How and When Psychotherapy Fails*. Champaign, Illinois: Research Press, 1971.

STUART, R. B.: Situational versus self-control. In R. B. Rubin, R. Fensterheim, J. D. Henderson, and L. P. Ullman (Eds.), *Advances in Behavior Therapy*. New York: Academic Press, 1972. (a)

STUART, R. B.: The role of social work education in innovative human services. In F. W. Clark, D. R. Evans, and L. A. Hamerlynck (Eds.), *Implementing Behavioral Programs for Schools and Clinics*. Champaign, Illinois: Research Press, 1972. (b)

STUART, R. B.: Behavioral control of overeating: A status report. In G. A. Bray (Ed.),

Obesity in Perspective. Washington, D. C.: U.S. Department of Health, Education and Welfare, 1975.

STUART, R. B.: Breaking the chain: Techniques for long-term weight control. New York: W. W. Norton, in press.

STUART, R. B. and DAVIS, B.: *Slim Chance in a Fat World.* Champaign, Ill.: Research Press, 1972.

STUART, R. B. and JACOBSON, B.: Sex differences in obesity. In E. Gomberg and V. Franks (Eds.), *Gender and Psychopathology: Sex Differences in Disordered Behavior.* New York: Brunner/Mazel, in press.

STUART, R. B. and LEDERER, W. J.: *Caring Days: Techniques for Improving Marriages.* New York: W. W. Norton, in press.

STUNKARD, A. J.: The success of TOPS, a self-help group. *Postgraduate Medicine,* 1972, 143-147.

STUNKARD, A. J.: Presidential address—1974: From explanation to action in psychosomatic medicine: The case of obesity. *Psychosomatic Medicine,* 1975, 37, 195-236.

STUNKARD, A. J.: *The Pain of Obesity.* Palo Alto, Ca.: Bull Publishing Co., 1976.

TAKE OFF POUNDS SENSIBLY. *What is TOPS?* Form PI-9A: Short Information Sheet. Milwaukee, Wis.: Take Off Pounds Sensibly, 1974.

TESSLER, R. C. and SCHWARTZ, S. H.: Help seeking, self-esteem, and achievement motivation: An attributional analysis. *Journal of Personality and Social Psychology,* 1972, 21, 318-326.

TORREY, E. F.: *The Mind Game: Witchdoctors and Psychiatrists.* New York: Emerson Hall, 1972.

WARREN, C. A. B.: The use of stigmatizing labels in conventionalizing deviant behavior. *Sociology and Social Research,* 1974, 58, 303-311.

WEITZ, L. J. et al.: Number of sessions and client-judged outcome: The more the better? *Psychotherapy: Theory Research and Practice,* 1975, 12, 337-340.

WIEBE, G. D.: Merchandising commodities and citizenship on television. *Public Opinion Quarterly,* 1951-52, 15, 679-691.

WILLER, B. and MILLER, G. H.: Client involvement in goals setting and its relationship to therapeutic outcome. *Journal of Clinical Psychology,* 1976, 32, 687-690.

WILLIAMS, A. E. and DUNCAN, B.: A commercial weight-reducing organization: A critical analysis. *Medical Journal of Australia,* 1976, 1, 781-785. (a)

WILLIAMS, A. E. and DUNCAN, B.: Comparative results of an obesity clinic and a commercial weight-reducing organization. *Medical Journal of Australia,* 1976, 1, 800-802, 1976. (b)

13

Power Reversal and Self-Help: The Vancouver Mental Patients' Association

FRANCES PHILLIPS, JACKIE HOOPER, CATHY BATTEN,
MOLLY DEXALL, DAVE BEAMISH, TOM POLLOK,
and GORDON McCANN

> *My day is a snare*
> *In which I am caught*
> *Struggling.*
> *At dawn I am revived*
> *To continue*
> *What life outside of life*
> *Where my soul screeches*
> *To unimagined heights*
> *And instinct holds me back,*
> *Puts on the brakes*
> *Till gathering strength*
> *I quietly descend to the glass surface*
> *and I remain,*
> *Healing myself*
> *By the steady routine*
> *Of my existence*

> DEXALL, 1974, p. 12

The Vancouver Mental Patients Association (VMPA) was formed in 1971 when a group of ex-mental patients decided that if they were going to get effective relevant help in the community they would have to instigate this help themselves. As a group they were confronted with inadequate services in all areas of community living and in the management of emotional stress. They found a lack of basic housing, disregard or even tyranny from certain professionals and agency personnel and ineffective therapies. All of these problems contributed to members' experiences of alienation and powerlessness and to their general lack of faith in the potential for gain through utilization of organized mental health services.

Against this background, the VMPA was formed with the objective of helping ex-mental patients to change their behavior relative to the community and to help the community to change its behavior relative to the ex-mental patients. Accordingly, it was formed in an effort to give members the knowledge and skills which they needed to control their own lives and to create an understanding among members of the community concerning the basic unmet needs of the former patients. VMPA members were to be taught how to make practical use of the available services and how to provide through self-help those services which were improperly administered or which were unavailable. The needed services ranged from help in finding suitable housing and jobs through the development of satisfactory recreational opportunities to help with dealing with the personal stresses associated with return to a hostile community environment.

RATIONALE

Members of VMPA had all been hospitalized in mental institutions whose services were recognized to be authoritarian, degrading, dehumanizing and illness-maintaining (Braginsky, Braginsky & Ring, 1969). Recidivism rates from these institutions averaged 60%, demonstrating that those who were discharged left the hospital without having been helped to develop the skills necessary for community adjustment.

Regrettably, the former patients found existing community agencies to be as inept as the institutions. Therefore they turned to self-help as a means of meeting their own needs much as they have seen Alcoholics Anonymous, Parents-in-Crisis and similar groups organize successfully to provide self-help for their members.

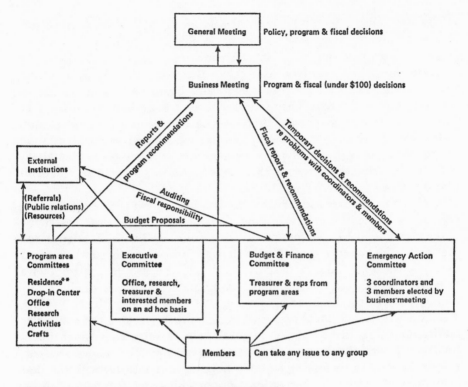

*Residences are autonomous except where M. P. A. policy is concerned

FIGURE 1

ORGANIZATIONAL STRUCTURE

A group of ex-patients banded together, deciding to form an organization in which bureaucracy, rules and structure would be kept to a minimum while individual freedom would be promoted to a maximum. A democratic process was established in which members made and enforced their own rules. Acceptance of the rules was established as a criterion for continued membership while violation of the rules was a basis for expulsion from the group.

Decisions are made on a collective basis by a general meeting held every three weeks and by business and committee meetings of smaller groups of members who get together more often. The general meeting makes major policy decisions, including the expenditure of $100 or more for any single project. The committees make implementation decisions which can be appealed by members of the general meeting. (The organization is outlined in Figure 1.)

Believing that members' ability to make decisions was eroded by their hospital experience, the VMPA was designed as a means of stressing the members' responsibility for their own decisions concerning all aspects of their lives. The Association recognizes that not all members are ready at the same time for the same amount of self-management authority and, therefore it designed a system which permitted the maximum possible level of individual variation. More skilled members focused their attention upon attacking community problems while those with less sophistication and less energy worked to deal with shorter-term, more immediate problems.

Recognizing that the group did not have within its members all of the necessary skills, coordinators who may or may not have had patient backgrounds were hired as resource persons. Their employment required termination and rehiring every six months so that the organization's needs would be met on a flexible, ongoing basis.

Members and coordinators together worked toward the creation of five semi-independent residences. Support for members in their residences is provided by their earnings and by the social assistance which they receive, supplemented by general funds from VMPA. Each residence is set up like a community family of both men and women. Entry to the houses is made by self-selection and by referral from social agencies. Anyone who is interested in the aims of the Mental Patients' Association and wishing to become a general member may do so by coming to the Drop-in Center two times and then by attending one General Meeting. Members wishing to live in one of the residences are chosen from among the general members of the Association and by referral from social agencies. All prospective live-in members are required to participate in a house meeting after which they must be approved by a majority of the current residents of the house. The House Coordinator does not have a vote in either this or any other house decision. Once admitted, residents typically remain for three to four months, with two years being the usual maximum stay.

Group decision-making prevails in the residences with members encouraged to offer one another maximal support. Specialized activities are offered and transportation is available to major events. Residents are prohibited from drinking, using illicit drugs and physical violence. They are also prohibited from interfering with the quiet enjoyment of others. Violation of the first three prohibitions can result in immediate expulsion.

Violation of the fourth can lead to lesser penalties. All sanctions can be reviewed at the business and general meetings.

In addition to the residences, VMPA also offers the services of a Drop-in Center to all former patients in the Vancouver areas. With a staff of five office workers (three of whom are former patients) and six service workers (four of whom are former patients), the Center offers housing referral, financial counseling and advocacy services to the needy. It has a large living room for social activities, a pool table, crafts room, music room, television room and dining room for a regular Wednesday free supper and for holiday meals.

Members of the VMPA do all of the cleaning, cooking and janitorial work in both the residences and the Drop-in Center. Office coordinators are responsible for securing necessary funds for salaries, operating expenses, mortgage payments on nearly half a million dollars worth of real estate and an ever-increasing number of projects, such as helping to set up a sheltered workshop for mentally and physically handicapped persons. In addition, the staff helps members to find employment, mans an information service at a large provincial hospital and publishes a bi-monthly newsletter with a circulation of over 2,000 copies distributed throughout Canada and to many foreign countries.

LINKAGE WITH EXTERNAL ORGANIZATIONS AND PROGRAMS

VMPA seeks help for its members from the surrounding community. Help comes in the form of vocational training, jobs, funding and assistance in dealing with legal matters such as licensing and regulation. It makes presentations before the Canadian Mental Health Association and various community meetings of interest to mental patients. At these meetings, it both offers information about the plight of former patients and gains information about how emerging problems can be met. In all of its dealings with community agencies, it is careful not to allow a conservative social norm to undermine its radical organization, process and objectives. A dialectic between the pressure to conform and the availability of support and information constantly exists and the VMPA makes a steady effort to preserve its values while expanding its effectiveness (see Figure 2).

BIRTH OF THE VANCOUVER MENTAL PATIENTS ASSOCIATION

The VMPA was born during the latter months of 1970. Lanny Beckman and later Roy Hunter offered articles in the local newspaper urging

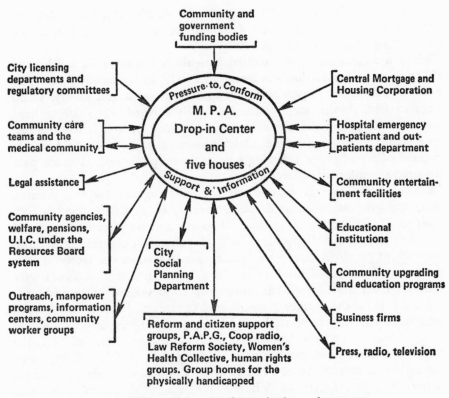

FIGURE 2. Linkage with external organization and programs.

mental patients to form a collective. A house was offered at low cost and in February, 1971, over 70 people attended an organizing meeting in the house. By March, caretakers occupied the house and the VMPA was underway. The name was chosen hastily and, at first, no rules were posed. Problems with violence developed when two members got involved with what they called "attack therapy" in which they yelled, screamed and pushed other members around. Following this incident, the four house rules were developed.

Volunteer mental health professionals offered seminars on mental health problems and were promptly rejected on the grounds that they were irrelevant to the true needs of association members. Volunteers with special skills helped with crafts projects and cooking. Members were offered meals for $40 per month or $0.75 for dinner, but many did not pay and much food was stolen. Gradually, more order came into the the handling of money and food.

When a second house was offered, neighbors protested its use by the VMPA and the Association was forced to vacate. In the existing house, 16 residents shared their space with up to 40 transients and at first social chaos existed. Again, social order gradually merged when all realized that survival of the Association was jeopardized by too much trouble-some behavior. Despite the difficulties, however, the members held strictly to their policy of never referring anyone to hospitals and as much peer support as possible was offered.

Limited funding was secured from a social agency for two salaries, while the graduation class of the University of British Columbia con-tributed $1,000. At the same time, furniture and supplies were donated in increasing amounts. By May 1972, the British Columbia Provincial government provided short-term funding for 10 salaries and later (1973) a federal grant provided funding for 20 salaries. In addition, funds were obtained from the City of Vancouver and from various private founda-tions. By 1973, the former patients had organized, funded and housed their own self-help association which was running in an orderly and effective way true to the traditions of self-help. By the end of 1973, the Association was so well developed that it was able to obtain 100% mort-gaging for its acquisition of two new houses and it was able to purchase rather than to rent its third house. While solvent, however, it faced perennial conflicts over licensing and it faced constant pressure from citizen groups in the neighborhood which were fearful and resentful of the presence of former mental patient living groups.

MEMBER CHARACTERISTICS

Almost all members of the Association have undergone recent hospital-ization. Many are males, with social agencies still reluctant to refer women to VMPA. Workers have been concerned about the fact that more men than women reside in Association houses and they are fearful that women may have difficulty in handling complex relationships with men whose quarters are not segregated along sexual lines. Aware of this reluctance, the Association has done all that it can to promote com-fortable relationships between its male and female residents and to apprise agency workers of the fruits of this effort.

TABLE 1

RESIDENCE PROGRAM—A History of Residents at the Mental Patients' Association:

January, 1974-December, 1975

These statistics were compiled by residence coordinators from each house and a strong effort was made to keep them as similar in structure as possible. Variations do occur, however, because of the difference in information available.

For the purpose of determining individual's "State of Departure" we set up some basic guidelines to go by which ars as follows: 1) Deteriorated; 2) Hospitalized; 3) Unimproved; 4) Slightly improved; 5) Improved; 6) Greatly improved; 7) Smashing success.

Dashes are used to indicate that information is unknown.

We hoped that these statistics would show similarities and a success rate, which they have done, in all five residences. We feel this is due to our common operating philosophies and the nature of our program.

Results were tabulated for individual houses and collectively based on the attached tables. They are as follows:

Residence	No. of Residents	Average Stay	Employed	*Hospitalized	Returned to Community	Showed Improvement
West 7	23	5 months	6/27%	3/13%	8/30%	16/70%
West 10	27	5 months	7/26%	1/ 4%	13/52%	20/74%
West 11	29	4.8 months	9/31%	3/10%	12/42%	21/72%
East 8	21	8.5 months	9/43%	4/14%	8/38%	15/72%
East 4	29	7 months	9/31%	2/ 7%	15/55%	23/79%
Totals	129	6 months	40/31%	13/10%	56/43%	95/74%

* The category for re-entry to hospital does not include those residents who went in and out of hospital for a few days only.

The Association members resist psychiatric labeling and stereotypic social descriptions and therefore prefer not to define member characteristics in stereotyped terms.

In the words of the association, "VMPA is not for everyone. It is an alternative community organization dedicated to providing choices and power to ex-mental patients and to setting up a variety of situations based upon the philosophy of self-help and self-government." Former patients must first choose whether or not to become part of the organization. Their decision to join is then reviewed by their peers as they seek to find a functional role in the structure of the group.

When members join the Association with a purpose in mind, and when they are willing to contribute to the organization, great success can be expected. But when they expect to take and not to contribute, problems often arise.

PROGRESS REPORT

The overall results of the residence program are summarized in Table 1. One hundred twenty-nine residents have an average stay of six months. One-third are employed and three-fourths showed improvement while only 10% returned to the hospital.

The VMPA has also worked toward the goal of progressive change in mental health legislation and patients' rights. Through careful research, it developed its own Mental Patients' Bill of Rights (see Table 2) and it succeeded in influencing the provincial government to adopt some of its recommendations in its Mental Health Act of 1973. It also has had significant impact on conferences on mental health legislation held in the two major cities of the province, Vancouver and Victoria.

In addition to its newsletter, its *Anti-Psychiatry Bibliography* (Frank, 1974) is a widely consulted guide to the literature, films and tapes in mental health. Its second work, *Madness Unmasked* (Dexall, 1974), contains the creative writing and sketches of former patients. It received critical acclaim. Finally, its book *Women Look at Psychiatry* (Smith & David, 1975) champions successfully the rights of women who seek or who are offered mental health services.

As a result of community awareness of its results, the VMPA has enjoyed increasing, albeit reluctant, respect from the mental health professionals working in the community. A survey of these professionals (Parfitt, 1974) showed that all of those surveyed were aware of VMPA,

TABLE 2

Mental Patient's Bill of Rights

Each person detained in a mental health facility shall have the following rights, a list of which shall be prominently posted in all wards of all in-patient faciilties and in all mental health centers. The Legal Aid Committee in each facility shall cause these rights to be brought to the attention of and explained to any person being treated or detained in the facility. Each person in the facility shall have the right to

a) refuse all forms of treatment or therapy;
b) to see visitors freely every day;
c) to have a reasonable access to a private telephone, both to make and receive confidential calls;
d) to have reasonable access to writing materials including stamps;
e) to mail and receive unopened correspondence;
f) to have provisions made so the person may register and vote;
g) to have ready access to printed and verbal information to explain thoroughly the various treatments, their methods, procedures, benefits and effects;
h) to have the choice of physician or other persons providing services in accordance with the policies of each agency and within the limits of available staff;
i) to solicit and use independent medical and other professional opinion at public expense if necessary;
j) to wear one's own clothes and use personal possessions and to keep and be allowed to spend a reasonable sum of the person's money;
k) to have access to individually locked storage space for his own use;
l) to have privacy within the space limitations of the facility;
m) to be notified of the whereabouts and availability of services within the facility;
n) to be given free access to reading materials from the library of the facility as well as publishers' book lists;
o) to be allowed wherever possible to continue with educational or employment training;
p) to refuse to work in the facility unless on a voluntary basis;
q) to receive new and suitable clothing upon discharge and to have social security arrangements made in the facility if the person in question has no visible means of support.

three-fourths had referred patients to the service and 40% found the service useful. The latter comments were, however, tempered by the use of such phrases as "anti-psychiatric trend," "disorganized," "too political," reflecting the fact that the activist sentiments of the association were also well known.

Finally, the VMPA, which sought consultation at its inception, is now a sought-after source of consultation. A member of VMPA sat on the steering committee of the Vancouver Handicapped Resource Center and made contributions to the meetings of the Canadian Mental Patients Association. Its members have also been asked to sit on committees at the city and provincial levels, giving the Association an increasing voice in the determination of policies relating to efforts to meet the needs of present and former mental patients.

CONCLUSIONS

The success of the VMPA demonstrates the vast potential which is to be found in the pooled resources of former mental patients working through a democratic self-help collective. If the judgment of the mental health professionals were correct—if these VMPA members were truly *non mens rae*—then the Association must be doomed to failure. But instead the Association is a success against overwhelming odds. Clearly, this is cause to question the original wisdom of hospitalizing its members, inasmuch as it shows the vast potential power inherent in collective action by patients. As the success of the VMPA becomes known throughout British Columbia, Canada and North America, the character of services to mental patients can be expected to undergo profound and radical change. Gone will be the dehumanizing and compromising practices of conventional mental health programs as innovative solutions to the problems of community living are developed in ways which enhance the dignity of the patients and which build their self-management and social skills. Only then will society fulfill its obligation to those suffering from emotional stress.

REFERENCES

BRAGINSKY, B. M., BRAGINSKY, D. D., and RING, K.: *Methods of Madness.* New York: Holt, Rinehart and Winston, 1969, p. 3.

DEXALL, M.: *"Beyond Sound," Madness Unmasked.* Vancouver, B.C.: The Vancouver Mental Patients Association Publishing Project, 1974.

FRANK, K.: *Anti-Psychiatry Bibliography and Resource Guide.* Vancouver, B.C.: Press Gang Publishers, Ltd., 1974.

PARFITT, H.: Psychiatry and the local initiatives program (L.I.P.). Paper presented to the Section of Psychiatry, B.C. Medical Association, August 13, 1974, p. 3.

SMITH, D. E. and DAVID, S. J. (Eds.): *Women Look at Psychiatry.* Vancouver, B.C.: Press Gang, 1975.

Much additional information about the Vancouver Mental Patients Association is available and may be requested by writing to the VMPA, 2146 Yew Street, Vancouver, B.C.

14

Behavioral Treatments of Obesity: Failure to Maintain Weight Loss

ALBERT J. STUNKARD

This review outlines first some of the biological boundaries of obesity—the growing evidence for the regulation of body weight, even by animals with damage to their hypothalamic weight regulatory centers, and even by ones made obese by such damage. It then reviews in a selective manner the brief but dramatic history of behavior therapy of obesity and the reasons for believing that it is superior to traditional approaches. It closes with a description of the few available studies of follow-up of behavioral treatments for obesity. A new analytic technique reveals that weight losses produced by these treatments are not maintained.

THE BIOLOGICAL BOUNDARIES OF OBESITY

Any consideration of a psychophysiological disorder such as obesity should begin with a consideration of the constraints within which efforts at behavior change must take place. It is timely to discuss the biological boundaries of obesity, since the nature of these boundaries has recently been delineated with increasing clarity.

Discussions of the biology of obesity have traditionally started with what seemed a truism: Obesity is due to a past or present disorder in the regulation of energy balance and/or body weight. In experimental

Supported in part by grant MH-28124 from the National Institute of Mental Health.

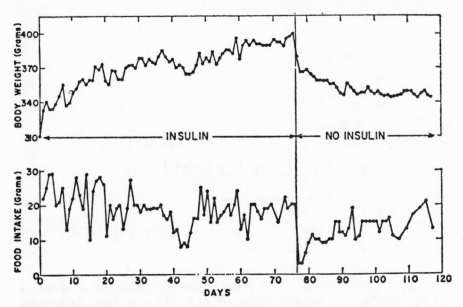

FIGURE 1. Effect of insulin injections on daily food intake and body weight of a rat. Body weight falls nearly to pre-experimental levels following cessation of insulin administration (Hoebel & Teitelbaum, 1966).

animals, at least, nothing seemed more evident than that obesity resulted from a disordered physiological regulation. Animals of normal weight quite clearly regulated their body weight with great precision. Animals with lesions of the ventromedial hypothalamus lost this capacity and, as a consequence, became obese. Or so it seemed.

The evidence for regulation in animals of normal weight is clear and unequivocal. Perturbations of body weight by a variety of experimental manipulations are followed promptly and predictably by a return to the previous weight when the source of the perturbation is removed. Figure 1 shows an increase in food intake and in body weight produced in a rat by the administration of insulin over a period of several weeks (Hoebel & Teitelbaum, 1966). Cessation of the insulin injections is followed by a prompt decline in food intake and a fall in body weight to pre-experimental levels. Increases in food intake and body weight produced by a wide variety of reversible manipulations show this same effect with remarkable predictability.

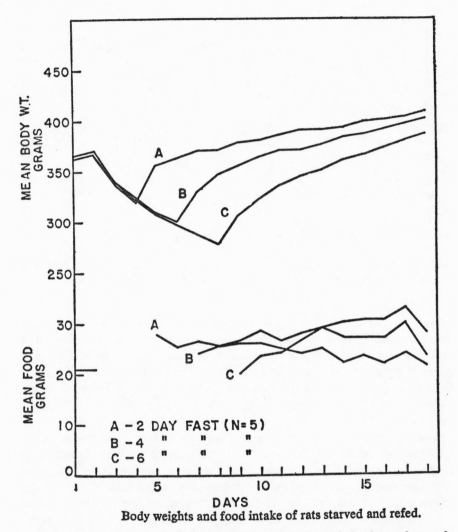

Body weights and food intake of rats starved and refed.

FIGURE 2. Body weights and food intake of rats starved for periods of two, four and six days and then refed. Rats rapidly regain lost weight when given free access to food (Hamilton, 1969).

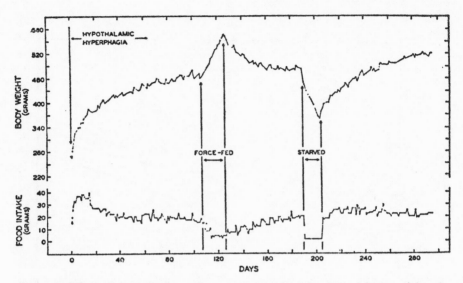

FIGURE 3. Effects of force-feeding and starvation on food intake and body weight of a rat with ventromedial hypothalamic lesions (Hoebel & Teitelbaum, 1966).

Body weight lost by reversible manipulations, most notably by restriction of food intake, is promptly regained when the animal again acquires access to unlimited food intake (Hamilton, 1969). Figure 2 shows the loss in body weight produced by starvation over a period of from two to six days. Renewed access to food intake is followed by an increase in food intake proportional to the amount of weight lost until the lost weight is restored.

The operations which establish regulation of body weight are, thus, quite straightforward. They consist of nothing more than determining that the animal can adjust food intake so as to return body weight to pre-experimental levels after removing the experimental conditions which either raised or lowered it. The very simplicity of this measure must have commended it to those intrepid investigators who first asked: Do obese animals also regulate body weight? Once the idea had been conceived, its implementation followed almost as a matter of course. Figure 3 shows the results of one of the first investigations of a rat made hyperphagic and obese by lesions in the ventromedial hypothalamus (Hoebel & Teitelbaum, 1966). Once the body weight of the animal reached its asymptote, the introduction of forced feeding resulted in a prompt and significant increase in body weight. Termination of the forced feeding brought about a compensatory fall in food intake sufficient to restore body weight to its pre-experimental levels. Similarly, we see that starvation for a period of 20 days resulted in a precipitate loss of weight. Free access to food was followed by an increase in food intake and restoration of weight to its pre-experimental levels.

The hypothalamic obese rat, thus, seems to meet the criteria for the regulation of body weight. But if there is no impairment in regulation, how do we account for its obesity? In terms of control theory, the answer is quite simple. The set point about which body weight is regulated is simply set at a higher level in the obese rat. Body weight is regulated about this higher set point fully as efficiently as it is in the nonobese peer with a lower set point.

An analogy with the home thermostat helps to convey this idea. A thermostat setting of 68°F. results in a room temperature which fluctuates within narrow limits about this set point. Elevations above this temperature can come about as a result of two different processes. The first, analogous to our former notions about experimental obesity, is a disorder in heat regulation which results in an elevated and wildly fluctuating room temperature. The second consists in an elevation of the setting of the thermostat whereby the room temperature is controlled within narrow limits about this elevated set point.

The experimental evidence clearly demonstrates the existence of regulation of body weight in the hypothalamic obese rat and regulation implies a set point. But is there evidence for the existence of a set point in such animals? Or, to phrase the question in another way: Are they fat because they overeat, or do they overeat in order to become fat?

At first glance this would seem a well-nigh impossible question to answer. Until recently, it has had much of the elusive quality of "Which came first, the chicken or the egg?" But a classic ingenious experiment has probably answered it: Rats overeat to become fat (Hoebel & Teitelbaum, 1966). What is the evidence?

Figure 4 depicts the production of obesity by the method shown in Figure 1—insulin injections to increase food intake. At the point when the rat had reached the obese weight of 460 grams, the ventromedial nucleus was destroyed. There were two possible outcomes: 1) If hypothalamic obesity were a simple consequence of neural damage, additional, incremental hyperphagia and increase in body weight should ensue. 2) If, on the other hand, the body weight of hypothalamic obese animals is

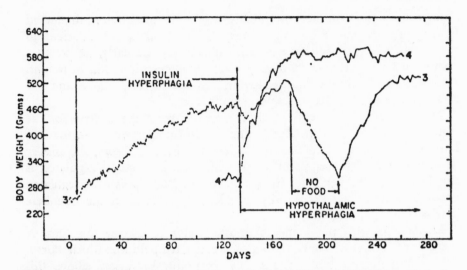

FIGURE 4. Failure of rat to increase body weight following ventromedial hypothalamic lesions when obesity had already been produced by chronic insulin injection. The usual course of increase in body weight following such lesions is seen in the second rat (Hoebel & Teitelbaum, 1966).

regulated about a set point, an increase in body weight sufficient to reach that set point prior to hypothalamic damage should result in no additional overeating and no further increase in body weight.

Figure 4 shows that the data favor the second alternative. Hypothalamic damage was followed by trivial increase in body weight. The existence of a set point at about 460 grams was further substantiated by the return of body weight to this same level following its reduction through temporary starvation. The more usual course of hypothalamic obesity is shown in the weight curve of a second rat whose normal body weight increased rapidly following hypothalamic damage.

Very recently evidence has been obtained for a gratifying symmetry in the ability to regulate body weight of rats made hypophagic and underweight by lesions in the lateral hypothalamus. Many years ago Anand and Brobeck demonstrated that lesions in the lateral hypothalamus resulted in cessation of eating and starvation of rats even in the presence of adequate amounts of nutritious foods (Anand & Brobeck, 1951). Subsequently, a series of classic experiments demonstrated that the use of heroic measures, such as tube feeding, was able to keep these animals

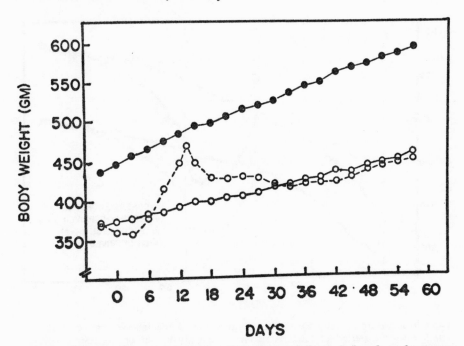

FIGURE 5. Reinstatement of anorexia in a lateral hypothalamic lesioned rat by means of force-feeding. An animal selected from the lesioned group (open circles) was force-fed until its body weight approached that of the control group (closed circles). When it was returned to *ad lib* feeding program, it reduced its food intake until its body weight had stabilized at a lower level (Keesey, Boyle, Kemnitz & Mitchell, 1976).

alive and even to permit sufficient restoration of eating to allow them a precarious, underweight, existence (Teitelbaum & Epstein, 1962). They remained, however, inordinately susceptible to unfavorable nutritional qualities of their diets, and readily susceptible to death from starvation. It was thus a remarkable feat that Keesey has been able to show that these animals, too, regulate body weight.

The following three figures illustrate experiments by Keesey and his co-workers with lateral hypothalamic-lesioned (LH) rats which reproduce in every detail the results obtained previously with normal weight and with ventromedial-lesioned rats (Powley & Keesey, 1970; Keesey, Boyle, Kemnitz & Mitchell, 1976). Figure 5 shows the weights of a group of control animals and a group of LH animals. The latter show the typical pattern of weight maintenance at a low level (79% of control animals).

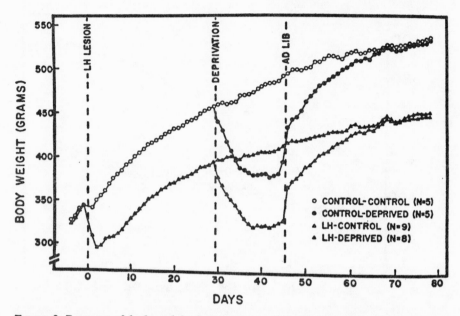

FIGURE 6. Recovery of body weight in lateral hypothalamic lesioned and control animals following a period of food restriction. The body weight of the lesion-deprived and control-deprived groups was first reduced to 80% of the value each normally maintained. When they returned to *ad lib* feeding each group increased food intake sufficiency to return to the level of the non-deprived groups (Keesey, Boyle, Kemnitz & Mitchell, 1976).

An animal selected from the LH-lesioned group was then force-fed until its body weight had increased to nearly that of the control group, at which time it was again permitted to feed *ad lib*. Note that the animal was anorexic after force-feeding until its weight had returned to the level of the LH group from which it had been selected. Once a reduced level of weight maintenance has been achieved by an LH-lesioned animal, it appears that elevating its weight to control levels by force-feeding reinstates the original anorexia. These findings make it appear that the primary effect of the LH lesions is upon the mechanism which sets the level of body weight. As with the ventromedial-lesioned obese animals, feeding behavior seems to be secondary to the achievement of this level.

Further support of this position comes from a technically difficult experiment which reduced the body weight of LH-lesioned animals by restricting their food intake. Figure 6 shows that the body weights of

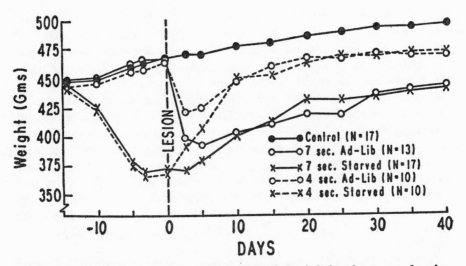

FIGURE 7. Body weight of control and lateral hypothalamic-lesioned rats as a function of lesion parameters and weight at the time of lesioning. The "4 sec" and "7 sec" refer to the duration of the 1 m/g electrolytic lesion. The body weight of the starved group was reduced to 80% of control by partial starvation prior to lesioning. *Ad lib* groups were allowed to feed without restriction (Keesey, Boyle, Kemnitz & Mitchell, 1976).

these animals, which had been maintained at 86% of that of a group of normal weight animals, was further reduced by restriction of food intake to body weights only 80% of those of LH animals which had remained on an *ad lib* feeding schedule. Some of the animals in the nonlesioned group were similarly deprived of food and similarly lost a significant amount of weight. Both deprived groups were then permitted to feed *ad lib*. Promptly both deprived groups, lesioned and unlesioned, returned to the weight levels of their non-deprived controls.

Figure 6 shows how closely the pattern of losing and regaining weight in the lesioned group parallels that of the nonlesioned animals. Both gained nearly identical percentages of the lost weight per day and took the same number of days to reach the levels of their nondeprived controls. The only difference between the LH-lesioned and normal animals was in the level of body weight which each defended.

Figure 7 compares the postlesion adjustment in body weight by LH animals lesioned at a normal body weight with that seen in animals lesioned while at a reduced body weight. Two groups of animals received lesions produced by either a seven-second or a four-second electrical current while on an *ad lib* feeding schedule. Both displayed a period of aphagia and then anorexia before finally regulating their body weight at a reduced percentage of the control level—88% and 93% respectively. Two other groups received equivalent lesions, but after reduction of their body weight to 80% of their usual level. These two groups showed a different pattern of weight change. Those which received a seven-second lesion displayed only very transient anorexia before increasing their food intake sufficiently to bring their body weight to a maintenance level of 88%. Animals receiving the four-second lesion while at 80% expected weight showed an even more unusual pattern. Not only were they not aphagic or anorexic following lesioning, but they ingested *more* food than a normal animal and gained 50 grams during the first week after the lesion. They then maintained their body weight at 93% of the control level.

This experiment showed that the food intake of animals following lateral hypothalamic lesions is apparently controlled in such a way as to produce a new body weight. If lesioned at a normal body weight, these animals were aphagic and anorexic, and achieved their new maintenance level by the loss of body weight. If lesioned when their body weights were below the new level, however, they were actually hyperphagic and gained weight to reach the new level. In each case the primary effect of lateral hypothalamic lesions seems to be to set a new reduced level of body weight; the changes in food intake appear to be secondary—in order to achieve this reduced weight.

The skeptic who questions the relevance of these experimental manipulations to the problem of human obesity may remain unconvinced. After all, the weight regulatory performances of brain-damaged rats may have little to do with the problems of human obesity and, in fact, there can be no wholly convincing counterargument. Yet the suggestions are tantalizing. For far from arguing against the possibility of the regulation of body weight in humans, the experimental evidence for weight regulation in experimental animals supports it. If damage to not just one, but to two, weight regulatory areas in the hypothalamus does not destroy the ability to regulate body weight, we are surely dealing with a very robust phenomenon. And if the phenomenon extends, as it appears to do, to every member of the animal kingdom in which it has yet been investigated, we would be hard put to claim exemption from such capacities for our own species. Clearly, far more numerous and more complex phenomena are involved in determining body weight in humans. But it is hard to ignore the strong likelihood that regulation of body weight may underlie these many phenomena.

What, in fact, is the evidence of regulation of body weight in humans? Although confined to two studies of normal weight men, it is impressive.

During World War II, an ambitious study of the effects of undernutrition and subsequent refeeding was carried out at the University of Minnesota and published in the monumental, two-volume *Biology of Human Starvation* (Keys, Brozek, Henschel, Mickelson & Taylor, 1950). Young men of normal weight were subjected over a considerable period of time to diets low enough in calories to reduce their body weight to 75% of its pre-experimental level. When these subjects were subsequently refed they overate in such a way as to restore their body weight to almost precisely its pre-experimental level. None seemed to have to pay any particular attention to their caloric intake or their body weight in order to achieve this precise regulation.

Several years after the Minnesota experiment, Sims showed that normal weight men could restore body weight after overnutrition as easily as subjects in the former study did after undernutrition (Sims & Horton, 1968). A group of 22 volunteers of normal height and weight were paid to eat a diet containing as much as 8,000 calories a day for a period of 40 weeks. During this time their body weight increased from 15 to 25%. When these men were permitted to eat *ad libitum* they underate for a period of time sufficient to restore their body weight to its pre-experimental level. As after experimental undernutrition, there was no evidence that they paid any conscious attention to either food intake or body weight in order to achieve this result. Thus, two well-designed experiments have made it appear highly probable that persons of normal weight maintain it at this level by an active process of regulation.

Do obese humans also regulate body weight? As yet, there is absolutely no evidence that they do. The most relevant information bearing upon this point—the lifetime weight history of obese humans—is equivocal. On the one hand, lifetime weight histories often show such an erratic course that one would be hard put to determine any weight, or even any range of weights, that is constant enough to argue for regulation. On the other hand, there is a strong tendency for the body weight of obese persons to return to its previous level after a wide variety of weight reduction regimens. This phenomenon is the more pronounced the more unphysiological the weight reduction efforts. Thus, a return to pretreatment weight occurs most prominently following therapeutic starvation. The question as to whether obese humans regulate their body weight cannot, therefore, be answered at the present time. But it would be remarkable if obese humans alone among the members of the animal kingdom failed to possess this capacity. How, then, can we explain the course of their weight history over the years?

One promising theory has been put forward with particular persuasiveness by Richard Nisbett (1972). According to this theory, obese persons may well possess the capacity to regulate body weight. However, the set point about which this weight would be regulated by purely physiological pressures is higher than that which is tolerated by social pressures. The result is the paradox of obese persons whose body weights are still, despite their obesity, below their physiological set points. In other words, persons who are statistically obese may still be biologically underweight. Indeed, Nisbett has described at least seven ways in which the biology and the behavior of obese persons resemble that of persons whose usually normal body weight has been reduced by starvation or less strenuous caloric restriction.

Our esthetic appreciation of this delightful theory must be tempered by a recognition of its failings: The theory is not directly testable. The only way of determining that an obese person is, in fact, below his biological set point would be to first encourage him to eat his fill. Then, when his body weight has reached an asymptote, it would be further increased, or decreased, by stuffing or starving as Sims and Keys had done with normal weight subjects. Finally, the presence of regulation would be assessed by the disposition of body weight to return to pre-experimental levels when subjects ate *ad libitum*. The experiment is, unfortunately, not feasible on ethical grounds.

Although the theory that obese persons may be below a putative body weight set point cannot be tested directly, it can be tested indirectly. And two such indirect tests support the theory. The first such test revealed that some obese persons, particularly those whose obesity stems from earlier periods in their lives, contain a larger number of fat cells than do nonobese persons or obese persons whose obesity began in adult life (Hirsch & Knittle, 1970). This larger than usual number of fat cells, with their added capacity for storing neutral fats, provides a plausible explanation of why some obese persons contain a greater than average amount of body fat. Reduction of their body weight to statistically normal levels might well leave them undernourished, with individual fat cells containing less fat than those of their normal weight peers.

The second line of evidence supporting the theory has recently been adduced by Peter Herman in a series of ingenious experiments (Herman & Mack, 1975; Herman & Polivy, 1975). These experiments have shown that persons, obese and nonobese, who habitually exercise restraint in the amount they eat share psychological characteristics which distinguish them from persons who do not restrain their food intake. Since such restraint may serve the function of preventing obesity in persons of normal weight and mitigating it in those already obese, it suggests that the body weight of these people is below set point.

Having outlined a theory which seems fully capable of explaining each and every treatment failure, let us consider the current status of behavioral treatment for obesity.

THE PROMISE OF BEHAVIOR MODIFICATION FOR OBESITY: TREATMENT RESULTS

Effective control of obesity is, above all, long-term control. Indeed, the health benefits of weight reduction for obesity depend entirely upon maintenance of weight loss. The process of repeatedly losing and then gaining weight has more deleterious effects upon health than maintenance of obesity; further, the more often this sequence occurs, the more deleterious the effects.

These facts have been known for many years and during all of this time there has been concern with the long-term results of weight reduction. In fact, we have been exhorted time and again to report the results of follow-up along with the results of treatment, but these exhortations have seemed gratuitous and hardly relevant to the problem. With treatment results as poor as they were, it seemed a futile exercise to follow-up almost nonexistent successes.

The situation is exemplified by one of the few two-year follow-ups of treatment for obesity (Stunkard & McLaren-Hume, 1959). This study showed that of 100 persons treated in the specialty clinics of a large city hospital, only 12 lost as much as 20 pounds in weight. In the face of this kind of treatment inefficacy it is anti-climactic to learn that only two of these 12 persons had maintained that weight loss at the end of two years.

This situation is now changed. The application of behavioral approaches to the treatment of obesity has significantly improved the expectations of favorable outcome. In 1967 Richard Stuart reported an uncontrolled study in which each of eight obese persons lost 25 pounds, a result surpassing that of any reported up to that time in the outpatient treatment of obesity (Stuart, 1967). In the past two years, no less than six reviews covering over 30 controlled clinical trials agree that behavioral treatments of obesity have produced consistently greater weight loss than a wide variety of alternative treatments (Abramsom, 1973; Jordan & Levitz, 1975; Stuart, 1976; Stunkard, 1975; Stunkard & Mahoney, 1976). This improvement in the results of treatment makes it reasonable to return to the question of long-term results. The rest of this paper deals with this question. Granted the greater efficacy of behavioral treatments in achieving weight loss, what is their effectiveness in maintenance of this weight loss?

We will begin with a highly selective review of five studies. As background for interpretation of the results of treatment, as well as the later, more vexing, interpretation of results of follow-up, we will refer to some considerations raised in a literature review of some time ago, which has been kindly dealt with by the years (Stunkard & McLaren-Hume, 1959). This review noted that out of the hundreds of articles on the treatment of obesity, only eight provided enough data to assess adequately the outcome of treatment. The criticisms of the literature at that time still apply to all too many reports.

> Most [reports] do not give figures on the outcome of treatment, and of those that do, most report them in such a way as to obscure the outcome of individual patients. Some authors, for example, report the total number of patients and the pounds lost without making clear how many patients achieved satisfactory results. Others report rates of weight loss for groups of patients for whom the duration of treatment was short or even unspecified. Still others use as their standard the percentage of excess pounds lost, without noting the amount in pounds. Perhaps the greatest difficulty in interpreting weight-reduction programs, however, is due to the exclusion from the reports of patients who did not remain in treatment, for such patients almost invariably represent treatment failures.

The five behavioral studies to be reported meet these criteria. The first is the aforementioned study by Stuart (1967). His results are summarized in Figures 8 and 9 which show the weight loss, over a one-year period, of eight patients who remained in treatment. (The initial study

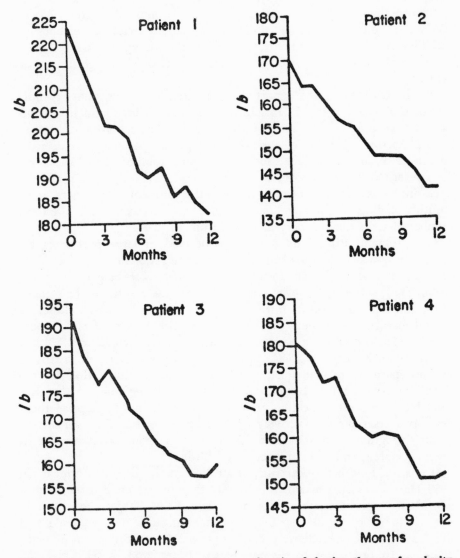

FIGURE 8. Weight profiles of four women undergoing behavior therapy for obesity (Stuart, 1967).

group had included 10 patients). Three, or 30% of the original sample, lost more than 40 pounds and six lost more than 30 pounds. These results are the best ever reported for the outpatient treatment of obesity, and they constitute a landmark in our understanding of this disorder. Even the absence of a control group does not vitiate the significance of the study.

Certain features of the report deserve attention. First, the expenditure of time was not exorbitant. In fact, time spent in treatment was no greater than that in a number of other studies that achieved far poorer results. At the beginning of the treatment period patients were seen in 30-minute sessions held three times a week, for a total of 12 to 15 sessions. Thereafter, treatment sessions were scheduled as needed, usually at two-week intervals for the next three months. Subsequently, there were monthly sessions and, finally, "maintenance" sessions as needed. The total number of visits during the year varied from 16 to 41.

The program utilized by Stuart was derived in large part from an earlier study which described in great detail the rationale and procedures of a behavioral approach to obesity (Ferster, Nurnberger & Levitt, 1962). These authors, however, never reported the results of their treatment, and a personal communication revealed negligible weight losses. A critical feature of the approach is the specification of a rigid set of "how to do it" instructions for each of the 10 or 12 patient contacts. Within this framework, there is great opportunity for the exercise of creativity by both patient and therapist. For example, Stuart noted that for patients suffering from a "behavioral depression" eating may be the only available reinforcer. Effective treatment depends upon helping them develop a reservoir of positively reinforcing responses. Two persons in Stuart's program were helped to develop such responses—an interest in growing violets, and in caring for caged birds.

It was not long before carefully controlled studies began to appear. In 1969 Harris reported a controlled study that utilized a behavioral program based upon Stuart's approach (Harris, 1969). Subjects were mildly overweight college students. Two treatment groups of three male and five female students each were compared with a control group of eight students. In order not to discourage the latter, and thereby bias the results, the control patients were told that they could not enter treatment at once because of conflicting schedules but that they would receive treatment later. Treatment sessions were held twice weekly for the first two months and then on irregular basis for the second two months.

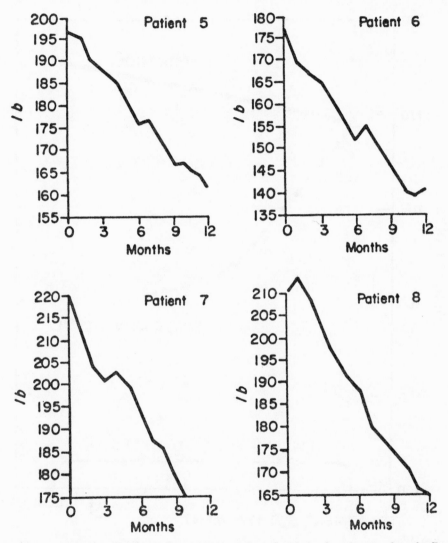

FIGURE 9. Weight profiles of four women undergoing behavior therapy for obesity (Stuart, R. B., 1967).

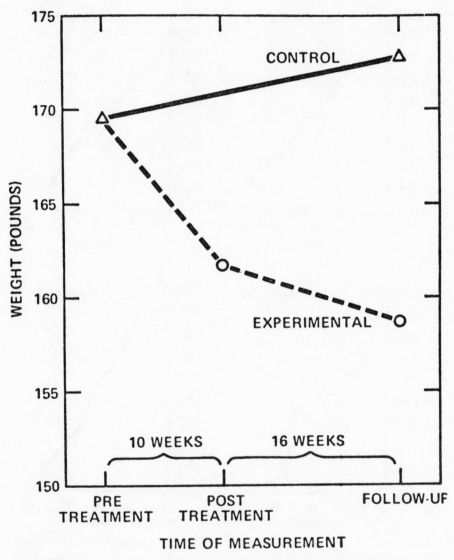

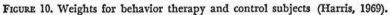

FIGURE 10. Weights for behavior therapy and control subjects (Harris, 1969).

The results are illustrated in Figure 10. The mean weight loss for the experimental group was 10.5 pounds, compared with a weight *gain* of 3.6 pounds for the control group, a highly significant difference (p < 0.001).

Although the results in the treatment group are clearly superior to those in the no-treatment control group, they are not as good as others reported in their literature: Only 21% of Harris's subjects lost 20 pounds and none lost as much as 40 pounds. The main reason for the modesty of these results is the relatively small degree of obesity of the subjects.

Two additional features of this study are worthy of note. The first is the finding that weight loss continued following the end of treatment. As we have noted, with traditional therapy, most obese persons regain most of the weight they have lost in treatment. For an obese person to continue to lose weight following treatment is uncommon; for a group to do so may well have been unprecedented.

The second feature of the study is the light that it throws upon the the problem of controls in psychotherapy research. Harris's control group consisted of subjects who were promised treatment and received it later. This procedure was quite acceptable, indeed, it was methodologically advanced for psychotherapy research in 1969. Yet the use of a no-treatment control group has serious disadvantages. Refusing treatment to someone who has come seeking it is far from a neutral event. Deterioration in the condition of members of a control group who have been disappointed in their expectation of treatment could give the false impression that a treatment was effective. Such a possibility may seem remote, yet it was precisely the weight gain in Harris's no-treatment control group that rendered statistically significant the modest weight losses in her active treatment condition.

The problem calls for the use of a placebo control condition to match the attention and interest that is received by patients in the active treatment condition. Precisely such a placebo control was introduced by Wollersheim in an elegant factorial design (Wollersheim, 1970).

Wollersheim's study contained four experimental conditions: 1) "focal" (behavioral) treatment, 20 patients; 2) non-specific (traditional psycho-dynamic) therapy, 20 patients; 3) social pressure (based upon TOPS—Take Off Pounds Sensibly), 20 patients; and 4) waiting list control, 19 patients.

The study thus contained three treatment conditions (1, 2, and 3) and three control conditions (2, 3, and 4) for behavior modification. The 79 subjects were mildly (29%) overweight female college students. Four therapists each treated one group of five subjects in each of the three treatment conditions for a total of ten sessions extending over a three-month period.

Wollersheim's findings are illustrated in Figure 11. At the end of treatment and at the end of eight weeks follow-up, subjects in the behavioral condition had lost more weight than those in the no-treatment condition. In addition, they had lost more weight than those in the two placebo control conditions who had themselves achieved respectable weight losses. The behavioral treatment clearly contributed something to the outcome that was over and above the usual effects of psychotherapy. This contribution seems to have resulted from the specific effects of the behavioral intervention, since this condition not only produced greater weight loss, but it also produced major changes in self-reports of eating behavior.

Wollersheim's study brought into focus a problem which resulted from the very advances in her experimental design. It is the problem of experimenter bias, one that had seemed mercifully distant in psychotherapy research. For although Wollersheim's placebo treatments controlled for the patients' expectations of treatment, they could not control for the therapists'. This is hardly a trivial matter. A large measure of therapeutic effectiveness is that conveyed by the therapist's expectations. Development of the methodology of the double-blind experiment in psychopharmacology has shown how powerful this influence can be in the case of drug treatments. It is surely more powerful in the more emotional case of the psychotherapies.

It is unlikely that psychotherapy research will ever attain to the elegance and economy of the double-blind methodology of the psychopharmacologist. To control experimenter bias will require methods tailored to the specific needs and opportunity of this kind of research.

One such method, deceptive in its simplicity, was introduced by Penick et al. (1971). The essence of this method was to give up at the start the notion that therapists could be unbiased in the use of therapies that they favored and disfavored. Instead, the therapists were selected on the basis of their commitment to either a behavioral or a traditional approach to therapy. Penick further biased the outcome against the behavioral approach by selecting therapists of vastly different experience for the two conditions. For the behavioral treatment, the therapists were beginners; for the control condition, they were experts.

This study is worthy of note also for the character of its patients. A great many of the trials of behavior modification have been carried out

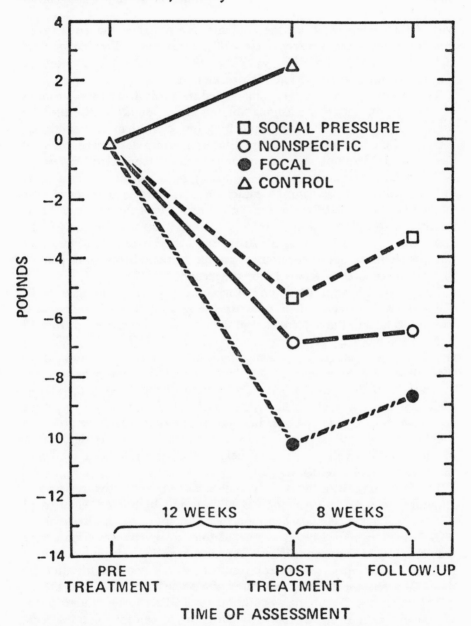

FIGURE 11. Mean weight loss of the focal (behavioral) treatment group, the two alternative treatment control groups and the no-treatment control group (Wollersheim, 1970).

with mildly overweight college students. By contrast, the patients in Penick's study were severely obese—78% overweight. Two cohorts, of eight and seven respectively, were treated in weekly group meetings lasting two hours for a period of three months.

The results of treatment are summarized in Table 1. The weight losses of the control group are comparable to those found in the medical literature—none lost 40 pounds and 24% lost more than 20 pounds. By contrast, 13% of the behavior modification group lost more than 40 pounds and 53% lost more than 20 pounds. Although the difference between the experimental and the control groups for these weight losses did not quite reach statistical significance, that for weight losses of over 30 pounds did: $p = 0.015$ by the Fisher Exact Probability Test. These findings were reflected also in more traditional methods of analysis. In each cohort the median weight loss for the behavior modification group was greater than that of the control group: 24 pounds versus 18 pounds for the first cohort; 13 versus 11 for the second.

The results of follow-up at one year and five years are also shown in Table 1. The percentage of patients losing 20 pounds has increased from 53 to 62 and the percentage losing 40 pounds has increased from 13 to 31. Although these percentages had decreased at the five-year follow-up, respectable percentages of patients were still 20 and 40 pounds below their pre-treatment weight. It should be noted that the superior performance of patients in the behavioral treatment condition at the end of treatment no longer obtained at the one-year follow-up. The apparent advantage was lost, it appears, because of unexpectedly large losses of weight after the end of treatment in the control group. The significance of these findings will be discussed below when the results of follow-up investigations are considered.

The fifth and last of the studies considered in this selective review was an ambitious program involving 234 subjects and 16 different chapters of TOPS (Take Off Pounds Sensibly), a self-help program. Each of 16 TOPS chapters was assigned to one of four treatment conditions, with four chapters in each condition: 1) behavior modification conducted by a professional therapist (psychiatric resident); 2) behavior modification by the TOPS chapter leaders, who used the same manual as the professional therapists; 3) nutrition education by TOPS chapter leaders given special instruction on this topic (in an effort to control for nonspecific effects of training and attention, these leaders received the same amount of nutrition education as the other leaders had received in behavior

TABLE 1

RESULTS OF TREATMENT

Percent of Groups Losing Specified Amounts of Weight

(1) BEHAVIOR MODIFICATION

WEIGHT LOSS	AFTER TREATMENT	1-YEAR	5 YEARS
40 or more lbs.	13	31	17
20 or more lbs.	53	62	25
n=	15	13	12

(2) TRADITIONAL THERAPY

WEIGHT LOSS	AFTER TREATMENT	1 YEAR	5 YEARS
40 or more lbs.	0	13	13
20 or more lbs.	24	60	20
n=	17	15	14

Summary table of results of behavioral and traditional treatment for obesity. Numbers represent percents of each group losing 20 and 40 pounds at the end of treatment and at one-year and five-year follow-up.

modification); 4) continuation of standard TOPS techniques—weekly weigh-ins, announcement of weight changes, and group discussion. Treatment of all 16 chapters was carried out once a week for one and a half hours over a period of 12 weeks.

The first major finding of this study was that far fewer subjects dropped out of the behavior modification treatments. Figure 12 shows that at nine-month follow-up 38% and 41% of the behaviorally treated subjects had left the program compared to 55% for the nutrition education and 67% for the standard TOPS program.

Second, despite the bias against the behavioral modification treat-

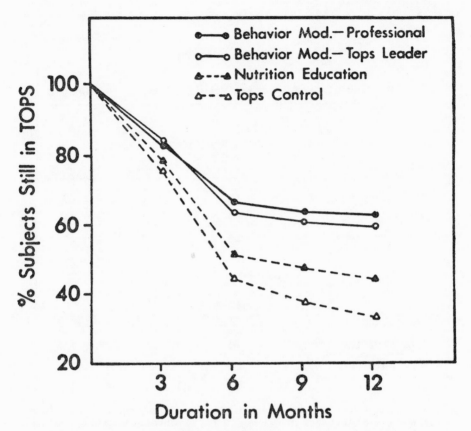

FIGURE 12. Attrition rates of TOPS subjects over a one-year period under four experimental conditions (Levitz & Stunkard, 1974).

ments resulting from their lower attrition rates (of presumably poorer weight losers), behavior modification produced greater weight losses than either of the two control treatments. The chapters in which behavior modification was introduced by professional therapists lost a mean of 1.9 kg., significantly more ($p < .001$) than the weight loss in both the nutrition education (0.1 kg.) and the TOPS control condition, in which subjects actually gained 0.3 kg. Chapters in which behavior modification was introduced by professionals lost significantly more weight ($p < .05$) than those taught the same program by the TOPS chapter leaders.

Figure 13 shows that the relative superiority of the behavioral groups

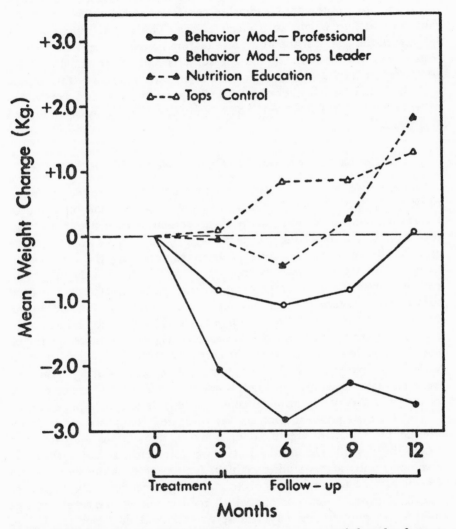

FIGURE 13. Weight loss of TOPS subjects over a one-year period under four experimental conditions (Levitz & Stunkard, 1974).

further increased at the nine-month follow-up assessment. The groups which had had professional leadership continued to show lower attrition rates and to lose weight to a mean 2.6 kg. The initial weight loss of subjects in the behavior modification program conducted by TOPS group leaders was not maintained, and the subjects' weights returned to their pretreatment levels. These subjects, however, did better than the control and the nutrition education groups. Subjects in these two conditions actually gained 1.3 kg. and 1.8 kg. in the nine months following treatment.

Behavior Modification for Obesity: Follow-Up Results

We discussed earlier the problems of reporting the results of treatment for obesity. These problems are compounded in the reporting of the maintenance of weight loss. With no consensus even about the most useful method of reporting treatment results, how do we cope with the equally elusive and interactive problem of reporting the sequelae of these results? As one simple example, how do we compare the efficacy of two regimens: one with a high drop-out rate during treatment, but good subsequent long-term survival, the other with a low drop-out rate during treatment but poor subsequent long-term survival? Then, for drop-out rate, substitute pounds lost, percent excess weight loss, reduction index, mean weight loss per unit time, or percent of subjects reaching various weight loss criteria. Finally, recognize that, whereas during treatment weight usually decreases, during follow-up it may either decrease further or increase. The permutations become too terrible to contemplate.

The increasing use of controls has mitigated the problems of interpreting the results of treatment of differing populations with differing susceptibilities to treatment. But these problems remain when we compare results across studies. Which, for example, is the more potent treatment: one which reduces obese middle-age housewives by 20 pounds and 25% excess weight, or one which reduces mildly overweight college men by 10 pounds and 50% excess weight? And does not the former find it easier to maintain pounds lost, and the latter percent of weight lost?

We propose here a new method of analyzing the long-term maintenance of weight lost in treatment. It is a scatter diagram which plots for each individual on the horizontal axis the difference between weight at the outset of treatment and at its conclusion. On the vertical axis we plot

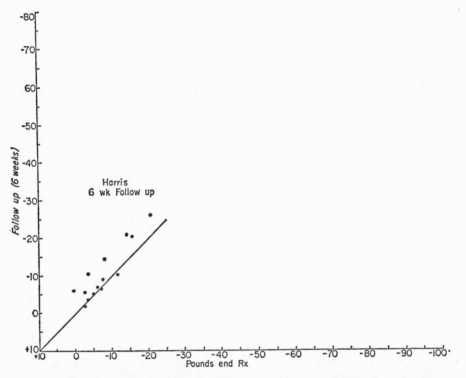

FIGURE 14. Follow-up of weight loss by individual subjects in the Harris study shown also in Figure 10. Note the distribution of points along or slightly above the main diagonal, indicating maintenance or slight increase of weight lost at the end of treatment.

the difference between weight at the outset of treatment and at follow-up. The characteristics of the method are best illustrated by examples from those reports in the behavioral literature which provide sufficient data for this purpose. The first is the study by Harris described above (1969). Figure 14 shows data points for the individual subjects arrayed along the main diagonal. This display illustrates an outcome in which weights at follow-up match those at the end of treatment. In fact, the individual data points are slightly above this diagonal, illustrating the effect shown in the earlier illustration of the mean weight change—weight loss continued after the end of treatment. The display also highlights the very modest changes in weight achieved by treatment and at follow-up, which

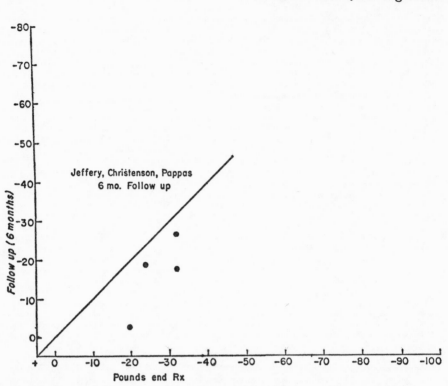

FIGURE 15. Six-month follow-up of weight lost by four subjects. Note the varying extent of weight regained, as indicated by data points below the main diagonal.

were noted in the earlier description of Harris's study. Finally, note the very limited duration of follow-up.

Figure 15 shows the results of a longer follow-up period, in this case, six months. This study was designed "to combine some of the most effective, positive control procedures of existing behavioral therapy weight reduction programs and was carried out in a group format with four persons who averaged 50 pounds over ideal weight (Jeffrey, Christensen & Pappas, 1972). The four subjects lost from 20 to 33 pounds in weight at the end of treatment, and the authors reported that "two subjects maintained their weight loss, one regained a portion of the loss, and one returned to baseline weight." Figure 15 summarizes rather more precisely than the verbal description the fact that each of the subjects regained some weight at follow-up, as manifested by the data points below the main diagonal. It further shows that those who lost more weight during treatment were more successful at maintaining the weight loss.

A study with an even longer follow-up—one year—was reported by Foreyt and Kennedy (1971). This study was notable in that it is the only behavioral one which exclusively utilized aversive control. A plot of the data of this study reveals that the mean change of weight in pounds reflects the authors' interpretation of the results. Thus, the experimental group lost 13.3 pounds during treatment and at 48 weeks was still 9.2 below a starting point. Mean weight changes in the control group were insignificant.

Use of this analytic technique highlights two issues which were not mentioned by Foreyt and Kennedy. For example, the authors state that at follow-up "five of the six subjects still showed some weight loss, although not as much as right after the conditioning." In fact, the data points of two of the experimental subjects above the main diagonal attest to the not inconsiderable feat of continuing weight loss following treatment. And the plot illustrates the interesting performance of one control subject who lost nine pounds during follow-up after a six-pound loss during treatment.

Figure 16 illustrates the results of a two-year follow-up of 10 obese women treated by behavioral methods. At the time that it appeared in 1973 it was the longest follow-up yet reported for the behavioral treatment of obesity and it attracted considerable attention. Reviews of the study agreed with the authors' conclusion that there had been a "failure to find long-term effects" and that "the results do not indicate a long-lasting effect resulting from behavioral treatment of obesity" (Hall & Hall, 1974). Figure 16 suggests a different interpretation. First, the distribution of data points on the horizontal axis reveals the very limited weight loss during treatment. Second, by contrast, the five data points lying above the main diagonal reveal not only maintenance, but even continuation, of weight loss following treatment. As in Jeffrey's study, a straight line describing these data points is steeper than the main diagonal, suggesting that the more subjects lost during treatment the better they performed after treatment. The usefulness of this method of displaying data is best exemplified in this study. Earlier applications had confirmed the authors' impressions as to the significance of their data; at most they drew attention to finer aspects of interpretation. In this

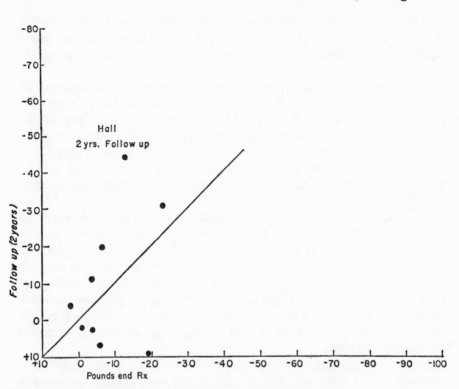

FIGURE 16. Two-year follow-up of ten women treated by behavior therapy. Note the limited degree of weight lost during treatment and the reasonably good maintenance indicated by the five data points above the main diagonal.

study, however, the display suggests conclusions contrary to those both of the authors and of others who have cited their work.

Let us now analyze in greater detail the one-year and five-year follow-ups of the study reported by Penick et al. (1971). Figure 17 shows the one-year follow-up of the results of treatment by behavioral and traditional approaches. Two previously well-established findings are clearly illustrated. The first is the somewhat greater weight loss of the behavioral group at the end of treatment, shown in the distribution of its data points further to the right along the horizontal axis. The second is the greater variability in weight change in the behavioral group during treatment. This display shows also that such greater variability is present one year after treatment. In addition to confirming earlier im-

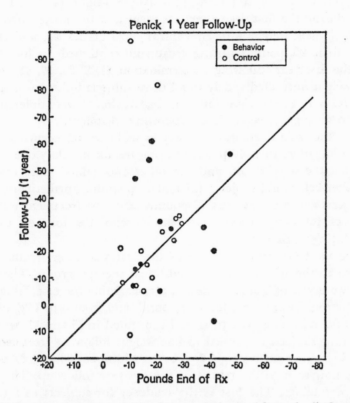

FIGURE 17. One-year follow-up of data from study by Penick et al., displayed earlier in Table 1. Note the apparently random distribution of data points for both the behavioral and control treatments, indicating failure to maintain weight loss by others during the follow-up period.

pressions, Figure 17 demonstrates relationships which are not apparent from presentation of the data in tabular form. Indeed, it demonstrates relationships which are quite different from those that had been inferred from the group data. Those data show that subjects losing more than 20 pounds increased from 50 to 62% during the first year after treatment. We had inferred from these data that loss of 20 pounds in a behavioral program was a powerful predictor of maintenance of that loss. Figure 17 shows a far different pattern. Of the seven subjects who had lost more than 20 pounds during treatment, four gained weight (8, 17, 21 and 47 pounds) during the first year after treatment and the other three barely maintained their weight loss. By contrast, five of the six subjects who lost less than 20 pounds during treatment continued to lose weight during the first year following its termination (1, 2, 35, 37, 43 pounds). Clearly weight fluctuated widely in all these subjects following treatment. Those who were good weight losers during treatment were different from those who were good weight losers following treatment.

Some of the wide fluctuations in weight maintenance occurred in subjects who lost more than 40 pounds during treatment. Only one of three maintained the weight lost, and the other two gained more than any of the other behavioral subjects (21 and 47 pounds). Furthermore, of the four subjects who were at least 40 pounds below pretreatment weight at the end of follow-up, three were persons who had lost less than 20 pounds during treatment.

For the most favorable outcome of the first year after treatment, we must turn to the subjects in the traditional therapy group. These subjects, as we noted in Table 1, showed a remarkable increase, from 24 to 60% of persons losing more than 20 pounds and from 0 to 13% of those losing 40 pounds. This pattern is well illustrated in Figure 17, where we see that nine subjects continued to lose weight following treatment, two of them increasing their weight loss by an additional 66 and 87 pounds.

Let us now turn to the results of the five-year follow-up. They show two major findings. The first is the tendency for subjects to return to their pretreatment weight. This tendency is seen in Table 1 by the attrition in subjects losing specified amounts of weight. The second major finding at the five-year follow-up is the same pattern of continuing fluctuation in body weight which was observed at the one-year follow-up.

SUMMARY AND CONCLUSIONS

In recent years investigations of experimental obesity in animals have given us a much clearer idea of the biological boundaries of obesity. We now know that the body weight of obese animals is regulated just as is that of animals of normal weight and that efforts to reduce the weight of obese animals face formidable pressures towards maintenance of the obesity. We do not know whether the body weight of obese people is similarly regulated. But, if it were, the poor results of treatment would have a ready explanation.

Improvement in these poor results has been achieved by the introduction of behavior therapy and a few examples from this literature were cited. But the major thrust of this paper is the introduction of a new method of analyzing the maintenance of weight lost during treatment. This new method has been applied to the few studies of weight reduction which report data on the extent to which individuals have maintained weight lost during treatment. It shows that behavioral therapies have been no more effective than traditional ones in this regard.

These results contradict earlier, more optimistic reports on the maintenance of weight lost during behavioral treatments. These earlier reports were based upon mean weight changes, which obscured the curious finding that persons who lost weight in behavior therapy tended to regain it after treatment, while those who had not lost weight during treatment did so thereafter. We close this account with the question, "Why?"

REFERENCES

ABRAMSON, E. E.: A Review of Behavioral Approaches to Weight Control. *Behavior Research & Therapy*, 1973, 11, 547-556.

ANAND, B. K. and BROBECK, J.: Hypothalamic control of food intake in rats and cats. *Yale Journal of Biology & Medicine*, 1951, 24, 123-140.

FERSTER, C. B., NURNBERGER, J. I., and LEVITT, E. B.: The control of eating. *Journal of Mathetics*, 1962, 1, 87-107.

FOREYT, J. P. and KENNEDY, W. A.: Treatment of overweight by aversion therapy. *Behaviour Research and Therapy*, 1971, 9, 29-34.

HAGEN, R. L.: Group therapy versus bibliotherapy in weight reduction. *Behavior Therapy*, 1974, 5, 222-234.

HALL, S. M. and HALL, R. G.: Outcome and methodological considerations in behavioral treatments of obesity. *Behavior Therapy*, 1974, 5, 352-364.

HAMILTON, C. L.: Problems of refeeding after starvation in the rat. *Annals of the New York Academy of Science*, 1969, 157, 1004-1017.

HARRIS, M. B.: Self-directed program for weight control: A pilot study. *Journal of Abnormal Psychology*, 1969, 74, 263-270.

HERMAN, C. P. and MACK, D.: Restrained and unrestrained eating. *Journal of Personality*, 1975, 43, 647-660.

HERMAN, C. P. and POLIVY, J.: Anxiety, restraint, and eating behavior. *Journal of Abnormal Pesychology*, 1975, 84, 666-672.

HIRSCH, J. and KNITTLE, J. L.: Cellarity of obese and non-obese human adipose tissue. *Federal Proceedings*, 1970, 29, 1516.

HOEBEL, R. G. and TEITELBAUM, P.: Weight regulation in normal and hypothalamic rats. *Journal of Comp. Physiology and Psychology*, 1966, 61, 189-193.

JEFFREY, D. B., CHRISTENSEN, E. R., and PAPPAS, J. P.: A case study report of a behavioral modification weight reduction group: Treatment and follow-up. Research and Development Report No. 33, University of Utah Counseling Center, 1972.

JORDAN, H. A. and LEVITZ, L. S.: A behavioral approach to the problem of obesity. *Obesity/Bariatric Medicine*, 1975, 4, 58-68.

KEESEY, R. E., BOYLE, P. C., KEMNITZ, J. W., and MITCHELL, J. S.: The role of lateral hypothalamus in determining the body weight set point. In D. Novin, W. Wyrwicka, and G. A. Bray (Eds.), *Hunger: Basic Mechanisms and Clinical Implications*. New York: Raven Press, 1976. Pp. 243-255.

KEYS, A., BROZEK, J., HENSCHEL, A., MICKELSON, O., and TAYLOR, H. L.: *The Biology of Human Starvation* (2 vols.). Minneapolis: University of Minnesota Press, 1950.

LEVITZ, L. S. and STUNKARD, A. J.: A therapeutic coalition for obesity: Behavior modification and patient self-help. *American Journal of Psychiatry*, 1974, 131, 423-427.

NISBETT, R. E.: Hunger, obesity and the ventromedial hypothalamus. *Psychological Review*, 1972, 79, 433-453.

PENICK, S. B., FILION, R., FOX, S., and STUNKARD, A. J.: Behavior modification in the treatment of obesity. *Psychosomatic Medicine*, 1971, 33, 49-55.

POWLEY, T. L. and KEESEY, R. E.: Relationship of body weight to the lateral hypothalamic feeding syndrome. *Journal of Comp. Physiology and Psychology*, 1970, 70, 25-36.

SIMS, E. A. H. and HORTON, E. S.: Endocrine and Metabolic adaptation to obesity and starvation. *American Journal of Clinical Nutrition*, 1968, 21, 1455-1470.

STUART, R. B.: Behavioral control of overeating. *Behavior Research Therapy*, 1967, 5, 357-365.

STUART, R. B.: Behavioral control of overeating: A status report. In G. Bray (Ed.), *Obesity in Perspective*. Fogarty International Center Series on Preventive Medicine. Vol. 2, Part 2. Bethesda, Maryland: DHEW Publication No. (NIH) 75:708, 1976.

STUNKARD, A. J.: From explanation to action in psychosomatic medicine: The case of Obesity. *Psychosomatic Medicine*, 1975, 37, 195-236.

STUNKARD, A. J. and MAHONEY, J. J.: Behavioral treatment of the eating disorders. In H. Leitenberg (Ed.), *Handbook of Behavior Modification and Behavior Therapy*. Appleton-Century-Crofts, 1976.

STUNKARD, A. J. and McLAREN-HUME, M.: The results of treatment of obesity: A review of the literature and report of a series. *Archives of Internal Medicine*, 1959, 103, 79-85.

TEITELBAUM, P. and EPSTEIN, A. N.: The lateral hypothalamic syndrome. *Psychological Review*, 1962, 69, 74-90.

WOLLERSHEIM, J. P.: The effectiveness of group therapy based upon learning principles in the treatment of overweight women. *Journal of Abnormal Psychology*, 1970, 76, 462-474.

Author Index

Subject Index

Italic page numbers indicate material in tables or charts.

359